Jan Hendrik Hessels, Antonius van der Linde

The Haarlem Legend of the Invention of Printing

by Lourens Janszoon Coster

Jan Hendrik Hessels, Antonius van der Linde

The Haarlem Legend of the Invention of Printing
by Lourens Janszoon Coster

ISBN/EAN: 9783337155087

Printed in Europe, USA, Canada, Australia, Japan

Cover: Foto ©ninafisch / pixelio.de

More available books at **www.hansebooks.com**

THE
HAARLEM LEGEND

OF

The Invention of Printing

BY LOURENS JANSZOON COSTER,

CRITICALLY EXAMINED

BY

DR. A. VAN DER LINDE.

FROM THE DUTCH

BY

J. H. HESSELS,

WITH AN INTRODUCTION, AND A CLASSIFIED LIST OF THE
COSTERIAN INCUNABULA.

London:

BLADES, EAST, & BLADES.
11. ABCHURCH LANE.

1871.

CONTENTS.

		PAGE
INTRODUCTION		v
THE AUTHOR'S PREFACE		xxvii
I.	WRITING, XYLOGRAPHY AND TYPOGRAPHY	1
II.	GUTENBERG'S PREPARATION	12
III.	GUTENBERG AT MENTZ	21
IV.	THE MEMORY OF GUTENBERG	29
V.	SPREAD OF TYPOGRAPHY IN THE NETHERLANDS	34
VI.	GERRIT THOMASZOON	40
VII.	VAN ZUREN AND COORNHERT	48
VIII.	LUIGI GUICCIARDINI	54
IX.	HADRIANUS JUNIUS	56
X.	1440	66
XI.	A BEECH IN "DEN HOUT."	72
XII.	SPECULUM NOSTRÆ SALUTIS	80
XIII.	JOANNES FAUSTUS	89
XIV.	THE BOOKBINDER CORNELIS	96
XV.	QUIRIJN DIRKSZ.	101
XVI.	THE REVELATIONS OF SCRIVERIUS	110
XVII.	LOUWERIJS JANSZOEN	116
XVIII.	COSTERIANISM	126
XIX.	GERARDUS MEERMAN	136
XX.	A HERALD OF LIES	147
XXI.	METAMORPHOSIS OF THE LEGEND	155
XXII.	A MUNICIPAL SHOW-BOOTH	164
XXIII.	CONCLUSION	167

INTRODUCTION.[1]

The original Dutch work, of which we here offer an English translation, was commenced, as the author tells us in his preface, in the "Nederlandschen Spectator" of 4th December, 1869, and continued in the weekly numbers of that periodical till its completion, 28th May, 1870. Afterwards the author considerably altered and extended the work, republishing it as a second edition in August, 1870, under the title of : *de Haarlemsche Costerlegende.*

The minds of many of those who took an interest in this subject had been prepared for this sweeping essay of Dr. Van der Linde, by the publication, in 1867, of some documents, by M. A. J. Enschedé, the archivist of Haarlem, and by M. J. A. Alberdingk Thijm, in a preface which the latter wrote for a Dutch translation of Paeilo's work: Essai hist. et critique sur l'invention de l'Imprimerie. 8vo. Lille, 1859.

These documents had been found by M. Enschedé, in the archives of Haarlem, and contained evidence that Lourens Janszoon Coster, the so-called Dutch inventor of printing, was alive and selling candles in 1447, while, according to the system of his worshippers, he had, and really ought to have, died at the end of 1439.

Jac. Koning—after Junius the chief author on the Haarlem invention of printing, whose book : Verhandeling over den oorsprong, de uitvinding, verbetering en volmaking der Boekdrukkunst, &c., was published in 1816, and later (1819) in the shape of an abridged French translation—had also made researches in the Haarlem archives, and, as it now appears from a MS. left by him (see page 91, note 3, of the present book), noticed all items relating to the so-called Haarlem inventor, but used only those which served his purpose, which was to write a book on the Haarlem invention and its inventor, Lourens Janszoon Coster, as he had been revealed to the world by Junius. Koning wisely concluded that his hero should die at the proper moment. Now, as the proper moment for the death of the Dutch inventor was the end of 1439, and as some person called Lourens Janszoon (this is the name by which the inventor was also known ; that of Coster or Koster, meaning a sacristan, being derived from the office he is said to have held), did die, or at least was buried, about that time, Koning took no further notice of other items which might have interfered with his work. In this way he made his system complete, wrote his book, and reaped great glory as the fruit of his patriotic labour.

Later writers on the same subject, Dr. A. de Vries, Noordzick, &c., seldom omitted to say that Koning's book had become obsolete and was defective in many respects ; but they never took the trouble of verifying his annotations with regard to Coster. At last, in 1840, M. Joh. Enschedé, the uncle of the above-mentioned M. Enschedé, examined the Haarlem archives, and found the same documents which Koning had found before him, but had not used. This M. Enschedé, however, happening

---

[1] I must ask those who have not made a study of the *minutiæ* of the history of the invention of printing, and do not wish to do so, to read of this Introduction only as far as the end of the first paragraph of p. vii. before they proceed to read the book itself. The greatest part of what follows can have no great importance to them ; and even those who are acquainted with the controversy, or wish to make themselves acquainted with it, would do well to read the Introduction last of all.

to be a great friend of Dr. Abraham de Vries, *the* champion of the Haarlem claims, and unwilling to annoy him, resolved never to reveal the documents he had found, so long as his friend was alive. His death took place in 1864, but M. Enschedé never even then told the secret,[1] until his nephew, after making independent researches, again discovered the above-mentioned documents. It was then that this part of the history became gradually known; and when, after the death of M. Enschedé, the uncle, in 1867, M. Rutjes translated into Dutch the French work of Pacile, and M. J. A. Alberdingk Thijm was writing an introduction to this book, M. A. J. Enschedé communicated his discovery to M. Thijm, who now enriched his introduction with the five documents which the reader will find on page 42 of the present book, together with a few more.

M. Thijm reasonably concluded that he could not publish these entirely new documents without some remarks, and wishing to give M. Enschedé all the fame of the discovery, he expressed himself thus: "I agree with my esteemed friend M. A. J. Enschedé, to whom I am indebted for these indications, that Lourens Janszoon Coster, the chandler of 1441 [— 1447] . . ., Lourens Janszoon, the sheriff in 1425—1431 [who really died at the end of 1439, see pages 116 and 119 of this work], and Lourens Janszoon Coster, who invented the art of printing in the Wood near Haarlem, are one and the same person. I also agree with M. Enschedé, who remarked to me in a letter, that ' he saw no objection whatever to take a Haarlem chandler of the 15th century to be identical with a sheriff, as we have had many burgomasters, who were brewers, coopers, or the like, at the same time. That Junius makes no mention of this circumstance, proves nothing against his account; it was, perhaps, a particular of very little value in his eye, but it does not appear so trifling to me. I can understand that a man like Gutenberg, who was acquainted with several industries, improved the art of printing; or that a chandler, acquainted with founding in moulds, among which were, perhaps, marks, conceived the art of printing, rather than a sheriff, conversant with judicial matters. I, for one, believe that Coster got first of all the idea by moulding candles; that thereupon he made experiments by cutting letters out of beech-bark in the Wood and printed from them; that he did not do so by accident, but that the invention was the fruit of an idea living in him, and which even accompanied him on his walks in the Wood.' "

"I have," said M. Alb. Thijm, "nothing to add to these words of the Haarlem archivist."

This is said in the preface to the very book (of Pacile) in which six pages (62—67) are devoted to demonstrating that Coster died at the end of 1439, where a document is given of Coster's burial, and where it is distinctly pointed out, that this event (the death of Coster in 1439) is in perfect harmony with the account of Junius. Moreover, among the notes at the end of the same book, is one which refers to what is demonstrated in these six pages, and where it is said that M. A. J. Enschedé (the man who had sent the five documents proving that L. J. C. was alive in 1447) confirmed the genuineness of the document of Coster's burial at the end of 1439!

The above remarks and inconsistencies, although coming from such well-known, learned men, did not satisfy all persons, and especially those who could not believe that a man, who was buried at the end of 1439, sold candles till 1447. The whole case soon brought down a shower of ridicule upon the Dutch in general, and upon the chief actors in the dispute in particular, as may be seen in the Nederl. Spectator (29th Feb. 1868), and more especially in "Le Bibliophile Belge," 1868, No. 2, pp. 152—183, where M. C(harles) R(uelens) severely criticized the proceedings of the Costerians in an article headed : " L'Odyssée de Laurent Coster en Hollande."

---

[1] "Except" thus Dr. Van Meurs, of Haarlem, wrote to me, "to some of his relations and also to myself, about 1861, under condition of never speaking about it. Dr. Van der Willigen, of Haarlem, also knew it, and when he, with the assistance of Dr. A. J. Enschedé, made researches in our archives about Haarlem painters, he found the places where the items occurred."

The question was now subjected to a new inquiry, the fruit of which is Dr. Van der Linde's book, wherein he strikingly exposes many other curious proceedings of the Costerians which were hitherto entirely unknown. His book has already called forth several articles in different periodicals and newspapers in Holland and in other countries. They are mostly confirmatory, but I do not think them important enough to be translated here; the majority of them hardly touch the question at issue. Only one *brochure* entitled: De Keulsche Kronick en de Coster-legende van Dr. A. Van der Linde te zamen getoetst door Dr. P. Van Meurs. 8°. Haarlem, 1870 (The Cologne Chronicle and the Coster-legend of Dr. A. Van der Linde tested by each other), deserves somewhat our attention, as it probably expresses the opinion of the present Costerians in Holland; although the author, who is a physician at Haarlem, tells us in his preface that he speaks only for himself. I will give the cream of this *brochure* while treating of some passages of Dr. Van der Linde's book. But before I do so I wish to make one general remark: no one who has written against Dr. Van der Linde has attempted to say one word in behalf of Coster, only Dr. Van Meurs, the title of whose *brochure* sufficiently indicates its object, says in his preface, that " he considers it a secondary question whether the statue erected at Haarlem in 1856, bears the name of Laurentius Johannes or Laurentius Johannes Cognomento Ædituus, Custosve, or any other name."

I said before that the minds of many of those who took an interest in this subject had been prepared for Dr. Van der Linde's essay, but I must not forget to say that to many others there was hardly a time that the cause of Haarlem seemed so strong as during the last twenty or thirty years. This was owing to the works of Ottley, Bernard, Sotheby, Berjeau, Noel Humphreys, Blades, &c., who are all in favour of Haarlem. It would, perhaps, be unjust to blame these authors for having so entirely relied upon what had been advanced by Junius, Koning, De Vries, Noordziek, &c. It was only natural that foreigners, who did not give way to patriotic prejudices, should fall into the trap, so long as Dutch authors, who enjoyed the highest reputation in their own country and whose honesty could not be suspected, published documents by which they, to all appearance, proved the soundness of Coster's history, as far as the time of his life and death was concerned. Whatever may be said about the discrepancies and absurdities of the Coster-legend, now that we possess a full knowledge of it, there is one circumstance which has given, and will give, an air of probability to the story, even now that it is deprived of its hero, so long as this circumstance cannot be sufficiently accounted for. I mean the existence of a comparatively large number of works—block-books and incunabula—which are of an incontestably early, and Dutch origin, and which cannot, even at present, be ascribed to any known printer, but of which it is certain that they belong to the printer who produced the four editions of the *Speculum Humanæ Salvationis*, the book referred to by Junius (see page 61.)

A great part of these works—which we might still call, for the sake of convenience, *Costeriana*—consists of different typographical editions of *Donatus*, the very book in which, according to the famous passage in the Cologne chronicle on the invention of printing (see page 8), "the first prefiguration (die eyrste vurbyldung) [for the invention at Mentz] was found, and which was printed in Holland before that time " [the invention at Mentz].

We find, moreover, among those Costeriana a goodly number of different editions of *Alexander Gallus' Doctrinale*, a little school-book, of which it seems that copies, *gette en molle*, were sold at Bruges and Valenciennes in 1446 and 1451 (see page 6), and which is also mentioned by Junius as being the first book printed at Mentz with the types stolen from Coster (see page 61).

Those who do not believe in an Haarlem invention of printing with moveable types, argue that the *Doctrinales* referred to in the Cambray MS., and the *Donatuses* spoken of in the Cologne chronicle, must have been *xylographic*. The reader may find *this* view more broadly expressed by our author (on pp. 6 and 7 with regard to the Doctrinales and on p. 10 with regard to the Donatuses) than in any other book on the question.

The partizans of Haarlem, on the other hand, argue that in both cases *typographic* productions must have been meant, and this, they say, is all the more evident, as no *xylographic* copy of either of these little works has ever been discovered, which could reasonably be put so early as c. 1440, while a great number of *typographic* Donatuses and Doctrinales has been found which bear the stamp of great antiquity.

There is no technical term in the passage of the Cologne chronicle to qualify the Donatuses mentioned there, and we can, therefore, not be surprised that that account has continually been interpreted in favour of either party, although Dr. Van der Linde points out that the whole passage would be perfect nonsense, if we asserted that the Dutch Donatuses mentioned in it were typographic ones (see p. 8 (note 5), 10, and 142, note).

We find, however, a technical term "*gette en molle*" in the Cambray MS., which seems to be applicable to either mode of printing (xylography or typography), while it appears also capable of being interpreted in a way disconnecting it altogether from our subject.

Those who are desirous of going a little further into this matter may compare with Dr. Van der Linde's arguments on page 7, regarding the Cambray document, Bernard, *de l'origine de l'imprimerie en Europe.* Paris. 1853. Vol. I. pp. 97 sqq.

Bernard, who is in favour of a separate invention of typography, at Haarlem and at Mentz, but earlier at the former place than at the latter, sees in the little books, mentioned in the Diary of Jean Le Robert, typographical productions of the press of Coster, or at least of one of his workmen. According to him they could only have been printed with *moveable types*, for the terms *gette en molle, jettez en molle* could only have regard to books printed with movable types, cast in a *mould*, and he refers to several documents in support of his opinion, among which are the very same quoted by Dr. Van der Linde, in favour of a contrary opinion. Bernard, moreover, asserts that not a single instance can be found where these terms refer to xylographic productions, whereas it is constantly applied to typographically printed works. He argues further that these terms could not be interpreted otherwise, for moveable cast types only made the use of a mould necessary; that they were borrowed from the scholars, or at all events from the merchants, who had to employ particular terms to designate the new products of typography; that the books of which Jean Le Robert speaks, were on vellum, except the last; and no one could print on vellum with the *frotton*, an instrument used for printing xylographic productions, &c. &c.; concluding that if it is proved that xylographic Donatuses were productions posterior to the invention of typography, it is also proved that the Dutch Donatuses of which the Cologne chronicle speaks are printed with moveable types, and not with wooden blocks.

In Trübner's American and Oriental Literary Record, No. 72 (June 30, 1871), we find an article of Mr. William Skeen, in which he says that the term *gette en molle* "certainly has no meaning as applying to manuscripts, but that . . . it is pregnant with meaning in regard both to block-printing and stencilling . . . . The assertion that *jettez en molle* means, and can only mean, printed from cast types, has no weight, and the phrase itself is valueless as an evidence that cast types were in use at the time when Abbé Jean Le Robert wrote his diary." This article is a chapter of Mr. Skeen's "Work on Early Typography, which will soon be ready, and which will throw very considerable light on several obscure points connected with the early history of typography, and in connexion with the work of Dr. Van der Linde . . . will confound not a little the Costerians at home and abroad." The book is being printed in Ceylon.

Finally, Dr. Van Meurs expresses himself on page 14 of his *brochure* as follows: " These Doctrinales (mentioned in the Diary of Jean Le Robert), are arbitrarily[1] declared by Dr. Van der Linde to be the Doctrinale of Alexander Gallus, but which exegetical dexterity allows him (Dr. Van der Linde) to distort the text of the Cologne chronicle, and to place the Donatuses, alluded to by Zell as having been printed already before 1440, in Flanders rather than in Holland, because (observe!) in 1446 two copies of a Doctrinale, *gette en molle*, were sold at Bruges for 20 pence, and because in 1451 again the same work *jettez en molle* was exchanged for one *en papier*? What right has he to make xylography of that *gette en molle*, after Bernard has pointed out that it could not have that signification? Or does Dr. Van der Linde think—because there is question in 1514 of *lettre mollé*, which undoubtedly refers to a typographical missal, and because Philip de Commines mentions in 1498 the Sermons of Savonarola, *qu'il a fait mettre en moule*, by which are perhaps meant the 'Prediche raccolte per Ser Lorenzo Violi,' which were published at Florence, probably in 1496 or 1497, and had, no doubt, nothing to do with xylography—that the term *gette en molle*, which he applies so arbitrarily to the *printed* Bible of Gutenberg and the *printed* Donatuses, could have been applied in 1446 also to xylography?

"The application of the words *gette en molle*, as meaning xylography, to any book, is pure fancy of those who wish to find that meaning in it. So long as not a single xylographic book can be produced to which the words *gette en molle* are unmistakeably applied in that way in the 15th century, so long is the whole manufactory of xylographic school-books in Flanders, which is only founded on those Doctrinales, nothing but a chimera. The remark that a copy *ne falloit rien et estoit tout faulx*, is already sufficient to put the idea of xylography out of the question; and we may say this with the more right, as not a single xylographic Doctrinale has come down to us, or exists otherwise but in the obscure words of the Cambray MS. The explanation has, therefore, no foundation.

"If we can, however, point out no xylographic, but typographic books, to which the words *mettre* or *jeter en moule* have been applied, I think it still more probable—at least as long as this question has not incontrovertibly been settled—that a *livre gette en molle*, has nothing to do either with *xylography* or *typography*. Who does not perceive, while reading the Cambray document, that in 1451 the term *gette en molle* is used in contradistinction to *en papier*? The same is the case in the ordinance of Louis XI. of 1474, in which he granted naturalization to Friburger, Gehring, and Mart. Crantz, and where we read: ' Quo ilz sont venuz demourer en nostre royaume puis aucun temps en ça, pour l'exercise de leurs ars et mestiers de faire livres de plusieurs manieres d'escriptures *en mosle* et autrement.'

"Do not these terms make us rather think of books in loose sheets or bound? In this way the Sermons of Savonarola, *qu'il a fait mettre en moule*, would simply mean that they were collected in some form, *i.e.* put together to one whole, or bound. In 1498 the art of printing was sufficiently known, and it would appear strange if Philip de Commines had spoken of it in metaphorical terms. He, therefore, means something else. And what can *molle* be but a form, and what is therefore a book *gette en molle* but a book brought together in a form or in a binding, in contradistinction to another *en papier*, *i.e.* in a paper cover? By this interpretation, the expensive (written, but bound) Doctrinale, which was exchanged for a much cheaper (unbound) copy, gets a natural sense; but that very sense would be unnatural when, by a most forced explanation, we declare the Doctrinale *en papier* to be a MS. copy, in *contradistinction* to a printed one; for, in this case, the MS. copy would probably have been the most expensive.

"If, notwithstanding this, the author of 'the Coster-legend' abides by his *xylographic* Doctrinale of Alex. Gallus, of which never any trace has been found, it is then his duty to produce evidence not only that really such a Doctrinale was meant, but also

---

[1] "It appears to me much more rational that a 'Doctrinale de Sapience' is meant; a work written in 1388 by Guy de Roye, and much used in convents; it commences thus: 'E qui est en ce petit liure doibuent ensainger les prestres a leurs parochiens. Et aussi pour les simples prestres qui n'entendent pas bien les escriptures,' &c. The first edition with a date was printed in 1478."

a fragment of such an edition; or to show, with undeniable proofs, that such works were printed, by the side of the *typographical* fragments which do exist, and of which the Costerians have spoken over since three centuries. The words of Paeile are, therefore, based on some foundation. But, however this may be, if Paeile had no right to invent, on the authority simply of that *gette en molle*, a whole bookseller's correspondence between Haarlem and Bruges; yet Dr. Van der Linde has much less right, on the same authority, 1st, to give to a word a meaning for which hitherto not the least logical reason exists, and which is, therefore, based on nothing but arbitrariness; 2nd, to represent a whole shop and manufactory of xylographic school-books in Flanders as a proved fact; 3rd, to represent xylographic Donatuses as having been published by the same firm some years earlier; 4th, to metamorphose typographical Donatuses into xylographic ones; 5th, to represent Donatuses, which ' an admirably accurate author, from whose credibility we may not deduct anything,' unconditionally ascribes to Holland, as having been born in Flanders, and all this because, according to a MS. annotation, Jean Le Robert, abbat of the convent St. Aubert at Cambray, had bought for him at Bruges, in January, 1446, by means of a writer of Valenciennes, a Doctrinale *gette en molle*, for which he paid twenty pence tournois, and also because later a similar copy had been sent by him to Arras, which had been bought at Valenciennes for twenty-four groots (the market was therefore higher there). This last copy, however, was full of misprints (of course a second, but not corrected, xylographic edition !). It was not accepted, and the Doctrinale *gette en molle* was exchanged for one *en papier*. Would it not be desirable to establish a professorship for Dr. Van der Linde's special criticism and exegetical dexterity ?"

It will be observed that Dr. Van Meurs does not apply the words *gette en molle* to the mode by which the books of the Cambray MS. were *printed*; but that he considers them to have been *manuscripts*, bound (*gette en molle*) or in loose sheets (*en papier*). If his interpretation were right, the Cambray document would lose all its value with regard to the invention of printing.

It would be rather difficult to give another opinion on these terms; nor is it necessary to do so; whatever may be their meaning, so long as we do not find early *xylographic* Doctrinales and Donatuses, it will be necessary to study the typographical ones, not with the avowed object of trying whether we could ascribe them to the Haarlem Coster, *but simply in what period we may place them*, and whether we could put them so early as 1446 or even before 1440. By this investigation we may safely leave the printer in the back-ground; for, although his discovery would be of great importance, inasmuch as it would, perhaps, enable us to settle *at once* the difficult question of the date of the books, yet if the books themselves do really prove to be executed after 1470, or I will rather say, if it cannot be proved (by documentary evidence and not by speculation), that they were printed before 1470, nothing is left to us, now that the man, to whom they have all been ascribed, is removed from the scene of his imaginary labours, but to treat them as we treat all other books of the same kind: that is to say, ascribe them to an unknown printer, and regard all the accounts of the Cologne chronicle, of Junius; &c., about them, as mere stories, which obtained, through certain circumstances, a remarkable air of probability. And if, in the course of time, we should be able to find any evidence of these books having been printed at an earlier date than the Mentz invention, then so many questions are set at rest that that of the printer can only be secondary.

For the convenience of those who might wish to interest themselves in this subject, I give here for the first time a :

CLASSIFIED LIST OF THE COSTERIANA.

[N.B.—Where a book is described in Mr. Holtrop's *Catalogus* of the fifteenth century books in the Royal Library at the Hague (Hagae Comitum. 1856, 8vo.), I have given the reference (BRH.), which indicates at the same time that a copy or fragment of the work is preserved in that Library. Where there is a facsimile or a description of any book in the same writer's *Monumens Typographiques des Pays-Bas* (La Haye, 1868. 4to.), I have referred to the plate or the page (MT.). I have also referred to Meerman (*Origines typographicae*, 2 vols. 4to. Hagae Com. 1765); Sotheby (*Principia typographica*, 3 vols. fol. Lond. 1858); Bernard (*De l'Origine et des Débuts de l'Imprimerie en Europe*, 2 vols. 8vo. Paris, 1853); Ennen (*Katalog der Incunabeln in der Stadt-Bibliothek zu Köln*, herausg. von Dr. L. Ennen); Wetter (*Kritische Geschichte der Erfindung der Buchdruckerkunst*, 8vo. Mainz, 1836.)]

Type I.

1. Speculum Humanæ Salvationis (unmixed Latin edition).
    Described BRH. No. 561; Sotheby I., p. 145; Bernard I., p. 17.—Facsimiles MT. pl. 17; Sotheby I. pl. xxix. and xxx.
    Sixty-four anopisthographic leaves (of which the first is blank). The work is divided into 5 quires, of which a contains 8, b, c and d, each 7, and the last, 8 sheets; the preface occupies the 5 last leaves of the first quire.
    Copies: 1. Museum Meerman-Westreenen at the Hague (wanting preface); 2. (John B. Inglis, at present) Mr. B. Quaritch; 3. Imperial Library at Vienna; 4. Library in the Palace Pitti at Florence; 5. Town Hall at Haarlem (wanting preface); 6. Library of the King of Hanover (?) (only 44 leaves); 7. Royal Library at Brussels (5 leaves wanting).

2. The same work (mixed Latin edition).
    Desc. BRH. 560; Bernard I. 13 sqq.—Facs. MT. pl. 20, 21; Sotheby I. pl. xxxii.
    This edition contains the same number of anopisthographic leaves, divided in the same way, as No. 1, but 20 of them are printed xylographically, viz. (in quire b) leaves 6-19, 7-18, 9-16, 10-15, 11-14, 12-13; (in quire c) ll. 21-32, 22-31, 26-27; (in quire c) ll. 51-60.
    Copies: 1. Museum Meerman-Westreenen; 2. British Museum (Grenville Collection); 3. Bodleian Library, Oxford; 4. and 5. Paris Library (2 copies); 6. Mr. Holford; 7. Earl Spencer; 8. Pembroke Library at Wilton House.
    Bernard says: "On connaît une dizaine d'exemplaires de cette édition." But I do not know where they all are.

3. The same work (mixed Dutch edition).
    Desc. BRH. 562; Bernard I. 17.—Facs. MT. pl. 18; Sotheby pl. xxxi. and xxxiv. 3; Ottley, Inquiry, I. 249.
    This edition consists of 62 anopisthographic leaves, which are divided as in the Latin editions; the first quire, however, has only 4 leaves. The 49th and 60th leaf are printed with a different type (see type II., No. 17). These two pages differ, moreover, among themselves in some of the copies (See Meerman, Origg. typogr. I. 121, note cl).
    Copies: 1. Museum Meerman-Westreenen; 2. Earl Spencer; 3. (Enschedé, afterwards bought by Mr. Quaritch, but now in the possession of ?).

4. The same work (unmixed Dutch edition).
    Desc. BRH. 563; Bernard I. 17.—Facs. MT. pl. 22; Sotheby I. pl. xxxiii. 1.
    This edition contains the same anopisthographic leaves, divided in the same way, as No. 3.
    Copies: 1. Museum Meerman-Westreenen (only leaf 42); 2. Town Hall

at Haarlem; 3. Public Library at Haarlem; 4. Library at Lille. (N.B.—This copy has two leaves printed on both sides; namely, on the reverse of pp. 25 and 26, are (re-)printed the pp. 47 and 62; they were probably proof-sheets of the printer); 5. Pembroke Library at Wilton House.

General remark on the Speculum: I cannot tell whether Nos. 1—3 are placed in the right order; this much I may say, that it is now pretty certain that No. 4 is the *last* edition, and that one of the Latin editions should come first. The work has been copiously described by almost every author on the history of printing; Bernard's description, however, is the best of all.

5. Donatus (Ælius) de octo partibus orationis—28 lines.
   Desc. BRH. 2.—Facs. MT. pl. 13^d.
   One leaf, on vellum, which was found pasted in a volume belonging formerly to the Sion Convent at Cologne, containing several treatises of Ulr. Zell, among which was: Augustinus de singularitate clericorum, 1467.

6. Donatus—28 lines.
   Desc. MT. p. 18.—Facs. Meerman VI.*
   One leaf, on vellum, preserved at the Town Hall at Haarlem, and found pasted in the original binding of an account-book of 1474 of the cathedral of the same town, in which an item occurs from which it appears that Cornelis the bookbinder had bound this volume.
   [N.B.—Five leaves of this Donatus are in the Paris Library (See Van Praet, Velins, IV. Belles Lettres No. 10)].

7. A Liturgical book—12 lines.
   Desc. MT. p. 18.—Facs. MT. 14^{ab}.
   The Royal Library at Brussels possesses of this work the leaves 2 and 3 (ll. 1 and 4 are wanting), printed on vellum. They were found by M. Ruelens in the cover of an old book.

8. A Dutch version of the seven penitential Psalms—11 lines.
   Desc. MT. pp. 18 and 19.—No facs.
   One sheet, on vellum, printed on *one* side, but containing 4 pages. It was found in the Royal Library at Brussels, where it is still preserved.

9. Donatus—30 lines.
   Desc. BRH. 5; MT. p. 19.—Facs. MT. 14^b.
   Three leaves, on vellum, found in the old binding of a copy of: Exhortationes Noviciorum, Deventer (R. Paffroed), 1491, in 4to.

10. Donatus—30 lines.
    Desc. BRH. 564.—No facs.
    Fragment, on vellum.

11. Donatus—30 lines.
    Desc. MT. p. 19.—Facs. Meerman IV.
    Two leaves (pp. 19—22), on vellum; discovered in 1750 by M. Enschede in a MS.: Handvesten en Privilegien van Kennemerland, 1330—1477. At the sale of his library in 1867, the fragments remained the property of the family Enschede. There are two leaves of the same edition in the Paris Library (See Van Praet, Velins, Belles Lettres, No. 8).

12. Donatus—27 lines.
    No description; no facsimile.
    Two leaves (pp. 3 and 4, and 13 and 14) and a small fragment (of pp. 7 and 8), on vellum, preserved in the British Museum (12932c), stuck in another edition of the same work (Reutlingen, 1495).
    [N.B.—There are 4 leaves of a Donatus of 27 lines in the Paris Library (See Van Praet, Velins, Belles Lettres No. 9).]

13. Alexandri Galli Doctrinale—32 lines.
    Desc. BRH. 558; MT. p. 19.—Facs. MT. 15^a.
    Two leaves, on vellum, 4to.

14. Alexandri Galli Doctrinale, 32 lines.
    Desc. BRH. 557; MT. p. 19.—Facs. MT. 15ᵇ.
    Two leaves, on vellum, 4to.
    [N.B.—3 leaves of a Doctrinale, on vellum, of 32 lines, are preserved in the Royal Library at the Hague (BRH. 3); they were found in the binding of a: Gemma Vocabulorum, printed by Paffroed at Deventer, 1495 (Qy., which edition do they belong to, either No. 13 or 14, or to an edition different from both?—Mr. Campbell answers: "Impossible to find it out, as the pages are not the same.")]
15. Catonis Disticha—21 lines.
    Desc. MT. p. 19; Dibdin, Bibl. Spenc. IV. 474—76.—Facs. Cat. Spencer IV. 474; Sotheby, I. pl. xxvi. 1; MT. 16ᵃ.
    Perfect (?) copy (4 leaves), on vellum, in 8vo., in Earl Spencer's library.
16. Alexandri Galli Doctrinale—32 lines in 4to.
    Desc. BRH. 559; MT. p. 20.—Facs. MT. 16ᵇ (27 lines).
    Fragment, on vellum, in 4to.

Type II.

17. Two leaves (the 49th and 60th) of the mixed Dutch Speculum (Cf. No. 3).
    Desc. BRH. 562.—Facs. MT. pl. 19.
    Mr. Holtrop (Mon. Typ. p. 21) points out that the type of these two leaves resembles that of Laur. Valla [type III.] (see Mon. Typ. pl. 25). The capitals A and N seem to be *nearly* the same. No trace of this type has hitherto been found in any other book.

Type III.

18. Laur. Vallae Facetiae morales et Franc. Petrarcha de salibus Virorum illustrium ac faceciis Tractatus—25 lines.
    BRH. 8; MT. pp. 29 and 30.—Facs. MT. pl. 25.
    Twenty-four leaves.
    Copies: 1. Royal Library at the Hague; 2. Town Library at Haarlem (Enschedé's copy); 3. British Museum (Grenville Collection).
    Mr. Holtrop, describing this book in his Cat. of the Incunabula at the Hague, said that this type was identical with that of the two leaves 49 and 60 of the mixed Dutch Speculum (see No. 17). In his Monuments (p. 29), however, he says it is different. The capitals resemble those of No. 19, while the B and the M of these two founts are identical.

Type IV.

19. Ludovici (Pontani) de Roma Singularia Juris. Pii Secundi Tractatus et Epitaphia.
    Desc. BRH. 13; MT. p. 26 sqq.—Facs. MT. pl. 23 (recto); Sotheby I. 181; Ill. 182; Wetter.
    Sixty leaves (the first blank) divided into three quires (of 8, 14, 8 sheets), in small folio, 26 lines. The tract of Pius II., with 34 lines to a page, commences on leaf 45ᵇ in Type V.
    Copies:—1. (Enschedé, at Haarlem) Asher & Co. (?); 2. Earl Spencer; 3. Royal Library at the Hague (wanting first leaf [blank]); 4. British Museum (Royal Library); 5. Royal Library at the Hague (BRH. 13, only 4 leaves); 6. British Museum (only leaf 24).
    N.B.—In No. 1 and 3 the versos of the 55th leaf present some variations (see MT. p. 27).

20. Donatus—24 lines.
    Desc. BRH. 11; MT. p. 28.—Facs. MT. pl. 13 and 24.
    One leaf, and part of a second, on vellum, 4to.
21. Donatus—24 lines.
    Desc. BRH. 576; MT. p. 28.—Facs. MT. pl. 13 and 24.
    Four leaves, on vellum, 4to.
22. Donatus—24 lines.
    Desc. MT. p. 29.—Facs. MT. pl. 13 and 24.
    Fragment, on vellum, 4to., formerly in the possession of Mr. Fred. Muller, but now in the Town Library at Haarlem.
23. Donatus—24 lines.
    Desc. Van Praet, Velins IV. No. 12; Bern I., 154 (but he is mistaken in saying that it is an ed. of 27 lines)—Facs. Bernard I. pl. iv.
    Four leaves, on vellum, 4to., preserved in the Paris Library.
    [N.B.—There are two leaves and a fragment of a Donatus of 24 lines in this type in the Cologne Town Library (see Ennen, pp. 7 and 8).]

Type V.

24. Pii Secundi Tractatus et Epitaphia.
    Desc. MT. p. 27.—Facs. MT. pl. 23 (verso).
    This tract commences on the verso of the 45th leaf of Lud. de Roma (see No. 19).
    Copies: (see No. 19).
25. Guil. de Saliceto de Salute corporis; Turrecremata de Salute animae; Pii II. Tract de Amore, &c.; Homeri Yliada, &c. in folio.
    Desc. BRH. 572; MT. p. 30 sqq.—Facs. MT. pl. 26; Renouard, Bibl. d'un Amat. II. 152—8; Sotheby, I. p. 183 (note).
    24 leaves (of which the first is blank), divided into two quires of 6 sheets each; 34, 35 and 36 lines.
    Copies: 1. Museum Meerman-Westreenen (in this copy, the MS. date 1474 occurs, of which I speak below, p. xvii.); 2. Earl Spencer (wanting first [blank] leaf); 3. Paris Library; 4. (M. Libri, perfect—Qy. where now?); 5. (the Hibbert [Hobert] Copy—Qy. where now?).
26. The same work (different edition).
    Desc. MT. p. 32.—No facs.
    The two fragments on vellum of this edition, different from the preceding one, were (1858) in the possession of M. Cohn (Asher & Co.) Berlin, but are now in the British Museum. They were found in the binding of a copy of the: Formulae Noviciorum, Haarlem, Joh. Andreae, 1486 (which is also in the British Museum). The side on which at present no printing is found seems to have been scraped, to give it the appearance of a blank page.
27. (Incerti auctoris, vulgo Pindari Thebani), Iliados Homericae Epitome abbreviatum (Metrice), cum praefatione Pii II. in laudem Homeri.
    (4 + 4 + 2) 10 leaves, 34 and 35 lines.
    Desc. BRH. 10; MT. pp. 33, 34.—No facs.
    Copies: 1. Royal Library at the Hague (wanting the 10th leaf); 2. British Museum (Grenville Collection).
28. The same work—17 leaves, 34 and 35 lines.
    Desc. BRH. 573; MT. pp. 33 & 34.—No facs.
    Copy: Museum Meerman-Westreenen.
    Mr. Holtrop, in his MT., p. 32—34, has given a most minute and clear description of No. 27 and 28, which are great bibliographical curiosities.

Donatus minor *or* abbreviatus—26 lines.
   Desc. BRH. 4; MT. p. 34.—Facs. MT. pl. 27.
   Two sheets (4 leaves; 1, 2, 7, 8 ?), on vellum.
   Mr. Holtrop, in his Monuments, states that the sheet which contains the first page, commencing with the words "Partes orationis quot sunt," contains also the last page, which ends thus: "Explicit." This edition was therefore composed of a single quire, and must have been a Donatus minor.
Donatus—27 lines.
   Desc. BRH. 565; MT. p. 35.—Facs. MT. pl. 28.
   Perfect copy (8 + 6), 14 leaves, on vellum.
Donatus—27 lines.
   Desc. BRH. 6, 566; MT. p. 35.—Facs. Wetter, XII. 2.
   The leaves (3, 6, 9, 14) in the Royal Library at the Hague (BRH. 6) and those (1, 2, 4, 5, 7, 8, 10, 13) in the Museum Meerman-Westreenen (BRH. 566) make together one copy of Donatus of 27 lines, of which only ll. 11 and 12 are wanting. With the leaves in the Royal Library are two more fragments.
Donatus—27 lines.
   Desc. BRH. 568; MT. p. 35.—Facs. MT. pl. 28^b.
   Leaf 4, on vellum.
Donatus—27 lines.
   Desc. BRH. 567; MT. p. 35.—Facs. MT. pl. 29.
   Two leaves and a part of a third (ll. 2, 7 and 8), on vellum.
   [N.B.—There is another fragment, on vellum (BRH. 7), which may belong to another edition of 27 lines.]
Donatus—27 lines.
   Desc. BRH. 569; MT. p. 35.—Facs. MT. pl. 29^b.
   Three fragments, the lower parts of ll. 1 and 8, and the upper part of leaf 8, on vellum.
   [N.B.—There are 8 leaves of a Donatus of 27 lines in this type in the Paris Library (see Van Praet, Velins, Belles Lettres, No. 7). There is also a fragment of a leaf, printed on *one* side, in the Cologne Town Library (see Ennen, p. 7). And several leaves of editions of Donatus of 27 lines in this type are in the Bodleian Library.]
Alexandri Galli Doctrinale—26 lines.
   Desc. BRH. 9.—Facs. Wetter xi. 9.
   Fragment, on vellum.
Alexandri Galli Doctrinale—28 lines.
   Desc. BRH. 570.—Facs. MT. pl. 30.
   Two leaves, on vellum.
Alexandri Galli Doctrinale—29 lines.
   Desc. BRH. 571.—Facs. MT. pl. 30.
   [N.B.—There are two leaves of a Doctrinale of 29 lines in the Cologne Town Library. (See Ennen, page 8.) Also two leaves in the Paris Library (See Van Praet, Velins, Belles Lettres, No. 16), and some leaves at Oxford.]
Alexandri Galli Doctrinale—32 lines.
   Desc. Van Praet, Velins, Belles Lettres, No. 17.—No facs.
   Two leaves in the Paris Library, on vellum.
   [Visser possessed also 2 leaves, and there are 2 leaves of an edition of 32 lines in the Cologne Town Library (See Ennen, p. 8.)]
Catonis Disticha—21 lines.
   Desc. MT. p. 36.—Facs. Sotheby I. 135, pl. xxiv. 4.
   Fragment.

Type VI.

40. Donatus—27 lines.
Desc. BRH. 556; MT. p. 36.—Facs. MT. pl. 31; Meerman, pl. II.
One leaf (the 11th), on vellum.
Fragments are also preserved at Haarlem. Dr. Kloss possessed the 4th and 5th leaves. Weigel also possesses two leaves (See Collectio Weigel. II. 165).

Type VII.

41. Donatus—27 lines.
Desc. MT. p. 36—Facs. MT., pl. 32ª.
Four leaves, on vellum, found in the old binding of a: Durandi Rationale, printed at Strasburg, 1493, belonging to the library of the Convent of the Holy Cross, at Uden, in North Brabant. These 4 leaves (2 sheets) contain the same text, and belong, therefore, to two copies of the same edition. The type resembles much that of the Saliceto.

Type of the Enschedé Abecedarium (See pag. xviii).

42. Abecedarium.
Desc. MT. p. 16.—Facs. MT. pl. 12.
Two leaves, printed on vellum. They were found in 1751 by M. Enschedé, in a MS. Breviarium of the XVth. century, originating from the family of Berestyn, related to Jan van Zuren, printer at Haarlem in 1561.

43. Donatus—31 lines.
Desc. BRH. 1.; MT. p. 15.—Facs. MT. pl. 11; Meerman, Tab. 1.
Two leaves, on vellum, printed on *one* side, found in 1844, by Mr. Campbell, the present Librarian of the Royal Library at the Hague, in a "Getydenboeck" printed at Delft, 1484.

[N.B.—There are two leaves of a Donatus of 27 lines, printed on *one* side, in the Paris Library. (See Van Praet, Velins, Belles Lettres, No. 11, where he says that they belong "à une édition en caractères mobiles de fonte très-bien gravés; ils ne sont imprimés que d'un seul côté, et paroissent sortir d'une presse des Pays-Bas.")]

I have arranged these books according to the types which were in all probability in the possession of the printer of the Speculum, there being such an unmistakeably close resemblance between the seven several founts of type, which I have enumerated above, and of which facsimiles have been given by Mr. Holtrop on pl. 13—32 of his splendid work: Monuments Typographiques des Pays-Bas. La Haye, 1868, that it is impossible to separate them. 1st, the types of the Yliada and of the Ludovicus de Roma are found in the same volume (see No. 19, and 23 & 24), and there can, therefore, be no doubt that they belonged to the same press; 2nd, Mr. Holtrop points out that some capitals of the Ludovicus type are identical with some which occur in the Facetiæ morales, which serves to connect these two; 3rd, the type of the Facetiæ morales resembles so closely that of the two stray leaves in what is called the mixed Dutch edition of the Speculum, that these two also must be connected; 4th, the two stray leaves in the Dutch Speculum issued undoubtedly from the same press as the rest of the book, although it may be difficult to assign the true reason for the printer's using a different type for this sheet; 5th, Mr. Holtrop gives on pl. 31 the facsimile of a Donatus, printed on vellum, with a type which differs from the others by its size and the shape of the capital P; but it is of Netherland fabrication, and is related, by its final t with the perpendicular bar, to the Donatuses and other books, which offer the same particulars; 6th and lastly, we find on pl. 32 of Holtrop's Monuments a facsimile of a Donatus, discovered in a convent at Uden in South Brabant, the types of which have a great family-likeness with that used for the Saliceto.

Whether type 1, 2, 3, 4, 5, 6 and 7, are really the printer's first, second, third, &c. type, I am unable to say. I have, with the exception of the type of the Abecedarium (see next page), merely followed the order in which Mr. Holtrop has given them in his Monuments, and which is also adopted by Mr. Bradshaw in his "List of the Founts of Type and Wood-cut Devices used by Printers in Holland in the 15th Century," just published by Macmillan and Co., and from which he kindly allowed me to borrow some of the above particulars. My only object for the present was to collect materials for further researches, and to arrange them into some shape, which enables any one to see at a glance what there is. The list is no doubt imperfect, but I have done all I could to make it as complete as possible, although I have abstained from all speculations, and simply confined myself to a query where the description from which I got my information was not clear enough. The forty-three works I have enumerated are, therefore, all different editions, except No. 17, which is the two leaves occurring in the mixed Dutch Speculum (No. 2). I have made no attempt to describe the books, and only given the barest information as to what they are, what has been preserved of them, where the remaining copies or fragments are to be found,[1] where they are described, and where (the best) facsimiles may be found. There are a number of fragments of Donatus in the Paris and Bodleian libraries which I have not yet been able to examine.

As to the number of these *Costeriana*, it has always been under-stated, by Costerians as well as Anti-Costerians. M. Ruelens, the present librarian of the Royal Library at Brussels, reached the highest statement in his article in *Le Bibliophile Belge*, mentioned above, yet he speaks only of "une vingtaine d'ouvrages." This under-statement, although never intentional, has often been the cause of the false argumentation with which the books on the subject abound.

As to the date—1470—which the Anti-Costerians usually ascribed to these works, this was in most cases a mere conventional one, and generally applied to incunabula which looked "very old." The history of printing at Strasburg (see page xxi of this Introduction) affords an example of the little confidence we can put in the dates usually assigned to some of the incunabula. The earliest date of printing at Strasburg was given by Panzer (1793) as 1471; Hain (1831) put it at 1473; Namur (1834) at 1471, and, of course, every early undated Strasburg book was put about that time. Bernard knew in 1853 already 1466 as the earliest date, and at present that date has to go back till 1460. It is a matter of course that if we have to put one work ten years earlier, the other undated works of the same printer, which follow it in workmanship, must go back at the same rate. Just now as we do with the Strasburg books, so may we proceed with the Costeriana as soon—— But I have avoided speculations in compiling the list, and there is certainly nothing which would justify my making them here. The earliest date we can assign for the present to the Costeriana is 1471—74. Mr. Holtrop tells us on p. 31 of his Monuments that the Hague copy of the Saliceto (see No. 25) contains two MS. annotations: 1st, "Hunc librum emit dominus Conrardus abbas hujus loci XXXIIII., qui obiit anno MCCCCLXXIIII, in profesto exaltationis sanctae crucis, postquam profuisset annis fere tribus." Another inscription indicates that this copy had belonged to the convent of St. James, at Lille.

---

[1] I have not been able to give a complete list of all the existing copies of the different editions of the Speculum. I have some hope that in the course of time I shall be able to find out where they are.

Now, the abbat Conrad, who bought this book for his convent, was Conrad du Moulin, who was abbat only from 1471 to 1474.

This is the only date we can use at present.[1] It is, as Mr. Bradshaw observes in his "List," mentioned above, "a singular circumstance that this one fact should compel us to place the printer of the Speculum at the head of the Dutch printers, though it only just allows him to take precedence of Ketelaer and De Leempt," from whom we have the date 1473, found in Peter Comestor, Scholastica hystoria.

At the end of the list I have put the celebrated Enschedé Abecedarium and the Donatus of 31 lines, both printed in the same type. Although this type, according to Mr. Holtrop (Mon. Typogr., p. 16) betrays its Dutch origin, and the final t, with the perpendicular bar, assigns it a place among the so-called Haarlem editions, it was, I thought, advisable to separate these two little works, to a certain extent, from the others. The family-likeness between them, however, is too great, and the controversy about this Abecedarium and Donatus has been too much bound up with the other Costeriana (Cf. Holtrop's Mon. Typogr., p. 15—17, and other authors), to omit them from this list. Some, indeed, who are of opinion that this Abecedarium and Donatus are the first productions of the Dutch inventor, would place them at the head of all the Costeriana, as, for instance, Mr. Holtrop does; but for this there is, I think, hardly any reason, for the even edges of both these little works, and especially the efforts made by the printer to space out the words, so as to make the lines in the Abecedarium even, betray too much skill and progress in workmanship, to place these books before the productions of which we find facsimiles on pl. 13, 14, 27, 28, &c., of Mr. Holtrop's work. The fact of the Donatus fragment being printed only on one side, can be no argument as to its great antiquity, for the fragment may have been a simple proof-sheet. On this head Mr. Bradshaw writes in the above-mentioned brochure, " Many specimens of early printing have been recovered from the bindings of other books, and these sometimes afford a very valuable evidence as to their history. Such fragments in the binder's hands are either sheets of books which have been used up and thrown away, and may be called *binder's waste*; or else they are spoilt sheets or unused proofs from a printer's office, and may be called *printer's waste*. In early times the printers were frequently their own binders; many instances can be found to confirm Mr. Holtrop's interesting notice of Veldener being his own bookbinder. It becomes, therefore, a matter of considerable importance to use all endeavours to ascertain where the volume was bound which contains any such fragments. If a fragment is found printed on one side only it has hitherto been described as ' a remarkably interesting specimen of anopisthographic typography, probably executed in the infancy of the art, &c. &c.,' instead of which it is simply a proof-sheet of the most commonplace description; and in no case does it seem to have inspired the discoverer to follow up the scent, or to inform the world of the one single fact which might give his discovery any real value. Surely there must be some trace of the binders who used some of the many fragments now existing in Holland, such as the Enschedé Abecedarium and the Donatus fragment in the same type, or any of the innumerable fragments of Donatuses and Doctrinales which exist in various collections. If it is not thought unreasonable to spend large sums of money upon such specimens, it seems at least reasonable to devote a little trouble towards ascertaining what they really are. This portion of the inquiry, however, seems at present almost wholly unattempted even in Holland."[2]

---

[1] It will be observed that this date is found in one of the books printed in type V. (see No. 25). But I have said before that I do not know whether the types are arranged in their proper order. For, if that were the case, it would follow that all the books printed in types I—4 had been printed before 1471; but such an idea is altogether out of the question. No attempt has hitherto been made to investigate in what order the types of the printer of the Speculum should be put: or if it has been made, it has been without any result. Let us hope that Mr. Bradshaw will be able, some day, to settle this question.

[2] Mr. Campbell writes to me, "I wonder whether there exist in any collection Donatuses, or fragments of Donatuses, *printed* on one side only. The vellum would not, I believe, allow the leaves

INTRODUCTION.

Here, then, we have the present state of the Coster-question, which could hardly be called by this name any longer. Its hero, or heroes, have been put on a firm, historical ground; the mystery which has hitherto surrounded him has been cleared up, and it is very improbable that either Lourens Janszoon, the sheriff, or Lourens Janszoon Coster, the chandler, will ever make their appearance again as inventors of printing. And for the forty-three different so-called productions of the reputed Dutch inventor, we have the date 1471—74, found in one of them, which is the earliest we can at present ascribe to them, and which puts a Dutch invention, prior to that of Mentz, entirely out of the question. There is not a single circumstance which would give us a right, at present, to place the Costeriana in an earlier period; the workmanship of the book on which the date is found, is quite in harmony with the date found in the Saliceto, and the workmanship of the other Costeriana is not materially different from No. 25. At any rate it would be impossible to separate some or all the Donatuses, and put them some thirty years earlier, for the sake of the passage in the Cologne chronicle. And yet this is what Dr. Van Meurs wishes us to do, as I learned from a letter of his, written in answer to an article I wrote on this subject, in July last, in the "Nederlandschen Spectator."

And why?

It is here the place to quote the celebrated passage of the Cologne chronicle, and to say a few words about it:—

"... Itē dese hoichwyrdige künst vursz is vonden aller eyrst in Duytschlant tzo Mentz am Ryne.... Ind dat is geschiet by den iairen uns heren, anno dn̄i MCCCCXL. ind vā der zyt an bis men schreue. L. wart undersoicht die kunst ind wat duir zo gehoirt. Ind in den iairē uns heren do men schreyff. MCCCCL. do was eyn gulden iair, do began men tzo drucken ind was dat eyrste boich dat men druckde die Bybel zo latyn.... Item wiewail die kunst is vonden tzo Mentz, als vursz vp die wyse, als dan nu gemeynlich gebruicht wirt, so is doch die eyrste vurbyldung vonden in Hollant ryss den Donaten, die dae selfst vur der tzyt gedruckt syn. Ind vā ind ryss den is genōmen dat begynne der vursz kunst. ind is vill meysterlicher ind subtilicher vonden dan die selue manier was, und ye lenger ye mere kunstlicher wurden ... der eyrste rynder der druckerye is gewest eyn Burger tzo Mentz. ind was geboren vā Straiszburch. ind hiesch joncker Johan Gudenburch.

"Itē vā Mentz is die vursz küst komen alre eyrst tzo Coellē. Dairnae tzo Straisburch, ind dairnae tzo Venedige." (A translation will be found on page 8 of the present publication.)

I have divided the passage into two parts; the first treats of the *invention* of the art of printing, the second of its *spread*.

With respect to the first part it will be observed that Dr. Van der Linde, having asserted on page 6 that the Doctrinales mentioned in the Cambray MS. were xylographic productions printed in Flanders, points out on page 8 (note 5) and on p. 142 (note), that by the Holland spoken of in the Cologne chronicle, *Flanders* was meant, and that this error is a "geographical inaccuracy, a confusion between Holland and Flanders, which may not surprise us in an author of the middle ages."

Dr. Van Meurs, who sees in the Cologne chronicle, together with the existing typographical Donatuses, the sheet-anchor of the claims of Holland, objects, just as he has done with regard to the Cambray MS., also to this interpretation; indeed, his

---

being pasted together, as was done in the anopisthographic block-books and Specula Humanæ Salvationis which are printed on paper. I know there are found fragments supposed to have been printed on one side only, and I myself discovered two leaves (Cf. No. 43 of the List); but the more I think on this point, the more I come to the conclusion that the very imperfect ink, used for the printing of these works, has been washed off from one side by the binder, in order that it might look like new vellum. Mr. Holtrop's facsimile (Mon. Typ. pl. 11) shows that even a part of the printed side of one of the leaves is blank now. No. 26, (the Saliceto) which Mr. Cohn was so kind as to send over for inspection, shows evidently that the not pasted part of the leaf has been scraped. Very likely this has been also the case with the two leaves in the Paris National Library (Van Praet, Belles Lettres, No. 11) and so many more which have been, or will be, found.

whole brochure was written with the intention to oppose it. He says, "the honour of Holland with respect to the invention of printing is founded on the account in the Cologne chronicle."

Now, as the truth of that part of the passage in the Cologne chronicle, which refers to Holland, cannot be proved by any authentic document, Dr. Van Meurs throws himself on the credibility of its author. He observes that: the account came from Ulr. Zell, who was probably a disciple of Gutenberg,[1] and still living in 1499, when the chronicle was published; a man who could know every particular of the event; who was a German, and gave his account to a German, and had, therefore, no reason whatever to speak of Holland as the country where the "vurbyldung" had been printed, if he had not felt bound to acknowledge the truth, &c. As to the "geographical inaccuracy," of which Dr. Van der Linde speaks, this explanation has, according to him, no foundation at all, and is totally in opposition to the geographical accuracy which the author of the Chronicle observes everywhere, in a manner really remarkable for his time. "Every man," thus we read on page 4, according to Dr. Van Meurs, "feels, by nature, more inclined to his own country, and everything connected with it, and more especially does he learn the manifold honourable deeds and histories of his ancestors, rather from one who was born in the place where he himself was born and brought up, than from a stranger. On that account, I will describe the principal and most remarkable events of Germany. But I will also write of the Roman emperors, and of the year in which they ascended the throne, in order that the events connected with every one of them, may be in harmony with truth. For, as Hugo of Florens says, those events of which cannot be said in which year or when they happened, will be regarded as fables or stories. And in order that no one may doubt the truth of what we intend to write down, be it known that this book is compiled from truthful historians. Also from the chronicles of the archbishop of Cologne, of the kings of France, of Saxony, of Treves, of Strasburg, Mentz, Brabant, Holland, Flanders, &c.

"It is evident from this," Dr. Van Meurs continues, "that we have here to do with a conscientious author, who has regard, in the first place, to patriotism; but who wishes, at the same time, to be as accurate as possible, and for that reason mentions his sources. The several countries which are connected with the question of the invention of printing, are specially named by him. And so it is in the whole chronicle. He always speaks of Flanders just in the same way as it is done at present; he speaks of Bruges as Bruges in Flanders, of Antwerp as Antwerp in Brabant. Whenever there is question of Holland, he means the Holland as we still know it; nay, even the bishopric of Utrecht is accurately defined. It would lead me too far, to quote all these passages, but I should be able to do it, and doubt therefore whether Dr. Van der Linde would be able to point out an example of this pretended geographical inaccuracy. To suppose so little knowledge, or an error in the author of the chronicle, that he would speak of Holland while he meant quite a different province, or to suppose that between him and Ulr. Zell, in their discourse on the

---

[1] In a brochure entitled: Lettres d'un Bibliographe (M. J. P. A Madden), published by Tross, at Paris, in 1868, the author (page 40) says: "Ulr. Zel de Hanau, était un élève non de Gutenberg, mais de Schoeffer . . ., je n'en veux d'autre preuve que la ressemblance des caractères de Schoeffer et de Zel, ressemblance qui a fait attribuer au premier ce qui appartient au dernier . . . . Il y a même plus que la ressemblance, il y a identité de certains caractères chez l'imprimeur de Mayence et celui de Cologne . . . . Remarquez d'ailleurs que si Ulric Zel eût appartenu à l'atelier de Gutenberg et non à celui de Schoeffer, il est peu probable qu'il eût quitté Mayence pour Cologne, et qu'il eût dit, dans la Chronique de Cologne, que Gutenberg était de Strasbourg." He further argues that Gutenberg printed the bull of Pius II., of 12th Sept. 1461, in favour of Adolph of Nassau; for at the capture of Mentz, Oct. 28, 1462, by the partisans of Adolph, the house of Fust was reduced to ashes, but that of Gutenberg and his workmen were respected. Adolph, moreover, created Gutenberg, in 1465, one of his courtiers, and rewarded his zeal and talents in divers other ways. Ulric Zel, *therefore*, belonged to the atelier of Fust and Schoeffer, he escaped from the fire and ruin when he arrived at Cologne and founded there the first printing-office, &c., &c.

Dr. Ennen, in his "Katalog der Inkunabeln in der Stadt-Bibliothek zu Köln," page II., says : "Ulr. Zell . . . learned his art at Mentz, and was probably the first composer and superintendent in the printing-office of Gutenberg and Fust."

origin of Donatuses, a sort of quiproquo had taken place, and that he had been mistaken, only on that occasion, in the term Holland—and all this without any evidence, and because it suited his purpose—is somewhat more than a sophism or distorting of the text. Indeed, it is the system of the anti-Costerians that at every troublesome place in the chronicle, either Zell or the author made an error."

After this and many more assertions as to the credibility of the author of the chronicle, Dr. Van Meurs concludes: "I consider the Cologne chronicle to be the strongest historical authority in favour of an invention of printing in Holland." "The account in the Cologne chronicle is the earliest and most important document for the invention of printing in Holland. If we will not accept it, and say: 'the whole is a lie,' be it so; but then there is henceforth no longer any history but an arbitrary one: let then every one heap the one false argument upon the other, with addition of the most hateful abuses and exclamations of indolence and bad faith, &c."

There is, I think, no reason whatever for distrusting Dr. Van Meurs' statement as regards the geographical accuracy of the author of the Cologne chronicle. On the contrary, every one will be grateful to him, for having ascertained it, for it is certainly no agreeable work to go through that old, quaint dialect of the book. Unfortunately, the labour of Dr. Van Meurs cannot benefit us. Real evidence (*i.e.* authentic documents) are required to substantiate the truth of the first part of a passage, of the second part of which we are able to point out the palpable *inaccuracy*.

In the second part of the passage it is said that "from Mentz the art was introduced first of all into Cologne, then into Strasburg, and afterwards into Venice."

Suppose now we had to make a chronological catalogue of all the incunabula, then, if we could accept the "historical authority" of the Cologne chronicle as the only valid one, we should have to put the towns in the following order: 1. Mentz, 2. Cologne, 3. Strasburg, 4. Venice.

But every one who has followed until our time the history of the invention and the progress of the art of printing, knows that—even if we adopt Bernard's opinion, and attribute the Calendars of 1455 and 1457, which are generally ascribed to Pfister at Bamberg, to a printer at Mentz—there is the date of 1461 (one in MS. on a duplicate copy of the last leaf of the Bible of thirty-six lines, printed by Pfister, in the Paris library; another, printed, in the colophon of Boner's Edelstein of the same printer), which compels us to put Bamberg before Cologne; for, the earliest date of Ulr. Zell, which has hitherto come to our knowledge, is 1466.

At the time Bernard wrote his book (1853), he placed Strasburg before Cologne, as he was aware of the copy of a Bible printed by Mentelin, preserved at Stuttgard, on which is written: "Explicit liber iste anno Domini Millesimo quadringentesimo sexagesimo sexto &c." And in a note on page 61 of his second vol., he says: "L'Auteur de la Chronique de Cologne, par patriotisme, fait passer sa ville avant Strasbourg," for knowing the Cologne date of 1466, and considering that it occurs in a thin and small work in 4to., he naturally concluded that the printer of a folio Bible, which was ready in 1466, had begun earlier than this year.

This circumstance, however, was not yet so prejudicial to the authority of the Cologne chronicle, for we could hardly demand from its author that he would know the progress of the art within a day or two. But a few months ago, Mr. Bradshaw called my attention to a note, added to a copy of the same Bible in the sale catalogue of Culeman's library, where it was said that the copy of the Freiburg library was rubricated 1460. Dr. Van der Linde, who lives at present in Berlin and was so kind as to write for me to Freiburg, received a letter from Dr. Dziatzko, the librarian of the university of that place, confirming the contents of the above note. At the end of the first volume he finds written in a contemporary hand with red ink: "Explicit Psalterium, 1460;" at the end of the second volume: "Explicit Apocalipsis. Anno dñi M°.CCCC.LXj°." And on some sheets of paper of the same manufacture, only a little different in colour, which contain the tables of contents in MS., he finds the dates

1462 and 1464.[1] There is no doubt that Strasburg should be placed before Cologne, even before Bamberg, as hardly any doubt remains with respect to this date.[2] It is also well-known that in the convent of Subiaco printing went on already in 1465, at Rome in 1467, at Augsburg and Basle in 1468, and at Venice not before 1469. These facts *compel* us to place the towns in the following order: 1. *Mentz*, 2. *Strasburg*, 3. Bamberg, 4. Subiaco, 5. *Cologne*, 6. Rome, 7. Augsburg, 8. Basle, 9. *Venice*; and the natural inference we may draw from them is, that the author of the Cologne chronicle was very *imperfectly* informed about the events he recorded. Now, an author who is so palpably inaccurate with respect to one thing, is liable to say something in another place which we may not unconditionally accept as "historical authority." For the present, therefore, we may regard the history of the *invention* and *spread* of the art of printing in this chronicle as a well-meant account of it; but which failed, either by the author being misinformed, or by some other circumstance which has hitherto not come to our knowledge.[3]

That the author of the Cologne chronicle wrote anything which he did not implicitly believe himself, or which he had not heard from Ulr. Zell, no one would think of asserting; but it happens not unfrequently that utterly wrong statements are made by authors, who by their position and learning find great credence, and thereby spread

---

[1] It will not be superfluous to give a translation of Dr. Dziatzko's letter. "Under the press-mark 17089 (Real Cat. vol. 3, p. 57) of our library, I find: Biblia sacra latina. Tomus I. continet Pentateuchum usque ad Psalterium. S. l. 1460. Tomus II. continet Proverbia Salomonis usque ad librum secundum Machabocorum novumque testamentum. 2 vols. fol.

"The copy itself (not long ago, it seems, rebound, or at least repaired) is labelled on the back with gilt letters: Biblia sacra latina Argent. per Mentelin, 1460. Tom. I., and . . . 1461. Tom. II.—Place and printer are not indicated in either of the volumes, but the description which Panzer (Annal. typogr. vol. I. p. 69) gives of the Strasburg Bible agrees *entirely* with our copy.

"Both volumes are ornamented with beautiful initials (if I am not mistaken, then those of the second volume have another character than those of the first). At the end of the first volume is written by the rubricator (apparently the same who worked the initials in the same volume):

𝕰𝖝𝖕𝖑𝖎𝖈𝖎𝖙 𝖕𝖘𝖆𝖑𝖙𝖊𝖗𝖎𝖚
. 1460

"At the end of the second volume:

𝕰𝖝𝖕𝖑𝖎𝖈𝖎𝖙 𝕬𝖕𝖔𝖈𝖆𝖑𝖎𝖕𝖘𝖎𝖘
𝕬𝖓𝖓𝖔 𝖉𝖓𝖎 𝕸𝖔. 𝖈𝖈𝖈𝖈. 𝖑𝖝𝖏

"I see a confirmation of these years in the following facts: In front of the first volume are bound eight leaves of the same size and of the same paper, only a little whiter, which contain tables of contents in MS. On these we find now and then dates (apparently every time when the epitome was finished). For instance, we find on leaf 4, col. 1, line 38, with black ink, the year 1462 (on both sides are dots with red ink); on leaf 6, col. 4 (at the end of the continuous table of contents; the following two leaves contain on the two opposite pages a review of the contents, arranged in the form of a genealogical table) . . . año dñi 1464. j die Junij, underlined with red, and with a red stroke through the a of anno . . . At the end of the second volume are again thirty-two written leaves, containing matters of a religious character. In the second half we find again, at the end of a division, the date 1464 . . . ."

[2] It is highly interesting, at present, to read Bernard's chapter on the introduction of printing into Strasburg, in his second volume, page 61 sqq.

[3] Dr. Van Meurs wrote to me: "Granted that it was an inaccuracy of Zell to place Cologne before Strasburg, I think it hypercritical to compare this with the main question of which I speak. If we go as far as that, then there is no reason why we should not reject Mentz and Gutenberg also when that were necessary [Dr. Van Meurs forgets that this is not necessary, as there is abundant evidence for the invention at Mentz, and that we object only to accepting those informations of the Cologne chronicle, which we cannot make agree with *facts*]. I am, however, not at all disposed to admit that it is an inaccuracy. The towns are at present arranged according to the dates of the works, printed in each of them. At the infancy of the art, however, a great many books were published without date or place. As contemporary, Zell was perfectly capable of knowing where and when these works were printed, and he had no interest whatever in giving wrong information about them. I consider it therefore a false science and ridiculous pedantry, to exclaim, four centuries later, simply because it suits one's purpose, without further evidence, and contrary to his (Zell's) account : 'We have changed all this.'" I need not add one word to this note, as the facts I have given above speak for themselves. The earliest date of Ulr. Zell we know of is 1466, but some authors suppose, and it is quite probable, that he arrived at Cologne already in 1462, after the capture of Mentz. But even if this were true, Strasburg and Bamberg would come before Cologne.

opinions which it takes a long time to eradicate. A striking proof of this we find in Bernard, whose book I admire for its charming style and the mode in which the author worked. He was an "*experienced* typographer," but, notwithstanding this capacity, of which he was perfectly aware himself, he made some errors from which it is clear that this very experience as a modern typographer, had led his judgment on the early printed books astray. One of these errors, I speak of, is his supposition that the earliest printers did *not* print their works page by page, and required, therefore, a great quantity of type before they could think of beginning to print. We find on page 164 of his first volume, a calculation as to how many thousands of letters Gutenberg required in order to be able to begin the printing of his Bible, and his result was: 120,000 at least. With respect to this calculation he says in a note on the same page: "Il y a des personnes qui croient qu'on imprimait les pages une à une dans les premiers temps de l'imprimerie. Cette idée n'a pu venir qu'à des gens tout à fait étrangers aux travaux de la typographie. Un semblable procédé aurait annulé tous les avantages que l'imprimerie avait sur la xylographie . . . .". Bernard returns to this subject on page 233 of his first, and on page 9 of his second volume, and perhaps in some other places of his work; but it is not worth while to look them out for—Bernard is here decidedly wrong. Mr. Bradshaw, the Librarian of Cambridge, whose bibliographical talents are too well known than that I should venture to praise them, often pointed facts out to me, during the time that I had the great fortune of seeing my study of incunabula guided by him, which left no doubt but that the earliest printers printed their works page by page.

I may also say that Mr. Winter Jones, the Principal Librarian of the British Museum, whose long experience and intrinsic bibliographical knowledge give great weight to his opinion, told me not long ago that he had always been of the same opinion, and that he had met with several proofs which confirmed it.

Bernard, when he says: "Un semblable procédé [printing page by page] aurait annulé tous les avantages que l'imprimerie avait sur la xylographie," overlooks the fact that the great advantage of printing with moveable type over xylography is that it allows the same types to be used over and over again.

I should wish to give the titles of a great many incunabula in which I have found myself evidence for this mode of printing; but in order not to swell this introduction to an unnecessary length, I must refer for the present those who wish to be enlightened on this subject, to Mr. Blades' excellent work on the life and typography of W. Caxton, where on page 29 Vol. I. and p. 6 Vol. II. the author adduces facts which absolutely settle the matter.

It was only natural that Bernard, who spoke with so much authority, should find followers. In the "Lettres d'un Bibliographe" (M. Madden) referred to above, the author, treating of some incunabula, generally attributed to Ulr. Zell, makes, on page 47, a somewhat similar calculation as Bernard, and, thinking that Ulr. Zell was not rich enough to have cast for him such a great quantity of types, as were necessary for the three quarto volumes, which he argued were printed at one and the same time, he comes to the conclusion that the books in question were issued, not by U. Zell, but by a convent at Cologne.

On page 78 (second line from bottom) of the present book, we find an expression in which Bernard's unfortunate theory is visible also. Here it may pass without doing any harm; in M. Madden's case it may lead to great mischief, however necessary and good his other investigations may be.

The task which remains to me is to call attention to the pedigree of Gerrit Thomasz., spoken of on pp. 41—47. As Dr. Van Meurs declared this document to be spurious, and being unable to say anything myself about it, I asked Dr. Van der Linde to explain this point further before this work was published, and I received the following reply:

"My dear Sir,—In connexion with the brochure of the new *Costerless* Costerian, the Haarlem Dr. Van Meurs, you ask me a few words in explanation of Lourens

Jansz. Coster's pedigree, mentioned in my work, which is preserved at Haarlem, and is exhibited to the public as a valuable argument for Haarlem's claim. For the unprejudiced it is sufficient to let the facts speak for themselves.

"This vellum document, unique among forgeries of this kind, has been declared to be:

'a pedigree of Lourens, on *very old vellum*, leaving off about the year 1585,' by Koning, in 1809.

'the *original* pedigree of L. J. Koster, written before 1560,' by the same, in 1816.

'the *original* pedigree, written in or about the year 1550, and continued after 1560 by another hand,' by the Haarlem Committee of the Typographical Exhibition of 1823.

'the *original* pedigree, written on vellum, which has become dark brown by time, and from which oldest part it is *sufficiently evident* that it was written before 1560,' by the archivist Scheltema, in 1834.

'an *old* pedigree of L. J. C., written between 1550 and 1560,' by Dr. De Vries, in the *official* List of Documents in the Town-Hall at Haarlem, in 1862.

'an *old* and *highly interesting* document,' by the present archivist of Haarlem, Dr. A. J. Enschedé, in 1870.

'a pedigree *certainly not much younger* than 1520, although the dates were falsified,' by the Rotterdam archivist, M. Scheffer, in 1870, in presence of me and the Haarlem archivist.

"Compare with this the exact description of the document in my book (p. 41—47), and you will agree with me, that the only answer Dr. Van Meurs deserves, is, to quote what he says (also in 1870) about the same document, *now* that I have exposed the shameful abuse made of it, and when evasions can no longer be of any use.

"On p. 57, note, he (Dr. Van Meurs) says: 'For those who are not living in Haarlem, and yet might feel inclined to study the Coster-question, I think it necessary to say a few words regarding this document, which Dr. Van der Linde uses frequently, and in connexion with which he creates a new witness, who has hitherto been unknown, and who now becomes the whole cause of the deception, namely Gerrit Thomasz., mentioned by Junius, *honoris causâ*. It would appear that this old man has really been *the* arch-rascal, but at the same time a biologer. He had a pedigree written for him on vellum, with the words that Laurens Jansz. Coster brought the 'first print into the world anno 1446'; he bribed Van Zuren; he shewed the pedigree as the 'memorie' (see page 54, 4th line from bottom) to Guicciardini; in honour of him Junius wrote the whole Haarlem story, nay, it is even probable that he bribed Coornhert to ignore the names of Bellaert and Andriessen in 1483—1486. I answer: that it is by no means certain yet that the pedigree was made for Gerrit Thomasz. One must be totally ignorant of the writing and the peculiar look of old documents, or never have had the document in his hands, not to see that its spuriousness is evident from all sides. I consider this pedigree, which was unknown to Scriverius, of which no one had ever spoken, until it dropt as it were from the sky in 1726, and which, therefore, possesses not the least authenticity—I consider this pedigree hardly of the 17th, much less of the 16th century. So long as practised, impartial antiquarii, acquainted with old manuscripts and similar documents, have not decided this question, so long do I deny Dr. Van der Linde the right of drawing conclusions respecting the Coster-question, on the authority of this document.'

"Therefore one must not have had this document in his hands not to see that its spuriousness is evident from all sides!? My respectful compliments again to Koning, who bought it (already in 1809!) for a long price; to the government of Haarlem, who bought it at the sale of Koning's effects; to the archivist Scheltema, who was so well acquainted with 'the writing and the peculiar look of old documents' that he made pedigrees to order; to Dr. De Vries, who had the thing under his care for half-a-century; to the government of Haarlem, who, till this very day, show this document to strangers as a weapon against the Mentz theft of Haarlem's glory!

"The thing is very plain. The 'document,' although it originated in the 16th century, can be of no use any longer, and they would fain disavow the exposed deceiver with one or two ungrateful dicta. . . .

Yours sincerely,

Berlin, Oct. 1, 1871.   VAN DER LINDE."

The history of the Coster-legend, and the exposal of all that has been said or written on the subject, is not calculated to inspire any one with a high opinion of the scholarship of those who have written on it; but we must not forget that the question of the invention of printing (palæotypography) and bibliography in general has hitherto very seldom been a field on which we could hope to encounter brilliant talents. A little theoretical knowledge of the subject was all that was cared for, and all the authors who have written on the question, whether they be Dutch, English, French, or German, always thought that the mere sight of one or two Donatuses, Doctrinales, &c., combined with some notion of modern printing, had given them a sufficient knowledge of palæotypography to enable them to give an opinion on this subject.

At present, a happy change for the better has set in, especially with respect to palæotypography; for some highly important works have been published in Holland, France, Germany, and England during the last few years, which must inevitably make the subject better known and more respected.

In Holland Mr. Holtrop, assisted by the present Librarian of the Royal Library at the Hague, Mr. Campbell, published a "Catalogus librorum Saec. XV° impressorum quotquot in Bibl. Regia Hagana asservantur." Hag. Com. 1856; and "Monuments Typographiques des Pays-Bas au 15e siècle," La Haye, 1868, which will be lasting monuments for the author and his country. In England Mr. Blades' Life and Typography of William Caxton, 2 vols., Lond., 1861, is a monograph which may safely be said to have exhausted the subject, and which may confidently be recommended to all practical students of incunabula. Mr. Bradshaw's "Memoranda," of which No. 1—3 have been published, are compiled with his usual consummate skill and accuracy, and contain rules and directions for the study of incunabula, which have called forth already the admiration of those who wish for a more exact study of this subject than exists at present. Their only fault is that they follow each other at such long intervals. The "Collectio Weigeliana : Die Anfänge der Druckerkunst" (written in German), by T. O. Weigel and Dr. A. Zestermann, 2 vols. fol., is written with a knowledge and accuracy which cannot fail to command the respect of all students of the subject.

I wish to make some general observations as to the proper names, &c., occurring in this work. As I had to leave some Christian names untranslated, I thought it better to leave them all in their original state. So for John the reader will find Johan and Hans (German), Jan (Dutch) and Johannes. The name of the hero, or rather heroes, Laurens Janszoon Coster (or Koster) and Laurens Janszoon, is spelt in various ways: Lou, Lourens, Laurens, Louwerijs, Louris, Lourijs, &c. Quotations from the Latin, French, and Italian, I have mostly given untranslated, as these languages are sufficiently known in this country. Extracts from Dutch account-books, &c., are generally given in their original, with an English translation added to it, as far as the phrase was capable of being translated. I have left untranslated the word "print" in the pedigree (see page 41). It will readily be understood that some impression is meant, although we do not know to what kind of impression allusion is made.

With regard to my translation, I hope it will not be found too faulty. I undertook it because I thought it required one who had some knowledge of the subject, and was thoroughly acquainted with the Dutch language. The subject itself has interested me for many years; and Haarlem is my birth-place, just as it is that of the author. I have done my best, but cannot avoid the conviction that I have sinned against the idiom of the English language. But those who go through the work and the accompanying notes will see that my task has not been one of the easiest. The style of the author himself was striking and terse, but at the same time idiomatic to the last degree. The thousand-and-one quotations, however, from French, German, Italian, and especially Dutch authors of the 17th, 18th, and 19th centuries, who all wrote in a different, and very often most tedious and prolix style, were exceedingly trying to me. Their translation required the utmost precaution, as they were full of technical terms and descriptions of different modes of printing, which had to be distinguished carefully one from another, and they demanded an equal amount of patience, in order to be able to read and translate what I could not help regarding as rubbish, but which it was necessary to give for a full understanding of the case. I had wished myself to abridge the work, as it contained, I thought, many things which are absolutely unknown, and which will even now be imperfectly understood, in this country. And I had more particularly wished to omit that part of the book which refers to the works of Pfister and Gutenberg, as Bernard has made important researches concerning these works, which differ altogether from those authors from whom Dr. Van der Linde's description is derived. As I was unable, however, to make just now the necessary investigations to see who is right, I have not touched this subject. Moreover, some friends, whose advice I could not disregard, wished to have the book complete. Hence it is that I have given the text intact, except a few expressions which I omitted, as they could only be understood or appreciated by a native of Holland. Of the notes I have only omitted those portions which were written exclusively for the Dutch. Every one in this country will therefore be able to study, in his own language, a subject which he could hitherto only have learnt at second hand from translations.

Several kind friends have assisted me, either in the revision of the proof-sheets, or in answering my questions with respect to the various difficulties which I now and then experienced in the translation. I am sorry that the conviction that there are still many expressions in the book which are "not English," prevents me from mentioning their names.

But I may be allowed to express my gratitude to the authorities of the British Museum, Mr. J. Winter Jones, the Principal Librarian, and Mr. W. B. Rye, the Keeper of the printed books, for the kind and liberal manner in which they place everything at my disposal which can further my studies of the early printed books, &c. Indeed, they give me so many facilities, that I often think, with some anxiety, that much will be expected from one to whom so much is given. And when I beg to thank Mr. E. Roy, the Assistant-Keeper, under whose more immediate care I am placed, for the kindness and never-failing accuracy with which he answers my manifold questions, I only wish to add that he is not the only gentleman of the British Museum to whom I am indebted for information.

J. H. HESSELS.

London, Oct. 5, 1871.

ERRATUM.

Pag. 35—In Chronological Table: 1473, for "Aalst" read "Alost."

THE AUTHOR'S PREFACE.

This book originated from a revision and amalgamation of my article on Gutenberg, inserted in the "Vaderlandsche Letteroefeningen" of July, 1870, and my essay on the famous Coster-question, published in the "Nederlandschen Spectator," from December, 1869, till May, 1870. It is no mere reprint, but a new work.

If I had written for any other public but that of Holland, much of what I have said about Gutenberg could have been omitted, that being better known elsewhere; but the bad faith of the Costerians has obscured and distorted all this for the Netherland public. It ought to be enabled to compare *history* and *fable*. The so-called arguments for Haarlem, placed by the side of the historical documents for Mentz, would be already a condemnation of the Costerian misleading demagogues. *All documents are here together for the first time.* Whoever has no leisure to make a study of the subject, let him read the book without the notes; by a simple reading he will be convinced that the Haarlem statues are crumbled down before criticism, like Dagon before the ark of the covenant. Let us watch how long the Haarlem people will remain deaf to the truth!

Sagacious readers will probably come to the conclusion that we could hardly speak of a Haarlem *legend*, as the inventions of Junius and Scriverius do not satisfy the scientific notions of a legend. Those who think thus are right. But the more exact title, *Coster-villany*, instead of *Coster-legend*, is a little hard, not for the case, but—for an advertisement in the newspapers. Posterity, not led astray by all sorts of personal reminiscences and acquaintances, will blame me for the too great forbearance of my polemics. *For, in the Coster-question, no Costerian ever spoke a true word.* Neither does posterity know that I have already been compelled to listen to communications from all sides in the interest of the Boscos and Barnums whom I have exposed.

Science may now proceed to a more accurate examination of all the secondary questions concerning the history of the invention of typography. It is, for instance, not impossible that some book has wrongly been attributed to Pfister; it even appears to me that the thirty-six line Bible was not printed by him, but by Gutenberg. But all these secondary questions could not be clearly stated and impartially examined, so long as Costerianism clouded our heads with the prejudice of a plurality of the invention. Its removal is, therefore, a revolution in bibliography, which promises a surprisingly plentiful harvest to a renewed, strictly scientific, exclusively historical and typological investigation.

VAN DER LINDE.

The Hague, Aug. 14, 1870.

I.

WRITING, XYLOGRAPHY AND TYPOGRAPHY.

Every revolution in history is the result of a long preparation, the necessary fruit of time, and has as condition the causes which bring it about. This law of history, observed by every one in the religious revolution of the first centuries of the Christian era, in the ecclesiastical revolution of the 16th century, in the social revolution of 1789, is forgotten whenever there is question of the invention of typography. "How is it possible that it was not invented *earlier?*" is the exclamation of popular surprise, the fact being that it did not appear earlier for the same reason that Christianity did not arise earlier, that America was not discovered earlier, and that the Church was not revolutionized some centuries earlier. No scientific man asks how it is possible that Luther was not born earlier, that the feudal system did not fall to pieces earlier. And yet the invention of typography is something more than all revolutions: an event, therefore, which could only be born from "the fulness of time."

It has waited already much too long for a purely scientific treatment. For my present task, however, it will suffice to give a sketch of the event and its cause, and of its connexion with the literary development of the middle ages, in order to enable the reader sufficiently to judge of the value of the fable, which represents typography, only long after, and in opposition to history, as having been invented at Haarlem. This fable, which rests on nothing but an artificially and deceptively-fostered popular belief, deserves to be struck at last by the justice of criticism. But it must be placed immediately in the light of history, in order to make its utter worthlessness manifest. I will, therefore, sum up as many of the facts as will be necessary to test the component parts of the legend.

The researches of our time have already brought to light so much as may assure us of the existence of a kind of book-trade in the *thirteenth* century. Sworn scriptores, illuminatores, and stationarii librorum, librarii, pergamenarii (transcribers, illuminators, lenders and sellers of books) belonged, at that time in Italy, and soon afterwards in France, to the organization of a university. The supply of books of that period, mostly of a juridical and theological nature, amounts to above one hundred different works. Notwithstanding the abstract contents of this literature, a book was seldom liked without some ornamented title and illuminated initials; hence the fact that there was no want of illuminators already at that time.[1]

The workmen-scriptores developed into calligraphers, the illuminatores into artists. Magnificent manuscripts on vellum became objects of luxury at the courts of princes and among people of distinction, especially in Italy, France, and England. But this development reached its highest point of prosperity in the Burgundy of the 15th century. The chivalrous-romantic element in the literature, the wealth of the towns of the Southern Netherlands, the love for art among the princes, the magnificent rise of the Flemish school of painting, the use of the living language of the country, the liberal reward of artists; all these beams united made Burgundy the lustre of Europe. The library of Philip the Good, at Brussels, was in 1443 said to be the largest and richest in the world. More than three thousand beautifully illuminated manuscripts were found in the libraries of the dukes of Burgundy at Bruges, Antwerp, Brussels, Ghent and elsewhere.

---

[1] Beiträge zur Geschichte des deutschen Buchhandels, Von Albrecht Kirchhoff, I. Notizen über einige Buchhändler des xv and xvi Jahrhunderts. Leipzig, J. C. Hinrichs, 1851. 8vo.

By the side of the calligraphers were developed the special transcribers of the universities, especially at Paris, Cologne, Heidelberg, Leipzig and Vienna. A third class, exempt from the privileges, but at the same time from the obstructive rules, of the universities, thronged the populous capitals and commercial towns, and worked, not like the calligraphers, for people of distinction, or, like the university transcribers, for the scholars, but for the people in general. In 1405 the Company of Stationers (Stationarii) existed in London, which supplied transcripts of several kinds of books, also ABC books, paternosters, credos, and similar trifles. Just as the university-quarter of the Paris booksellers and transcribers of the middle ages is still called the *pays latin*, so London places derive their names from the labours of the said Company—Paternoster Row, Creed Lane, Amen Corner, Ave Maria Lane. Even at present the association of typographers and booksellers in London is called "The Stationers' Company."[1]

We find an example of a busy trade in manuscripts in Germany in Dypold Lauber, teacher and transcriber in the free town of Hagenau, whose formal advertisements, in the handwriting of the middle of the 15th century, have been discovered with the notification, "Item welcher hande bücher man gerne hat, gross oder clein, geistlich oder weltlich, hübsch gemolt, die findet man alle by diebold louber, schriber, in der burge zu hagenow." This remarkable earliest stock catalogue commences with, "Das gross buch genannt Gesta Romanorum mit den viguren gemolt." After this, poetical works appear (Parcival, Tristan, Freidank); romances of chivalry (der witfarn ritter, *i.e.* the knight from afar; von eime getruwen ritter der sin eigen hertze gab umb einer schönen frowen willen; der ritter unter dem zuber, *i.e.* the enchanted knight, &c.); biblical and legendary works (ein gerymeto bibel; ein salter latin und tütsch; episteln und evangelien durch das jor; vita christy; das gantze passional winterteil und summerteil); edifying books (Bellial; der selen trost; der rosenkrantz; die zehn gebot mit glosen; cleine bette bücher); books for the people (gute bewehrte artznien bücher; gemolte lossbücher, *i.e.* fortune-telling books; schachtzabel gemolt), &c.[2]

The transcriber of school-books stood lowest in the scale. The education of that time was exclusively in the hands, *i.e.* in the fetters, of the Church. The lower educational books were the so-called Abecedaria, which contained the alphabet, the Lord's Prayer, the Creed, and one or two prayers. In the Netherlands are well known the "little book of the mass," and the "little book for blessing the table." The Museum Meermanno-Westreenianum at the Hague possesses a manuscript copy of the Abecedarium with alphabet, paternoster, ave-maria and credo. It was still used during the reign of Charles V., for in an ordinance concerning the schools of Leeuwarden it was enjoined by him that a sworn printer should furnish, without any alteration "the little book commencing with the alphabet; the little book which directs how to bless the table (graces at meals); the little book which directs how to answer at the holy mass." In the list of prohibited books of 1546 the alphabet, paternoster, ave-maria, credo, confiteor, and the seven penitential psalms are exempted for educational purposes.

Fragments have been discovered of all of them, except of that which directs how to bless the table. In a school-ordinance of Bautzen, of 1418, we find even the prices of these little manuscript books :—

---

[1] Aelteste Gesch. der Xylographie und der Druckkunst überhaupt; besonders in Anwendung auf den Bilddruck. Ein Beitrag zur Erfindungs- und Kunst-Geschichte, Von J. D. F. Sotzmann. (Histor. Taschenbuch . . . herausgeg. Von Fr. von Raumer. Leipz. F. A. Brockhaus, 1837. Sm. 8vo, pp. 449—599.)

[2] Die Handschriftenhändler des Mittelalters. Von Albrecht Kirchhoff. Zweite . . . Ausgabe. Leipzig, 1853. 8vo.
Weitere Beiträge zur Geschichte des Handschriftenhandels im Mittelalter. Von A. Kirchhoff. Halle, H. W. Schmidt, 1855. 8vo.

Item vor ein ABC und Pater noster und Corde benedicite icgliches 1 gr.
Vor einen guten Donat 10 gr. eine Regulam moralem und Catonem [Cato's Disticha] 8 gr.
Vor ein gantz Doctrinale, das man nennet einen gantzen Text, eine halbe Marck.
Vor primam partem 8 gr.
Welch reich kind von seinem Locato nicht kaufet ein Buch, das gebe ihm 2 gr. im Anheben, ein mittelmässiger 1 gr., der arme nichts.

In this list other educational books are mentioned, of which we desire to know a little more. From the works of a Roman grammarian of the 4th century, Aelius Donatus, an extract had been compiled to serve as guide to the teaching of Latin, and was used during the middle ages all over Europe, and called "Donatus pro puerulis." A minorite of Brittany, Alexander Gallus or De Villa Dei, wrote in the 13th century a Latin grammar in barbarous (leonine) verses extracted from Priscianus (5th century). This little book, too, was used in schools for centuries. Nay, the Abecedarium and Donatus (how strikingly conservative!) are used in conventual schools in Italy to this very day. I look with melancholy respect at an Abecedarium, a little octavo book of four leaves (Il Sillabario), printed in our time, in 1862, at Asti (presso Borgo e Raspi Librai). Beneath the heading Jesus Maria the alphabet follows, and after that the pater noster, ave and credo. But the Ave salus mundi is replaced by the Salve Regina Mater misericordiae. Besides the Sillabario I have a Latin grammar, entitled: Donato ad uso delle scuole secondarie. Nuova edizione accresciuta e riformata. Pinerolo, tipografia Giuseppe Lobetti-Bodoni, 1865. 8vo.

The esteem in which these Catholic school-books, those foul springs from which, for instance, Erasmus drew the first elements of Latin, were held, was so great, that the first efforts of the humanists to improve them were regarded as heresy, and heaven and earth were moved against such dangerous destroyers. It is clear at first sight that no books were more likely to be so numerously multiplied than these, either by means of writing, wood-engraving or typography. We know already, besides some xylographic, more than *fifty* typographical editions of the 15th century from all the civilized states of Europe at that time. Donatuses were printed in every place where schools were established, and where the art of printing was introduced.

For logic and dialectics, the Summula Logica of Petrus Hispanus (perhaps Pope John XXI., elected in 1276), who was styled after this book the Summulator, was used. The chief books for morals were the "Disticha de Moribus" of a certain Dionysius Cato, not to be confounded with Cato the Censor; the "Facetus," a supplement to the preceding book; the "Floretus S. Bernardi," and some others, afterwards all printed under the collective title of "Auctores Octo Morales." Notwithstanding the reforming influence of Reuchlin and Erasmus on philology, it took a considerable time before these barbarous remains of Christian darkness were superseded for good.[1]

The rest of the education of the people was chiefly confined to the addresses of the travelling mendicant friars, who had, since the 13th century, gradually monopolized preaching and the pastoral work of the settled clergy. Provided with nothing but a little Church Latin, and therefore too ignorant to derive their discourses from original sources, they felt the want of homiletic and catechetical assistance, as a help for their understanding and memory.

Picture-books, with a brief explanatory text, were the best means of supplying this want. Hence originated representations of the mystic relation between the Old and New Testament (typology), of which the "Biblia pauperum" is the first fruit. We

---

[1] Gutenberg und seine Mitbewerber, oder die Briefdrucker und die Buchdrucker. Von J. D. F. Sotzmann. (Histor. Taschenbuch, 1841, pp. 516—676.)

find manuscripts of this work, sometimes with beautiful illuminations, as early as the 13th century. A re-modelling and development of this book is the "Speculum humanae salvationis," a work in rhyme of the 14th century in barbarous Latin, which in 45 chapters typologically represents the Bible-history, interwoven with Mariolatry and legend. The commencement gives us title and method :—

> Incipit speculum humane salvacionis
> In quo patet casus hominis & modus reparacionis
> In hoc speculo potest homo considerare
> Quam ob causam creator omnium decreuit hominem creare.

The writer of the preface says at the end, that he has added it to the work for the sake of poor preachers, to enable them to preach even from the table of contents, if the whole work should be too expensive to them :—

> Predictum prohemium huius libri de contentis compilaui
> Et propter pauperes predicatores hoc apponere curaui
> Qui si forte nequierint totum libri sibi comparare
> Possunt ex ipso prohemio si sciunt historias predicare.

The character of the theology of this celebrated book is distinctly laid down in the preface of the Dutch translation of 1464. Especially remarkable is the frankness with which the secret of all "biblical theology" is babbled out. Holy Writ is as wax, which reflects the figure of every impressed stamp. A genial expression indeed! One may judge from the preface to the first edition. "This is the preface of the 'Spieghel onser behoudenisse,' which will teach many people righteousness, and to shine as the stars in eternal eternities. It is for this reason that I have thought of compiling, as an instruction for many, this book, from which those who read it, will give and receive instruction. I presume that nothing is in this life more useful to mankind than to acknowledge his creator, his condition, his own being. Scholars may learn this from the scriptures, and the layman shall be taught by the books of the laymen, that is by the pictures. Wherefore I have thought fit, with the help of God, to compile this book for laymen to the glory of God, and as an instruction for the unlearned, in order that it may be a lesson both to clerks and to laymen. It will be sufficient to explain the matter briefly. I mean first to show the fall of Lucifer and the angels. Then the fall of our first parents and their posterity. Thereupon how God delivered us by his assuming flesh, and with what figures he whilom prefigured this assuming. It is to be observed that many histories are given in this work, which could not be explained from word to word, for a teacher does not want to explain more of the histories than he thinks necessary for their meaning. And in order that this may be seen better and clearer, I give this parable : There was an abbey in which stood a large oak, which, on account of the narrowness and smallness of the town, they were compelled to cut down. When it was cut down the workmen came together, and each of them chose whatever he thought would suit his trade. The smith cut off the undermost block, which he thought suitable for a forge ; the shoemaker takes the bark for making leather ; the swine-herd the acorns for the pigs ; the carpenter the straight wood for a roof; the shipwright the crooked wood ; the miller digs the roots up, as they are fit, on account of their solidity, for the mill ; the baker uses the thin twigs for his oven ; the sexton of the church the leaves for decorating the church at festivals ; the butler the branches for barrels and mugs ; the cook the chips for the kitchen." (The German Speculum adds to all this : "Der buchschreiber nam die aychöpffel damit macht er die dintten.") "Just now as here every one chose his liking from the hewn tree, so they do with Holy Writ. The same method was followed as regards the histories which will be explained. Every teacher collects from them what he thinks proper and useful. I shall follow the same way with regard to this work, leaving out altogether some part of the histories, that it may not offend those who will hear and read it. Let us also observe that Holy Writ is like soft wax, which assumes the shape of all forms impressed upon it. Does, for instance, the stamp contain a lion, the soft wax will contain the same, and if it bears an ear, the soft wax will bear the same figure. So one thing signifies sometimes the devil and sometimes Christ. However, we need not be astonished at this manner of the Scriptures, for divers significations may be ascribed to divers performances of a thing or person. When David, the king, committed adultery and manslaughter, he represented not Christ but the devil. And when he loved his enemies, and did them good, he bore within him the figure of Christ and not of the devil." (In the German text: "when David violated his oath, and killed a man, he represented the devil and not God. But when he loved his enemy, he represented God and not the devil." In the same manner follows the prefiguration of Absalom and Sampson.) "This is why I have noticed these remarkable things here, for I thought it useful to those who study the Holy Scriptures, that they should not judge me, if they happened to find such things in this book, for the manner of translation and exposition is so. O good Jesus, give me works and a Christian devotion which may please thee."

Equally curious is the explanation of the marriage of the mother of God with Joseph. It appears from this, that it was not thought superfluous to justify a fact somewhat strange in regard to the doctrine of the supernatural incarnation of the second person of the godhead. The author of the Speculum assigns eight reasons for this marriage: The first was that Mary should not be suspected of unchastity; the second, that she might want the help of a man during her travels as well as elsewhere; the third, that the devil might not become aware of the incarnation of Christ; the fourth, that Mary should have a witness of her purity; the fifth, that God wished that his mother should be married; the sixth, to prove the sanctity of marriage; the seventh, to prove that marriage is no impediment to blessing; the last, that married people should not despair of their salvation. Catholicism had then already brought the world to the possibility of that despair.

After this digression on manuscripts, let us look at xylography so far as it stands in connexion with our subject, in so far, namely, as not only pictures, but texts also were made by this process. The researches of this century, which have thrown new light on the history of block- and metal-printing, compel us to look for the practice of xylography as early as the second half of the *fourteenth* century. Its origin is still enveloped in mist, but we know that it was already busily employed between 1400 and 1450. At that time it was less an art than a trade, and became a means of communication at a time when there was no book or newspaper. All papers of this nature, generally of the size of one leaf, first drawn or painted, afterwards cut on blocks and printed, were called *briefs*, from breve (scriptum), as every small document was named in the Latin of the middle ages, in distinction from a book. In this manner every separate leaf, no matter whether it contained a picture, a text, or both together, was called a brief; and so, at length, all advertisements, records, diplomas, even a pack of cards, were called briefs; as for instance, *vracht brief* (bill of freight), *kaper brief* (letter of marque), the German *gült brief* (bond), &c. The printers of these leaves (brief *malers* and printers) may be here and there pointed out, with name and date, *e.g.* Wilhelm Kegel, Brief Printer, at Nördlingen, in 1428; Henne Cruse, Printer, at Mentz, in 1440; Hans von Pfedersheim, at Frankfort, in 1459; Peter Schott, at Strasburg, in 1464.[1]

With the sculptors (pyldsnytzer, boeldesniders), engravers (plaet-snyders), and the artificers of other connected trades, these printers (prenters) constituted gilds, as, for instance, at Augsburg already in 1418, at Nördlingen in 1428, at Ulm in 1441, St. Luke's gild at Antwerp in 1442, and St. John's gild at Bruges in 1451. The celebrated Brussels Mary-engraving, with the date 1418, predecessor of the beautiful engraving, of which the only known copy, in the Museum at Berlin, is figured in the Monumens typographiques of Holtrop, indicates a fairly well

---

[1] Geschichte der Buchdruckerkunst in ihrer Entstehung und Ausbildung von Karl Falkenstein . . . Leipzig, Teubner, 1840. 4to.

advanced Flemish art of wood-engraving in the first years of the 15th century.[1] The Berlin engraving contains the following dialogue in verses, scattered over several places :—

<pre>
(W)ie es dese coninghinne die hier staet
Het es alder werelt toeverlaet
Hoe es haer name my des ghewae(cht)
Maria weerde moeder ende maecht.
Hoe es sy gheraect aen desen state
Bi minnen oetmoet ende karita(te).
(Wie) wort met haer meest verhoven
Die haer best dient in syn leven.
</pre>

Mr. Holtrop says truly, on the connexion of these two engravings, "Ces deux estampes se complètent mutuellement ; celle de Berlin annonce leur origine, celle de Bruxelles indique leur date. On peut admettre qu'elles ont été gravées dans les Pays-Bas, probablement en Flandres, et peut-être à Bruges, au commencement du 15e siècle." The "Pomerium spirituale," c. 1440, the "Exercitium super Pater noster," the "Alphabet grotesque," are Flemish too.[2] In the Museum at Haarlem, a xylographic work of 16 pages is preserved, containing meditations in Flemish, addressed to the Holy Virgin, on the seven deadly sins.

A wood-engraving of the sower, in the Imperial library at Paris, contains five lines xylographic, purely Flemish, text :—

<pre>
Ic saey goet saet suuer ende rene . . . . cristus van nasarene Die
es dit sact dat ic mene Et valt in dorne distelen ende in steue
(sic) Oft aen yemant mocht becliuen Die waerheit moet die waer-
heit bliuen Daer dit sact an blyft verloren wee hem dat hi noyt
was gheboren.
</pre>

The artists of such wood-engravings were, as has been said before, included in the first half of the 15th century, in the South Netherland gilds of St. Luke, together with the painters, illuminators and sculptors, and were called *prenters* (engravers and printers of picture-books). Hence the first typographical productions were said to have been *prented*, and Schöffer calls Mentz in 1492, "Eine anefangk der prenterye." Even if there existed no historical evidences, yet from this process of development of xylography, in connexion with the requirements of the time, we might safely presume that the prenters, brief printers, would get at last the idea of engraving the text of school-books on wood as well as prayers. This, in fact, happened, and, of course, in Flanders, where xylography had first of all made progress. In this connexion the well-known discovery of Ghesquière at Cambray (1772) gets its real signification. The Abbat Jean le Robert wrote in his diary, "Item for a Doctrinale *yetté en molle*, which I sent for from Bruges, by Marquart, the first writer of Valenciennes, in Jan. xlv. (*i.e.* 1446), for Jacquet, 20 sols tournois. Little Alexander got a similar one, which was paid for by the Church. Item, I sent a Doctrinale to Arras to instruct Dom Gerard, which was bought at Valenciennes, and was *gettez en molle*, and cost 24 groots. He returned me the said Doctrinale on All Saints day, in the year 51, saying, that it was of no value and full of mistakes. He had bought one of paper."[3]

---

[1] Monumens typographiques des Pays-Bays au 15e siècle. Collection de fac-simile d'après les originaux conservés à la Bibliothèque Royale de la Haye et ailleurs. Publiés par J. W. Holtrop, La Haye, 1868. Folio.

[2] Documents iconographiques et typographiques de la Bibliothèque Royale de Belgique. Fac-simile photo-lithogr., avec texte hist. et explicatif, par MM. les conservateurs et employés de la Biblioth. Royale . . . Bruxelles, 1864, Fol.

[3] Item pour. i. doctrinal *gette en molle* anvoiet querre a Brug. par Marq. i. escripvain de Vallen. ou mois de jenvier xlv. pour Jaq. xx. s. t. Sen heult Sandrins. i. pareil q. leglise paña . . . (Fol. 158 recto). Item envoiet Arras. i. doctrinal pour apprendre ledit d. Girard qui fu accatez a Vallen. et estoit *jettez en molle* et cousta xxiv. gr. Se me renvoia led. doctrinal le jour de Tonss. lan. li. disans quil ne falloit rien et estoit tout faulx Sen avoit accate. i. xx. patt. en papier . . . (Fol. 160 recto.)

The Abbat of St. Aubert, at Cambray, therefore, had bought for him in 1446 the school-book of Alexander Gallus, in Bruges, which was thirty-six hours distance from his place, and six years later it was to be had at Valenciennes, but useless. These Doctrinales were printed from a (wooden) form, *jeté en moule*. As had been the case in German and Dutch, so, in the French language, the terminology of xylographic works (drucken, trucken, pronten, printen : to print, printer), was also at first applied to typography. In the privilege granted by Louis XI., in 1474, to the first printers of Paris, it is said that they receive it "pour l'exercise de leur ars et mestiers de faire livres de plusieurs manieres d'escriptures *en mosle* et autrement." Philippe de Comines wrote in 1498 in his *Mémoires* on frère Heronyme (Savonarola) : "tous ses sermons premiers, et ceux de present, il les a fait *mettre en moule* et se vendent," which is changed in the edition of Petitot into "il les a fait *imprimer*."[1] This question, however simple and plain it may be, has been the cause of much (and often intentional) confusion, for which, however, there is in the present condition of science fortunately no longer any occasion.

Therefore *Flemish xylography* was so far developed as to be applied to the making of school-books towards the end of the first half of the 15th century, *i.e.* towards the time that *typography* was invented. According to the earliest polemic and apologetic account of this invention, given in 1499, in the Chronicle of Cologne,[2] it was such xylographic school-books which suggested to the inventor the idea of a new means of multiplying books. This curious account deserves to be read in full. It forms a separate chapter in the chronicle mentioned.

"When, where, and by whom was found out the unspeakably useful art of printing books.

"Here we have especially to observe that of late the love and ardour of mankind have decreased very much, or have been polluted, at one time by vain glory, at another time by covetousness, idleness, &c., particularly reprehensible in the clergy, who are more watchful and anxious to gather temporal good, and to seek the enjoyments of the flesh than the salvation of the soul ; whereby the common people fall into great error, for they and their leaders seek only temporal good, as if there were no eternal good or eternal life hereafter. In order, therefore, that the negligence of our leaders, and the evil example and corruption of the divine word by all preachers in general, who cause their immoral covetousness to be heard and observed, at the same time might not be too great an impediment and injury to good Christians ; and in order that nobody might excuse himself, the eternal God has produced out of his impenetrable wisdom the present excellent art whereby books are printed and multiplied, so that every person himself is able to read, or to hear read, the way to salvation. How should I attempt to write or to relate the praise, the advantage and the bliss which arise, and have arisen from this art? for they are inexpressible. Let all who love letters testify it. God gives it to laymen who are able to read German, to the learned who make use of the Latin language, to monks and nuns, in short to all. O, how many prayers, what unspeakable edification is derived from printed books ! How many precious and wholesome exhortations are given in preaching ! All this arises from this noble art. O, how great an advantage and blessing proceed, if they choose, from those who either make, or are instrumental in making, printed books. And he who wishes to read about this may peruse the little book, written by the great and celebrated Doctor Joh. Gerson, De laude scriptorum,[3] or the book of the spiritual

---

[1] Collection complète des mémoires relatifs à l'histoire de France . . . par M. Petitot. Tome xiii, Paris, 1820. 8vo.

[2] Cronica van der hilliger Stat van Coellen. oder Tzytboich van den geschichten der vergangen jairen in Duytschen landen und sunderlinge der heiliger stat Coellen und yrer Busschove (Coellen, 1499). Folio 312b.

[3] Joh. Koelhoff, of Lubeck, who published the Chronicle in 1499, printed at Cologne from 1472—1500. Like Zell, he published works of Gerson, the first collection of whose works was published by him, in four folios, in 1483 and 1484. The treatise of Gerson, De laude scriptorum, was printed at Cologne by an unknown printer.

father and abbat of Spanheim, Joh. von Trittenheim.¹ This highly valuable art was discovered first of all in Germany, at Mentz on the Rhine. And it is a great honour to the German nation that such ingenious men are found among them. And it took place about the year of our Lord 1440, and from this time until the year 1450, the art, and what is connected with it, was being investigated. And in the year of our Lord 1450 it was a golden year (jubilee), and they began to print, and the first book they printed was the Bible, in Latin; it was printed in a large letter, resembling the letter with which at present missals are printed.² Although the art (as has been said) was discovered at Mentz, in the manner as it is now generally used, yet the first prefiguration (die erste vurbyldung) was found in Holland (the Netherlands), in the Donatuses, which were printed there before that time. And from these (Donatuses) the beginning of the said art was taken, and it was invented in a manner much more masterly and subtle than this, and became more and more ingenious. One named Omnibonus, wrote in a preface to the book called Quinetilianus, and in some other books too, that a Walloon from France, named Nicol. Jenson, discovered first of all this masterly art; but that is untrue, for there are those still alive, who testify that books were printed at Venice before Nic. Jenson came there and began to cut and make letters.³ But the first inventor of printing was a citizen of Mentz, born at Strasburg, and named Junker Johan Gutenberg. From Mentz the art was introduced first of all into Cologne, then into Strasburg,⁴ and afterwards into Venice. The origin and progress of the art was told me verbally by the honorable master Ulrich Zell, of Hanau, still printer at Cologne, anno 1499, by whom the said art came to Cologne.⁵ There are also some confident persons who say that

---

¹ The treatise of Trithemius alluded to, is entitled: De laude scriptorum pulcherrimus tractatus, and was printed in 1494 in 4to, at Mentz, by Petrus Friedberg.

² Some inferred from this that Zell did not allude here to the Bible of 42 lines, because its types are not large enough for a comparison with missal-types. The greatest part, however, of the contents of the missals published in the latter part of the 15th century, was printed in a small type. Only the Canon of the Mass and some prayers, which were to be read at a distance, have larger type. Zell printed in 1466 and 1467 at once with a small type, of the size of those in Gutenberg's Catholicon and Schöffer's Rationale Durandi. Only the types of his Latin Bible and "Gesta Romanorum" are somewhat larger. In contrast with his small type he might, therefore, have called the type of the first Mentz Bible large, and compare it with missal-type, of which it has the form.

³ This mistake of Ognibene de Lonigo (Omnibonus Leonicenus) rectified here, appears in the edition of Quinctilianus of 1471. But Johan de Spira printed already at Venice in 1469. An edition of Jenson (Decor puellarum), with the date 1461, rests on a misprint; the book was only published in 1471.

⁴ As we know that Gutenberg was about a quarter of a century absent from Mentz, and returned thence from Strasburg, it gave rise afterwards to the error that he was sometimes taken for a Strasburger.

⁵ Ulrich Zell, a clerk of the diocese of Mentz, published the first dated Cologne work in 1466 (Chrysostomus supra Psalmo quinquagesimo). Panzer supposes (Ann. typogr. i. 274) that Zell brought the art of printing to Cologne as early as 1462; at least he published there several books without date. The earliest printed Strasburg date, the Decretum Gratiani of Eggesteyn, is 1471, but Mentelin printed much earlier at Strasburg, although the earliest date on any work of his, 1466, is only written; the earliest printed date is 1472. Taking everything together, the information of the Cologne chronicle seems to be correct in the main, and it was a colossal error in the polemics of the French and German Gutenbergians to deduct anything from its credibility. An earlier imprint of Trechsel will afterwards assist to explain much of this account. The substitution of Dutch for Flemish, of North for South-Netherland Donatuses, may easily be explained in a Cologne author of the latter part of the 15th century, and this provincial term, moreover, must be explained by him from the geographical and political notion of that time ("Hollandia . . . . whose capital is called *utrecht* in the German tongue, or trajectum inferior in Latin, for it belongs to Germania, i.e. to the German land, and it belongs all to Germany by its situation, habits, government, and language." Haerlem, 1485). Just as the prosperity of the South-Netherland wood-engraving falls into the *first half* of the 15th century, that of the North-Netherland occurs in the *second* half, and we know, moreover, that xylography continued to assist in the production of school-books when typography was in full vigour. A xylographic Donatus, for instance, in the Library at Deventer, was published only at the *end* of the 15th century (according to Meerman, even 1499—1503); the letters of a xylographic

d already before, but this is not true, for we find in no country
;ime. Moreover many books have been lost, which we can find
little was written, as for instance the large volume of Titus
the gods, written by Tullius; the books of the wars of the
ians, by Plinius; of which few or none are found. This useful
ilumniators, as all other things, but this is, as seems to me,
hings which we learn, and which are worthy of being read and
not be prohibited. What is more useful and salutary than to
things which regard God and our salvation? Not all under-
;ures, who read them in Latin, neither do those who read the
into German. But if both will be diligent, they will then
and delight from the Latin as well as from the German
ieard from clergymen who discoursed of spiritual things with
e. But this disfavour is mostly on the part of the unlearned,
ise of their great lukewarmness and ignorance to answer when
y well-disposed persons about those things, and thus become

errors arise (from the art of printing). But even if this were
soon be refuted by the scholars. It is seldom seen or heard
from the common people, but generally and most of all from
re also who think that the multiplication of books is injurious:
hy. For those who love art and honour, it is now an agreeable,
me, in which they can plant and sow the field of their under-
able wondrous seeds, or enlighten it with many heavenly
rays. ve neither the art nor their soul, I say, if they choose, they
imo, with half the labour, as much as one could do formerly in
ises from the great diligence, in multifarious ways, of those who
re infinitely better than those which were written in former
any use to one who will injure himself? Æsop tells us that a
cious stone on a dunghill, but did not know it, and threw it
er to cast pearls before swine. Blessed be they who use the
as given them, and thereby gain still more." Thus far the

that we have here to do with a clear mind, who is perfectly
tes, who understands the far-reaching influence of typography,
of his time. He not only dares to chastise a corrupted clergy,
is valid against censure and newspaper taxes. The author of
, knew quite well what he was about, when he asked for informa-
nd the value of his arguments cannot be appreciated too highly.
ist of this account, in order to view with one glance what it
e that the art of printing was invented *first of all* at Mentz;
y were *ready* with the invention in 1450, and they began then
—a Latin Bible; the art with which this was effected was the

---

n, have the greatest resemblance to those of Willem Vorsterman, who printed
ing of the 16th century. A similar xylographic fragment in the Museum
n is not much older. A great number of typographic Donatuses were printed
also exported to foreign countries. Add to this the lively commerce between
ich belonged to the Hanza; that the art of printing spread itself over the
Cologne, and the geographical inaccuracy, the confusion between Holland and
se us in an author of the middle ages. We may, therefore, read unhesi-
accepted, that also this particular originated from Zell, and not from the
of the chronicle may have been the first who ignored the exact relation
typography): Junker Johan Gutenberg conceived, *about* the year 1440 (the
ind number, not exactly in that *year*), by means of Netherland woodcut-
ur present (typographic) mode of printing books. He devoted some years
s new idea, to experiments, and was *ready* with his invention in 1450 (repeated

art of printing, " in the manner as is now generally used " (*i.e.* typography); the model, pattern of this art was got from the Donatuses, printed before in Holland in a manner (*i.e.* xylography) not so " masterly and subtle " as the Mentz art, which was perfected more and more; it is an untruth that Jenson, at Venice, should have invented " first of all this masterly art"; no, THE FIRST INVENTOR OF TYPOGRAPHY WAS JOHAN GUTENBERG, AT MENTZ; indeed, there are pedants who say that books were printed before, but that is not true, for in no country are found (even) contemporaneous books.

Such are the contents of the celebrated account of Zell, with the addition only of two technical terms. For it is indisputable, that without the contrast of two modes of printing, the account would only be utter nonsense. The author simply tries to explain psychologically the great fact of the invention of which he speaks. The look of a xylographic Donatus suggested to the inventor the idea of typography, *i.e.* the look of a *book* not written but printed, kindled the lightning flash of the invention in his mind, the idea of a more easy multiplication of books by means of *loose* letters.

Whenever an invention is made language tries to find words to define it, and it is a very natural phenomenon that the poor style of the middle ages especially, was not very soon ready with this work. To expect in the Cologne chronicle a clear, terminologically accurate, distinction between typography and xylography, would only betray ignorance. There is question there of two (different) *modes* of printing; the one masterly, subtle, now generally used and perfected by degrees, and *another* by which the first prefiguration (die eyrste vurbyldung), the suggestion (admunitio) had been printed. What is meant by that mode of printing at present in use? Nothing else but typography proper, printing with moveable, cast types. Guicciardini still used in 1567 a similar definition. He calls typography, " l'arte dello imprimere e stampare lettere e carattere in foglio *al modo d'oggi*," (according to the present mode) and Eytzinger translates " die kunst der Truckerye auff unser jetzige weiss mit Buchstaben und Caracteribus, auff papir oder sonst zu trucken." We could even give quotations from the 17th century to confirm this mode of expression. So Scriverius wrote in 1628, " The praiseworthy and valuable art of printing arose and came to light, not in the mode and manner as is usual at present with types cast of lead and tin, which are separately taken by the compositors out of a box, and put together on a composing-stick, first a word, afterwards a line or verse, finally a whole form. No, but a book was cut leaf by leaf on wooden blocks." For the " other mode," therefore, for those Dutch (Flemish, Netherland) Donatuses, nothing remains to us but xylography, but the prefiguration of the product of the new art in a little book, printed from engraved wooden blocks.

The idea of Gutenberg to multiply books in a manner *different* from the former (xylographic), more masterly, subtle, ingenious, the means of having always serviceable (*i.e.* moveable, cast, metal) letters, *that* is his invention. To make any one invent typography by seeing a *typographically* printed book, is raising him, not to the " very first inventor," as is pleonastically expressed in the style of the middle ages, but to a wholly independent post-inventor. Every one might have seen a thousand times, letters printed on playing cards, pictures of saints, letters of indulgences; in short, in all the xylographic and chalcographic texts of the (14th and) 15th century. But Gutenberg was the first who arrived at a *second* idea, after xylography had begun to omit gradually the pictures, and expand more and more the text of its productions. On the other hand, many little xylographic works appeared after the invention of typography, simply out of a principle of economy; an engraver could cut more cheaply and easier a few pages in wood, than procure the furniture of a printing-office. Books which were continually used, *i.e.* bought, were generally selected for such block printing. Here is, for instance, the subscription of a xylographic Donatus, in small folio (of 27 lines), printed on paper c. 1475: " Octo parcium oracionis donatus. Per Cunradum dinckmut Vlmensis Oppidi Ciuem impressus finit feliciter." Also that of a German Biblia pauperum : " Friedrich walthern mauler/ zu Nördlingen und Hans Hürning habent das buch/ mit einander gemacht 1470." There exists even a xylographic "Ars moriendi," with the date 1504. The block-printing of the latter part of the 15th century may therefore be regarded as the stereotype of that period. It is of no importance whether such block-books originated before 1450 in Holland, in the South-Netherlands, or in Germany, for the maker of xylographic works invented *nothing*. And those who represent Gutenberg as having not only practised, but even invented xylography, prove that they did not understand the question at all, and had therefore no right to judge. Biassed and ignorant partizans of Mentz have confused xylography and typography, have made Gutenberg cut wooden blocks, and thereupon print with the pieces; but history, the authentic documents relating to the fact of the invention, know *nothing* of a xylographer Gutenberg, either at Strasburg or at Mentz.

God, art, and typography—these three are one, namely in this respect, that every one pretends to know equally much of them, that every one has a so-called opinion, those too who have not laboured in the sweat of their brow to find the way to the temple of knowledge. The atheism of the philosopher, who has scrutinized the history of human knowledge and thought, is judged in absolute ignorance by the thoughtless and heartless philistine; the wonderful creations of a genius are reduced to a flat nonentity which stupidity calls "taste." Every noodle is a fellow-creator, a *post*-inventor in his own way, of the spiritual cosmogony comprised in the invention of printing. Just as Noodle, who hears people talk about printing, knows at once how *he* would have invented it, so it *was* no doubt invented. Of course, Noodle! nothing is more simple than that art of printing; it is *printing*, you know, and a great quantity has already been printed, and very early too, on this earth. And Noodle nappingly goes on, perplexed with astonishment, that blunt humankind had to wait so many centuries for that simple printing. Had it not been, properly speaking, the duty of Adam to invent it the first time he saw the impressions of Eve's little feet on the ground, after he had been raking Paradise? Or when Cain and Abel came from school on a snowy day? At such questions Noodle becomes a perfect misanthrope. O, those miserable prejudices, quite ready before all investigations, and which plunge all questions into a chaos. The most common prejudice is the supposition à priori, legitimated strictly scientifically by nothing, that printing with moveable types was only an improvement on that with wooden blocks in which the letters were cut; that it originated from wood-engraving; that it was a development of it, an extension, a fortunate application, the highest step of the ladder, consisting of playing-cards, images of saints, pictures with super- sub- and other scriptions, text without pictures. In short: xylography, in a technical, logical, and reformatorical sense, would be the mother of typography. But it is such only in the sense of an external impulse, of an external push to meditating on quite *another* means than wood- or metal-engraving, on *another* mode of obtaining books. Zell finds that push in block-Donatuses, but the inspiration of genius, the first invention of a quite independent art, of a totally new principle, which has nothing in common with wood- and metal-engraving, he ascribes, in accordance with the universal opinion of the 15th century and of all Europe, to Gutenberg. In Gutenberg's mind the grand idea arose that all words, all writing, all language, all human thoughts could be expressed by a small number, a score, of different letters arranged according to the requirements; that, with a large quantity of those different signs, united to one whole, a whole page of text could be printed at once, and repeating this process continually, large manuscripts could swiftly be multiplied in as great a number as was wanted. *This thought, this idea begot the invention of typography.* In *that* moment, it was conceived in Gutenberg's mind, and it was born when "the fulness of time" had come. Every other explanation is at once unhistorical and unpsychological. Granted that Zell's explanation of the inspiration of printing by "Dutch" Donatuses is perfectly correct, then these Donatuses stand to the idea which we have described in the same relation as the traditional falling apple stands to Newton's theory, as the dancing lid of the kettle with boiling water to the discovery of steam. But a statue to a gardener who shakes a fruit tree empty, or to an honest girl who brings the tea-kettle into the room, would be, notwithstanding the universal importance of gravitation and steam, a somewhat foolish whim. However, not so foolish that it were not capable of being surpassed! And would this not be the case, when the centripetal and centrifugal force according to imminent laws of nature, were to be glorified on account of tradition by an artificial tree with golden apples, and—there arose then at the same time a lively dispute between kinds of apples mutually, whether the falling apple, which caused the English philosopher to reflect, was a pomegranate, a sweet or a sour one, a grey or a green one? The Cologne chronicle mentions two things: a *fact*, the invention of the art of printing, and an *explanation* of that fact. The objective fact is of importance to us, not the subjective explanation of it which may be true, but also false, without altering the fact a bit. The qualification, *Holland* Donatus, this innocent geographical limitation which is of no importance, is a provincial mistake; these Donatuses of the first half of the 15th century, which the chronicle mentions at the end of that century, were no more *Dutch*, than the Mentz patrician Gutenberg was of *Strasburg*, and had been in Mentz in 1440: all inaccuracies which occur also in that celebrated account.

Once more, the short Latin grammar printed from wooden blocks (Donatus de octo partibus orationis) stands with typography in no other but this historical-psychological connexion; that *small books* had already been printed with wooden blocks when the inventor, Johan Gutenberg, was devising typography, *perhaps* ex donato Hollandiae (*i.e.* Flandriae) prius impresso *in tabula incisa* (Mariangelo Accorso).[1] As to their value to the invention of typography, they might have been just as well German, French, or English books.

II.

GUTENBERG'S PREPARATION.

THE immortal inventor of typography was born at Mentz at the end of the 14th century, as second son of the patrician Frielo zum Gensfleisch, and of Else zu Gudenberg. In consequence of one of those many broils between the nobility and the citizens, his family emigrated in 1420, and went (probably) to their property at Eltvill; at least his elder brother Frielo lived there still in 1434. Ten years later (18th March, 1430) the archbishop of Mentz, Conrad III., decreed a reconciliation between the noble families and the gilds, in which document, of which a transcript is preserved in the town library at Frankfort, Henne (Johan) zu Gudenberg, is mentioned for the first time. He made no use, however, of this decree by which his kinsman George Gensfleisch was banished. We meet him for the first time at Strasburg in the year 1434. As his native town had neglected to pay him interests due to him, he had caused the recorder of Mentz, Nicolaus, to be imprisoned. But on the intercession of the great council of Strasburg he released the prisoner by this document:—

"I, Johan Gensfleisch the younger, called Gutenberg, declare by this letter, that the worshipful sage burgomaster and the council of the town of Mentz owe me every year a certain interest, according to the contents of letters which contain, among other things, that, if they do not pay me, I am at liberty to seize and imprison them. As I have now to claim much rent in arrears from the said town, which they were hitherto not able to pay me, I caused M. Nicolaus, secretary of Mentz, to be seized,

---

[1] Angelus Roccha: Bibliotheca Vaticana, Romae, 1591. 4to, Appendix.

whereupon he promised me and swore to give me 310 valid Rguilders, to be paid at Oppenheim, before the following Whitsuntide. I acknowledge, by this letter, that the burgomaster and council of Strasburg have induced me to relieve of my own free will, in honour and love of them, the said M. Nicolaus from his imprisonment, and from the payment of the 310 florins. Given on Sunday (12th of March), 1434."

The ease with which Gutenberg relinquishes his monetary claim, and which at once shews him to be a better knight than financier, exhibits a trait of character which explains much in his later fate.

Lady Ennelin (Anna) zu der isern thüre accused him in 1437 before the episcopal judge at Strasburg of breach of promise of marriage—an infidelity which was afterwards expiated by marriage.

Of more importance is a law-suit of George Dritzehn against Gutenberg in 1439, at Strasburg, the protocol of which was discovered in that town by Professor Schöpflin in 1745, and published in 1760.[1] It is written in the Elzas dialect, and has, as all the other documents relating to the life of Gutenberg, so little attraction for those who do not wish to make a careful study of the origin of printing, that but a few know it, and people generally content themselves with reading partial accounts of that process. However, the knowledge of it is indispensable to form an independent judgment. I have, therefore, taken the trouble to translate it, trusting that the diminished difficulty of reading it will deter no one from becoming acquainted with it.

The document preserved in the "Dicta testium magni consilii, Anno dni. MCCCC, Tricesimo nono," runs thus:—

Barbel von Zabern, the "trading woman," also called "the little woman," said, that she, on a certain night, spoke about several things with Andreas Dritzehn; she said, for instance, to him, "Won't you go and sleep now?" to which he replied, "I have to finish this first." Thereupon said this witness, "But good gracious! you squander much money; that thing must have cost you more than 10 guilders." To this he answered, "You are a fool; do you think it has cost me only 10 guilders; look here, if you had what it has cost me more than 500 guilders ready money, you would have enough for your life; and what it has cost less than 500 guilders is very little, except what it will cost me besides; I have, therefore, mortgaged my house and my ground." Then this witness said to him, "Holy passion! what will you do if you fail?" He answered, "We cannot fail; before we are one year further, we have back all our capital and are all safe then, unless God be against us."

Ennel (Annie) *Dritzehn*, wife of Hans Schultheiss, wood merchant, said, that *Lorenz Beildeck* called once at her house for *Claus Dritzehn*, her cousin, and said to him, "Dear Claus Dritzehn, the late *Andreas Dritzehn has four pieces lying in a press; now, Gutenberg has requested that you will take them out of the press and separate them, that no one may know what it is, for he would not like anybody to see it*." This witness also said, "when she stayed with Andreas Dritzehn, her cousin, she had often assisted him in the same work day and night." She also said, 'that she knew quite well that Andreas Dritzehn, her late cousin, had, at one time or other, mortgaged his income; she knew not whether he had used this for the work."

Hans Sidenneger declares, that the late Andreas Dritzehn had often told him, 'that he had spent a great deal of money on the said work, and that it cost him much money, and that he did not know how to act in it." Whereupon this witness answered him: "Andreas, if you have been caught, it is necessary that you should get out again." Then Andreas said that he ought to pawn his goods. Witness then advised him to do it, and to tell nobody anything about it, which Andreas did; he did not know, however, whether the sum and the time were great or small.

Hans Schultheiss said, that *Lorenz Beildeck* came once at his house to Claus Dritzehn, when this witness had seen him home, after Andreas had died, at which occasion Lorenz said to Claus: "*Andreas Dritzehn, your late brother has four pieces*

---

[1] Jo. Dan. Schoepflini Vindiciae typographicae. Argent, 1760. 4to.

lying underneath a press; now, Hans Gutenberg has requested you to remove them, and to put them separated on the press: no one is able to see then what it is." Thereupon Claus Dritzehn went and looked for the pieces, but found nothing. This witness, too, heard a long time ago from Andreas Dritzehn that the work had cost him more than 300 guilders.

Conrad Sahspach said, that Andreas Heilmann came once to him in the Kremer Street, and said, "Dear Conrad, Andreas Dritzehn has died, *and you have made the press and know of the business; go there, take the pieces out of the press and separate them: nobody knows then what it is.*" Now, when this witness went to do so, and looked for the work, on St. Stephen's day last, the thing was gone. This witness said also, that Andreas Dritzehn had once borrowed money from him, which he used for the work. He knew also that he had mortgaged his income.

Werner Smalriem says, that he made three or four purchases, but he knew not whom they concerned. One purchase was to the amount of about 113 guilders, for which money three of them remained securities; Andreas Dritzehn for 20 guilders. Afterwards a sum had been paid at the house of Anton Heilmann, and the rest by Fridel von Seckingen.

Mydehart Stocker said, that Andreas Dritzehn, on St. John's day, at the time of Christmas, when they made the procession, got ill and was laid up in witness's room. Witness came to him and said, "Andreas, how are you?" Whereupon he answered, "I am dangerously ill; if I were to die, I should wish never to have joined the partnership." "Why?" "Because I know that my brothers never agree with Gutenberg." Witness asked him, "Is then the partnership not put on paper, or have no people been present?" Andreas—"Yes, it is written down." Witness asked further how the partnership was made, whereupon he told him that Andreas Heilmann, Hans Riffe, Gutenberg and he (Andreas Dritzehn) had made a partnership, to which Andreas Heilmann and he had contributed each 80 guilders. While they were in partnership Andreas Heilmann and he went to Gutenberg, at St. Arbogast, *where the last concealed many arts from them,* which he was not compelled to show them. They did not like this, so they had broken up the partnership, and concluded a new one on condition that Andreas Heilmann and he should each supply, besides the first 80 guilders, so much that the sum would amount to 500 guilders, and they together would be counted in the partnership as one man. Gutenberg would *then conceal from them none of the arts he knew.* A contract had been made on this point. If one of them died, the remaining partners would pay his heirs 100 guilders, while the rest of the money should remain in the partnership. This witness, too, knew of Dritzehn's pawn.

M. Peter Eckhart, pastor of St. Martin's, said, that the late Andreas Dritzehn sent for him during the Christmas days to hear his confession. When he came to him he confessed freely, and witness asked him whether he was in debt to somebody, or others to him. Andreas answered, that he entered into a partnership with some, with Andreas Heilmann and others, and that he had paid more than two or three hundred guilders, and possessed at present not a penny.

Thomas Steinbach said, that he named to the commissioner Hesse, at his asking him whether he knew something for him to buy, Johan Gutenberg, Andreas Dritzehn, and a certain Heilmann, as they were sure to want money.

Lorenz Beildeck said, that Johan Gutenberg sent him once to Claus Dritzehn, after the death of his brother Andreas, to say *that he should not show to any one the press which he had under his care:* witness did so, and added, *that Claus should go to the press, and open the two little buttons, whereby the pieces should fall asunder. He should then put those pieces in or on the press, that nobody should afterwards make out anything of it.* And if he happened to go out, he should call on Gutenberg, as he had something to talk with him. This witness knew that Johan Gutenberg owed nothing to Andreas, but that Andreas was indebted to Gutenberg, and was to pay him by instalments, but that he died before he had paid the debt. Witness had often seen Andreas Dritzehn dine with Johan Gutenberg, but never seen him pay a penny

Reimbolt, of Ehenheim, said, that he came at Andreas's before Christmas, and asked him what on earth he did with those nice things with which he was busy? Andreas answered, that it had cost him more than 500 guilders, but he hoped, if he succeeded, to get a good quantity of money, with which he should pay witness, and see all his trouble rewarded. Witness then lent him eight guilders, and spoke also of presents of wine, made by the partners to Gutenberg.

Hans Niger, of Bishofsheim, said, that Andreas came to him, and told him he wanted money, for he was working at something, for which he could not collect too much money. Witness asked him what he was working at? Andreas answered that he was *a manufacturer of looking-glasses*.

Fritz von Seckingen had been a surety for Gutenberg, Heilmann, and Dritzehn, to an amount of 101 guilders, for which he held a sealed bond. Andreas, however, had kept this to himself and not sealed, but Gutenberg had afterwards paid everything.

M. Anton Heilmann said, when he saw that Gutenberg was willing to accept Andreas Dritzehn for a third part *in the journey to Aix-la-Chapelle* (die Ochevart) *with looking-glasses*, he urgently requested him to accept his brother Andreas, too, as a partner. Gutenberg, however, intimated his apprehension that the friends of Andreas should take it to be a deception (witchcraft), and could therefore not well give his consent. Anton thereupon prayed again Gutenberg, and made out a contract which he could show to both the partners, that they might think about it. The consent was given. On this occasion Andreas Dritzehn begged this witness to assist him with money, whereupon he helped him, on security, with 90 lbs., which money he brought to him at St. Arbogast. Witness asked him, "What do you ask so much money for, as you don't want more than eighty guilders?" Andreas said that he wanted money, as he had to pay Gutenberg eighty guilders two or three days after the beginning of Lent, before Lady-day (25th March); witness had to pay the same sum, as each of them had, according to their agreement, to pay eighty guilders for the other third part in the profits which was still at Gutenberg's disposal. This money was given to Gutenberg for his share in the undertaking and instruction in the art, but was not paid into the common purse. Thereupon Gutenberg said to witness, that he had to make him another proposition, namely, that there should be equality in everything, because he (Anton) had done so much for him; *nobody should conceal anything from the other*, whereby the progress of the other arts would be expedited. According to this promise, Gutenberg made a record of it, and said to Anton, "Tell the others that they should think well about it, whether it pleases them as it is." This he did, and thereupon they had a long conference; at last he said, "*Although there is at present so much in store, and we are still making more, that your share in the work comes very near the amount of the money you advanced, yet the art will be communicated to you.*"

So they agreed with him on two points, the one of which was to be quite settled, the other to be explained well. The matter which was to be regarded as settled, was that they wished to be under no obligations whatever to Hans Riffe, as they had nothing from him, but everything from Gutenberg. The matter which was to be explained, was that if one of them happened to die, exact explanation should be given, and they decided that they should, at the end of the five years, pay to the heirs of deceased *for all things made or still to be made*, for the money advanced which every partner had to pay in the expenses, *and for the forms, and for all tools, nothing excepted*, 100 guilders. This was stipulated in order that, if any one died, they should not be under the necessity of *showing, telling, or revealing the art* to all the heirs.

Thereupon the two Andreases told witness (Anton Heilmann) that they had come to an understanding with Gutenberg upon the document. Andreas Dritzehn had given to Gutenberg forty, Andreas Heilmann fifty, guilders, as the agreement was, for this term, fifty guilders, before next Christmas, twenty guilders, and afterwards, in March, as much as was stipulated by the record, signed also by witness. Witness acknowledges the contract, and that the money had not been paid into the common purse, but should be for Gutenberg. Neither had Andreas Dritzehn paid any money into their partnership, and had never paid for the meals they had taken (in the neighbourhood of the town at St. Arbogast, where Gutenberg lived).

This witness knew also very well that Gutenberg, shortly before Christmas, sent his servant to the two Andreases, *to fetch all the forms; these were melted before his eyes, which he regretted on account of several forms.* Witness knew that when Andreas died, *they should have liked to see the press, and that Gutenberg said, that they should send for the press, for he feared that any one should see it. Thereupon he sent his man to take the press to pieces.* He had also asked his brother, when they did begin to learn, whereupon he answered, that Gutenberg still claimed 10 guilders from Andreas Dritzehn of the 50 which he had to pay on the day of St. Henry.

Hans Dünne, the goldsmith, said that he had earned some three years ago about 100 guilders from Gutenberg, *only for that which belonged to printing.*

JUDGMENT.

We, Cune Nope, burgomaster and councillor of Strasburg, make known to all who will see this letter, or hear it read, that Jerge (George) Dritzehn, our citizen, appeared before us for himself, and with authorization of Claus Dritzehn, his brother, and made a claim against *Hans Gensfleisch, of Mentz,* called *Gutenberg,* our townsman, thus: Andreas Dritzehn, his late brother, had put a large amount of his paternal inheritance into a partnership with Hans Gutenberg and others.; *they had also exercised their trade with each other for a long time.* Andreas Dritzehn, too, had been security in many places, *where they had bought lead and other things wanted,* and had redeemed his bail. Now, after Andreas had died, George and his brother Claus had often demanded of Gutenberg that he would accept them, instead of their brother, into partnership, or else repay the money advanced, which he declined. To this Hans Gutenberg answered, that the demand was unreasonable, and not in accordance with the schedules which George and Claus Dritzehn found after the death of their brother. For Andreas applied to him some years ago to learn some arts; *at his request Gutenberg taught him to polish stones.* A considerable time afterwards Gutenberg and Hans Riffe came to an understanding about an art, *which was to be used at the occasion of a pilgrimage to Aix-la-Chapelle,* on condition that Gutenberg should get two, and Riffe a third part of the profits. Andreas Dritzehn became aware of this fact, and asked him to be allowed to learn this art also. M. Anton Heilmann made the same request on the part of his brother Andreas, whereupon Gutenberg promised them both to instruct them, and to yield the half of such an art and undertaking, namely, that these two should have one share among them, Hans Riffe the other part, and Gutenberg the half. They were to pay him 160 guilders for the instruction. He received, indeed, 80 guilders from each of them, as the pilgrimage would take place that year, and they had learned their art. *When the pilgrimage was put off for one year, they urgently begged him to instruct them in all his arts and undertaking of which he knew, and to conceal nothing from them.* Thus they persuaded him, and came to an understanding, on condition that they should pay him, besides the amount mentioned already, 250 guilders, 410 guilders in all. Of this Gutenberg was to receive 100 guilders in ready money, of which he got 50 guilders from Andreas Heilmann, and 40 from Andreas Dritzehn, so that the last owed him still 10 guilders. They would, moreover, pay him each 75 guilders in three instalments. Andreas Dritzehn, however, died within this time, and the partnership was made for five years, and if it happened that one of the four died within that time, *then all their art, tools, and work made already, should remain with the others,* and after the expiration of five years the heirs of deceased should receive 100 guilders. All this was put on paper, *whereupon Gutenberg instructed them in this art and undertaking, which Dritzehn had acknowledged on his death bed.* Therefore, he wished that George and Claus Dritzehn should deduct from the 100 guilders the 85 guilders which he had still to claim from their brother; he then would pay them the remaining 15 guilders, although he was in no hurry about them for some years. If Andreas Dritzehn borrowed, as his brother said, much money on his father's goods, or pawned or sold of them, that did not concern Gutenberg, for he received nothing but what has been mentioned before. Nor had Andreas been his security for lead, or for anything else, except once by Fritz von Seckingen, of which, however, he had relieved him after his death. On account, therefore, of claim, answer, assertion, &c., George and Claus Dritzehn are denied their claim; to Gutenberg his contra-claim is adjudicated. Dated (12 Dec.) Anno XXXIX.

Later, but also in 1439, Lorenz Beildeck, Gutenberg's servant, instituted, in consequence of this process, a law-suit against the petitioner, George Dritzehn, who, after the process, accused him of perjury. The accusation is as follows :—

"I, Lorenz Beildeck, accuse, before the lords of the high council, Master Jörg Dritzehn, who had summoned me before you, my gracious lords, to tell you the truth, while I have said on my oath what I knew of the business. Thereupon the said Jörg Dritzehn has summoned me again before you to give evidence, and by doing so he had given to understand that I had not told the truth before. Moreover he had said to me in public: 'Thou witness, thou shalt tell the truth for me, even if we should go together to the gallows;' thereby maliciously accusing me of being a perjured criminal; whereby he has, by God's grace, done me wrong," &c.

It appears from the list of witnesses that the protocol has not come down to us perfect. Both the parties had summoned Lorenz Beildeck, Werner Smalriem, Fridel von Seckingen, Ennel Dritzehn, Conrad Sahspach, Hans Dünne, and Master Hirtz (whose evidence is wanting). Dritzehn moreover had caused to be summoned the pastor of St. Martin, Hans Sydenneger, Hans Schultheiss the wood-merchant, Thomas Steinbach, Reimbolt von Ehenheim, Berbel das clein fröwel, whose evidence has been given ; Jacob Imerle, Midhart Honöwe, Heinrich Bisinger, Wilhelm von Schutter, the wife of Lorenz Beildeck, Stösser Nese von Ehenheim, M. Jerge Saltzmütter, Heinrich Sidenneger, Hans Ross the goldsmith and his wife, M. Gosse Sturm, at St. Arbogast, and Martin Verwer, whose evidences are wanting. It is especially a pity that the evidence of the second goldsmith is wanting. Gutenberg's witnesses à decharge, besides the above mentioned, with M. Anton Heilmann and Mydehart Stocker, are wanting in the protocol; they were Andreas and Claus Heilmann, Heinrich Olse, Hans Riffe, and Johan Dritzehn. I doubt, however, whether if complete, the evidence would have enabled us to draw *decisive* inferences as regards the technical work mentioned in the partnerships discussed. The council of Strasburg looked exclusively on the judicial side of the question which it had to solve ; to us the industrial question is of importance, and we will see how far it may be explained.

After the development of the towns, all members of the nobility did not seek their occupation exclusively in deeds of knighthood. Industry, art, and the refinement of town-life gradually superseded the warlike spirit of the nobility, to whom the town offered distinguished dignities and situations, while enterprises of commerce and industry gave them distinction and riches. The privilege of coining money, especially, was often farmed out to an association of ancient families. At Mentz this association consisted of twelve families (Münzer-Hausgenossen), among whom was also the family of Gensfleisch. They possessed, moreover, the privileges of the valuation of coin, of the assize of weights and measures, of offices for the exchange of money and of the sale of gold and silver staves to the mint. Such employment brought them chiefly in connexion with the goldsmiths, whose work consisted, at that time, of one of the most considerable trades, which comprised mechanics and chemistry, nay, the whole dominion of plastic and graphic art, in its application to metals, whether separate or in conjunction with diamonds and other precious materials. With the mint, bank money and commerce-affairs were connected, which were transacted at Nuremberg, Augsburg, and elsewhere, by similar associations. From the fourteenth century they were even mostly patricians who established powder-mills, paper-mills, and similar new manufactories.

It is as such a noble worker that the law-suit of the heirs of Dritzehn reveals

Gutenberg to us. Without making conjectures on the financial question, we will endeavour, with strict self-constraint against every wish to help exegesis by imagination, from the standpoint of absolute impartiality, to get some notion of the nature of the work done by Gutenberg at Strasburg. In the first place, as to the facts, it is plain that Gutenberg is in everything the chief person, the teacher, requested by others to communicate to them his knowledge, for payment. Some years before the law-suit he entered into partnership with Andreas Dritzehn to instruct him in the polishing of stones. "Under polishing of stones we could not yet understand the cutting of jewels; it is most probable that ornamental stones are meant, as the Hundsrück, and the so-called Westrich, in the neighbourhood of Mentz, produced. According to Seb. Münster, chalcedony was broken in the river S. Wendel; and Oberstein on the Nahe, where agate, onyx, and other similar ornamental stones are found, is still the place where they are cut on a great many mills, and polished by means of tripoli or tin-ashes."[1] This industry was exercised to the mutual profit of the partners. About the same time the goldsmith Hans Dünne earns much money from Gutenberg for what belongs "to printing." As this expression is not explained more fully, we have no right to infer more from it, than that the work of Gutenberg stood also in connexion with the working of *metal*.

While the partnership with Andreas Dritzehn had existed for a considerable time, Gutenberg made, in 1438, another agreement with the judge, Hans Riffe, to instruct him also in some art. As soon as Dritzehn became aware of this, he asked to be admitted into this new partnership. The same request was made by Anton Heilmann, a friend of Gutenberg, in behalf of his brother Andreas. He was persuaded by them; and thereupon Gutenberg, Riffe, Dritzehn, and Heilmann entered into a partnership for the manufacture of looking-glasses, destined to be sent to Aix-la-Chapelle at the time of the pilgrimage, which was to be expected in 1439.

The looking-glasses of the 15th century were silvered by means of pouring melted lead or tin on the heated glass. The frames were broad, gilt, and richly adorned with carving-work, "en bas-relief;" such a looking-glass frame of the 15th century is described in Reinaerd de Vos of Hendrik of Alkmaar:—

> Dat holt, dâr dat glas inne stôd,
> Was brêd anderdhalven mannes fôt
> Buten umme gânde alle rund,
> Dâr mannige frômde historien uppe stund.
> Under itliker historien de wôrde
> Mit golde dorgwragt, so sik dat behôrde
> Siet dese historien end noch mêr
> Stunden uppen *spegel* umhêr
> Gewragt, *gesneden* en *gegraven*
> Mit bylden end guldenen bôkstaven.

We find lead (which is also mentioned in the law-suit) spoken of already, as used for the manufacturing of looking-glasses, in the 13th century. In the "Speculum naturale" of Vincentius Bellovacensis (c. 1240) it is said: "Inter omnia melius est speculum ex vitro et plumbo. . . Quando superfunditur plumbum vitro calido, efficitur altera parte terminatum valde radiosum." And in the "Perspectiva communis" of Peckham: "Specula consueta vitrea sunt plumbo obducta."

The pilgrimage to ancient Aix-la-Chapelle took place every seventh year, and, commencing on the 10th of July, lasted fourteen days, during which time the ordinary service in the church did not take place, but a free market was held. The concourse of people was uncommonly great on that occasion, so that, for instance, in the year 1496, 142,000 pilgrims were counted in the town and 80,000 guilders in the offering-boxes on one day. Aix-la-Chapelle possessed relics of the first rank, as the swaddling-clothes of Christ, his body-cloth at the Crucifixion, the dress worn by Mary at his birth, and the cloth on which St. John the Baptist was beheaded. The Strasburg partnership, therefore, was looking forward to an advantageous speculation, when it resolved to manufacture looking-glasses for the pilgrimage of 1439. The

---

[1] K. Falkenstein, Gesch. der Buchdruckerkunst, &c.

festival, however, was put off for one year, which seems to have involved the partners in pecuniary embarrassment. Meantime this delay afforded their enterprising genius an opportunity for entering into a *third* partnership for a period of five years, Gutenberg binding himself to reserve nothing of his industrial skill to himself, but teach the partners everything he knew. This contract, therefore, would last till 1448.

As decisively as we learn from the law-suit the object of the first agreement (Gutenberg-Dritzehn), and that of the second (Gutenberg-Riffe-Dritzehn-Heilmann), so uncertain is it which art is meant in the third quinquennial contract. The verdict, which has, of course, only regard to the judicial, that is, to the monetary question, describes it in general as "art and enterprise" (kunst und afentur). Schöpflin has translated the word "afentur" incorrectly by "secret art," ars secreta et mirabilis. The word signifies nothing but an enterprise in general, a risk, a commercial business which is undertaken, *i.e.* risked. In a judicial compact of 1477, between Peter Schöffer and his brother-in-law, Johan Fust, it is stipulated: "Dieselben Bücher sal der genaunte Peter in Zyt und die wyle er den Handel mit Bücher trybet, dem obgenannten Johannes sinem schwager zu Fruntschaft und zum Besten uff sinen kosten und uff Johannes *abentur und wagnisse* synen eygen büchern, als ferne er verwag, vertryben und verkauffen." The printer, Friedrich Pfister, at Regensburg, complained in 1494 to the bishop that Joh. Pfeyl, and not he, had been entrusted with the printing of prayer-books; whereupon he was answered, "Man mag niemand drucken wehren, es drucke der auf sein eigen *abentuer*."

It is clear from the evidences of the witnesses, 1. that Sahspach made a *press* for the partners; 2. that this press was placed, not at Gutenberg's, in the convent of St. Arbogast, in the neighbourhood of the town, but at Dritzehn's, who lived with Mydehart Stocker; 3. that this press could be opened by means of two buttons; 4. that underneath the press were four *pieces*, which would come down when the buttons were unfastened; 5. that the *secret* of this press (which Gutenberg and Heilmann wished to have kept after the death of Dritzehn) consisted in the *manner* in which the whole machinery was put together, not in its *contents:* separating the thing was sufficient to keep the secret. Now what did this press mean; what were these four pieces? Schöpflin translates them by "four pages" (quatuor paginas), and sees through this prism of an arbitrary translation the beginnings of the *art of printing*. Meerman even, copying him, says: "Every one sees that there is question here of the art of printing." *Every one* namely to whom the sound of the word is sufficient, but *nobody* who attaches more value to meaning than to sound. The character of typography is not pressing and printing, but mobilisation; the winged A is its symbol. The elements unchained; the letters freed from every bond in which the pen or chisel of calligrapher or xylographer held them entangled; the cut character risen from the tomb of the solitary tablet into the substantive life of the cast typos—that is the invention of printing. But the sound of the word *printing* fosters the current misunderstanding as regards *typography*. The uninitiated, misled by the sound, thinks that every kind of *printing*—all that is connected with the impressing of some figure (be it an image or a word) from some form upon some one or other material —belongs to it. And especially a *book*, even if the text is only an impression from engraved wooden blocks, and, therefore, only a specimen of wood-engraving and figure-printing, is not doubted for a moment to be a production of the art of printing. And yet such a book is altogether out of the question.

I cannot repeat often enough that, when we speak of typography and its invention, nothing is meant, or rather nothing must be meant, but printing with *loose* (separate, moveable) types (be they letters, musical notes, or other figures), which, therefore, in distinction from letters cut on wooden or metal plates, may be put together or separated, according to inclination. Even if we discovered a folio, printed from engraved plates, it would signify nothing with respect to typography, but would belong to the history of metallo- or xylography. One thing, therefore, is certain: he who did not invent printing with moveable types, did, as far as typography goes, invent *nothing*. What material was used first of all in this invention; of what metal the first letters, the patrices (engraved punches) and matrices were made; by whom and when the leaden matrices and brass patrices were replaced by brass matrices and steel patrices; by what process the printing-ink, the press, the chases, and other tools were improved— all this belongs to the secondary question of the technical execution of the principal idea: multiplication of books by means of multiplication of letters, multiplication of letters by means of their durability, and repeated use of the same letters, *i.e.* by means of the independence (looseness) of each individual letter (moveableness).[1]

It is necessary to repeat these elementary notions, until they at last are regarded as axioms, for there are still some who pretend, with genial impudence, that printing did not require to be invented, because—it had always existed. Certainly, *printing* has existed always (immemorably long); for the brands, stamps, tiles, the coins of the ancients, and some illuminated manuscripts of the middle ages, exhibit artificially impressed letters. But *no* book was printed with *loose* (*i.e.* cast) *types* before the second half of the 15th century.

To return again to Gutenberg. We understand now that he would *not* have concealed from the uninitiated the real contents of the press by taking it out and putting it upon it, but, on the contrary, by doing so, would have revealed the matter.

Neither do we find here the least connexion with xylography. The press did not replace the *frotton* by xylography before the 16th century. An important evidence, moreover, of one of the witnesses proves, beyond contradiction, that our Strasburg mechanics worked in *metal*, and not in *wood*. I mean this clause: "Dirre gezuge hat ouch geseit das er wol wisse das Gutenberg unlage vor wihnahten sinen kneht sante zu den boden Andresen, *alle formen zu holen, und würdent zurlossen* das er ess sehe, und in joch *ettliche formen ruwete*."[2] Wetter, the most learned writer on the Strasburg process, and who applies it to "Tafeldruck" (block-printing), says of it, and gives, at the same moment, the lie to his own words: "Diese Worte sind viel zu dunkel, als dass sich etwas Bestimmtes daraus folgern lassen könnte. Unter dem wort *Formen* aber sind in keinem Falle einzelne Buchstaben zu verstehen, sondern ganze Tafeln. Daher hiessen die Holzschneider schon früher in ganz Deutschland *Formschneider*. Die folgenden Worte der Aussage sind so dunkel, dass sie schwerlich je befriedigend werden erklärt werden können."[3] A German ought not to give it up so soon, especially not in this case, for the words are plain. They stopped at the words *zurlossen* and *ruwete*, which have been martyred already many times. Zurlossen—zerlassen, means *melting*, and ruwete is still (in Alsace, in Switzerland, and elsewhere) dialect for *reuete*, repeated. Anton Heilmann, therefore, declares that Gutenberg, shortly before Christmas, sent for all forms at Dritzehn's and Andreas Heilmann's, and had them melted in his presence, which he (Gutenberg or witness) regretted, on account of some of them. There is, therefore, no question at all of *wooden* printing-forms; nor do the four pieces of the press, each of which make one whole by themselves, refer to typography. We do not know what these *forms*, these *pieces* (metal-plates?), this *press*, really were. In scientific, objective investigation, we have no right to ask whether an uncertain thing

---

[1] Some idea of typography is already found in Cicero's De natura deorum, II. 20, where he makes the stoic Balbus reply to the epicure Vellejus: "He who fancies that a number of solid and indivisible bodies could be kept together by gravitation, and a world full of order and beauty formed from their accidental meeting together, from such a man I cannot understand why he should not believe also that, if we threw a surprising number of the 21 letters, either of gold or some other material, pell-mell, the annals of Ennius could be legibly put together from these forms scattered on the ground." Here we have indeed the loose metal letters to oppose atomism; but the idea of printing is wanting, and as many thousands of letters are supposed as a whole book contains.

[2] This witness knew also very well that Gutenberg, shortly before Christmas, sent his servant to the two Andreases, *to fetch all the forms; these were melted before his eyes, which he regretted, on account of several forms.*

[3] These words are too obscure, for us to infer anything definite from them. We are, however, in no case to understand by the word *Formen*, separate letters, but whole blocks. Hence, the wood-engravers were formerly called in Germany *Formschneider*. The following words of the evidence are so obscure, that we shall hardly ever be able to explain them satisfactorily.—Kritische Geschichte der Erfindung der Buchdruckerkunst durch Johann Gutenberg zu Maintz, mit einer . . . Prüfung und . . . Beseitigung der von Schöpflin und seinen Anhängern verfochtenen Ansprüche der Stadt Strassburg, &c. Von J. Wetter. Mainz, 1836, 8vo.

may be this or that, but what it really is. The Strasburg law-suit, however, is, even without positive technical result, important enough for an historical investigation; it reveals the future inventor of typography to us as a nobleman, who is, at the same time, an industrial genius; as one who psychologically and technically satisfies the condition, the individual predisposition of the invention. He is no inventor by accident, or by a whim of fate, but by serious *study*, by technical *reflection*. This single fact is of more value to science than a whole ship-load of paper, filled with tiresome suppositions, which advance knowledge not one step further.

Let us follow Gutenberg by the help of positive documents. Evidences of pecuniary embarrassment present themselves afterwards also at Strasburg. The 2nd of January, 1441, Gutenberg and the Knight Luthold von Ramstein gave security for an annual rent of 5 lb., which Johan Karle had sold to the chapter of St. Thomas', at Strasburg, for the sum of 100 lb. On the 15th of December, 1442, he and Marten Brother, citizen of Strasburg, sold to the same bishopric an annual rent of 4 lb. from the revenues of the town of Mentz, which he had inherited from his uncle Johan Lehheimer, judge in that town. Both acknowledge to have received the price in ready money, and to have employed it to the sole use of Johan Gutenberg (quam pecuniam ipsi venditores confessi fuerunt se a Dominis Decano et Capitulo pleno recepisse, sibique numeratam, traditam et solutam fore, ac in usus praefati Joannis Gutenberg totaliter convertisse.) The records of these bonds are preserved at Strasburg, in the church of St. Thomas. Gutenberg is described in them thus: *Johannes* dictus *Gensefleisch* alias nuncupatus *Gutenberg de Moguntia*. Finally, the following annotations have regard to his residence in that town: In the Helbeling-Zollbuch (register of the receipts of the helbeling, or penny-tax, raised from every measure of wine), which is still preserved at Strasburg, we find in the volume, containing the years 1436—40: " Item Hans Gutenberg i voer and iiii aam. Settled with him on Thursday before St. Margaret A. 1439; still due xii s. and when he pays these, he has paid till St. John's till St. Agnes last. Item has given xii s. on the same day."

In the volume of 1442 and following years we find: " Item Hans Gutenberg. . . . on St. Matthias A. 1443. Has given 1 guilder on St. Gregorius A. 44." In another place it is said that this tax was paid by " Ennel Gutenbergen;" but as this annotation has no date, we are unable to infer from it since when Ennel resided alone at Strasburg.

III.

GUTENBERG AT MENTZ.

It is not before 1448 that we know for a certainty that Gutenberg was again living in his native town. On the 6th of October of that year he borrows 150 guilders, which his relative, Arnold Gelthuss, borrows for him from Rynhard Brömser and Henchin Rodenstein on security of the rent of some houses, which Gelthuss possessed at Mentz.[1] It is very probable that this continual pecuniary embarrassment had something to do with Gutenberg's indefatigable industrial experiments. Without knowing of course the exact moment in which the first idea of typography enlightened his mind, without knowing his first efforts, of more importance to curiosity than to science, we have approached however the year in which the celebrated invention was an accomplished fact. Gutenberg was *ready* in the year 1450 with the invention of

---

[1] Die Geschichte der Erfind. der Buchdruckerkunst durch Johann Gensfleisch genannt Gutenberg zu Mainz . . . von C. A. Schaab. Mainz. 1830—31. 8vo. III.

the art of printing, according to Luther, "Das letzte Auflodern vor dem Erlöschen der Welt," but in reality the first glimmer of a new creation. The vellum documents which prove this are still preserved at Frankfurt and at Mentz. They prove that Gutenberg, instead of having any longer recourse to small pecuniary loans, could make the rich Mentz citizen, Johan Fust (dialect for Faust), understand the importance of his invention so clearly, that he supplied him, in August, 1450, first with the funds necessary to the establishment of a printing-office, and afterwards with a sum of money to make it work. For the first amount the established printing-office remained security; for the second Gutenberg gave the value of his discovery and his labour, of which the profit and the loss would be divided.

There was therefore a twofold (simply *financial*) connexion between Fust and Gutenberg. Fust was 1. holder of the mortgage on the printing-office and its appurtenances, 2. partner in the projected business. The second sum therefore could have been supplied just as well by another than Fust. All this will soon be evident.

The first work to which the new art was applied, was the Bible in the language of the Church, a gigantic labour, worthy the genius which discovered it. Some years were spent on the two folios, 324 and 317 leaves, of which it consists, but they were decidedly completed in 1455, for the copy of the Library at Paris contains the following inscriptions of the rubricator : " Et sic est finis primæ partis bibliæ, scilicet veteris testamenti, illuminata seu rubricata et ligata per Henricum Albech alias Cremer Anno Dni. MCCCCLVI. festo Bartholomei Apli . . . [24 August] Deo gratias . . . . Alleluja." And at the end of the second vol.: " Iste liber illuminatus,ligatus et completus est per Henricum Cremer Vicarium ecclesiæ collegiatæ Sancti Stephani *Maguntine* sub Anno Dni. Millesimo quadringentesimo quinquagesimo sexto, festo assumtionis gloriosæ Virginis Mariæ, deo Gratias Alleluja." These authentic dates, in connexion with the time absolutely necessary for such a work, bring us to the year 1455 as the positive date of its *completion*. Every page, printed in 2 columns, contains, except the ten first, 42 lines, whereby it is known among the bibliographers as the Bible of 42 lines. The ink, probably soot and gum, is dissoluble by water. Of this admirable monument there exist, as far as I am aware of, still sixteen copies in the public libraries of Europe, of which seven are on vellum and nine on paper.

While Gutenberg was occupied with this bible, he executed also smaller works, of which the most however have been lost. This appears from the still existing letters of indulgence on vellum. Pope Nicolas V. decreed an indulgence, in order to support with the produce John II., king of Cyprus, against the Turks. He sent the agent of the king, Paulinus Zappe, to the Archbishop of Mentz, with an authority dated 6th January, 1452. The name of this deputy appears on the printed letters of indulgence, whereby it is beyond doubt that they were printed at Mentz. These letters consist of three parts: the first commences with the words : " Universis Christi fidelibus presentes litteras inspecturis Paulinus Chappe consiliarius ambasciator et procurator generalis Serenissimi Regis Cypri," and concludes with the date, which shows the place, year and day of the delivery of the letter ; the second part contains a form of absolution for life (Forma plenissime absolutionis et remissionis in vita) ; the third at the point of death (Forma plenissime remissionis in articulo mortis). The headings of these forms and the words Universis and Paulinus in the first part, are printed with missal-types, but all the rest with a smaller type. Space is left for the name of the receivers, their place, and the exact day. The year, however, was printed. The Museum Meermanno-Westreenianum at the Hague possesses a copy with the year Mcccliiii., *the earliest typographically printed year in existence.* Lord Spencer possesses a copy of another edition, as well as a second with the year 1455.

It lies in the nature of the case that since the erection of this printing-office, workmen were engaged, *i.e.* apprentices were educated. Among them, we know in the first place, Peter Schöffer, an excellent calligrapher, born at Gernsheim, a small town on the right bank of the Rhine, between Worms and Oppenheim, and which at that time belonged to the archbishopric of Mentz. In the year 1449 this Schöffer lived as a scriptor at Paris. The town-press at Strasburg possesses a work written by him, with the calligraphic inscription, "Hic est finis omnium librorum tam veteris quam nove loice completi per me Petrum de Gernsheim, alias de Moguntia, anno MCCCCXLIX., in gloriosissima universitate Parisiensi." In the illumination of this inscription the future artist of the beautiful initials in the Psalter of 1457 is already visible.

Another disciple of Gutenberg was Albert Pfister, originally a xylographer, and the first who established a printing-office outside Mentz; he settled, perhaps already in 1453, at Bamberg, and published at that place, a year later, *the first book with a year*, it being at the same time the first book in *German*. The only copy known of this work, 6 leaves, in 4to., of which 9 pages have been printed upon, is preserved in the Royal Library at Munich. The text, divided into the twelve months of the year, contains: Eyn manung der cristenheit widder die durken (an appeal to Christendom against the Turks, who had conquered Constantinople on the 18th of May, 1453.) At the end we find the year: "Als man zelet noch dni geburt offenbar MCCCC.LV. jar." The following year he printed with the same types a kalender on one sheet in folio, printed on one side, but with the year for which it was destined, namely, 1457. About the year 1460, Pfister also completed a great typographical work, a Latin bible, a vellum and paper folio of 881 leaves, each of 36 lines, hence its name among bibliographers of the bible of 36 lines. In the rubricated copy of the Library at Paris the year 1461 is written with the same red ink with which all the rubrics of the whole work have been done. This bible has been ascribed to the press of Pfister on account of its identity with the types of the "Fabelbuch," printed at Bamberg in 1461, and known to bibliographers under the name of Boners Edelstein. This work consists of 88 leaves in 4to, with 85 woodcuts and (continuous) rhymed text. The imprint of this first book in German, with indication of the *place* where it was printed, runs thus, as taken from the only copy known, in the library at Wolfenbuttel :—

> Zu Bamberg diss puchleyn geendet ist
> Nach der geput unsers herren ihesu crist
> Do man zalt tausent unde vierhundert jar
> Und ym ein und sechzigsten das ist war.
> An sant valenteins tag
> Got behut uns vor seiner plag. Amen.

The name of the printer at Bamberg is revealed last of all in the imprint of the so-called "Buch der vier Historien," with the year 1462. This work, consisting of 58 leaves, small folio, with 61 woodcuts, contains the histories of Joseph, Daniel, Esther and Judith. It concludes with the (continuous) lines :—

> Tzu bambergk in der selben stat.
> Das albrecht pfister gedrucket hat.
> Do man zalt tausent und vierhundert jar.
> In zweiund sechzigsten das ist war.
> Nit lang nach sand walpurgen tag.
> Die vns wol gnad erverben mag.
> Frid und das ewig leben.
> Das wolle uns got allen geben. Amen.

Printed with the types of the bible of 36 lines, but without a date, appeared also a German translation of the Belial of Jacobus de Theramo, 90 leaves in small folio, on the last of which we find the name of the printer: Albrecht Pfister zu Bamberg. According to the types, the following undated editions should also be ascribed to the press of Pfister: 1. Die sieben Freuden Mariä, 9 leaves in 12mo. with 8 woodcuts; 2. Das Leiden Jesu, 21 leaves with 20 woodcuts (if they were printed before 1460, then these are the first typographical books with woodcuts); 3. Klagen gegen den Tod, 24 leaves, small folio, with 5 woodcuts; 4. Rechstreit des Menschen mit dem Tode, 23 leaves, small folio; 5. Die Armenbibel, 17 leaves, folio, with 170 woodcuts; and 6. the Biblia Pauperum, the same work as No. 5, but with Latin text and printed ib. 1462. While history knows nothing about it, the librarian J. H. Jäck, at Bamberg, has been so good as to raise Albrecht Pfister almost to the inventor of the art of printing, and has caught indeed, in his tissue of conjectures, a few weak minds (as for instance Dr. Karl Falkenstein),[1] who, not being able to ignore the documents regarding Gutenberg, have begun to acknowledge Pfister as an independent inventor of typography, contemporary with Gutenberg. Not a single date however exists which compels us to this arbitrary supposition. Science has nothing to do with the psychological *possibility* of a simultaneous invention of two geniuses unknown to each other. The question is not what *could* have happened, but what really did happen. Now, a simultaneous invention of typography at Mentz and at Bamberg, situated not far from the first place, is even psychologically improbable. Inventions of this importance are not epidemic. Lessing has truly said: " It is perhaps possible to show more or less of all inventions, that somewhere somebody must have been very near to it. To prove of any one, whichever it may be, that it could or should have been invented long ago, is nothing but chicane; we are to prove incontrovertibly that it was really invented, or to be silent."

Let us return to Gutenberg. Genius and talent for pecuniary administration, which are seldom found together in one man, do not seem to have combined in Gutenberg. At least in the year 1455, Fust seems to have felt it necessary to force him judicially to produce an account of the money advanced. The very important act of the Mentz notary, Ulrich Helmasperger, dated 6 Nov. 1455 and preserved on vellum at Frankfort and at Mentz, the first record which treats of the art of printing, deserves to be known by every one who takes an interest in the history of the most important of inventions.[2] I have tried to facilitate this by giving an intelligible translation of it.

" Instrument of a certain day, when Fust produced an account and confirmed it by an oath.

" In the name of God. Amen. Be it known to all who shall see this public document or hear it read, that, in the year of our Lord, 1455, on Thursday the 6th of November, between eleven and twelve at noon, at Mentz, in the large dining hall (refectorium) of the convent of barefooted friars, appeared before me notary, and the witnesses to be mentioned hereafter, the honorable and prudent man Jacob Fust, citizen of Mentz, and has, in behalf of Johan Fust his brother, also present, shewn, said and exposed, that to the said Johan Fust on one side and Johan Gutenberg on the other, should be administered the oath, according to judgment passed on both the parties, and for which this day and this hour had been fixed and the hall of the convent assigned. In order that the friars of the said convent, who were still assembled in the hall, should not be disturbed, the said Jacob Fust did ask through his messenger, whether Johan Gutenberg or any one for him were present in the convent, in order to finish the matter. At this message came into the said refectorium the reverend Heinrich Gunther, pastor of St. Christopher's at Mentz, Heinrich Keffer [one of the first printers at Nuremberg] and Bertolf von Hanau [one of the first printers at Basle] servant of Johan Gutenberg, and when they had been asked by Johan Fust whether they had been authorized by Johan Gutenberg, they answered that they had been sent by Junker Johan Gutenberg to hear and to see what should happen in this case. Thereupon Johan Fust begged leave to conform to the stipulations of the verdict, after he had waited for Johan Gutenberg till twelve o'clock, and was still waiting for him. He reads the sentence passed on the first article of his claim, from word to word, with it pretension and response, which runs as follows: first, that he, according to thei written agreement, should lend Johan Gutenberg about 800 florins in gold, *with whic*

---

[1] In the work quoted already before, and which is only valuable on account of the beautif facsimiles. The critical part is very uncritical, as we might expect from the natural disposition of th author to insanity, which does not go hand in hand with acute criticism. The work of Sotzmann suffer from the same confusion. The heads of these authors were clouded by dark, wandering, undetermined ideas of transitions from xylography to typography, so that the invention, repeated more tha once, took, properly speaking, place *unwittingly*, and the fictitious inventors must have discovered years afterwards, with surprise, that—they *had* invented typography.

[2] Hochverdiente und aus bewährten Urkunden wohlbeglaubte Ehren-Rettung Johann Guttenberg ... wegen der ersten Erfindung der ... Buchdrucker-Kunst in ... Mayntz ... von Johann Davi Köhler. Leipz. 1741. 4to.

he was to finish the work, and whether it would cost more or less was no matter to Fust; and that Johan Gutenberg was to pay six per cent interest for this money. He had indeed lent him these 800 guilders on a bond, but Gutenberg was not satisfied, but complained that he had not yet received the 800 guilders. For that reason, Fust, being desirous of doing him some service, lent him 800 guilders more than he was bound by his contract to do, for which 800 guilders Fust had to pay forty guilders as interest. And, although Gutenberg had bound himself by contract to pay six per cent interest on the first 800 guilders, yet he had not done so for a single year, but Fust had to pay this interest himself to the amount of 250 guilders. For, at present, Gutenberg having never paid interest and Fust having been obliged to borrow this interest from Christians and Jews, for which he had paid about thirty-six florins, his payments, together with the capital, amount to about 2,020 guilders, of which he demands reimbursement. Thereupon, Johan Gutenberg answered that Johan Fust had agreed to lend him 800 guilders, *with which money he was to arrange and make his tools*, and that these *tools* should remain a security for Fust. But Fust had moreover agreed to give him every year 300 guilders for *expenses*, and to advance also *wages, house-rent*, VELLUM, PAPER, INK, &c. If, afterwards, they did not agree, Gutenberg should then pay the 800 guilders back and the tools should be free from mortgage; it should be understood, that with the 800 guilders he had to make the *machine*, which was to be a pledge. He hopes not (that any one shall pretend) that he was obliged to spend these 800 guilders *on the work of the books* (i.e. on vellum, paper, &c.) And, although in the contract it is said that Gutenberg was to pay six per cent interest, Fust had told him that he had no intention of accepting this interest from him. Moreover, he had not received the 800 guilders in full and at once according to agreement, as Fust had pretended in the first article of his claim, and as for the second 800 guilders, he is ready to give an account of them, but declines to give him interest or usury for them, and hopes that he is not bound by law to pay them. We pass therefore sentence according to pretension and response:—When Johan Gutenberg has submitted an account of all receipts and disbursements spent *on the work to their common profit* (i.e. printing), this work shall be added to the 800 guilders; if he has spent more than the 800 guilders, which did not belong to their common profit, he should pay it back; if Fust is able to prove on oath or by witnesses, that he has borrowed the money on interest and did not lend it out of his own resources, then Gutenberg is bound by contract to pay it.

"Now, after this sentence had been read in presence of the aforesaid witnesses, Johan Fust has, with raised fingers, in the hands of me, public notary, taken the oath by all the saints, that everything was comprised according to truth and sentence, in an act which he placed in my hands. He confirmed it (the act) on oath, as truly as God and the saints may help him; and the contents of this document was as follows:—

'I, Johan Fust, have borrowed 1,550 guilders, which have been received by Johan Gutenberg, and spent on our common work, for which I have paid an annual interest, and still owe a part of it. Therefore, I count for every hundred guilders which I have borrowed in this way, six guilders per annum; and for the money spent on our common work, I demand the interest according to judgment passed.'

"The said Johan Fust demands from me, public notary, one or more public acts of this matter, as many and as often he should want them; and all these matters recorded here, happened in the year, indiction, day, hour, papacy, month, and town aforesaid, in the presence of the honest men, Peter Grauss, Johan Kist, Johan Knoff, Johan Ysencck, Jacob Fust, citizens of Mentz; Peter Gernsheim and Johan Bone, clerks of the city and diocese of Mentz, asked and summoned as witnesses. And I, Ulrich Helmasperger, clerk of the diocese of Bamberg, by imperial authority, public clerk of the Holy See at Mentz, sworn notary, have been present at all the aforesaid transactions and articles with the witnesses mentioned. Therefore, being requested to do so, I have signed with my hand, and sealed with my common seal, this public act, written by another, as testimony and true record of all the aforesaid matters.

"ULRICUS HELMASPERGER, *Notary.*"

After this law-suit, Gutenberg's printing-office came into the possession of his money-lender, who found in the talented Peter Schöffer, instructed by the inventor, and surpassing him in the particulars of the execution, the most proper person to carry it on. Their interests were afterwards bound up together, when Fust gave him, c. 1465, his only daughter, Dyna (Christina), as wife.

There is material in this event for an affecting drama: a genial inventor, indefatigably occupied in realizing an idea, an usurious and crafty money-lender, abusing the financial carelessness of a genius, to get him more and more into his power; a clever servant, courting the daughter of the usurer, and conspiring with him against the great master; the inventor robbed of all the fruit of his exertions during many years, at the moment that it was ripe to be gathered!

But history has to submit to the oath of Fust. Free from Gutenberg, he published with Schöffer, in 1457, the magnificent Psalter (properly an officium divinum), *the first printed book with a complete date.* The translation of its curious imprint, in red ink, is as follows :—" The present codex of the psalms, adorned by the beauty of the capitals and sufficiently rubricated, has thus been made by the masterly invention of printing and the forming of characters (types) (adinventione artificiosa imprimendi ac caracterizandi) without any writing of the pen, and, with much labour and industry, completed to the honor and service of God, by Johan Fust, citizen of Mentz, and Peter Schöffer, of Gernsheim, in the year of the Lord thousand CCCCLVII., on the eve of the assumption of Mary" (14 Aug.).

(With that prefix "ad," the bad latinity of the 15th century meant to strengthen the substantive, inventio. So in the pandects, adinventio means simply *inventio*, not additional invention. When Gebwiler in the 16th century was desirous of ascribing to the Strasburg printer, Mentelin, the invention of typography, he expressed himself (Panegir. Carolin. Edit. Argent. 1521, 19) thus : "Primus autem ante 64 annos in hac urbe—*adinvenit.*" If, however, deep philosophy *must be* concealed in this " ad," it was then a measure against the inventor, whose printing-office they had succeeded in securing. The inventor, Gutenberg, at least has never made use of the term adinventio. He says *inventio.*)

The Psalter is a masterpiece of typography, difficult, even at present, to be imitated, hardly to be surpassed. It is a folio of 175 leaves, on vellum, printed with five kinds of letters, large choral types, for church use, 228 beautiful initials in colours (blue, red, and purple), of which the first capital, the B (Beatus vir) is a real work of art. The copy of Count Mac-Carthy, of Toulouse, was sold, in 1807, for 12,000 francs; but it is worth much more now.

The Psalter was reprinted, with the same types, in 1459, 1490, 1502, and 1506. In 1502 it was the last publication of Peter Schöffer, just as in 1457 he had opened his typographical career with it. About a month after the second edition of the Psalter, a folio of 169 leaves appeared, printed with a new and much smaller type, on vellum and on paper, the Rationale divinorum officiorum, a liturgical work of the most flourishing period of Catholicism, by bishop Durandus (Durant, † 1294), on the origin and signification of ecclesiastical ceremonies. The imprint (6 Oct. 1459) is almost the same as that of the two Psalters. In 1460 (25 June) Fust and Schöffer published their fourth book with a complete date, 51 leaves in folio, again printed with new types, the Constitutiones of Clement V.

The inventor meanwhile, assisted with money by Dr. Humery, had bought new typographical furniture. He completed a gigantic work, a folio of 373 leaves, printed on vellum and paper, namely, the celebrated Catholicon, an elaborate Latin grammar and etymological dictionary in five divisions, by Joh. de Janua de Balbis. The Museum Meermanno-Westreenianum possesses *two* copies of this splendid monument of the grand invention, where the inventor himself speaks in the imprint. A law-suit may have been the reason why he does not call himself the printer, but he speaks of the *invention* in the most unequivocal, dignified manner. In the theological language of his age, he speaks of himself as of the chosen instrument of God, by whom the glory of His people is raised. Gutenberg concluded his work with the following prophetic lines, alluding at the same time to the contents of the book, a grammar:—"By the assistance of the Most High, at whose will the tongues of the children become eloquent, and who often reveals to babes what he conceals from the wise, this excellent book, Catholicon, has been printed and completed, in the year of the Incarnation 1460, in the town of Mentz (which belongs to the glorious German nation, and which God has consented to prefer and to raise with such an exalted light of the mind and free grace, above the other nations of the earth), not by means of reed or pencil, or pen, but by the admirable harmony, connexion and regularity of the punches (patrices) and forms (matrices). Therefore, to thee, Holy Father, Son, and Holy Ghost, threefold and only God, be given praise and honour. Let those who never cease to praise Mary, accord also by this book, with the universal anthem of the Church. God be praised!"

With these thanks the typographical career of the inventor nearly concluded; at least we know nothing more of him but a letter of indulgence, printed in 1461 with the types of the Catholicon, and described by Van Pract (Cat. des livres imprimés sur vélin, I. 218). The same cause which put a temporary stop to the work of Fust and Schöffer, prevented also Gutenberg's press from working.

Meanwhile the year of the general spread of the art had arrived. Aeneas Sylvius, who ascended the Papal throne on the 27th of August, 1458, as Pius II., removed, in 1461, the Mentz elector-archbishop Diether von Isenberg, from his office, whereupon the canons elected Adolph von Nassau, although the town maintained the authority of Diether. This event was the cause of the first papers printed of a controversial, political nature, of which the researches of the 19th century have discovered the following:—

I. A German "Brieff" of the emperor Frederick III. (8 Aug. 1461), whereby the archbishop Diether von Isenberg is removed, and Adolph von Nassau elected in his stead; 28 lines on one sheet.

II. A Latin bull of Pius II. (21 Aug. 1461), on the removal of Count Diether; 87 lines on one sheet of paper, in which is found the well-known water-mark, representing a bull's head, with the bar and the cross of St. Andrew (×).

III. A Latin bull in favour of the new archbishop Adolph (12 Sept. 1461); two editions, each of 27 lines on one sheet, containing the aforesaid water-mark.

IV. A Latin bull to the chapter of Mentz, about Diether and Adolph (12 Sept. 1461); 24 lines on one sheet.

V. A Latin bull to the chapter, provosts, &c. of the church and diocese of Mentz on the removal of Diether (12 Sept. 1461); 18 lines on one sheet, with the bull's head.

VI. A German proclamation of Adolph against Diether; 58 lines on one sheet. It appears from the beginning that Diether, too, had written polemic papers. "(W)yr haben vernummen das Diether von Isenberg der sich etzliche zyt des stiffts czu Mentz underwunden hait fast mancherley schrift habe laszen vszgeen die auch etzlich an uch gelangt mugen," &c. We know of those "mancherley schrifft" of Diether hitherto only:

VII. A German proclamation of 6 April, 1462; 106 long lines on one sheet, with the bull's head with a short bar as water-mark.

The texts of No. I.—VI. have been reprinted in full in the Collectio Weigeliana.[1] No. II.—VII. are printed with the types of the Rationale Durandi (1459), as also an epistle of Pius II. to all prelates, princes, &c. concerning the mission of cardinal Bessarion, and the Turks' tithe (28 lines on one sheet, dated 1st Sept. 1461). All these documents therefore originate incontestably from the press of Fust and Schöffer. Only the types of No. I. were new and appeared soon in a large work. They printed on the 14th of August, 1462, namely, with these types the first *Bible with a date*, two

---

[1] Die Anfänge der Druckerkunst in Bild und Schrift. An deren frühesten Erzeugnissen in der Weigel' schen Sammlung erläutert von T. O. Weigel und Dr. A. Zestermann. Mit 145 Facsimiles und vielen in den Text gedruckten Holzschnitten. Leipzig, T. O. Weigel, 1866. Fol. II.

folios in Latin, of 481 (242 and 239) leaves, on vellum and paper, again a typographical masterpiece. The imprint is, with a trifling alteration, the same as before. Strangely enough, the publishers call their work in this imprint, somewhat humorously, "opusculum"; in the second edition, however, of 1472, this word was changed into "opus."

Meanwhile the archiepiscopal quarrel was not to be decided by the pen or press. Both the parties took up arms. Schaab describes the consequences of this contest thus: "This enmity between two archbishops was the cause of one of the most terrible days to the town of Mentz. It was the 28th of October, 1462, the day on which Christianity celebrated the anniversary of the apostles Simon and Judas. Mentz had remained faithful to the archbishop Diether. Adolph therefore tried to conquer it by stratagem and treason. Traitors were gained over in the town, who entailed upon a half thousand of their fellow-citizens death, and endless misery on many more. By this treachery of some wicked persons the town was assaulted during the night between the 27th and 28th of October 1462, by the followers of Adolph; its noblest citizens were murdered, the most of them robbed of their possessions, and driven from the town. All kinds of mischief was committed towards those who remained behind. Neither age, rank, nor sex was excepted. The booty was sold publicly in the cattle-market, and the money divided between the soldiers. Of the expelled citizens only a few gradually returned in secret to their relations. But the town, so populous before, remained empty, and all industry was destroyed. The elector Adolph II. found it necessary, on the Saturday after St. Thomas' day of the same year, to issue a proclamation whereby he promised to all who wished to trade or to exercise a profession in Mentz, protection for their persons and possessions, to induce a few to return. A town, a short time before flourishing with commerce and industry, had been robbed in a few days of its privileges and utterly destroyed. It remained long in this miserable condition, and even the elector Diether, when he had been restored, after the death of Adolph, if we except the university which he established at Mentz, did nothing for the restoration of its liberties, which it had lost in his cause; he even abandoned it to the rule of the cathedral chapter, and when the citizens declined to acknowledge its authority, he did all he could for their oppression, and caused even a fortified castle to be erected within its walls. It could not but fail that in these days of misery and anxiety the work-places of the two printers of Mentz should be abandoned, that all workmen should leave the town and bring their art to countries where it was yet unknown."

Indeed, from this moment we see everywhere presses established under the direction of Germans. The Mentz presses, however, remained inactive for nearly three years on account of the expulsion and flight of the workmen. We know at least only a bull of the year 1464 against the Turks. Two Mentz typographers, Conrad Schweynheym and Arnold Pannartz, had already brought the new art into Italy, and published, 29th of October, 1465, the celebrated edition of Lactantius Firmianus, printed in the convent of Subiaco, near Rome, after which date, on the 17th of December of the same year, Fust and Schöffer produced again a folio: Bonifacius VIII., Liber sextus Decretalium. In some copies of this work we find the ordinary imprint mixed up with the panegyric on Mentz of Gutenberg's imprint of the Catholicon. Schöffer did this regularly after the death of Fust, until, in 1472, he began to call Mentz unreservedly the inventress of the art of printing (impressoriæ artis inventricem eliminatricemque primam). In the same year, 1465, the father and his son-in-law published their first edition of a Latin author, Cicero de Officiis, reprinted on the 24th of February, 1466. The imprint of both these editions indicates for the first time a close relation between Fust and Schöffer; Fust calls him for the first time "puerum suum." (Presens Marci Tuly clarissimum Opus. Johannes Fust Moguntinus civis, non atramento plumali cana neque aerea. Sed arte quadam perpulcra. Petri manu pueri mei feliciter effeci finitum.). Formerly Schöffer was called clericus (writer, clerk). The last work published during the lifetime of Fust, was the Grammatica vetas rhythmica, 11 leaves small folio, in the year 1466.

IV.

THE MEMORY OF GUTENBERG.

MEANWHILE the inventor himself was no longer at Mentz. On the 17th of January, 1464, he was admitted by the elector Adolph II. among his courtiers or chamberlains. The act of appointment has been preserved:

"We, Adolph, elected and confirmed archbishop of Mentz, acknowledge that we have considered the agreeable and voluntary service which our dear and faithful Johan Gutenberg has rendered to us and our bishopric, and have appointed and accepted him as our servant and courtier. Nor shall we remove him from our service as long as he lives; and in order that he may enjoy it the more, we will clothe him every year, when we clothe our ordinary suite (unsern gemeinen hoffgesind), always like our noblemen, and give him our court dress; also every year twenty mout of corn and two voer of wine for the use of his house, free of duty, as long as he lives, but on condition that he shall not sell it or give it away. Which has been promised us in good faith by Johan Gutenberg. Eltvill, Thursday after St. Antony, 1465."

"An aristocratic appointment at the court," says Schaab, "procured this nobleman a comfortable life. Voluntarily he followed the princely court, where he had a free table and fodder for his horses. Even for his dress he received cloth in the court colours, and generally wore a kind of mantle, called Tabard. It was in accordance with the morals of that time to carouse at court. They went there with empty cups and returned with full ones. The princes tried not before the sixteenth century to put a check to this excess by special orders. The elector Johan Schweikard von Kronenberg ordered, even in the year 1605, to leave the 'grossen Saumagen'—this was the name of the cups then used—for the future at home."

However comfortable and German-like all this may look, miserable were these court-wages, this dress, these alms presented to the inventor of typography. But no, it is perfectly in harmony with the general course of earthly things.

As Gutenberg stood in relation to the municipal syndicus, Dr. Conrad Humery, one of the principal followers of the expelled archbishop (while the Fusts on the other hand had belonged to the adherents of Adolph), the distinction of the conqueror can have had no connexion with Gutenberg's partizanship during the archiepiscopal rupture. The service, therefore, rendered to the bishopric, to which the act of appointment alludes, must have been the grand invention. At least the interest of Adolph in the exercise of typography will be evident presently from another particular.

Adolph II. had established his court at Eltvill on the Rhine, three hours distance from Mentz. The greatest part of Gutenberg's printing-office was removed thither. At Eltvill lived the brothers Heinrich and Nicolaus Bechtermüntz, who belonged to the ancient nobility of Mentz, and were related by marriage to Gutenberg. They were instructed by him in the new art, and he gave them, at least the use of, his press. When the eldest brother, Heinrich, died in July, 1467, another patrician, Wiegand Spies von Ostenberg, succeeded him. On the 4th of November of the said year, therefore during the lifetime of Gutenberg, these noble typographers published an extract of the large Catholicon, of 165 leaves, in small 4to., printed with the same types and known among bibliographers as Vocabularium ex quo. It is the first dated book of Gutenberg's press with a plain statement of the printer. The late Heinrich Bechtermüntz, according to the imprint, began to print the work at Eltvill, but it was completed on St. Leonard's day by Nicolaus Bechtermüntz and Wiegand Spies von Ostenberg. Refreshing sight! Three noble, distinguished, rich men, every one of whom had been sheriffs of Hechtsheim, situated in the neighbourhood of Mentz, call themselves here publicly printers. And the nature of their work was so clear to the minds of these noble disciples of the noble inventor that they unequivocally called their art a *nova artificiosaque inventio*. N. Bechtermüntz alone reprinted the book in 1469. The publication of this work (the only copy known of the first edition is preserved in the Library at Paris) was the last joy of Gutenberg. He died before the 24th February, 1468, for his second money-lender, the aforesaid Dr. Humery, bound himself by an act of that date, to print only in Mentz with the typographical instruments which by the death of Gutenberg devolved upon him. The contents of the said act run thus :—

"I, Conrad Homery, Doctor, acknowledge by this letter that . . . Adolph, archbishop of Mentz, had given me a great many formes, types, instruments, tools, and other things connected with printing, which Johan Gutenberg left when he died, and which have been my property and still are; that I have bound and bind myself by this letter to use those forms and instruments only for printing within Mentz, and nowhere else; if I had occasion to sell them, and a citizen were willing to give me as much for them as a stranger, I shall give the preference to an inhabitant of Mentz. Given in the year 1468, the Friday after St. Matthew."

Johan Gutenberg, the last descendant of a branch of the family of Gensfleisch, the discoverer of gold mines, died, burdened with debts, unmarried and childless, and was soon forgotten. Without the epitaph, made not long after his death by his kinsman Adam Gelthuss, and fortunately printed in 1499 at Heidelberg, we should not even have known that he was buried in the church of the Minorites at Mentz. The epitaph alludes to an unexecuted plan of erecting a monument in honour of him, and runs thus :—"To Johan Gensfleisch, inventor of the art of printing, deserving well of all nations and languages, Adam Gelthuss has erected this monument to the immortal memory of his name. His remains rest peaceably in the church of St. Franciscus at Mentz."

While Gutenberg was alive, Fust and Schöffer appropriated nothing of the glory of the invention to themselves. After the death of the inventor in 1468 (Fust had died already before) Peter Schöffer was free to indulge his vanity. Characteristic is the elaborate imprint of the Institutiones of Justinianus, published (24th May) 1468 : his first work after Gutenberg's death. With an allusion to the history of the resurrection in the Gospels (John xx. 2—6) he says, that "God has sent the excellent masters in the art of cutting letters, both Johanneses (Gutenberg and Fust), born at Mentz, the celebrated first printers; he, Petrus (Schöffer), came indeed later than they to the grave, but he entered it first, as he is their master in the art of cutting letters." As however his great taste and the technical improvement introduced by Schöffer after Gutenberg's invention have altered *nothing* of the real nature of things, we observe here, for the first time, the intention of raising those improvements in the *execution* of the discovery at the cost of Gutenberg's immortal *invention*. The imprint, consisting of twenty-four verses in barbarous Latin, is too curious not to be translated :—"Moses completed not the plan of the tabernacle, nor Solomon the building of the magnificent temple, without skilful artists. More exalted than Solomon the glory of the Church came renewing and calling forth also Bezaleël and Hyram. He who is pleased to gird mighty men with wisdom, sent those two excellent in the art of engraving, the first celebrated printers of books; both called Johannes, born by Moguncia. Petrus came with them to the long wished-for grave, reaching it later, but entering it first, surpassing them in the art of cutting letters, through Him, who gives us light and knowledge. Every nation may now make its own character, for the art prevails everywhere with all-creating pencil. The labours of the scholars to prepare writings and to make them ready for the press, are many; just as Franciscus, whose work enlightens the earth, has prepared this. I, too, am attached to him, not by vile profit, but by the love of the common weal and the glory of my paternal country. That they who prepare the work and read the proofs may distinguish the false from the true (things). The friends of letters will undoubtedly gratify them with a laurel, for with their books they instruct thousands of cathedras."

The gist of the poetical envelopment is of great importance. While Fust's son-in-law calls him protocaragmaticus, it is historically true, as we know from the process of 1455, that he was exclusively the money-lender, and Gutenberg the soul of the undertaking. Here therefore we detect family pride in the very fact, and are able to reject at once, on incontestable authority, the first effort of making an original typographer of Fust. And as for Schöffer himself, his own confession (repeated in 1472), that he entered, *later* than Johannes, the sanctuary of the art, and improved it *after* him in the application (the designing of letters);—this involuntary homage to truth triumphantly maintains Gutenberg's priority. In striking harmony with this is Schöffer's verbal account to Trithemius, between 1480 and 1490:— "About this time (1450), the admirable, and formerly unheard-of, art of composing and printing books by means of letters was *conceived and invented* at Mentz *by a Mentz citizen, Johan Gutenberg.*" All that Trithemius says more than this is nonsense, for which he is responsible, and with which a serious investigation needs not trouble itself.

Schöffer has not said any more about Gutenberg, nor appropriated to himself the *invention*, but in the imprints of his numerous works glorified distinctly, and perfectly in accordance with truth, *Mentz as the town of the invention*. This he did in plain words, before the whole of civilized Europe, and, of course, contradicted by no one, in the year 1468 (Grammatica rhythmica), 1469 (Thomas de Aquino, Expositio quarti lib. Sent.), 1470 (Bonifacius VIII. Lib. VI. Decretal.), 1471 (Clemens V. Constitutiones and in the first edition of Thomas de Aquino, Prima pars secundae partis summae), 1472 (Biblia sacra, and in the Decretum of Gratianus), 1473 (Gregorius IX., Nova compilatio Decretal.), 1474 (Herp, Speculum aureum decem preceptorum Dei) and so on.

In accordance with all this, Matthias Palmer (born at Pisa as early as 1423) said, in 1474, that Johan Gutenberg zum Jungen, a knight of Mentz, had invented the art of printing books; confirmed (*not* copied) in 1499, by the Mentz disciple Ulrich Zell, in 1504 by Sabellicus, in 1517 by Vergilius. The account of the last-named is important, because Vergilius in the first edition of his work (De inventoribus rerum, Ven. 1499), mentioned, on the authority of a verbal information of another German, "a German, a *certain Peter*," as the inventor of printing; but he corrected the mistake in the edition of 1517, at a time when the legend of Faust began already to show itself. The correction of Vergilius therefore rests on investigation, and on investigation in a good quarter. The memory of Johan Gensfleisch Gutenberg was preserved during the fifteenth century, although he left no heirs who could maintain his reputation; although his invention had got into the hands of the antagonistic firm of Fust and Schöffer; although the true documents of his right existed only in manuscript. In 1494, two professors at Heidelberg wrote each a Latin panegyric on Johan Gutenberg, *the inventor of typography.* The first consists of thirteen distichs, with the heading: Ada Wernheri Temarensis Panegyris ad Joannem Gensfleisch primum librorum impressorem. The commencement travesties the Latin name Ansicaro (Gensfleisch):—

> Ansicaro vigili praestantior ansere : Romam
> Qui monuit gallos limine inesse canens.
> Arcem is servabat. Vasto tu consulis orbi
> Qui se felicem non negat arte tua.

The eighth distich raises Gutenberg above all geniuses of antiquity:—

> Tanti est, te literis sculpta excudisse metalla
> quae effundant fidas tam cito pressa notas.
> Hinc tua si poscit dignus moguntia grates
> solveret, ante alia, quam colis ipse, loca
> Terraque jam multe germana volumine dives
> te colit, invento dicto beata tuo.

The subscription runs: Ex Heidelbergo III. Kalendas decembris 1494. The second panegyric has six distichs, under the title: "Ad Joannem Gensfleisch impressoriae artis inventorem primum Joannis Herbst Lutherburgensis Panegyris." Here also the inventor is called Ansicaro, and in the third and fourth distich it is said of him, that the vine which is watered by the waters of Rhine and Main, had caused a new shoot to sprout, had produced an excellent goose, whose flesh served all men as food :—

> Vitem que Mogano Rhenique liquore rigatur
> te (puto te) gemmam parturiisse novam,
> Anserem et egregium, qui carnem protulit illam
> quae lante exultans se cibat omnis homo.
> Invento palmam meruisti, nec negat ullus.
> germanum ingenium quid valet ecce patet
> Tu nostrae gentis decus admirabile quamvis
> Italia invideat emula vive vale.

The document is dated : Ex Heidelbergo III. nonas decembris 1494. Wimpfeling does homage to the inventor in the same spirit, in his epigram in honour of Gutenberg (Heidelberg, 1499): "Blessed Gensfleisch! Through you Germany reaps glory everywhere: for you, Johannes, supported by divine knowledge, printed first of all with letters of metal. Religion, the wisdom of Greece, the language of the Latins, is much indebted to you."[1]

Without name of the inventor, Mentz was praised everywhere as the cradle of the invention: in 1478 in the Fasciculus temporum of Werner Rolevinck van Laar;[2] in 1482 by William Caxton, at Westminster; in 1486 in the first censure-edict of the archbishop Berthold of Mentz, and in the same year by the abbot Trithemius, in a work printed at Strasburg; in 1494 by the Mentz typographer, Meydenbach (Hortus sanitatis); in 1497 by a typographer at Vienna; and afterwards by a cloud of witnesses, harmonizing with the song of Celtes : " You wind yourself already, O broad-waved Rhine! to the town of Mentz, which printed first of all with metal letters." The *century of the invention* did not uncertainly grope in the dark, did not ask bashfully, nor answer whisperingly, but *trumpeted Mentz about as the town where typography was born.*

But when Johan Schöffer, in 1503, succeeded his father in his printing-office, and published his first work (Mercurius Trismegistus), he could not resist the temptation to descend, not from the money-lender of the inventor, but from the inventor himself. He is, however, cautious enough to mention no name, and he only says: "The finishing hand has been put to this work by the venerable man Johan, called Schöffer, one of the principal citizens of the archiepiscopal town of Mentz, descended from the

---

[1] It is the writer of these beautiful lines who laid the foundation for the tradition of the invention at Strasburg. If he, in 1499, represents, perfectly in accordance with history. Johan Gensfleisch (Gutenberg) as having invented typography, printing with metal types, at *Mentz*, in 1501 it seems (videtur) that it had taken place already at Strasburg, but the art was *perfected* at Mentz; in 1502 he represents the art of printing as having been positively invented at Strasburg in 1440, by the Strasburg Johan Gutenberg; in 1505 he writes that it was invented under bishop Robertus, by a Strasburger, who went to Mentz, where he perfected the art with the help of a certain Joh. Gensfleisch (!) who lived in the house zum Gutenberg, and became blind in consequence of his old age. Where remained now the Fœlix Ansicaro, by which Germania omnibus in terris proemia laudis habet? Wimpfeling was copied in 1537 by the Strasburg theologian Caspar Hedion, who then said the art was invented in 1446 ; but in 1549 he mentioned Gutenberg, Mentz, and the year 1450. Daniël Specklin at last solved the question, c. 1580, in his chronicle. He said the art of printing was invented in 1440 by—*Johan Mentelin* (the first printer of Strasburg). Peter Schöffer is Mentelin's brother-in-law. His servant, Johan Gensfleisch, robs him of the art, goes to Mentz, and is assisted by the wealthy Gutenberg ! Mentelin dies of a broken heart on account of this theft, but Gensfleisch is punished with blindness.

[2] In the edition of Cologne, published by H. Quentell in 1478 and 1481, it is said : "Impressores librorum multiplicantur in terra, *ortum suae artis habentes in Moguntia.*" The last words are still wanting in the edition of Arnold ter Hoerne, Cologne 1474, which was imitated by Johan Veldener in his Latin edition, Louvain 1476, and in the Dutch translation, Utrecht 1480, so that we find there only: "Ende die boeckprinters worden seer vermenicht in allen landen." (The printers of books are increasing in all countries). By a trick of Koning this shorter reading was forged, in 1816, into an argument against Mentz. According to him, namely, it proved that Veldener *knew better* than that the art of printing had been invented at Mentz. As if Veldener could have reprinted in 1476, at Louvain, a Cologne text of 1478. As for the rest, the silence also, in the Dutch edition of 1480, of the man who at that time used the engravings of the Speculum, is no instructive way of knowing the invention of typography "*better*" than Rolevinck or his continuator.

fortunate race of those who, favoured by fate, invented the almost divine art of printing."

In 1509 (Breviarium Moguntinum) he goes already a step further, and says: "Printed at Maintz by Johan Schöffer, whose *grandfather* was the first inventor of the art of printing." Again, six years later, the liar completes his dishonest attack against Gutenberg's glory, in the elaborate inscription of the work of Trithemius: Breviarium historiae francorum. From this foul spring all later fables concerning the invention of printing were got. It deserves, therefore, to be well known; it runs as follows: "The present chronicle was printed and made in the year 1515 . . . in the noble and celebrated town of Mentz, the first inventress of this art, by Johan Schöffer, grandson of the venerable man, Johan Fust, citizen of Mentz, the first inventor of the said art, who began to conceive it by his own knowledge in 1450 . . . In the year 1452 only, he perfected it, with the help of God, and made it serviceable to the printing of books, but with the assistance, and many necessary inventions, of Peter Schöffer, of Gernsheim, his servant and adopted son, to whom he gave his daughter Christina as wife, as a reward of his labour and inventions. Both, Johan Fust and Peter Schöffer, kept this art secret, and bound all their workmen, and members of their house, by an oath not to make it known in any way. Which art, however, was spread, in 1462, by these workmen, in divers countries, and increased."

We see that Gutenberg, with despicable impudence, is completely ignored, and his merit wholly ascribed to the money-man. Even the story about the oaths of the workmen is invented. There is no trace of it in history—the printing-office of Pfister at Bamberg, the public law-suit of 1455, the great pecuniary difficulties of the erection of a printing-office, the corporations, the very rapid spread of typography over Europe, the want of any valid evidence, all this condemns this oath—emerging only in 1515 from the mouth of a wilful liar—to the empire of fiction.

The best punishment of Johan Schöffer is the homage which he was *compelled*, in 1505, to do to the truth. In that year he published the first German translation of Livy, by Ivo Wittig, with a dedication to Maximilian I. In this dedication he was obliged to say to the emperor: "May your Majesty be pleased to accept gracefully this work, which was printed in the town of Mentz; in which town also *the wonderful art of printing was first invented by the genial Johan Gutenberg*, in the year 1450, and afterwards improved and perfected with the industry, expenses, and labour of Johan Fust and Peter Schöffer." This dedication was reprinted unchanged in 1514, 1523, 1531, 1533, and 1551. Alas! the sixteenth and seventeenth century left this excellent antidote unused; they began to corrupt, to intricate, to mutilate the clear and indisputable history, and to make it serviceable to all local by-objects. Suppositions took the place of facts, the subterfuges and sophisms of the pleas that of investigation, unscientific prejudice that of scientific conception. But in the 18th century, the light of truth has begun to shine again, and the 19th buries all the fables of the 16th. Before its close, it will generally subscribe the artless words of the memorial-stone of the year 1507, consecrated to the memory of *Gutenberg of Maintz*, the inventor of typography:—

JO. GUTENBERGENSI MOGUNTINO
QUI PRIMUS OMNIUM
LITTERAS AERE IMPRIMENDAS INVENIT
HAC ARTE DE ORBE TOTO BENE MERENTI
IVO WITTIGUS
HOC SAXUM MONUMENTO POSUIT
MDVII.

V.

SPREAD OF TYPOGRAPHY IN THE NETHERLANDS.

The general spread of typography was brought about, as was only possible and perfectly natural, on account of its origin, exclusively by Germans. Germans (we mentioned them already) bring it, in 1465, to Rome (Subiaco); Ulrich Gering, Martin Crantz, and Michael Friburger transfer it, in 1470, to Paris; in 1473, Andreas Hess establishes it at Ofen; in 1474, a German was the first printer at Valencia; in 1483, at Stockholm. The first English book was, indeed, printed by an Englishman, named William Caxton, but at Cologne, where he had learned the new art, and whence he returned to his native country to establish, at Westminster, the first English printing-office. There, in 1474, his English translation of De Cessolis' "Meditations on the Game of Chess" was published. Finally, in 1478, Theod. Rudt (Rood), from Cologne, printed at Oxford.

The introduction and spread of typography in the Netherlands presents an image, each trait of which accurately agrees with what we have hitherto sketched in outlines from the sources of the 15th century. In the first place, the existing Dutch manuscripts, in so far they are dated and have connexion with the earliest printed books, present an historical line, which admirably agrees with all that is historically certain about the origin and era of typography. The most important which I have met with, and which are well known as incunabula, are:

1434. De LXV artikelen van der passie ons heren. 4to.
1437. Summe le Roy ofte die Coninx Summe. 4to.
1449. Die tafel van den kersten geloue. Folio.
1450. Passionael Somerstuck. Folio.
1451. Devote contemplacie op dz heren pr. nr. 12mo.
1461. Boeck van der natueren der Byen. Folio.
1463. Dat eerste stue van der vaderen Collacie.
1464. Dat boeck van den Spiegel onser behoudenisse. 8vo.
1467. Cantica canticorum Salomonis, gescreven &c. 4to.
1469. Die tafel van den kersten geloue. Folio.
1469. Der Byenboeck. 14. meye en 20 juny. 4to.
1470. Passionael Winterstuck. Folio.
1472. Ons liefs heren leven. Folio.

Typography did not at once annihilate the trade in manuscripts in the Netherlands, but we see it soon decay and disappear. Only the missals and legends, books of private devotion, and to the reproduction of which the monks had especially applied themselves, which, moreover, could not be made as handsomely as the printed ones in so short a time, maintained longest of all the competition. The printing-press, however, secured everywhere, in a short time, the large folios.

The curious manuscript of the "Spiegel der behoudenis," on vellum, of 290 leaves in 8vo., is preserved at Haarlem. The register of the chapters and the Prologhe of six pages is followed by the text. The first page is surrounded by an illuminated border, adorned with foliage in colours and gold, and has a beautiful initial in which Mary is represented as instructing the child Jesus in the Scriptures. At the end of the forty-five chapters we find: "Dit boec behoert toe Cayman Janszoen van Zerickzee, wonende met die Carthusers buten Vtrecht. God si gheloeft nu ende ind' eeuwicheit. Amen."[1] After this two other books follow: "Een goede oefening voor sieke menschen, die in hun uterste legen" (with the same subscription), and "Goede leeringhen ende gheboden voor sicken die menen te sterven." At the end of the volume we find: "Dit boec is gheeyndet int jaer ons heren MCCCC ende IIII ende tsestich opten XVI dach in jul. Een ave Maria om God voer die scrijver."[2]

Therefore, the Speculum was written, and finished in the Dutch language on vellum, at Utrecht, in 1464, in the days *before* the introduction of the art of printing. This circumstance harmonizes exceedingly well with the *fact*, that the *general* spread of typography over Europe dates only from the capture and plundering of Mentz in 1462.

It took its way to North-Netherland through Cologne. Even Colard Mansion of Bruges learned it there, just as William Caxton, of Westminster. Johan Veldener printed earlier at Cologne than in the Netherlands. At Deventer the art of printing was introduced (1477) by Richard Paffroed of Cologne. On the other hand, a Dutchman, Ter Hoorne, printed at Cologne, while his types were imitated again by the brethren of common life at Brussels. The types of Jacob de Breda, at Deventer, have the greatest resemblance with those of Zell, so that he also must have learned the art at Cologne, or from Paffroed of Cologne. This historical line points to the year 1470, or thereabouts, as the earliest period for the introduction of typography into the Netherlands. A chronology of the dated incunabula affords the following table:

1473. Utrecht, Aalst.	1482. Antwerp.
1474. Louvain.	1483. Leiden, Kuilenburg, Ghent, Haarlem.
1476. Bruges, Brussels.	
1477. Deventer, Gouda, Delft.	1484. 's Hertogenbosch (Bois-le-Duc).
1478. St. Maartensdijk.	1495. Schoonhoven.
1479. Nijmegen, Zwolle.	1498. Schiedam.
1480. Audenaarde, Hasselt in Overijssel.	

We see that we are behind Italy and France, and that, even at the commencement of the 16th century, there were still many Netherland towns destitute of a printing-office. For instance the earliest work printed at the Hague is dated 1518, and at Middleburg there was no printing before 1577. After the profound inquiries of Mr. Holtrop,[3] it may be considered certain that the so-called first printer in the Southern Netherlands, Thierry Martens, was a disciple of Johannes de Westphalia, born at Paderborn or Aix-la-Chapelle, who established himself at Louvain in 1474. From 1473—77, Johan Veldener, from the diocese of Würtzburg, printed there also; in 1475, Conradus Braem of Cologne; in 1476, Conradus de Westphalia, from Paderborn; in 1483, Herman of Nassau. The only possible way of coming to an accurate notion of the signification of German typographers for the Netherlands, is the study of Holtrop's Monumens Typographiques, for here especially it is a case of autopsy.

This magnificent work of the librarians of the Royal library at the Hague (for the dedication assigns also to Mr. Campbell his share in this meritorious work) is a brilliant example of what may be done in this branch of science. Here the results of infallible researches are laid down with accuracy. This book is a library in which we are at the same time taken round by the proprietor, who is intimately acquainted with all its treasures, and who is not only bibliophile, but also bibliologer. Without a serious study, therefore, of the Monumens Typographiques, there can henceforth be no question for any one of pronouncing an opinion on this subject. They have raised the history of the Netherland typography of the 15th century to the rank of a science, and have, as a fruit

---

[1] This book belongs to Cayman Janszoen of Zierickzee, living with the Carthusians near Utrecht, &c.

[2] This book was finished in the year of our Lord 1464, on the 16 day of July. An Ave Maria to God for the writer.

[3] Thierry Martens d' Alost. Étude bibliographique par J. W. Holtrop. La Haye. Nyhoff. 1867. 8vo.

of a lifelong, accurate study, chased away, for good and all, the fantastic dilettanteism from this dominion of our knowledge. The road to the only good system of treating and classifying incunabula, geographic-chronologically and typologically, namely, is paved now. We do not want, as a student of exact bibliography has very justly remarked,¹ the *opinion* or *dictum* of any bibliographer, however experienced. We have to study the types and habits of each printer of the 15th century, to scrutinize and to point out the characteristics of his work. Each press must be looked upon as a genus, each book as a species; and it is our business to trace the connexion of the different members of the typographical family. The study of palaeotypography has hitherto been abandoned to dilettanteism; it is time to apply to it also the method of natural history. Though this only true method was not applied in all its rigour, and adopted with all its consequences by Holtrop and Campbell, even Bradshaw acknowledges that the catalogue of our incunabula, compiled and published, in 1856, by the above-named gentlemen, is far the most valuable contribution to this class of literature which we have. And " except Mr. Blades' monograph of Caxton's press, the Hague *Catalogus* and *Monumens typographiques* are the only books existing in any literature, which render the study of palaeotypography possible on a proper basis."

It is of great importance to notice, besides the results of exact typological investigation, how the North-Netherland xylography also corresponds with the era, which the scientific method affords. It appears to belong to the *second* half of the *fifteenth* century. Holtrop has proved from Church history that the North-Netherland engraving of indulgence (in Weigel's collection), with eight lines of engraved Text, originated between the years 1455 and 1470. The North-Netherland incunabula since 1470, especially those of Leeu at Gouda, Veldener at Utrecht and Kuilenburg, Van Os at Zwolle, Barmentlo at Hasselt, show the presence in Holland of xylographers, artistically less developed, however, than the Flemish. While the purely xylographic illustrated books (Biblia pauperum, Canticum, Temptationes demonis, Ars moriendi, Historia Virginis in the North-Netherlands; Apocalypsis, Entkrist, Acht Schalckheiten, Dr. Hartlieb's Ciromantia, Ars memorandi, Salve Regina, Todtentanz, &c., in Germany; l'Art au morier, le Calendaire, in France; the Moral play in England), must be left to the history of wood-engraving, our subject is yet of great importance to it, because their connexion with typography assists us in determining their dates. Van Os, at Zwolle, for instance, used in nine different books of 1488, 1490, and 1491, *original* blocks of the Biblia pauperum, and in 1494, a block of the Canticum; Peregrinus Barmentlo, at Hasselt, a block of the Biblia pauperum in 1488. The *original* blocks of the Speculum are, in 1481, in the hands of Johan Veldener at Utrecht, who cut them afterwards into two, and, added to a number of other engravings, used them in 1483 for a quarto edition of the Dutch *Spiegel*, and sold them at last to Van Os, at Zwolle, in whose incunabula of 1487, 1488, and 1494, they appear. He who can place himself in the enormous activity of that time in the dominion of typography, must see that the dates in which the wooden blocks were used by the typographers in their original or reduced size, cannot be far from the moment the North-Netherland xylographers engraved them. Neither are there great distances of time between the undated and dated editions of the same works.

To our most celebrated, but not most known, undated incunabula, belongs the Speculum, mentioned already before, one of the earliest, but not the very earliest, North-Netherland incunabula. In this study we should not forget that the earliest typographers had to make everything themselves, so that much more depended at that time upon individual sagacity and good direction than at present. Disciples, moreover, do not always become masters, and disciples of disciples are often a degree worse. At least the first Netherland incunabula are bad, and the work gets only better by slow degrees. Let us examine, for instance, the Dutch folio of Jan de Mandeville,

---

¹ A classified index of the 15th century books in the collection of the late M. J. de Meyer, which were sold at Ghent in November, 1869. By Henry Bradshaw, librarian of the University of Cambridge. London. Macmillan and Co. 1870. 8vo.

ca 1470; as a work of printing it is so bad that the earliest
:ulum are masterpieces by the side of it. A "schoon spieghel
hen," probably printed at Louvain, is almost equally primitive,
.ter date; the line, " Ons daghelycxs broot gheeft ons heeden," is
e of the word gheeft (ghe-eft). A work of an unknown Schiedam
part of the fifteenth century, is equally bad. And so we find here,
, good number of works which betray want of sufficient preparation,
we can only trace dexterity in typography by degrees. Bad work-
es not yet prove great antiquity. The Brussels incunabula of the
itae are bad; those of Arnold ter Hoorne at Cologne (1471—83)
s. Heinecke mentions a book: " Passional des bitteren Leiden
s Herrn, getruckt zu Augspurg durch David Neckern, Form-
id says: " Si le nom du graveur en bois et l'année ne s'y trou-
:endrait pour le plus ancien livre du monde." Some time ago
which the word " Gricksz " was divided after the k and the sz
line. *That* ought to be very old! Oh no, the work was printed
. In a German Speculum I found in a moment the following
., sch-miden, me(n)-sch, gesch-lecht, tra-ckheit, ansy-cht, wa-rd,
ia-ch, br-acht, mi-ch; and yet this book was printed long after the
And any one who considers what letter-writers dare to do in this
time, will not be surprised at the mastery which the compositors of
possessed over the language. In the series now of the different
f this kind, the Speculum presents itself very favourably; it is not
.ed; it is not a first experiment, but the fruit of practice.
the Speculum four typographical editions in folio, two with Latin,
. The engravings have served for the *four* editions, but they were
es, for they have all a line as subscription in Latin. To this first
I we may add as a second one the worn look of the type, to that of
.kages in the lines. From these criteria together it follows that
iists of the Latin one with an entire typographic text; the second
with twenty xylographic leaves; the third the Dutch one with two
e Dutch edition, printed with very much used, worn types. The
iphic, because the engravings were printed after the method of the
e *frotton*, which prevented the paper being printed upon also on
rinted page would have been completely damaged by the printing
In the same manner, illustrated books were printed with dates,
2, 1473. Anopisthography and opisthography is not a chrono-
technical question, which, in its turn, is related to the corporations,
ween *prenters* and typographers. So also the light-brown colour,
:teenth century the engravings were printed, in order to impede the
s so much in favour at that time, as little as possible by sharp
se.
the Speculum is an abridgment of the text of the Utrecht MS.
already before, and which was of course not made *after* the book
dready some times. In 1481 the original woodcuts are there
e German typographer and xylographer, Johan Veldener. Com-
i, of which reprints followed each other at that time, within one,
ears, the *Spiegel* (62 or 63 leaves) was only a brochure. Ketelaer
ited probably already at Utrecht about 1470. At least the earliest
originates from them; their type is already, in 1475, in the hands
er Hees, and yet they printed at least thirty works without name,
these works, among which the Opera of Thomas à Kempis, not
(*without* the Imitatio), were published after the manuscripts, and,
donnent une idée avantageuse de l'état des Bibliothèques dans
à cette époque, et de l'encouragement que David de Bourgogne
s et aux belles-lettres, qui permit aux imprimeurs d'entreprendre la

publication d'ouvrages semblables." The types of the Speculum are related to those of Ketelaer and De Leempt (Meerman even attributed, on account of this resemblance, Utrecht incunabula to his fictitious Haarlem sub-sexton); at Utrecht the Dutch translation was written; Utrecht had an episcopal see, a gymnasium, a Burgundian prince,—indeed, if hypotheses are allowed, then is that of an *Utrecht* origin of the Specula provisionally the only reasonable one. However this may be, as far as regards science, the well-known quackery with the *Spiegels* is finished for ever.

In the types of the Speculum are also printed :—1. a Donatus of 28 lines, a fragment of which was used at Haarlem as cover for a service-book of 1474; another fragment, exhibiting difference of text, but not of types, was discovered at Cologne, in a volume of tracts printed by Ulric Zell, among which one of 1467; 2. the little book of the Mass, and 3. a Dutch translation of the seven penitential Psalms; fragments of both were discovered at Brussels. 4. a Donatus of 30 lines, discovered in an edition of Paffroed at Deventer, of 1491. 5. and 6. two editions of Alexander Gallus' Doctrinale, of 32 lines, found in a book printed by Paffroed in 1495. 7. The Disticha of Cato. This gives us, with the four editions of the Speculum, already eleven well-known works in those types, of which seven are on vellum.

Of the Abecedarium (wrongly called Horarium) also, a little schoolbook which, as we have seen before, was a link in the literature of the fourteenth, fifteenth, and sixteenth centuries, one copy has come down to us and is figured in extenso in the work of Holtrop. In the same type is printed a Donatus of 31 lines, discovered by M. Campbell in the binding of a Delft prayer-book of 1484.

In the third place comes the type of Ludovici (Pontani) de Roma Singularia juris, in which moreover three editions of Donatus of 24 lines were printed. Fourthly, the type of Laur. Vallae († 1458) Facetiæ morales and witty sayings of great men, collected by Petrarca.

Finally, the type of Pii II. Tractatus et Epitaphia, resembling that of the Speculum. The cardinal Piccolomini (Æneas Sylvius) was elected pope in 1458, as Pius II. *Before* that year of his elevation to the papacy, therefore, this edition is totally impossible. In this type we have several editions of Donatus and Doctrinale, an edition of Cato, the Latin translation of a fragment of the Iliad. Lastly, to this family of type the type of Saliceto, De salute corporis, belongs, in which were printed Turrecremata (Torquemada † 1468), a letter of Pius II. De amore, in the edition of his works (Basle, 1551) put at 1464. A fragment on vellum of the Saliceto was found in a volume of Jan Andrieszoon, Haarlem, 1486. We have in the same type :—1. a complete Donatus of 27 lines, 14 leaves; 2. a Donatus minor (Partes orationis quot sunt), 4 leaves; 3. an edition of the Disticha of 21 lines; finally, two Doctrinales of 28 and 29 lines.

By the side of this bibliographical review of some of our undated incunabula, which is necessary to test the town legend by history, a sketch also of the earliest typography at Haarlem is indispensable. We have already seen that Haarlem does not belong to the towns where printing was introduced very early. The earliest Haarlem date is of 1483. The 10th of December of that year a book was published there on "dat liden" of Jesus, with 32 woodcuts, used, the year before, by Gerard Leeu at Gouda in the same work. It is distinctly said in this edition that it was printed "tot haerlem in hollant." The same press produced successively, 15 Feb. 1484, Der sonderen troost; 31 May, Summe le roy; 9 Aug., Der Sielen troest; on sinte Crispyn, het Boek des gulden throens; in 1485 de Historien van Troyen and de Historie van Jason. At the end of this year we find for the first time the name of the printer in this imprint : "Hier eyndet dat boeck welck ghebieten is bartholomeus van de proprieteyten der dinghen inden iaer ons heren 1485 opten heylighen kersauont Ende is gheprint ende oeck mede voleynut te haerlem in hollant ter eren godes ende om leringhe der menschen van mi Meester *Jacop Bellaert* gheboren van zerixzee." This Jakob Bellaert of Zierikzee, published, moreover, the following year, 8 April, Epistelen ende euangelien; 24 July, Doctrinael des tijds; 20 Aug., het Boeck van den pelgherijm, after which we lose sight of him for ever. During the last year of his activity at Haarlem the second printer appeared there, namely Jan Andrieszoon, who published, besides three undated, four other works, 1 May, 31 May, 15 June, and 10 Aug. 1486, so that both seem to have printed for the last time in August of the same year. The only thing which is especially connected with Haarlem in their books are two family arms on a woodcut by Bellaert: the arms of Van Ruyven and of the knight Jakob van Cats, from 1484—89, bailiff at Haarlem. As for their types, Bellaert printed with types of Gerard Leeu at Gouda, and Andrieszoon with types which were already very much worn. They were therefore simply Netherland printers who came from elsewhere to try whether they could settle at Haarlem. How naturally therefore appears the *earliest* Haarlem date in a chronological series of imprints in the earliest Netherland incunabula :

1473. Impressa in traiecto inferiori per magistros . . .
1473. Impressum. Alosti. In Flandria. Anno.
1474. Imprime en la noble ville de Bruges en flandres.
1475. Louanii impressa. — te louen gheprint.
1476. Arte impressoria . . . bruxelle op. in brabancie.
1477. Dit boec is voleyndet ter goude in hollant.
1478. ghecyndt in die printe te delf in hollant.
1478. gheprint . . . tsentemertensdyck in zeelant.
1479. volmaket ende ghecynt in die stad van vtrecht.
1481. gheprent in die eerw. universiteyt van louen.
1483. geprent te leyden in hollant.
1483. Dit bouck is voleyndet tot *haerlem* in hollant.
1483. volmacet in die goede stede van culenburch.
1484. Gheprent tots hartogenbosch.
1485. Gheprendt tot Gendt.
1487. in die seer vermaerde coopstadt Tantwerpen.
1493. Gheprent te Deuenter inden stichte van Vtrecht.
1493. geprent te zwolle inden stichte van vtrecht.
1499. Ghedruct buten scoenhouen inden Hem.
? Imprime en la ville de Schiedam en hollande.

The first book printed at Haarlem, after Bellaert and Andrieszoon, places us in the 16th century. There exist, namely, two rare books, in small 8vo., with a crucifix in woodcut on the title, the one entitled " Een soete meditacie hoe dat die verloren siel van den sone Gods gevonden is met synre heiliger passion ;" the other, " Een boecxken van verduldich lijden dat sinte Bernardus bescrijft," &c. " Gheprint tot Haerlem." It was printed shortly after 1506, and by the same typographer, who published, in 1506, at Amsterdam, the " Wandelinghe in den hof der bloemen," in 8vo. The initial O, which occurs in this work, is also found in the others, only in a little more worn condition. The Amsterdam printer, who lived " bi der heiliger stede," departed probably very soon from Amsterdam, and made an equally fruitless effort to establish himself at Haarlem. The history of typography produces a number of such itinerant printers. We find, for instance, Veldener at Utrecht from 1478—81, at Kuilenburg in 1483 ; De Leempt in 1473 and '74 at Utrecht, in 1479 at Nymegen (?), from 1484—90 at 's Hertogenbosch ; Govert van Ghemen (Van Os), since 1486 at Gouda, afterwards at Leiden, and we see him, c. 1490, introduce typography at Copenhagen. Our unknown printer lived probably already before at Haarlem. In that case we would be able to discover his name. At least the registers of the cathedral at Haarlem contain the following entry :—

1502. Item *de Hasback* besteet hondert brieven te printen van onsse offclact om de priesters die biecht hoeren over hoer hoeft te setten, dat hondert voor vi. st. etc.

Between his residence in 1502 and that in 1506, we may suppose a temporary residence at Amsterdam ; at least, in 1504, the church at Haarlem had its letters of indulgence printed at Leiden : " Item Meester Hugo die printer te Leiden gegheven xx st. van de VIe copyen die hy geprint het nut der bullen." This Leiden printer is

Hugo Janszoon, of Woerden, since 1494 printer at Leiden, in 1517 at Delft, in 1518 at the Hague. After the first years of the 16th century follows again a long-continued cessation in the exercise of printing at Haarlem. All that we have found in the existing sources is confined to the following items in the treasury accounts:—

1546. De tresorier heeft betaelt . . . *Dirck Volckertz* [*Coornhert*] figuer-snyder . . . xvi lb. by hem verdient ende bedongen voor 't snyden van de figuere en chaerte van de lootherye . . .

1546. *Symon Claesz. Bybel* bet. de somme van thien ponde . . . van dat hy zekere chaerten van de looterye voors. gedruet heeft . . .

1557. *Claes Symonsz* bouckverkooper ende prenter betaelt de somme van zes ponden pryse als voren voir hondert vyftigh charten . . . roerende de contagieuse siecte der pestilencie . . .

1576. *Claes Jansz,* of Alkmaar, bookseller at Haarlem.

1578. Betaelt Louis Laeckeman om te betaelen in handen van den drucker tot Leyen over . . . duysent exemplaren van ossemaret . . .

Between the years in which the government of the town could have their printing executed at Haarlem and those in which they were obliged to have it done at Leiden—1557 and 1578—we find the printing-office, established in 1561, with other partners, by the burgomaster Jan van Zuren, "sworn bookprinter at Haarlem;" but which does not seem to have worked much longer than the following year. Only in 1581 we find again a printer at Haarlem, Anthonis Ketel, and, since 1587, Gillis Rooman, who was succeeded, in 1611, by Adriaen Rooman.

The harvest of history on the field of typography concerning Haarlem may be scanty; it does not yield *anything*, as far as xylography goes. There existed there already very early a Lucasgild, like that at Antwerp, and like the Johannesgild at Bruges; but, however rich in painters, sculptors, and goldsmiths, the Haarlem corporation may have been, it produces, notwithstanding the most patient researches, not a single *prenter* (*briefprenter*) or xylographer.[1] The manufacture, therefore, of a whole series of blockbooks of the 15th century, ascribed, two, three, and four centuries afterwards, without any shadow of evidence, to a Haarlem innkeeper, has to be referred to the empire of fiction.

VI.

GERRIT THOMASZOON.

There died about the year 1563 or '64, at Haarlem, a certain Gerrit Thomaszoon (son of Thomas), who occurs as sheriff of the town in 1545, and who was churchwarden from 1547—52. He had lived in the market-place and kept an inn. My researches in the archives at Haarlem, in order to know more of him, were in vain. The following lines are the only thing I found in the sheriff registers, but they are of no importance:—

"Van Geryt thomas cum sosijs van alle die achtergheleten goeden van wijlen Mr. Jacob Deyman, Licenciaet, die gestorven is anno 1541 . . . alst blijct bij een Inventaris . . . die de selve Geryt thomasz bij eede verclaert heeft goet ende deuchdelijcke te zijn, sonder dair inne yet achterhouden oft verzwhegen te hebben, welcke eedt hem afgenomen heeft Jan van Zuyren, burgemeester."

---

[1] Geschiedk. aanteeken. over haarlemsche schilders voorafgegaan door eene korte geschiedenis van het St. Lucasgild te Haarlem. Door A. van der Willigen Pz. Med. Doctor. Haarlem. Erven F. Bohn. 1866. 8vo. A French translation of this work was published (?) at Haarlem in 1870.

Thomas pieterszoons eerste wijf was Josina Janna van Alphen, die dochter Alijt van Alphen.	Janna van Alphen haer dochter van(s) Alphen	Thomas Pieterszoon	—	Sijn tweede wijff was Louwens Janssoens Coeters dochter die deerste print in die werlt brocht Anno 1440.	Lucija Lauris dochter waer bij hij had dese nageneveo(s) kinderen.	Len Corters Wupel.a, (Lints)	Pieter Thomass, Aendries Thomass, Thomas Thomass, Katrijn Thomasdr, Margriet Thomasdr.
Het tweede wijff.		Kathrijn Beerthous dochter sonder kinderen 1484.	Pieter Thomass bleeff in 's Cruws broottspel met sij(e) broeder Andries Thomass.	Sijn eerste wijf.	Margriet Jan Floris. dochter waer bij hij had deese kinderen 1440.	Thomas Pieterss, Margriet Pietersdr.	
		Thomas Pieterss.	Zijn eenighe wijff.	Claes Pieterss. dochter waer bij hij was deese.	Gerrijt Thomass. Margriet Thomasdr.		
			Gerrit Thomass.	—	Zijn eenighe wijff.	Ermingaert Jansdochter waer bij hij was dese onder geschreven.	
Marigien Gerrits. dr. had twee kinderen die storven terstond na den baringe. doot.	Alijt Gerrits. dr. starff jong. doot.	Margriet Gerrits dochter.	Gerrit Aeffgen Gerritsdochter sterff jong. doot.	Thomas Gerrits bij .... bleft claerdochter doese kinderen 1689.	Cornelia Gerrism. bij Geertenijn van Berckearo doese. 1680 den 14 Jannarij getruut.	Claes Gerritsdr.	Janna Gerritsdochter.	Anna Gerritsdochter.
Jacob Thomass starff jong met Dirckszen Thomas doot.	Marigien Thomasdochter.	Marritgen Thomasdochter alias Gerritsdochter.	Alijt Thomasdr. alias I'oouvsdr.	den 12 Januarij gehoren Anna Cornelia-dr. alias van Berckearo starff jong. doot 1641.	Margriet Cornelis dochter alias Bartenadr. 1682 den 10 Augusti.	Gerrit Cornelis. alias Thomas. 1663 den 30 Sept.	Willem Cornelis. alias van Berckearo 1665 starf den 14 Aug. 1666.	Cornelis Cornelis dochter 1666 den 7 Novembris Decembris.
								Willem Cornelis 1668 den 4 November.
								Op den (illegible).
				Margriet Cornelisdr. alias van Berckearo won bij Gerrit Pieterss. Wit dese navolgende kinderen, geb. 1683 1 Februarij.	Claes Gerrits dochter wert geboren Ao. 1682 den 1 December.	Eiken Gerrits dochter de Wit wert geboren An. 1685 den 12 October.		

Now, we could safely let him rest, had he not had, some years before his death, the strange fancy of having a pedigree made for him. This not uncommon and innocent amusement has had, in his case, such curious consequences, that we have to subject this family document to an accurate scrutiny. We are enabled to do so, as the document has not only not been lost, but—Gerrit Thomaszoon could not possibly have imagined it—was bought, as late as this century, by the town of Haarlem, and is exhibited in its museum as a very important document.

While the text of the document is printed herewith, it ought to be described somewhat in detail.

The pedigree seems to have been written by the same hand down to, and including, the fifth child of Gerrit Thomasz. This original part is calligraphic, and has, to all appearances, served as a picture on the wall. The whole is surrounded by embroidery, blackened by age. The centre is occupied by Gerrit Thomasz., the man who had the pedigree made. Underneath we observe three hills. Above the two lowest are two escutcheons: the one on the left has two quarters (the first quarter, on the left, is blank, as also the shields of the Thomases on the document have been left blank; the second has a dove); that on the right a lion rampant (arms of Ermingaerd, the wife of Gerrit Thomasz.). The middle (highest) hill, or mountain, encloses an oval crest of some woman, probably with the dove of Lucye Coster. Round the mountain a knotted riband is wound, on which there was originally an inscription with golden letters. Arms and inscription, however, have been artificially erased. But thus much is plain also here, that the whole was made for Gerrit Thomasz. and Ermingaerd, and that Lucye Coster formed the lustre of the document. In the last circle, after 1568, something was written in very fine letters, of which the word "baarnsteel" seems to be still legible; but this emendation was erased afterwards. By the side of the name Gerrit Thomasz., on the left, and above, by the name of Thomas Pietersz., are two blank scutcheons; by Ermingaerd Jans a scutcheon with a lion rampant. Further on, to the left, by the side of the scutcheons of the Thomases, an ornament is found. Above, in the border in the middle of the document, were the arms of Haarlem, but they have also been effaced.

Entirely intact is the representation of Lou Coster's arms, a *dove*, on an heraldic chart of Amsterdam, said to have been the arms of Mr. Marten Jansz. Coster, burgomaster in 1578. The first, fourth, and seventh division of the writing on the top, is written with beautiful Roman letters, the rest in italics. Only the year, on the top, by the name of Lucye L. J. Costersdochter (daughter of L. J. Coster), is in the handwriting of the maker. The numbers, by Baertoutsdochter and Margriet Jan Florisdochter, are written with different ink. In order, therefore, to avoid the possibility of making any mistake with regard to the determination of the time of the origin of the document, after the marriage of Gerrit Thomasz., and after he had had some children, we shall take the very liberal period of between 1520 and 1560.

We were already able to observe that the document is no longer in its original condition, but that it has been in the hands of later explainers, who effaced some inconvenient things, especially in the inscription around Lucye, which, among other things (ni fallor) contained a year in Roman numbers. The last figure of the date 1446 has been falsified; they have not only removed the inscription from the pedestal, but an original 6 changed into a 0, so that the careless visitor of the Haarlem townhall reads at present 1440. The record therefore of the famous Coster legend, which we shall have to speak of presently, runs, critically corrected, thus:—

> Zyn tweede wijff was
> Louris Janssoens Cos
> ters dochter die deerste
> print in de werlt br
> ocht Anno 1446.[1]

---

[1] His second wife was the daughter of Louris Janssoens Coster, who brought the first print into the world Anno 1446.

Thomas pieterssoens — Janna van Alphen   'eter Thomass.,
eerste wijf was Jouf-   haer dochter Alijt   lries Thomass.,
frou Janna van Al-   va(n) Alphen.   nas Thomass., Ka-
phen, die dochter Alijt   Thomasdr., Mar-
van Alphen.   Thomasdr.

                    Het tweede wijff. == Kathrijn B
                                           dochter sonde
                                           ren 1464.

                                        Thomas Pi

Maritgen Gerrits dr.   Alijt Gerrits. dr.   Margriet   G Gerritsdochter.
had twee kinderen die sturff jong. doot.   dochter.
storven terstond na den
haringe. doot.

Jacob Thomass.   Maritgen Thomas-   Marritgen Th rnelis Cornelis
sturff jong met Dirck- dochter.   dochter alias G ter 1566 den 7
gen Thomas doot.   dochter.   mbris.

                                                       illem Corneliss.
                                                       den 4 November.

                                                     ı den . . . .
                                                     ible).

Now, we could safely let him rest, had he not had, some years before his death, the strange fancy of having a pedigree made for him. This not uncommon and innocent amusement has had, in his case, such curious consequences, that we have to subject this family document to an accurate scrutiny. We are enabled to do so, as the document has not only not been lost, but—Gerrit Thomaszoon could not possibly have imagined it—was bought, as late as this century, by the town of Haarlem, and is exhibited in its museum as a very important document.

While the text of the document is printed herewith, it ought to be described somewhat in detail.

The pedigree seems to have been written by the same hand down to, and including, the fifth child of Gerrit Thomasz. This original part is calligraphic, and has, to all appearances, served as a picture on the wall. The whole is surrounded by embroidery, blackened by age. The centre is occupied by Gerrit Thomasz., the man who had the pedigree made. Underneath we observe three hills. Above the two lowest are two escutcheons: the one on the left has two quarters (the first quarter, on the left, is blank, as also the shields of the Thomases on the document have been left blank; the second has a dove); that on the right a lion rampant (arms of Ermingaerd, the wife of Gerrit Thomasz.). The middle (highest) hill, or mountain, encloses an oval crest of some woman, probably with the dove of Lucye Coster. Round the mountain a knotted riband is wound, on which there was originally an inscription with golden letters. Arms and inscription, however, have been artificially erased. But thus much is plain also here, that the whole was made for Gerrit Thomasz. and Ermingaerd, and that Lucye Coster formed the lustre of the document. In the last circle, after 1568, something was written in very fine letters, of which the word "baarnstoel" seems to be still legible; but this emendation was erased afterwards. By the side of the name Gerrit Thomasz., on the left, and above, by the name of Thomas Pietersz., are two blank scutcheons; by Ermingaerd Jans a scutcheon with a lion rampant. Further on, to the left, by the side of the scutcheons of the Thomases, an ornament is found. Above, in the border in the middle of the document, were the arms of Haarlem, but they have also been effaced.

Entirely intact is the representation of Lou Coster's arms, a *dove*, on an heraldic chart of Amsterdam, said to have been the arms of Mr. Marten Jansz. Coster, burgomaster in 1578. The first, fourth, and seventh division of the writing on the top, is written with beautiful Roman letters, the rest in italics. Only the year, on the top, by the name of Lucye L. J. Costersdochter (daughter of L. J. Coster), is in the handwriting of the maker. The numbers, by Baertoutsdochter and Margriet Jan Florisdochter, are written with different ink. In order, therefore, to avoid the possibility of making any mistake with regard to the determination of the time of the origin of the document, after the marriage of Gerrit Thomasz., and after he had had some children, we shall take the very liberal period of between 1520 and 1560.

We were already able to observe that the document is no longer in its original condition, but that it has been in the hands of later explainers, who effaced some inconvenient things, especially in the inscription around Lucye, which, among other things (ni fallor) contained a year in Roman numbers. The last figure of the date 1446 has been falsified; they have not only removed the inscription from the pedestal, but an original 6 changed into a 0, so that the careless visitor of the Haarlem town-hall reads at present 1440. The record therefore of the famous Coster legend, which we shall have to speak of presently, runs, critically corrected, thus:—

> Zyn tweede wijff was
> Louris Janssoens Cos
> ters dochter die deerste
> print in de werlt br
> ocht Anno 1446.[1]

---

[1] His second wife was the daughter of Louris Janssoens Coster, who brought the first print into the world Anno 1446.

My knowledge of this falsification dates only from the 28th February, 1870, but the falsification itself may be fixed, at least morally, in the sixteenth century already. We see here a fable arise before our very eyes. A Haarlem citizen has a pedigree made for him, probably to put it up in his inn; at least he occupies the house in the Market-place, which seems to have always been an inn. But the frame wants lustre, and so the pedigree is linked by the probably totally fictitious Lucye (the second wife, "*tweede wyff*") to a Haarlemer; to a Haarlemer who (the awkwardness and naïveté of the expression may not surprise us at all in such a product of family vanity) "deerste print in die werlt brocht." Such fabricators of pedigrees exist in multitude to this very day.

What was Gerrit Thomaszoon thinking about, in the middle of the sixteenth century, by that "eerste print" of a hundred years ago? What may have presented itself to his mind? An engraving? A drawing? Had his ancestor done something by way of pastime, which was preserved for a long time in the family as a relic of great-grandfather or grandfather? It can no longer be decided, for an authentic interpretation of that singular word "print" can nowhere be found. We have therefore to try and find light in the year 1446, in which, according to the descendant of Coster, "deerste print in die werlt" came. According to the bad construction of the expression, it was really *Lucye Coster* who brought "deerste print in die werlt" (and she is on the vellum document genealogically more the chief person than her father), but we will assume that *Lourens Coster* is the person meant, and therefore look for him in the archives of the fifteenth century.

With a zeal and patience, worthy of a better cause and of a better reward, this investigation took place, and has brought to light that there really lived at Haarlem a citizen in the fifteenth century whose name was Lourens Coster, son of Jan Coster, who died in 1436. All that we find in the archives of the town and church of Haarlem about this *Laurens Janszoon* [son of Jan] *Coster* is contained in the following chronologically arranged items—

1441. Item opten 13 auont gherekent met lou koster van 15 pont en 12 pont oly, ele pont een ouden buddrager en 34 stuvers van seep en van smeerkaersen te somme 22 guld. 3 stuvers (Item on the evening of the 13th settled with lou koster for 15 pounds and 12 pounds of oil, each pound an ancient buddrager, and 34 pence for soap and tallow candles, together 22 guilders 3 pence.) (In the registers of the church.)

1441. Item Louwerijs Janssoen geg. van lxxij pond kaersen die jn dit jegenwoerdige jaer opter stede Huys voir die wakers verbornt sijn van ele pont enen ouden butdrager fac. v lb. xij. (Item Louwerijs Janssoen for 72 pounds of candles which have been burnt by the guards in the town-hall during this year, for each pound an ancient butdrager . . .)

1441. Item Louwerijs Jans voirscr. van den kaersen die jn dit jegenwoerdige jaer juden thoorn voir onser liouer zoeter vrouwen verbarnt sijn so dat mit hem verdinct is iij gouden philippus scildo fac. iij lb. (Item Louwerijs Jans, aforesaid, for the candles burnt in the tower in honour of Our Lady during this year, as was agreed with him . . .)

1442. It. Lourijs Coster van dat hy die lantaern voir onser liever Vrouwen in den toern van nieuws opgemaect heeft geg. f. iii lb. (Item Lourijs Coster, paid for having repaired the lantern of Our Lady in the tower . . .)

1442. It. Lourijs Coster van xl lb. smeerkeersen die die wakers opter stede huyse gehadt ende verbarnt hebben coste ellic lb. een oude butdrager f. v lb. 2 st. viii d. (Item Lourijs Coster for 40 pounds of tallow candles which the guards in the town-hall burnt, cost each pound an ancient butdrager . . .)

1442. Tot lou coster betaelt 8 guld. van oely ende seep. (Paid to lou coster 8 guilders for oil and soap.)

1442. It. Van lou coster van seep en van keersen en van ander dinc 15 st. (Item to lou coster for soap and candles and other things 15 pence.) (Church of Haarlem.)

1447. It. opte xiiii dach in Maerte Louwerijs Coster betaelt en geg. van vijf pont kaersen die in den thoorn voir onser liever soeter vrouwen verbarnt waren van ele pont een stuver f. vi st. viii d. (Item on the 14th day of March, paid to Louwerijs Coster for five pounds of candles which have been burnt in the tower in honour of Our Lady . . .)

The thing is plain: Lourens Janszoon Coster, to whom a hundred years afterwards an unintelligible "eerste print" is ascribed at Haarlem, was, between the years 1440 and 1450, a tallow-chandler, and kept a shop for oil, soap, and similar articles connected with his trade. This business was afterwards continued by his sister Ghertruit Jan Costersdochter, who sells candles in 1452 and 1453 and died in 1456. Her brother had chosen another trade. At least we see Lourens Janszoon Coster make his appearance since 1451 as innkeeper, according to the following items in the treasury accounts at Haarlem :—

1451. Item betaelt lou' coster ii menghelen wijn, die on' (voor) een jair die burg'meister ghesedt werden. (Item lou' coster paid for 2 menghelen of wine which were sent to the burgomaster a year ago.)

1454. Item den grave van Oostervant viii daighe in Octobri anno Liii tot lou costers een maeltyt gheschenct wert, so bleef men den selven lou coster dair af sculdich xvii guld. (Item as a dinner was offered to the count of Oostervant on the 8th of Oct. '53 at lou coster's ; indebted to him for it xvii guilders.)

1468. Louris Coster and other citizens are summoned to the Hague.

1474. Louris Janszoon Coster pays war taxes.

1475. Louris Jansz. Coster pays a fine for "buyten drincken" (to drink beyond the premises).

1483. (Before September). Item van Louris Janszoon Coster van pondgelden van synen goeden dat hy wter stede mitter wone gevaren is viii. Rgl. (Item received of Louris Janszoon Coster for ferry-toll for his goods when he left the town 8 Rgl.)

As soon as Lourens Coster has paid his ferry-toll, duty of departure (exue, issue in Flanders), he disappears for ever from our sight. As the towns of Amsterdam, Delft, Gouda, and Dordrecht, had exempted the citizens of Haarlem from the payment of this duty, on condition of reciprocity, we can only infer from this item to which town he did *not* go.

We have now to prove that the innkeeper of 1483 is still one and the same with the chandler of 1447, and marked by Gerrit Thomasz. with the year 1446. We are able to do this from another source, as authentic as the archives.

At Haarlem the "*heilige kerstgilde*" (*Holy Christmas corporation*) still exists, one of those fraternities which had, according to Van Oosten de Bruyn (De Stad Haarlem, p. 107) the lofty aim of "eating and drinking." This corporation is already very old, for it celebrated its third jubilee[1] in 1606. Its 54 brethren and sisters possessed each a chair for their meetings. According to their statutes, these chairs, if they were not disposed of by a last will, were inherited by the eldest and nearest blood-relation in the branch from which they came, with the understanding that a younger son should always have the preference to the eldest daughter, and a younger man to an elder woman, if they were heirs in the same degree (Art. 10). The corporation remained in existence, the right of property in the chairs continued, by uninterrupted transmission, until our time.

M. G. P. van Roermund, at the Hague, possesses a manuscript, in folio, entitled: H. | Karsemis Gilts | Register Stoel Boeck | van de | Broeders en Susters | Namen | Zoo die van tijt tot tijt sijn verboeckt | volgens de drie registers noch in wesen | voor soo veel by leesbaar schrift of sin te sien is | geschreven ende vereert ten dienste van't | H. | Karsemis Gilde | By myn | 1669 | (21 Januari) J^sen. van Alckemade | van Berckenrode. (Chair-Register of the names of the Brethren and Sisters of the Holy Christmas corporation, as they have been transmitted from time to time, according to the three registers still existing, &c.).

---

[1] Beschryvinge ende lof der stad Haerlem in Holland. . . . . Door Samuel Ampzing. Haerlem. 1628. 4to., p. 434.

One leaf of this chair-book contains the following entries:—
29. Stoel

A°. 1421 (lib. 1, fol. 47 verso) Jan Coster, by . . . .
1436 (lib. 1, fol. 74 ,,) Lourijs Coster, by erfnis (by inheritance).
1484 (lib. 1, fol. 149 ,,) Frans Thomas Thomasz., by . . . .
1497 (lib. 1, fol. 156) Gerret Thomas Pietersz., by erfnis van zyn vader (by inheritance from his father).
1564 (lib. 2, fol. 140) Cornelis Gerritsz., by erfnis van zyn vader (by inheritance from his father).
1589 (lib. 2, fol. 206 verso) Anna Gerrits^{dr}, by koop van haer neef (by purchase from her cousin).
1620 (lib. 3, fol. 20 verso) Mr. Jan Hendriksz. Spoorwater, by erfenis van zyn oude Moeije (by inheritance from his old aunt).
1625 (lib. 3, fol. 45 verso) Mr. Thomas Spoorwater, by erfenis van zyn broeder (by inheritance from his brother).
1649 (lib. 3, fol. 157 verso) Mr. Henrick Spoorwater, by erfenis van zyn vader (by inheritance from his father).
1651 (lib. 3, fol. 164) Joh. Maria Spoorwater, by gifte van haar broeder (by gift from her brother).
1692 (lib. 4, fol. 12 verso) Mr. Hendrik Soutman, by erfenis van zyn moeder (by inheritance from his mother).
1738 (lib. 4, fol 52) Paulus a Roy, by testament van Mr. H. Soutman (by last will from M. H. Soutman).
1770 (lib. 4, fol. 62) Laurens a Roy, by versterf van zyn E. vader voorsz (by inheritance from his father aforesaid).
1806 (lib. 4, fol. 78) Mejuff. Antoinette Wilhelmina Coninx, huisvr. van den Heer Joan Paulus a Roy, by erf van voorsz (Mrs. A. W. Coninx, wife of M. J. P. a Roy, by inheritance from aforesaid (L. a Roy).
1820 Deze Stoel door de weduwe a Roy aan den Heer Cornelis Henricus a Roy present gedaan, die dezelve weder aan't Gild heeft afgestaan. (This chair presented to M. Corn. Henr. a Roy, by the widow of a Roy, who conceded it in his turn to the corporation again).

At present the chair No. 29 is the property of the family of Dommer van Poldersveld.

A comparison of the names in the pedigree with the proprietors of the 29th chair of the Christmas-corporation proves that we have here the same family before us, without our being able, or thinking it necessary, to disentangle the family-clew entirely. Lourens Coster inherits the chair in 1436 from his father, and leaves it, in 1484, i.e. after his departure from Haarlem in 1483, to Frans Thomas Thomasz., who gave mortgage to (his uncle?) Pieter Janszoon Coster, in 1492. As we have no right, without a valid reason, to assume a gap in this official gild-register, and the dates moreover perfectly tally with those of the town-archives, it is historically certain that the chandler-innkeeper, Lourens Janszoon Coster, was one and the same man until 1483, and was at that time not yet too old to leave Haarlem in order to settle elsewhere. What "print" that man now, according to the opinion of his descendant, Gerrit Thomasz., brought into the world in 1446 is of no importance to us in regard to science.

As for the other persons of the pedigree, a certain Thomas Pietersz. died, in 1492, as sheriff;[1] a Pieter Thomasz. was innkeeper and burgomaster at Haarlem in 1472 and 1489 ; and an Andries Thomas supplies, in 1457, a "banner, which has a lion underneath, in the new room" (die de leeu in die voet heeft op die nuwe camer) for a rynschen gulden (Rhenish guilder), iii s. iii d.,—and was burgomaster in 1473, '74, and '81. According to the "Diviziekroniek" of 1517 both were murdered in 1492. Finally, a

---

[1] Naamregister van de Heeren van de Regeering der Stad Haarlem. Haarlem. 1733. 4to.

Thomas Thomasz. became burgomaster in 1482. We are, at present, no longer able to decide whether they were all relations. The archives of the 15th century contain such a multitude of similar names, that no safe guide presents itself anywhere. The murdered Thomases may have been related to Gerrit Thomasz., but we may just as well suppose them to have been derived from the traditions of the "Diviziekronick," and that they were placed on the pedigree for the sake of ornament.[1] A synopsis of the sources, whose authority is so weighty that that of the pedigree is, even genealogically, nothing compared to it, allows us only to assume some or other relation between :

Lourens Janszoon Coster, chandler-innkeeper, departed from Haarlem in 1483 ;
Thomas Pieterszoon, sheriff, who died in 1492 ;
Gerrit Thomaszoon, sheriff-innkeeper, who died circa 1564.

The synopsis would be thus :—

Archives of Haarlem.	Chair-book.	Vellum Pedigree.
1441—83. LOURENS JANSZ. COSTER.	1436. LOURENS (JANSZ.) COSTER.	1446. LOURENS JANSZ. COSTER, father-in-law of
1492. *Frans Thomasz.*	1484. *Frans Thomas Thomasz.*	
1492. THOMAS PIETERSZ. died.		THOMAS PIETERSZ., father of five children : Pieter, Andries † 1492, Thomas, Katryn, and Margriet. Eldest son : Pieter Thomasz. ; † 1492, father of Thomas Pietersz., father of
1545. GERRIT THOMASZ., sheriff.	1497. GERRIT THOMAS PIETERSZ., father of	GERRITTHOMAS(Pietersz.), great-great-grandson of L. J. Coster.
	1564. *Cornelis Gerritsz.*, cousin of 1589. *Anna Gerrits*.	1560. *Cornelis Gerritsz.*, brother of *Anna Gerrits*.

Let us see, before we take leave of the piece of vellum—which has now been explained enough, and which would not deserve our attention had it not been the cause of the Haarlem Coster-legend, and an imposition upon the people for centuries —what have been its external adventures since its fabrication.

It remained unknown to the public during the 17th and 18th century ; but, in 1724, a pedigree of *Laurens Koster*, going down to Cornelis Willemsz. Kroon, who died unmarried, 24th March, 1724, was published at Haarlem, by W. van Kessel, on one folio leaf, and afterwards in the " Laurierkrans " of 1726, in 4to. Meerman (1765) translated it into Latin.[2] No one, however, gave any account whatever of the source from which it was derived. But, in 1809, at an auction at Haak's, at Leiden, suddenly the original document appeared. It came into the possession of Jacobus Koning, who described it in the " Konst en Letterbode " of the same year, thus : " Pedigree, written on very old vellum, but perfectly legible, of Laurens [?]. It commences with Louris Coster's *daughter, who brought the first print into the world* (die d'eerste print in die werlt brocht) *anno* 1441 [?], and concludes with his descendants, about the year 1585." The names, therefore, of the 17th and 18th century, occurring in the aforesaid editions of van Kessel, in the Laurierkrans, and by Meerman, are *not* derived from it. It was said that it had been preserved, together with a xylographic block (of the end of the 15th or beginning of the 16th century) which contained a part of an horarium, for about two centuries, by Haarlem families. As far as they could ascertain, it was, at the beginning of the 17th century, in the possession of Adriaan Rooman, town-printer of Haarlem, who had got it from one of the descendants of Coster (read : Gerrit Thomasz.), a man of great age. Dr. Johan Vlasveld, of Haarlem, got it from him, after whose death it came into the hands of his children ; and, on the 19th July, 1734, it was bought by Jan Maas, whose son-in-law, the Rev. Jacobus Mandt of Gorinchem, inherited it from him. After his death, it was bought, together with the

---

[1] At least, I found, in the archives at Haarlem, a Thomas Thomasz.. Feb. 1493, while an invasion of one of the parties of the civil war took place 3 May, 1492. I find Thomas Thomas Thomasz. in 1497.

[2] Origines typographicæ. Ger. Meerman auctore. Hag. Com. 1765. 4to. II.

block, for 400 guilders, by Jacobus Koning,[1] who said something further about it in his prize-essay, published 1816:[2] "On a certain original pedigree of Laurens Jansz. Koster, written before 1560, we find a dove on his coat of arms. Meerman is, indeed, of opinion that this shield was put afterwards on this pedigree by some ignorant person, but that is not at all apparent to me." Well, neither is it the case at all. In 1823, the document was exhibited at Haarlem, and described again differently: "This original pedigree, written on vellum, in or about the year 1550 [again ten years older!], commences with Louris Janssoens Coster, who brought the first print into the world [when?], and is continued, after 1560, by another hand."[3]

Scheltema said, in 1834: "*Thomas Pieters* and his family. All that may have been in the dark with respect to this subject, is cleared up at present, by the *discovery* of the original pedigree or genealogy, which belonged formerly to M. Koning, and is now the property of the town of Haarlem. It is written on vellum, which has become dark brown by time, but the writing is perfectly legible. It commences with *Thomas Pieters*, whose wife, *Lucie*, was the daughter of Lauris Coster, who brought the first print into the world [when?!]. The succession of the members of the family is, moreover, very accurately mentioned; and as it is sufficiently evident, from the document, that its eldest or upper part was written before 1560, and that, after that, a new series was begun with another hand, I have more than once represented this document in my letters to Koning, as of the greatest importance to the cause."[4] We shall very soon become acquainted with the bad "cause" which is here alluded to. But why did neither the verbose Koning, nor Scheltema—more verbose still—publish this genealogy? One page of printing alone was required.

At last, in 1862, an official list of documents,[5] preserved at the town-hall at Haarlem, was published by Dr. A. de Vries: "Old pedigree of Lourens Janszoon Coster, written on vellum, between 1550 and 1560, continued after 1660 (read 1560) by another hand, until the death of the last of Coster's descendants, Willem Cornelisz. Croon, who died 24 March, 1724." This last assertion is totally contradictory to the description of 1809, and—to the truth: the original does not go further than the *sixteenth* century. After the enumeration of all these descriptions, every one will ask with surprise, why this highly important document—even according to the assertions of Koning, Scheltema, and De Vries, the eldest evidence of the fable which they propagated—was systematically kept back and only exhibited at a distance? While search was made in all corners of the earth for supports of the Haarlem Costerianism; while they quarrelled with bitterness when any one objected that the historian Hadrianus Junius was the *first* who mentions the name of a Haarlem inventor of typography; while it was in their power to show triumphantly a vellum document, anterior to 1560, with the name of Coster on it;—they doggedly concealed this first leaf of his laurel, and covered him patiently with the dust of later chronicles, which prove *nothing*. Indeed, this circumstance is a matter for reflection. Sotzmann wrote already, in 1841: "We know (he speaks of the wrong representation, by Faust von Aschaffenburg, of the history of the invention of typography) what confusion at that time was put into genealogies, and how nothing was too fabulous or incredible, when there was a question of finding ancestors or to procure them some dignity. The genealogy of the Costerian family at Haarlem will afford another example. A distinguished family of Haarlem citizens, namely, has linked its pedigree already to the legendary Koster, ' die deerste

---

[1] Algem. Konst-en Letterbode voor 1809. Haarlem. 8vo. II. Wederlegging van het Geschrift van Jac. Koning over de Aanmerkingen wegens den Houten Drukvorm verkocht, 29 Apr. 1809, door Mr. G. van Lennep. 8vo.

[2] Verhandel. over den oorsprong, uitvinding, verbetering en volmaking der Boekdrukkunst. Door Jac. Koning. Haarlem. 1816. 8vo. There exists a French translation of this work.

[3] Gedenkschriften wegens het vierde eeuwgetijde van de uitvinding der boekdrukkunst door Lourens Janszoon Koster, gevierd te Haarlem, 10 en 11 July, 1823; byeenverzameld door Vincent Loosjes. Haarlem. 1824. 8vo.

[4] Geschied-en letterkundig mengelwerk van Mr. Jacobus Scheltema. 1816—36. 8vo. VI.

[5] Lijst der stukken betrekkelijk de geschiedenis van de uitvinding der boekdrukkunst, berustende op het raadhuis te Haarlem. Opgemaakt door Dr. A. de Vries. Haarlem. 1862. 8vo.

print in die werlt brocht,' and made him their ancestor. We see here, all at once, the source whence Junius derived the descendants of Koster, as well as his informations about them, and whence the confusion with the authentic sheriff, financier, and councillor, Laurens Janszoon, who lived from 1870—1439, arose. Scheltema is surprised that Koning mentions this pedigree only by the way, and attaches so little importance to it; but Koning was clever enough to conceal that only such a weak authority had been the cause of swelling the myth to the elaborate Coster-fable." I said before that this suspicion dated already from 1841; and now, of course, the champion of the foolish pretension of Haarlem, the librarian of the town, De Vries, who has read this, will put at once an end to such a suspicion by the publication of the important document? No, for—the Coster-document upsets his mendacious system.

Faithful to the principle of letting every one see with his own eyes, I have, as the fairest way, published, for the first time, number 13 of the Costeriana preserved at the town-hall of Haarlem. The reader may compare the document with the descriptions of Koning, Scheltema, and De Vries, given above.

In the first place, it is evident that in the editions of the pedigree published in 1724 and 1726, and not earlier, they supplied Lourens Coster with a wife, *Catarina Andriesdochter*; but on the other hand deprived him of the year of "the print." Meerman was polite enough, in 1765, to put on his genealogical table, "Laurentius Jo. fil. Aedituus [?] Harlemi, primus inventor Typographiae A°· 1440." Did he not discover the apparent falsification of the 6? He could not bring himself to dissolving that marriage of the eighteenth century, and he wrote calmly: "Uxor Catharina Andreœ filia." And what did Koning do, who had been for many years possessor of the vellum document? In his work he speaks of the difficulty that the wife of his sheriff Louwerijs Janszoon (who had nothing in common with Coster but the Christian name) was called in the archives Ymme Lourens Janszoon's widow; but, undauntedly, he answers: "I know very well [!] that our Louwerens Janszoon was married to Catharina Andriesdochter .... but this does not prevent that this Catharina may have been also called Ymme, or that Lourens Janszoon may have afterwards married this Ymme." This is said by Koning, who had in his hands the vellum document of the sixteenth century, on which Lourens Janszoon Coster has *no wife*. Yet he knows "very well," and gives in one breath not only two wives to the sheriff *Louwerijs Janszoon*, but at the same time two husbands to the fictitious Catrina: the sheriff, and his fellow-townsman of later date, *Lourens Janszoon Coster*.

In the second place we see how little right Scheltema had to say, "the succession of the members of this family has been accurately described." Yes, particularly accurate; so accurate, that even Scheltema, who was of opinion that Koning attached too little value to the document, dared not to show this excellent " genealogy" to the public. He himself was too willing to procure ordered pedigrees, not to know what was the value of the thing. On the contrary, the document has not the least genealogical value; but notwithstanding this worthlessness, it is of great use to remove a town-gossip, which has grown into a popular belief: it tells us the origin of the Haarlem legend at the time of Van Zuren, Coornhert, and Junius. "Lourens Janszoon Coster brings in 1446 the first 'print' into the world," *that* is the main question. In 1809, when Koning bought that patient piece of old vellum, he was either not yet contaminated strongly enough with the moral disease of wilful lying, or still so ignorant as to communicate in an unguarded moment of naïveté in the "Konst- en Letterbode" a dangerous date (1441!) Afterwards, however, the people resolutely concealed it. So the original legend decidedly takes Lourens Janszoon Coster to be the author of "deerste print," for it does not only call him so, but it assigns to him distinctly the arms of the family of that name.

VII.

VAN ZUREN AND COORNHERT.

JAN VAN ZUREN, who was born at Haarlem in 1517 and died there in 1591, Coornhert (born at Amsterdam in 1522, died at Gouda in 1590), and other partners, established a printing-office at Haarlem in 1561; and it is this association which, with full knowledge that the German invention of the art of printing was generally acknowledged, makes the first attack on Mentz, and endeavours in indefinite terms to transfer the honour of this invention to the town of Haarlem. Van Zuren made the first step. When we read later authors who are in favour of Haarlem, we get the impression that he explained in an elaborate work the history of the Haarlem invention, but which, alas! was lost during, or in consequence of, the siege of this town. Let us see what is the case. The only author who mentions that so-called book is Scriverius, in 1628.[1] He declares that he finds only the title, the preface, and the introduction, but the history itself and the evidences of his modest and clever explanation are not there; and we know not by what circumstances it is concealed or has been lost. And after having described the fragment he possessed, he says "that he found no more of it in the original papers, which were handed over to him by a good friend; neither does he see that the copy he used has been *continued* or *finished*." In these circumstances it is hopeless for *us* to discover the truth. If we now consider that Van Zuren in 1561, therefore *after* the time in which his book is put, had his own printing-office at his service, but did *not* publish his work, which was of course destined as a first undertaking of the new association; that he printed the vague evidence of Coornhert [in his edition of Cicero, to be mentioned hereafter], without making it more positive; that he was a contemporary of Junius, and lived even after the publication of the Batavia (1588), without Junius referring to his fellow-townsman, Van Zuren, an author on the question!—we have no right then but to take that "lost book respecting the Haarlem printing-office" as a first bashful, but abandoned effort, of depriving Mentz of the honour of the invention of typography. This is incontestably confirmed by the contents of the fragment described by Scriverius.[2] Van Zuren tried to write a

---

[1] Petri Scriverii Lavre-Crans voor Lavrens Coster van Haerlem, Eerste Vinder Vande Boeck-druckery. Haerlem, Adr. Rooman, 1628. 4to. 100 pp. First ed. increased the same year with 24 pp., and added to Ampzing's Beschrijvinge der stad Harlem.

[2] "Zvrenus Jvnior, sive De primâ, & inaudita hactenus vulgo & veriore tamen Artis Typographicae inventione, Dialogus, Nunc primum conscriptus, & in lucem editus, autore Joanne Zvreno, Harlemeo Ad ampliss. virum N. N. It appears from this title, and from what follows, that M. Zurenus treated this matter in the form of a dialogue between Zurenus, the father, and Zurenus, the son. In the preface he complains, and is surprised, that this so highly necessary and invaluable science came so late into light and to the knowledge of mankind. Declaring further that he took this treatise, "de subtili, ingenioso, solertiq. invento, non ita multis abhinc annis mortalibus divino consilio prodito, ac in hanc lucem ac hominum usum producto," to hand "tum ipsius veritatis amore, tum Patriae quoque studio, &c." Adding to it: "Quo ego protectò meo scripto, et si id facilè contemni potest, nihil tamen Maguntimensi quicquam Reipublicae unquam detractum volo, aut de illius etiam hujus inventi gloriâ diminutum tantillum, cujus ego quoque nomini faveo prae coeteris multum. Fruantur illi certè, idq. me nec invito, nec reluctante quidem, laude suâ praeclarâ certè, quâ jam annos multos, in hominum sermone ac scriptis, nec immeritò gaudent. Sit haec ipsis quoque quieta & justa longissimi temporis praescriptione possessio; quâ ipsos turbare, profectò nec justum, nec etiam humanum (arbitror) foret. Hoc tantùm (precor) animo ferant aequo, ut liceat mihi hanc Patriae fidem, ne an pietatem dicam? praestare, quae mihi certè hujus & lucis & institutionis nonnullae initium extitit primum, & causa praecipua, ut non sinam hoc patrimonium laudis, quod adhuc in recenti patrum memoriâ haeret, à genitoribus suis sibi per manus traditum, aliquando tandem perire, & ex omni hominum memoriâ extingui deleriq. ut perpetuis deinceps tenebris obruatur cujus ad seram posteritatis famam decebat nos praesertim memoriam conservare sempiternam. Illa quidem civitas, meritò praedicanda, olim hanc rem acceptam à nobis prima certè publici juris fecit, & in hanc lucem altius evexit, & rude admodum informeq. inventum in formam tandem redegit elegantiorem, ut quidem tum ferebat aetas. Quo nomine quis non insigni sarte laude ac merito perpetuò celebrandem ac praedicandum illam quoq. profectò judicet, quae etiam vel in primis, quamquam non sit difficile inventis aliquid addere, tanti tamen beneficii bonitate orbem sibi devinxit universum. Caeterum hoc teneat velim Amplitudo tua N. N. in hac urbe nostrâ Harlemensi prima esse jacta opificij hujus praeclari fundamenta, rudia fortassè, sed tamen prima. Hic nata & in lucem edita Typographica est (quod Maguntinensium

Dialogus de prima Artis Typographicae inventione. He will not deprive Mentz of a bit of its reputation; to supplant it in this possession which has, by long duration, become lawful, were—neither just nor humane. But he will prevent this inheritance of glory, still so fresh in the memory of our parents and transmitted to them by their fathers, being lost altogether and buried in eternal darkness. The town of Mentz, so justly lauded, first introduced this art, received from us, into public life. But the first, although crude, yet first foundations of this excellent art, were laid in our town of Haarlem. Here the art of printing was born . . . and it was no doubt long carefully cultivated and improved, and remained here for many years within its own walls . . . until at last, as if it despised the poverty of its native home, it accompanied a foreigner and . . . made at last its public appearance at Mentz. The doubt alone which makes itself master of Van Zuren with regard to his sad intention, is curious enough. He first acknowledges that the invention is unanimously ascribed to Mentz, and then proceeds thus : " I often used to consult in secret with myself, my son, whether it were not better to talk the matter over among ourselves, lest any one of those who would not remain passive when the *Mentzers were deprived of the glory of the invention* and turned out of a quiet and prolonged possession, should hear us." The other proposition of this comical dilemma puts the question : Whether it were, after all, not better to prove his love to his country, by placing it again in possession of the never-lost (!) paternal inheritance—advienne que pourra : whatever storm, or perhaps war (!), may be the consequence of it.

Such is the famous evidence of Jan van Zuren ! Without stating any date or

pace dictum velim) suisq. membris formata, ut succrescere posset; ac diu certè, ut nuper nati infantes solent, tractata figurataq. sedulò; multosq. hic annos intra privatos tantum parietes stetit, qui sunt modò, quamquam ruinosi, tamen adhuc salvi & incolumes, tanto pridem partu suo orbati ac spoliati miserè. Hic est profectò educata, sumptuq. tenui diu nutrita & alta parcius atque restrictè nimiùm, donec tandem tanquam privati laris angustias & paupertatem aspernata, extero cuidam se comitem dedit, sordibusq. patrijs majore sui parte relictis, nacta amplissimas opes, ad postremum apud Maguntiam se publici juris fecit ; ubi brevi adeo tempore in tantam excrevit amplitudinem, vt ea jam propemodum magnitudine laboret suâ. Quæ omnia tua Amplitudo, hunc nostrum cum filio Zureno Sermonem per otium aliquando legens, latius cognoscet." And finally, after a few pages, he continues thus : " Nam cùm res sit profectò non miraculo solùm, postquam est cognita, sed & utilitate quoque, non tam usu tamen sui quàm fructu, & summa per se, & hujusmodi merito etiam prædicanda semper; cujus item in amplitudine ac ubertate mirabili, ac omnem stylum superante, compendium tantum, & in angustum quoque, pro tam copiosi fructus magnitudine, contracta brevitas extat, varias sanè dabit nec inamœnas nobis multa & narrandi & disputandi occasiones : cùm & de commodis illius multiplicibus, tum incommodis quoque nonnullis intercurrent; quæq. sunt alia hujusmodi multa non contemnenda profectò : ut nihil dicam quoque de ejus inventione primâ, quam falsò hactenus totus propemodum orbis unanimi consensu (!) Maguntinensibus asscripsit. De quo vel solo negotio, fili, sæpè mecum multa soleo tacitus cogitare, ac nonnihil etiam subindè hæsitare, mussitandáne sit hæc res inter nos (!) clanculùm magis, ne quid quis fortè eorum exaudiat, qui hanc hujus inventi gloriam Maguntinensibus eripi, tamq. jucundâ ac diuturnâ possessione turbari, nunqua(m) æquo animo patientur ; an potius, manifestiùs nobis præsertim rei veritate subnixi, cujus adhuc recens in hominum memoriâ testimonium extat, Patriæ etiam hanc pietatem grati præstemus, ut ipsam tandem in avitæ hæreditatis possessionem, opinione nostrâ ac animo nunquam quoque deperditam, per reliquam etiam nonullam orbis partem aliquando tandem restituamus, eiq. hoc tanquam patrimonium laudis simul in hominum animis, ad posteritatis memoriam, confirmemus ; securi quæ nobis indè tandem nasci excitariq. possit tempestas, & fortassè etiam bellum nonnullum.

"I find no more concerning this matter in the original papers which have been handed to me by a good friend, nor do I see that the book I use has been continued or finished. Certainly a matter much to be regretted, because we observe the sincere proceedings of the man, endeavouring, by no by-ways (!) but by a straight way, to come to the truth. How modestly and laudably he speaks of those of Mentz (!) where, however, the printing-office is of no lawful, but adulterous, bed. He could easily have proved this (!) while it will be more difficult to us, as having come so much later into the world than he, and not being so well supported and provided [with arguments] as M. van Zuren was. We shall, however, lose no courage, and advance as much as is in our power, what we have been able to find or what we thought expedient and true . . . trusting that we shall be able to tell the reader something curious, which was unknown, perhaps, to Zurenus, and certainly (!) to Junius. The last mentioned may, according to my opinion, replace the lost book of the first, supplied with what we have given above. The passages of Zurenus . . . are but an argument of, and introduction to, his intended work, and only indicate that the author wished to treat of the matter elaborately, in defence of the Haarlem honour, and to express the truth freely . . . saying at present only : that the art of printing was first of all invented at Haarlem —that the house where the printing-office was first established still existed in his time, with what belonged to it—that the new, and still crude art was taken away by a foreigner and brought to Mentz ; where it was housed, maintained, continued, and greatly improved.

"These and similar points were treated by our Zurenus . . . But as all this has been neglected and lost (I know not by what catastrophe), we have to be satisfied with the faithful service of Junius, who has so manly fought in our behalf ; and, further, with what now has been done by us (!)."

H

name or book or anything else, nay, without giving anything which would resemble a *proof*, he *says* only that the whole world unjustly ascribes the invention of the art of printing to Mentz, because it was invented at Haarlem, crude and shapeless, but yet so developed that it could grow further (succrescere). To upset historical facts a *century* afterwards, I believe that every one will acknowledge that something more is wanted for that purpose than the chatter of a father with his son.

From the same source is derived the *earliest printed vindication* for Haarlem. Coornhert settled there at the age of twenty (c. 1542) and was an engraver in copper; he is even said to have been the instructor (at least the adviser) of the celebrated Goltzius. He became a notary in 1561, and associated himself with Van Zuren, who published the same year as first-fruit of their new press his Officia Ciceronis[1]. The dedication of this book to the municipal government deserves to be read in full.

" To the Burgomaster, Sheriffs and Councillors of the town of Haarlem, D. V. Coornhert wishes, as his honourable and commanding masters, salvation to soul and body.

" I was often told in good faith, honourable, wise, and prudent gentlemen, that the useful art of printing books was invented first of all here at Haarlem, although in a very crude way, as it is easier to improve on an invention than to invent ; which art having been brought to Mentz by an unfaithful servant, was very much improved there, whereby this town, on account of its first having spread it, gained such a reputation for the invention of this art, that our fellow-citizens find very little credence when they ascribe this honour to the true inventor, as it is believed by many here on incontestable information, and is undoubtedly known to the elder citizens. Nor am I ignorant that this fame of Mentz has taken so deeply root in the opinion of all, by the heedless carelessness of our forefathers, that no proof, however apparent, however clear, however blameless it may be, would be capable of removing this inveterate impression from the hearts of the people. But—for truth is no less truth when known only to a few, and because I implicitly believe what I have said before, on account of the trustworthy evidence of very old, dignified, and grey heads, who often told me not only the family of the inventor, but also his name and surname, and explained the first crude way of printing, and pointed with their finger the house of the first printer out to me—I could not help mentioning this in few words, not as an envier of another's glory, but as a lover of truth, and to the promotion of the honour of this town ; which proper and just ambition seems to have also been the cause for the re-establishment and re-commencement of this printing-office (as a shoot from the root of an old tree). For it often happened, when the citizens talked to each other about this case, that they complained that others enjoyed this glory unjustly, and (as they said) without anybody contradicting them, because no one exercised printing in this town.

" Induced by this daily talk, my partners and I (who always preferred an honest occupation to idleness) have thought it expedient to establish a printing-office in Haarlem in order to honour the town, to be of use to every one, and to strive for profit without anybody's loss. This our intention is not only not impeded by you, gentlemen (whose diligent willingness is always looking towards the honour and duty of this town), but so liberally promoted, that such a wise favour will be an imperishable example of modest love to the common well-being to all other regents. But as I, not only as a citizen and member of this town, but also as a partner in this business, have a share, generally, and in particular, in this favour, I was naturally induced to render some token of gratitude : which consists (as it ought to do) of the first-fruit of my first work not only, but also of the Haarlem printing-office. For this purpose I have chosen the three books written by the great philosopher and most eloquent orator M. T. Cicero de officiis ; seeing every day the life, conduct, and actions of you, gentlemen, teach the citizens that which these books are instructing, namely, virtue and honour. I have purposely abstained from the habits of translators, who laud the materials treated of by their authors, as I thought that I should not be able to do that

---

[1] Officia Ciceronis, Leerende wat yeghelyck in allen staten behoort te doen, bescreuen int Latyn door den . . . Orator Marcum Tullium Ciceronem, ende nv eerst vertaelt in nederlantscher spraken door Dierick Coornhert. Tot Haerlem, By Jan Van Zuren, 1561. Sm. 8vo.

properly, considering that even the most eloquent men may easily say much, but never enough, in praise of the charming expediency of these books. You, then, gentlemen, will (as I feel quite sure) accept this my trifling work with your usual benevolence, as from one who works with diligent willingness, which I hope to show in future times with still greater readiness, if God Almighty will spare me; Whose mercy I heartily pray will preserve you, gentlemen, in long prosperous health, to His honour and the well-being of this town. Amen."

Although Coornhert writes for the promotion of the honour of his town, although he alludes to: the family of the inventor, his name and surname, and the house of the very first printer, he is however (wise or awkward?) enough to keep all this fine knowledge for himself, and not to mention the name of the fictitious inventor. And this he does, although the citizens complained that others enjoyed the honour of the invention unjustly without contradiction. How was that? *Because no one exercised printing at Haarlem.* For *that* reason Coornhert and his partners establish now a printing-office for the *honour of the town*. The only thing he blabs out of the increase of the Haarlem gossip, is that the art of printing did not, as Van Zuren wrote, accompany a foreigner to Mentz (extero cuidam se comitem dedit), but that it was carried thither by "an unfaithful servant."

Coornhert calls his printing-office (firm Van Zuren) "a shoot from the root of an old tree, re-established and re-commenced." That *old tree* upon which the revived Haarlem typography sprouts, is the printing-office of *Bellaert* of 1483—1486. Scriverius had traced already, in 1628, this explanation of Coornhert's words. He says in the "Lauwerkrans":—"D. V. Coornhert writes to all appearances as if the printing-office established by him and his colleagues at Haarlem were new, and was a shoot from the root of an old tree. But did he mean and would he like to persuade us that, prior to the erection and opening of his shop, no printing-office has been here since the first inventor and establisher? really I cannot accept that, but *take it to be a great misunderstanding*, and the contrary is evident from the books (of Jacob Bellaert)."

In the sheriff-registers, under the year 1559, I found mentioned that Allart Willemsz sold a house, situated in the "Cruysstraat," with ground, a lane and a gate annexed to it, called *den bellaert*. Five years afterwards it was sold again, according to the following item in the aforesaid registers:—

"Henrick van Zwolle, Prior of the Convent of St. John, within this town, and Dirick Volckharts Coornhert, Secretary of the same town, as attorneys of our reverend lord, Nicolaes van Nyeuwelande, Bishop of Haarlem, sell, authorised by the sealed letters of procuration, with which this letter is transfixed, to Claes Ysbrantsz Huydecoper, a house, with ground, lane and gate annexed to it, called *den Bellaert*, situated in the Cruysstract, &c.; thus enacted before sheriffs within Haarlem, on the x Febr. anno xv^{c}Lxiiij." (Heere Henrick van Zwolle, Commandeur van Sinte Jans Convente binnen deser stede, met Dirick Volckharts Coornhert, Secretaris der selver stede, als volmachtichden van onsen eerwaerdighen heere, heere Nicolaes van Nyeuwe-lande, Bisschop tot Haerlem, vercoopen uyt crachte van de bezegelde Lru van pro-curatie, daer deure dese brieff getransfixeerd is, Claes Ysbrantsz Huydecoper een huys mitten erve stege en(de) poerte daer bezijden, genaempt *den Bellaert*, staende ende liggende in de Cruysstraet, &c., aldus gepasseert voor scepenen in Haarlem opten x Feb. anno xv^{c}Lxiiij.")

Now, whether the printer *Jacob van Zierikzee*, at Haarlem, gave, by means of his shield *den bellaert*, the name to this house, or whether Jacob Bellaert derived his name from the house in question, which was probably already called by this name—we have here really the house called by Coornhert "the house of the first [Haarlem] printer, often pointed out to him with the finger by many very old, dignified, and grey heads."

At Haarlem two stories have been afloat by the side of and through each other: the first of the real first Haarlem printer, of "his name and surname," and of "his house," in the remembrance indeed of the oldest citizens; the second of an imaginary "inventor," grafted on the first. Hereby the contradictory assertions of Van Zuren and Junius concerning his "decaying" and "splendid" house, and the strange silence of Van Zuren and Coornhert in respect to his name, are sufficiently explained. The town-gossip had not yet assumed a definite shape; it was not yet crystallized; it could not yet express itself but in vague, indefinite terms. As for what was "believed by many" at Haarlem in Coornhert's time, "on incontestable information," and what was "known to the elder citizens," it is of no importance to us. The "elder citizens" still believe that the little clocks which ring at Haarlem from nine till half-past nine every evening, were fetched by their forefathers from Damiate; they believed, in Coornhert's time, in a merman, caught in the Zuider Zee and brought to Haarlem; a century earlier they believed that they could conjure the evil spirits of thunder by the ringing of bells; and, again, a century earlier, they implicitly believed in a mermaid, caught in the Purmer and presented by the town of Edam to the town of Haarlem. And yet nobody hesitates to reject all those fables, although the evidences in favour of them are of infinitely greater weight than those in favour of the imaginary Haarlem invention.

The first Haarlem printing-office, therefore, the house Den Bellaert, the house of the *first* Haarlem typographer, not followed for many years by a printing-office of any signification, originated among the aged at Haarlem an obscure legend concerning this "first printer." This very vague popular legend, the remembrance of this first Haarlem printer, growing more and more obscure, *have been taken advantage of*, a generation afterwards, by a Haarlem citizen, Gerrit Thomasz., to ornament his pedigree. Just as the Strasburg bookseller Schott made of his grandfather on the mother's side, the printer Johan Mentelin, an inventor of typography, so Gerrit Thomasz., in the second quarter of the 16th century, placed his (grandfather or) great-grandfather, the chandler-innkeeper *Lourens Janszoon Coster*, on a calligraphic piece of vellum, as the man *who brought the first print into the world Anno* 1446.

Of such genealogical ostentation heraldry knows thousands and thousands of examples. And not only of early times. For are there not persons ready at any moment to convince those who are interested, that a certain crest of arms occurs in a certain book of such-and-such a year? What does this prove? Has not of late a bookseller of Haarlem filled an entire volume,[1] a real receptacle of refuse of chronicles, to prove that he descends in a direct line from the Counts of Holland; and was all this not figured on a lithographic pedigree? But what does this prove for the descent from a count of the namesake of the dapifer Brederode of the middle ages? And does not every literary man know the follies of Bilderdyk, who, in his History of Holland, besides from Jacqueline of Bavaria and Jan Wagenaar, descends almost from everybody whom he mentions? And does not every one know at least half-a-dozen anecdotes of this weakness for pedigrees? And would anybody feel inclined at present to submit, when some simple citizen stuck on his wall, in a frame, the assertion that (not Watt, but) his great-grandfather, an industrious linen-bleacher, had invented the steam engine?

The three lines of beautiful writing of Gerrit Thomasz., according to form and character belonging to the second half of the 16th century, are a simple *assertion* of an ignorant person, but by no means an historical *proof* of a thing which was said to have happened *a century before*.

What did the man mean by that "first print"? *Typography*, in the pure, scientific sense of the word? Not at all. The term of his pedigree, born in the 16th century, from the popular notion that every kind of *printing* belongs to the real art of printing books and preceded it, means, if it has any meaning, simply *block-printing—no* typography. We know how the authors of the 17th century lived entirely under that wrong impression; it prevailed in the 18th; they began to overcome it in the 19th; but there is still much to be done before it will be rooted out altogether. The word *prenten* for *drukken* (printing) is a purely Netherland term of the

---

[1] To my surprise, the Haarlem bookseller has in this compilation, which commences with the Dutch counts and leaves off with his own children, not known what to do with his bronze relative in the market-place, who was declared to be a descendant of the Counts of Brederode on equally valid grounds as a great number of his pedigree with or without bar-sinister.

15th and 16th centuries, derived by the typographers from the vocabulary of the prenters-gilds, of the xylographers, who printed "prents" with or without accompanying text. Hence, the well-known imprints of our incunabula. But even if these three words existed for the workman, the work and the work-place, the object, the fruit of the work, was a *book*, but never a *prent*. The addition of the notion BOOK to the words of Gerrit Thomasz. would make nonsense of them, or else one of those mistakes by which swindlers generally betray themselves. If, however, we have here not the nonsense of self-betrayal, we are then not allowed to go further than to the first *prent*, the first *woodcut*—but the first woodcut is *much* older than 1446.

Coornhert is, in 1561, not able to tell us anything more but that he was often *told*, in good faith, that the art of printing books was invented at Haarlem, although in a "very crude way" (= deerste print). What he means by his crude way, he does not say, neither is it clear. But his omitting every further indication of time, inventor, or production, proves that the conversations, held in a public-house at Haarlem, about a forgotten inhabitant of the past century, had not yet forged a perfect fable. Remarkable only is his naïve confession how, at Haarlem, local jealousy began to awaken; how vanity was on the alert to arrogate an undeserved honour.

We find, therefore, in the above dedication of Coornhert nothing but a reclamation of tradesmen, who open their new business; and in such reclamations we not seldom meet with one or other especially historical blunder. The great objection, that Coornhert saves himself the trifling trouble of mentioning name and surname of the inventor, is generally answered with the remark that it was totally superfluous to mention that name to the Haarlem burgomasters, as it was too well known. Superfluous? But the name had as yet *never* been mentioned in public! Superfluous? But then it was unnecessary for Coornhert to say *anything at all* to those Haarlem burgomasters, who were so well acquainted with the invention at Haarlem! The purpose of the preface was to conquer the claims of Haarlem to the honour of the invention of the art of printing from Mentz; and, considering this undeniable purpose, Mr. Ruelens[1] made a just remark when he said: "Cet oubli de Coornhert nous a toujours paru une des particularités les plus colossales de la légende Harlémienne. Comment! Voilà un homme très-savant, très-patriote, qui revendique avec fracas pour son pays l'honneur d'être le berceau de la plus grande des inventions modernes, qui apprécie l'importance de la découverte, il sait le nom, le prénom, la famille de l'inventeur et il ne les divulgue pas à ses concitoyens! C'est à ne pas y croire. Et que dire du bourgmestre Van Zuren? Il écrit un traité spécial pour revendiquer la gloire de l'invention, au profit de la ville dont il est le magistrat et l'idée ne lui vient même pas d'honorer la mémoire de l'inventeur, je ne dirai point, par quelque monument, ce serait exiger beaucoup de sa part, mais au moins par une mention, un souvenir quelconque, son nom donné à une rue, moins encore, simplement écrit dans un livre. On ne trouverait pas un second exemple d'un oubli aussi incroyable."

Oh, I perfectly understand Scriverius' lamentation over Van Zuren: "Alas! how much has he harmed and prejudiced us in the honour of such an invention by his silent mouth!"[2]

---

[1] (C. Ruelens) L'Odyssée de Laurent Coster en Hollande. (Extrait du Bibliophile Belge, Tome III.) 1868. 8vo.

[2] Eylaas! hoe heeft hy ons in d'eer van sulken vond
Verachterd en verkort door synen stommen mond!

VIII.

LUIGI GUICCIARDINI.

The Florentine nobleman, Luigi Guicciardini, who knew the Netherlands from having visited them, and who resided many years at Antwerp, finished there, in 1566, a "Descrittione di tutti i Paesi Bassi," in fol., and published it a year afterwards. As the contemporary of those who propagated the Haarlem story of a so-called invention of the art of printing, it came also to his ears, and in a shape in which the growing of the legend, but at the same time its hesitation and searching for a more distinct representation, was plainly visible. We may not always be able to point out everywhere the authorities for his informations, yet he now and then mentions them distinctly, from which it is evident that he, as he assures us in his preface, has purposely asked information about some questions. He also mentions the mermaid (donna marina) caught, in 1403, in the Purmer, and civilized at Haarlem. But, says Guicciardini, what is no less curious, forty years ago (therefore between 1520 and '30!) the citizens at Haarlem said, and believed, that a merman (huomo marino), of the same figure as we, was caught in the Frisian sea, and lived many years at Haarlem, and died of the plague. The author now produces, for this curious particular, this traditional proof: "M. Nicolaus Nicolai (Claas Claeszoon), a truthful and trustworthy man, has told me, besides many other evidences he had on the subject, that M. Jasper Lievenszoon, councillor in the council of Holland, and M. Peeter, secretary of the same council, told him that they often saw this merman, explaining many particulars about him." And who will be astonished, asks the author, at such strange things? For Pliny and other trustworthy(!) authors speak of the Tritons and other sea-monsters. St. Jerome, in his life of Paul the Hermit, speaks even, as of true and unquestionable things (per cosa vera ed indubitata), of satyrs, fauns, &c., and (adds Kiliaen, the Dutch translator of his work, Amst. 1648, p. 199,) of "wild Klaboutermen." However, notwithstanding Plinius and Kiliaen, notwithstanding the Dutch councillors, we shall not trouble ourselves further about the Haarlem monstrology, but examine the value of another Haarlem legend, more recent than that of the Triton, and which cannot refer to eye-witnesses. Guicciardini says: "Questa terra (Haerlem) è la maggiore di tutte le altre terre d'Hollanda &. è la seconda preferita. In questa terra non solo per voce publica de gli habitatori, & di altri Hollandesi, ma ancora per alcuni scrittori, & per altre memorie, si truoua che fu primamente inuentata l'arte dello imprimere, & stampare lettere & caratteri in foglio al modo d'oggi, impero venendo l'autore a morte innanzi, che l'arte fusse in perfettione, & consideratione, il seruidore suo (secondo dicono) andò a dimorare a Maganza, oue dando lume di quella scienza, fu rauolto allegramente, & quiui dato opera con ogni diligentia, a tanto negotio, ne vennero all' intera notitia, & total' perfettione, onde è poi volata, & inueterata la fama, che di quella citta vscita l'arte, & la scienza della stampa: quel que ne sia alla verità, non posso, ne voglio giudicare, bastandomi d'hauerne tocco vn motto, per non pregiudicare a questa terra, & Regione."

Guicciardini, therefore, on the occasion of describing Haarlem, speaks of the invention of printing there, but, just as Van Zuren and Coornhert, without the least indication of year or name, and simply according to the assertions of the inhabitants, the evidence of some authors, and other remembrances (Guicciardini has, perhaps, asked information in a direct way, and the "scrittori" he alludes to are no doubt our two Haarlem printers. The "memorie" are the pedigree and the wine-pots of the sheriff-innkeeper, Gerrit Thomaszoon). The inventor died before the perfection of his art; his servant went (as they say) to live at Mentz, and perfected there the art: hence the report that it was invented there. *On the truth of the subject Guicciardini is neither able nor willing to express an opinion ; it is enough to him to have touched it with a few words, in order not to prejudice Holland and Haarlem.*

Every one will easily see what is the value of such information. It does not prove anything but that the people at Haarlem were very busy in spreading, as much as possible, the report which had once got abroad, only they have as yet not been bold enough to accuse to the foreigner the unmentioned servant, called by Coornhert "unfaithful," of the unmentioned inventor. They represent him to the Italian author as having gone after, therefore *on account* of, the death of his master, to Mentz; as having been received there with open arms, and as having perfected there the art.

Meanwhile, the translation of Guicciardini's Descrittione di tutti i Paesi Bassi, in French (1567), German (1582), English (1593), Dutch (1612, 1648), Latin (1613), conduced much to spread the false report of a Haarlem invention, especially because it was literally *translated*, or liberally *copied*, by some compilers; by Braun (1570),[1] Eytzinger (1584),[2] Quade (1594),[3] and rendered entirely unintelligible by the addition of the year 1453, and the name of Johan Gutenberg! by Noël Conti (1572).[4] Thus mutilated by a countryman of the author, the evidence of Guicciardini was afterwards used again by another of his countrymen, Mirtius, in an abbreviated form, as note to his chronicle of the convent Subiaco.[5] Van Vaernewyck alluded in his book of fables

---

[1] Geo. Braunius: Civitates orbis terrarum. Col. 1570—88. Fol. Six volumes. The preface of the second vol., in which the map of Haarlem, No. 26, is found, is dated 1575. The translation from Guicciardini runs thus: "Haec (Harlemum) est omnium in Batavis urbium maxima et dignitate sane secunda. Typographicam artem, in ea, a quodam fuisse primum excogitatam constans ea urbe, totaque provincia Batavorum fama est. Quam opinionem scriptores nonnulli confirmant et quidam privatarum ejus loci rerum commentarii. Verumtamen antequam artem perficeret, et eam ipse in lucem proderet, e vivis excessisse, ejus famulum ob id Moguntiam concessisse, in qua urbe artem evulgaret, et eam ob caussam acceptis perbenigne fuerit." But translations grow also, just as news. To the scriptores belongs now, of course, already his source Guicciardini.

[2] Mich. Eyzinger: Niederländ. beschreib. auff den Belgischen Löwen: Cöln, 1581; 4to.; p. 75:— "Zum andern, so findt man auch, das in diser stat Harlem, die Kunst der Truckerey auff jetzige unser Weiss mit Buchstaben und Caracteribus, auff papir oder sonst zu trucken, durch einen daselbst erstlich erfunden. Darnach aber mit absterben solches Meisters, durch seinen knecht in der Churfürstlichen Reichstat Maintz, zu volkommener endtschafft ans liecht gebracht sey worden."

[3] Matth. Quadus Pictor Juliacus: Compendium Universi, sive Geographicae Narrationes; Col., 1600 (L. III., c. 38): "Harlemo expertissimorum (!) quorumque testimonio Typographicae artis inventio debetur. Ajunt enim ejus inventorem ante perfectam artem morte praeventum, ejusque deinde servum Moguntiacum profectum; ubi continuo exercitio ad perfectionem ars perducta est; ut haec altrix seu matrix, illa artis mater sit."

[4] Natalis Comes: Universalis Historia sui temporis. Venet. Varisci 1572. In edit. Ven. ap. Dam. Zenarum, 1581. Lib. xxiv., p. 521: "Memorabilis esse potest haec urbs (Harlemum) ob divinum prope inventum imprimendorum librorum: quod fuit Joannis Gutenbergii (!) primum excogitatum anno salutis nostrae 1453 (!), qui cum rudem quandam rationem prius invenisset, uti sunt res prope omnes recens ortae, habuit famulum satis callidum et artis domini observantem. Famulus, mortuo Joanne, ubi Moguntiacum adiisset, artem ad meliorem rationem perduxit: atque inde didita est fama, quod eius urbis fuit inventum."

[5] Chronicon Sublacense, per P. D. Cherubinum Mirtium Trevirensem monachum Sublacensem laboratum, Anno partus Virginis, 1629. MS. in 4to. On page 150, we read: "Non aegre ferat, quaeso lector, si inseruero ratione temporis rem non plane ab instituto nostrae alienam, nempe laudabile studium monachorum Sublacensium teutonicorum quod ad decus eorum, atque monasterii quodammodo spectare videtur. Nempe, quod nobilissima librorum typographia paucis ante annis in inferiori Germania enata est et in lucem * qua certe in mundo nulla dignior ars atque utilior exstitit," &c.

* HOLLANDIA.

A.D. 1453, in civitate Harlem par Joannem Cutembergam, quae tamen ars, postea Moguntiae per dicti inventoris famulum in meliorem redacta fuit excudendi formam.

It is clear that Mirtius copies in the note the mishmash of Conti, and ludicrous, therefore, is the reasoning with which M. J. H. Boucker Andreae (Herinn. aan Italie, Leeuw. 1856,) commented on it: "Everything is written by the same hand and well by that of Mirtius. As addendum he enumerates the works which these printers [Schweynheym and Pannartz] printed in this convent, until (?) 1465. Without venturing upon any hazardous guesses, it is, I think, not altogether unimportant that, in a chronicle of the convent of Subiaco, where the servants of Guttenberg had transferred and continued the art of printing, mention is made of Harlem, civitas Hollandiae; it is a matter of course that Guttenberg, when he continued (!) the invention at Mentz, did not tell his men in what way he had got the secret. This convent, therefore (!) retained the tradition of Haarlem, although the honour was ascribed to Guttenberg." Intolerably stupid! Because an Italian of the 17th century copies a confused account of a countryman of the latter part of the 16th century; because it is said, in this account, that Gutenberg, who was really ready in 1450 with his invention at Mentz, discovered it first, in 1453, at Haarlem; that his servant (!) transferred it to and perfected it, *after* that year, at Mentz, and Gutenberg, therefore, had never been at Mentz himself; it is for *that* reason that Gutenberg cannot have told the *Mentz* typographers, Schweynheym and Pannartz, in what way he had got the secret!" And *because* all this nonsense dates from the years 1572, 1581, and 1629, for *that* reason the convent of Subiaco "retained, since 1465 (since

(1568),[1] in the careless style of a rhetorician, to Coornhert's preface ; while, finally, Ortels (c. 1570)[2] simply said " that the inhabitants of Haarlem were convinced that printing had been invented first of all in that place." They have, however, not scrupled, until this time, to throw dust into the eyes of the people with this series of foreign authors. For an unproved assertion does not increase in strength at all by copying it, nor is town-gossip capable of being chattered to truth. And yet they have handled the quotation from Guicciardini as if they, in good faith, believed in the substantiating force of copying : the multiplication of the *same* intelligence of authors who consult one another, became, in the hands of misleading demagogues, a battery of so many *new* evidences. But, reduced to their real origin, all these evidences, which were a little increased every now and then, give this formula : Mirtius — Conti = Guicciardini -- (Braun = Eytzinger = Quade) = Coornhert (— Van Zuren) = 0. And the subject would never have been the cause of our ridicule in foreign countries and a flood of impostures in our own country, had not somebody come forth who, instead of a vague, ambiguous gossip, fabricated a somewhat elaborate story.

IX.

HADRIANUS JUNIUS.

HADRIANUS JUNIUS (Adriaen de Jonghe) was born at Hoorn on the 1st of July, 1511, and sent as a boy to the Latin grammar school at Haarlem. He completed his first studies at Louvain, made thereupon (1537) a tour in foreign countries, accompanied by Martinus Costerus, and got in 1540 at Bologna his degree as doctor of medicine.[3] The two following years he dates his letters from Paris ;[4] since 1542 he resided for six years on English ground, and as physician in ordinary to the Duke of Norfolk, after whose death he came back to his native country. But, reduced to utter poverty,

---

1465 !), the tradition of Haarlem !" Abr. de Vries willingly accepted the quotation of the chronicle (Eclaircissemens, p. 216), but omitted, according to his usual shameful tactics, the year 1629, frankly made the *Mentz* typographers the authorities of the passage, and added to it : " Or leur (!) témoignage peut être rangé parmi les plus anciens."

[1] De Historie van Belgis, diemen anders noemen mach den Spieghel der nederl. oudtheyt. Published first, without the name of the author, at Ghent, 1568. Afterwards : Ghent, 1574 ; Amsterdam, 1590 ; Antwerp, 1619, 1665 ; Brussels, 1619 ; Ghent. 1784. Under the description of Haarlem, we find nothing about the invention of printing. Chapter 70, on the contrary, forms a Balade, of which I quote the 4th couplet :—

" Van d'inventie der letteren, sullen wy hier swyghen,
    Oock van 't verkrijghen, van d'eerste Druckeryen,
    Diese som Joanni Faustino tot Mens optyghen :
    Andere Guttenberch, daer de Duytschen in verblyen
Daer synder oock die hier teghens stryen,
    En segghen : sy sou eerst vonden zyn al claer en plat,
    (Soo Dierick Coornhert schrijft in zijn poeterijen)
    Tot Haerlem, twelck is een Hollantsche stadt."

There exists no poetry of Coornhert on this subject. With his " poeterijen" he can have meant nothing but the dedication of Cicero. The invention at Haarlem, " al claer en plat," is Coornhert's " crude way," and Gerrit Thomaszoon's " eerste print " = 0.

[2] Abrah. Ortelius : Theatrum orbis terrarum. Antv. 1574. Fol. The dedication to Philip II. is dated 1570.

[3] Oud en Nieuw, uit de vaderl. geschied. en letterk. verzameld door P. Scheltema, Amsterdam, 1844. 8vo. In it we find : " het leven van Junius." P. Scheltema had published already before : Diatribe in Hadriani Junii vitam, ingenium, familiam, merita literaria. Amstelod. 1836. 8vo. cf. : Vita Hadriani Junii. Ex epistolis illius familiaribus, aliisque monumentis, quidquid eo pertinet, coll. G. W. ab Oosten de Bruyn (Miscellaneae observatt. criticae novae in auctores veteres et recentiores in Belgio collectae et proditae. x. xi, xii,). Amstel. 1751. 8vo.

[4] Hadr. Junii Epistolae. Dordr. 1652. 12mo.

and supported by nobody, he was compelled to return to London, where he published in 1548 the Greek Lexicon of Ceratinus, increased with nearly six thousand words. A letter of 1551 is dated again from Haarlem, but Junius wished to settle in his native place. His tonsure, however, caused him trouble there, and he was again reduced to poverty. In order to get money he wrote his Philippeis, a poem on the marriage of Philip II. and Mary of England. The hoped-for reward turned out not very princely, for he could hardly defray from it the half of the expenses of the voyage he had made to hand his poem over to Philip at London. He immortalized this delicate behaviour by the following choice comparison, which exposes all the unreasonableness of the better payment of a portrait ordered than that of unasked-for marriage hymns:—

> He who has painted the face so perishable,
> Got more for little work than he could wish;
> But he whose song gives life to princes,
> What is his reward? To return with empty hands!

In 1559, Junius resided at Haarlem, and married there M. W. Keizers. She was rich, and from that time his frequent complaints of want, and of being misunderstood, cease. He married after some years a second time with Hadriana Hasselaer, sister of the celebrated Kenau, who survived him. About 1562 he was invited by the ambassador of Frederic II. of Denmark, probably by the intercession of his friend Costerus (at that time physician in ordinary at the court of Copenhagen), to undertake the education of the crown prince. But the Danish climate and reception did not please him, and he returned without taking leave of the king. Not long after this repeated return, therefore c. 1563, he was appointed town-physician and rector of the Latin grammar school at Haarlem; this last appointment he held till 1569. On account of this appointment, Junius asked for freedom of duties on wine and foreign beer, but this request was unanimously declined by the town-council by its resolution of 23rd of November, 1564. At Haarlem he wrote his Nomenclator, a lexicon in eight languages, and the "Batavia," with which we have now to occupy ourselves. In the beginning of 1573, after the Spaniards had been besieging the town for two months, William of Orange sent for him from Delft, as the prince required medical assistance. When the town was captured his library was plundered and many of his manuscripts perished. In 1574, Boisot appointed him town-physician at Middleburg, with a liberal salary and free living in the abbey. But the climate of Zealand agreed with him as little as the Danish. He died 16th of June, 1575, at Arnemuiden, probably at the house of his sister-in-law, Kenau Hasselaer, who was married to Nanning Borst, and had for her services to her country very poetically been rewarded by the States of Holland and Zealand, among other things, by being appointed tax-gatherer of the peat at Arnemuiden. Junius's remains were transferred, four years after his death, to a church at Middleburg, where his son Petrus erected a stone to his memory, with an elaborate inscription, on which he is extolled, for instance, as the very trustworthy author of the "Batavia," and for his unlimited reading. This epitaph disappeared, but in 1842 it was (as a consequence of the Coster-literature?) renewed and simplified thus: "To the memory of Hadrianus Junius, by his learning an ornament of the sixteenth century, born at Hoorn and buried in this church, the Zealand Society of Sciences." (Ter gedachtenis van Hadrianus Junius, door zijne geleerdheid een sieraad der XVI. eeuw, geboren te Hoorn en in dit kerkgebouw begraven, het Zeeuwsch Genootschap der Wetenschappen.) When we add to this that Justus Lipsius declares him to be the most learned Netherlander after Erasmus, and Janus Douza addresses him in his Carmen inaugurale at the inauguration of the Leiden university: "Adsis alter Erasmus et secundus Nostri temporis, erudite Juni!" then at least nobody will doubt that we have in Junius an example of the learning of the sixteenth century. And now for his book.

At a meeting of the deputies of the States of Holland, which took place at the Hague, 14th of September, 1565, the president proposed, in the name of the Prince of Orange, as it was desirable to have all the matters and former events of Holland described in the form of a history, to entrust this work to a person of quality and learning, named Adriaen de Jonge, residing at Haarlem, who had been invited by other lords and princes, as the kings of Hungary, Poland, Denmark, to enter their service, but nevertheless rather remained here and be employed in the service of his native country. On that account the prince recommended him strongly to this committee, and urged that a salary should be granted him. The work would conduce to the honour and profit of the country, for it was to contain: " all its ancient histories and good descriptions of all its parts and quarters, all its situations, foundations, rights, and all that belonged to it." On the 26th of the same month the subject was discussed, as a " request of Dr. Adrianus Junius," and at the " recommendation of the Lord Stadtholder to charge him with the description of all the concerns of the country, in the form of a history, in Latin, to an overlasting memory." They put to the vote the appointment of Junius, at an annual salary of 200 pounds of 40 groots (= 200 florins). Haarlem, Delft, Leiden, and Gouda gave their consent, but Dordrecht and Amsterdam asked time for consideration ; Dordrecht wished to know further " what the nature of his work would be, and whether he would write and publish it according to his own pleasure." In answer to this question the plan was further defined as a description of " all towns, colleges, professions, deeds of the princes, compiled from other true histories, chronicles, and records, to be sent in to the States and to be arranged according to their advice." At the meeting of 17th November, Dordrecht gave its consent on condition that the money was to be found out of the taxes, and Junius should be bound to complete every year a volume of his work, but to publish nothing without permission of the States, who were to provide him with instructions. Gouda, however, withdrew, and the deputies of Amsterdam declared that they had no authority in these troublesome times to give their consent in anything respecting this matter, or to burden the country with it. Nor did they feel inclined to be bound by a vote of the majority. Therefore again no decision. On the 5th February, 1566, Amsterdam and Gouda gave their consent in so far that they submitted to letting Junius begin to " make something," in order to remunerate him properly after the completion. Junius began to write, but the payment failed already after the first year. At least there appears a request of his at the sitting of 13th March, 1570, begging payment of the pension, granted to him by the States in 1566, of 200 guilders a-year, as he had now finished and handed over to the States Primum Tomum Historiæ Bataviæ. It was deferred to the next sitting. On the 4th of April there was " great difficulty " about the request; they wished to have the first two hundred guilders regarded simply as a gratuity to induce Junius to begin the work, but not to be bound to an annual salary; nor did they think it advisable to publish such a History at that time, dedicated to the States, and which in any case should be examined by competent persons. But because Junius had incurred much work and expenses, they proposed to grant him for once a sum of two or three hundred guilders. " Opinion of Gouda. Is resolved that they should refuse Dr. Junius the pension he had requested, and pay him for the work done." After long deliberations they at last, on the 11th April, decided with a majority of votes to pay him by way of gratuity three hundred guilders, to prohibit him from publishing the first volume of his work with a dedication to the States, and to free him from continuing his work.[1]

Thus originated, between the years 1566 and 1570, the " Batavia," doomed to remain imperfect ; a work solicited by the author, ordered, not without opposition, by government at the intercession of the Stadtholder, in order to procure Junius a salary which would keep him in the country. These animating causes have given birth to a miserable book,[2] the more miserable because the work of Guicciardini, which was infinitely better, could already have been used by him. I know that most people, if

---

[1] Brief van A. de Vries aan A. D. Schinkel, over Guichard's Notice sur le Speculum humanae salvationis, met drie bylagen tot staving der naauwkeurigheid van het verhaal van Junius wegens de uitvinding der boekdrukkunst en ter wederlegging der meening : dat Coster koster zou geweest zyn. 's Hage. 1841. 8vo.

[2] Hadriani Jvnii Hornani, Batavia. In qua praeter gentis & insulae antiquitatem, originem, decora, aliaque ad eam historiam pertinancia, declaratur quae fuerit vetus Batauia, &c. Ex. off. Plantiniana. 1588. 4to. Reprinted in 1652.

there are some who would like to enjoy this "grand production of the mind," will succumb to the struggle, and I will therefore justify my opinion.

P. Scheltema, in his life of Saint Junius, says: "It appears unintelligible to some that the 'Batavia,' a work of such an extent and marvellous learning, was finished in the space of a few years." Nothing is more unintelligible to me than this want of comprehension on the part of some persons. The Batavia is simply one of those uncritical compilations, productions of mere book-learning, compiled according to the prescription of book-making: take three books and make a fourth of it. How little the historical value of the book is, is evident even to the most obstinate, when we see that Scriverius—observe: Scriverius, who was going to wreathe a laurel, in 1628, for the hero of the Haarlem story—published in 1611 the work of the geographer Cluverius, and admitted in this book without contradiction: "Hadrianus Junius melior medicus quam geographus aut historicus, male Batavorum fineis descripsit." One glance on the list, at the commencement of the book, of the authors used, quoted, and mentioned by Junius, among whom not even Jamblichus and Sextus Empiricus are wanting, is sufficient to give us a foretaste of the mish-mash which is given here as the history of the Netherlands. The "marvellous learning" of very cheap alloy, is only a musty classification, a show of mere formal Greek-Latin school knowledge, which chases away all that is fresh and alive. *Such* learning is calculated to make any one shudder, *such* a scholar hides himself under dust. I do not exaggerate. Or is Junius, for instance, in the description of his native town, satisfied with saying that it produces hoorn carrots (radices bulbosiores, Hornanæ dictæ). Oh no; we are to know also that Plinius says that Tiberius was so fond of them, that he every year sent for them from Rome to the castle Gelduba, situated on the Rhine. How marvellously learned and well-read, but how withered are at once those radices hornanæ! Junius describes the town of Edam. We hear in a few words that our forefathers called it Ydam after Ya or Yda, formerly a river; that it was celebrated for the quality of its cheeses (caseorum bonitate), and that there was an excellent wharf. Oh heaven, they built also ships in ancient times! Yes, that wharf of Edam, that fine wharf, quae digna iudices vbi Hieronis nauis illa, quam Alexandriam nominauit, mons verius quam nauis, fabricaretur; tanta mole ac capacitate fabricata isthic nauigia, summa naupegorum industria, in maris sinum deducuntur vt non minore in admiratione sit horum habenda industria, quam Philcæ Taurominitani, qui Hieroniam illam deduxit, aut quam Dioclidis Abderitæ, quod Helepolim immanis magnitudinis machinam ad oppugnandam Rhodum adduxisset.—Edam, Hiero, Alexandria, Philcas Taurominitanus, Diocles Abderites—and what is more classical: Edam is situated, by water as well as land, two miles from Hoorn. The climax would make you faint, and the revenues of the taxes were sometimes spent in a very wrong way, and two hundred pounds per annum of forty groots was marvellously expensive for this marvellous learning. "Well and good, but Junius is not above the bad taste of his time." Of course, neither is he above the superstition of his time, nor above the total want of his time of an accurate notion of history. And therefore we shall have to look very sharply to what is served up to us by this learned cook, but who does not understand cooking. Extensive reading is no science, a stuffed head is not necessarily a clear head, a faithful memory not yet a keen judgment. Even in our time, a learned is often mistaken for a scientific treatment. What is learned is on that account alone not yet scientific. Learning is only one of the indispensable component parts of science; but science itself is the unity and the fruit of knowledge, the result of a critical examination of the materials in store. Learning alone is a matter of memory, and establishes a literary huckster's shop; science is an action of judgment, and builds a cathedral. Learning is the fruit of zeal and patience; science a fruit of passion and character. In short, simple learning creates confusion, science creates order. The judgment required for this task we observe nowhere in the so-called historian Junius. On the contrary: when fables had only in their favour, that they had been written before him, or that their remembrance was still fresh, or that the "women" seemed attached to them, or that the story was guaranteed by—a painted board! it was a sufficient reason for our jobber to translate the gossip and to hand it down to "posterity." We have nothing to do with his social respectability and domestic trustworthiness, which are always pointed like pistols to our breast to make us succumb to his written fiddlefaddles. I am very willing to believe that Dr. Junius did not purposely poison one of his patients; but I am on that account not compelled to accept that the expenses for the building of the church at Dordrecht were paid by the virgin Soter, who possessed three pennies which always returned to her purse. I doubt not for one moment that Junius answered always honestly and to the point, when any one asked him the time; but it does not enter my head to believe on his authority that the Haarlemers captured Damiate. I am at once ready to suppose that the author of the Batavia has been very amiable, first to Wilhelmina and afterwards to Jenny; but that for that reason a ship with eleven thousand virgins from England had arrived in the port of Verona, a town which existed somewhere in the neighbourhood of Alkmaar, but has disappeared altogether—I take the liberty to accept such things as stories. Again: I take "Erasmus Secundus" to be an extremely learned, very honest man, but that the stone in the church of St. Pancras at Leiden has formerly been a loaf, changed at once by an imprecation—this transubstantiation Adriaen de Jonghe must relate when he rocks little Peter de Jonghe on his knee. And am I to speak of the miracle of Loosduinen—of the delivery of Margaret, Countess of Hennenberg, whose 365 babies make you think of an upset pot of shrimps? I know that people have been insolent enough to say that Junius calls this case a "partus incredibilis," an "omnem fidem superans miraculum," but they forgot to say that he adds to the first expression, "nisi publici monumenti autoritatem conuellere," &c., and afterwards says more distinctly, "Nos tabulae pensilis, quae in Losdunensi fano rei memoriae consecrata est, fidem sequimur." They, moreover, forgot to mention that he does not apply that "omnem fidem superans miraculum" to the Loosduin miracle, but to a similar prolific birth, related elsewhere, where the 350 babies were baptized according to the decision of the Sorbonne. But I leave to others a radical faith in wonders, and have no inclination to encounter Junius on clerical ground. I wish nothing but the acknowledgment that his standpoint has not necessarily to be ours; that the distinction between the man and his scientific judgment may not be imputed as a crime against the personal character of the author. When Junius derives Duyvenvoorde from *duw roort* (push on)! or says of Haga Comitis that it signifies "sepes e spinis dumisque opere topiario facta," I take the liberty to call this pedant amusement, albeit surrounded by panegyrics, epitaphs, and obsolete flatteries, ridiculous. Foolish etymologies remain foolish, even if they are served up by an honest man.[1]

When the Costerian Vlaming, in his edition of the "Hartspieghel,"[2] feels already bound to acknowledge that Junius was "somewhat addicted to childish fables and trifling gossip," then we claim at least the not very radical right of judging his stories without being persecuted with prolix and tiresome arguments on the "credibility of Junius." "*Ein Geist der stets bejaht*" is as superficial as "*der Geist der stets verneint*." As for the rest, there is no educated man in our time but is, at least with respect to a purely historical question, above the authority of an unproved tradition or legend. He who is satisfied, as regards a *fact* like that of the invention of typography, with a simple *assertion* of people who talk of things which are said to have happened more than a century before their time, is destitute of scientific morality; he is ignorant of the passion of truth; in short, he belongs to the plebeians. Therefore we have not only the *right* to reject the fable, fabricated by Junius on the pedigree

---

[1] On this dominion of his particular amusement, Junius is bold enough to criticize, and ludicrous is then the acuteness of his polemics. After having expatiated on the derivation of Leiden, and disapproving that of Noviomagus from Geleide, he continues: "quae conficta risum etiam ipsi illi Crasso, qui Agelastos dictus est, excutere posse putarim. a leo nullum tam impudens est mendacium, quod affertore careat." (Gerardus Noviomagus seems to have committed not only etymological, but also historical, errors; at least he writes, in 1520: "Et, ut quod verum est addam, maxima omnium saeculorum inventa Germanorum sunt; bombarda videlicet, Typographia, pyxis chartaque nautica." Published, without any contradiction, in 1611, by — Scriverius!)

[2] H. L. Spieghels Hartspieghel en andere Zedeschriften . . . Door P. Vlaming. Amsterd. 1730. 8vo.

of his friend and fellow-believer Gerri' Thomasz., with so many other stories of his Batavia, but as honest men we are b*und* to do it.

The said story runs as follows: "In the year 1440 a certain *Lourens Janszoon Coster* lived at Haarlem, a man who 128 years afterwards, by the mouth of Hadrianus Junius, reclaims the honour of having invented the art of printing, an honour unjustly robbed and possessed by others. The said *Lourens Coster* took one day after dinner (sumpto cibo), or on a feast-day, a walk in the "Hout" (a wood near Haarlem), and began to cut letters in the bark of a beech. He printed these letters reversed (sigillatim) on paper, and thus made, out of amusement, some lines, which were to serve as copies to his grandchildren. When this succeeded, he invented a better ink (more gluey and substantial than the common, which blotted too much,) assisted by his son-in-law (gener) *Thomas Pieterszoon*, who left four children (liberos), who nearly all held the dignity of burgomaster. Coster began afterwards to print whole sheets with pictures, to which he added the letters. Junius has seen a specimen of this printing, a book in the Dutch language, of an unknown author, entitled, "Spieghel onzer behoudenis (Speculum nostræ salutis)." This first production of the art was, as no invention is at once perfected (nunquam simul & reperta & absoluta), anopisthographic (printed on one side only), but they had concealed this unsightliness by pasting the backs of the leaves on each other. Afterwards (postea) Coster changed his letters (formas) to leaden ones, and these again to tin ones, in order that they might be more solid and lasting. From the remainder of these last letters winepots were made, which at the time of Junius were still to be seen in Coster's house, afterwards inhabited by his great-grandson (pronepos) *Gerrit Thomaszoon*, a respectable citizen, who died a few years ago in very advanced age, and mentioned, honoris causa, by Junius. The curiosity of the public was, as is generally the case, awakened by the news of the invention; the new merchandise, which they had never seen before, attracted purchasers from every side and produced great profits, whereby the love for the art became greater, the business was extended, and they were obliged to engage more men. But this was also a source of evil. Among the workmen, namely, was a certain Johannes; whether he was called Faust, as some suppose, or whether he was another Johannes, Junius will not scrupulously investigate this matter, *i.e.* he insinuates distinctly whom he means, but thinks it safer not to speak plainly. Now this John, sworn as printer, waited until he thought he knew the art of composition and casting, and everything which belonged to the business, perfectly. Arrived at that point, he took a fit opportunity [in 1441]—namely, Christmas-night, when all Christians used to go to the Holy Mass—broke into the printing-office, took the store of types and tools, manufactured with so much ingenuity by his master (choragium omne typorum invòlat, instrumentorum herilium ei artificio comparatorum convasat), and left the house with his booty as a thief. He fled by Amsterdam and Cologne to Mentz, where he opened a workshop and reaped the fruits of his theft. For it is certain that within a year after this event, in 1442, this Mentz printing-office published with the types of Coster: 1. The Doctrinale of Alexander Gallus, a grammar very famous and generally used at that time; 2. Tractatus of Petrus Hispanus. All this Junius says he had heard from old trustworthy people, as, among others, from *Claes [Lottynszoon] Gael*, a respectable old man with a retentive memory. A second authority is the burgomaster *Quiryn [Dirkszoon] Talesius*. These two persons knew a certain bookbinder, *Cornelis*, an old man of more than eighty years of age, who had been servant (sub-minister) in the workshop of Lourens Coster, had slept with the culprit John for several months in one bed, and could never speak of the affair without bursting into tears and into the most passionate imprecations against the villain who had so shamefully robbed his master's honour. Now, Junius is afraid that he will sing before the house of a deaf man; but, however this may be, he delights in having vindicated with all his power the memory of the inventor and the glory of the town of Haarlem. For among careless people, who do not desire to investigate the truth, prejudice will always prevail over sound reasoning and strong evidence (!). This misfortune has to be put up with, however hard it may be and however the people may complain about it. *This loss would be less painful if our glory had been transmitted to one of the celebrated towns of Germany by straightforward means, and not by theft.*

In the proceding translation I have given, without troubling myself about later exogetic falsifications of the text, the *real* meaning and the *true* coherence of the story of Junius, of which any one may convince himself, besides from the original text,[1] from translations by Boot,[2] Le Petit,[3] Van Meteren,[4] Montanus (by Guicci-

[1] Redeo ad vrbem nostram, cui primam inuentæ isthic artis typographicæ gloriam deberi, & summo iure asserendam aio, vtpote propriam & natiuam: sed luminibus nostris sola officit inueterata illa & quæ encausti modo inscripta est animis opinio, tam altis innixa radicibus, quas nulli ligones, nulli cunei, nulla rutra reuellere aut eruere valeant, quâ pertinaciter credunt, & persuasissimum habent apud Magonticum claram & vetustam Germaniæ vrbem primò repertas literarum formulas quibus excuderentur libri. Vtinam hic incredibilem illam dice(n)di vim, quæ in Carneade fuisse perhibetur, voto exoptare possem, qui nihil defendisse vnquam, quod no probarit, nihil oppugnasse, quod non euerterit, dicitur; vt saltem refugam illam laudem postliminio reuocare, & hoc quasi trophæum erigere possem, veri interpolator: quod ego non alio optarim, quàm vt veritas rectè à Poëta vetere Temporis filia nuncupata, aut (vt ego soleo) χρόνου ἔλεγχος, tandem detegatur, quæque iuxta Democritu, altissimo in puteo demersa hactenus delituit, in apertum proferatur. Si gloriosum certame(n) suscipere non piguit Ægyptios & Phœnicas de literarum inuentione, his Deo duce earum inuentum ad se trahentibus, quando tabulas θεοχαράκτους, hoc est, à Deo exaratas iactant: illis à se reportas Græciæ intulisse gloriantibus, quando Cadmus Phœnicum classe vectus, rudibus Græcorum populis artis illius auctor, eas commonstrauit. Rursus si Athenienses Cecropi suo, Thebani Lino, eandem laudem vindicant. Palamedi Argiuo excogitatorum characterum gloriam Tacitus & Philostratus deferunt: vt Hyginius Latinorum Carmentæ Euandri matri. Si itaque controuersam dubiamque gloriam cunctæ gentes ad se ceu propriam rapere non erubuerunt, quid vetat quo minus indubitandæ laudis possessionem, de qua per socordia(m) auitam (!) exturbati sumus, quasi postliminij iure (!) repetamus? Equidem non inuidia, aut maleuolentiæ studio transuersus agor, vt huic asseram, quod alteri derogem ac detraham. Crassi impudentia(m) non imitabor, hinc Scæuolæ sanctimoniam & grauitatem affecta(n)do, illinc prehensationibus fauorem hominum eblandiendo: haud is sum, corruptis arbitrijs planum agere non decreui, veritatem illam vnam perspicuam, quam vti cœleste Solis iubar, nulla nox, nulla caligo quantumuis alta obtenebrare potest, exhibiturus, quantum in me est, idque simplici ac minimè fucato orationis filo, quod illa amat. Quòd si optimus ille testis est, auctore Plutarcho, qui nullo obstrictus beneficio, neque alterius addictus studio, liberè quod sentit loquitur & intrepidè, meum testimonium meritò locum habent, qui nec mortuu(m) aut hæredes posterosve cognatione attingam, neq. gratiam aut beneficium inde expectem, qui quicquid huius feci, id totum sepultis Manibus pictatis ergò impendi. Dicam igitur quod accepi à senibus & auctoritate grauibus, & Reipub. administratione claris, quique à maioribus suis ita accepisse gnauissimo testimonio confirmarunt, quorum auctoritas iure pondus habere debeat ad faciendam fidem. Habitauit ante annos centum duodetriginta Harlemi in ædibus satis splendidis (vt documento esse potest fabrica quæ in hunc vsque diem perstat integra) foro imminentibus è regione Palatij Regalis, LAVRENTIVS Ioannes cognomento Æditues Custósve (quod tunc opimum & honorificum munus familia eo nomine clara hæreditario iure possidebat), is ipse qui nunc laudem inuentæ artis Typographicæ residiua(m) iustis vindicijs ac sacramentis repetit, ab alijs nefariè possessam & occupatam, summo iure omnium triumphorum laurea maiore donandus. Is fortè in suburbano nemore spatiatus (vt solent sumpto cibo aut festis diebus ciues qui otio abunda(n)t), cœpit faginos cortices principio in literarum typos conformare, quibus inuersa ratione sigillatim chartæ impressis versiculum vnum atque alterum animi gratia ducebat, nepotibus generi sui liberis exemplum futurum. Quod vbi feliciter successerat, cœpit animo altiora (vt erat ingenio magno & subacto) agitare, primumque omnium atramenti scriptorij genus glutinosius tenaciusque, quod vulgare lituras trahere experiretur, cum genero suo Thoma Petro, qui quaternos liberos reliquit omnes fernè consulari dignitate functos (quod eò dico vt artem in familia honesta & ingenua, haud seruili, natam intelligant omnes) excogitauit, inde etiam pinaces totas figuratas additis characteribus expressit, quo in genere vidi ab ipso excusa Aduersaria, operarum rudimentum paginis solùm aduersis, haud opistographis: is liber erat vernaculo sermone ab auctore conscriptus anonymo, titulu(m) præferens, Speculum nostræ salutis, in quibus id obscuratum fuerat inter prima artis incunabula (vt nunquam vlla simul & reperta & absoluta est) vti paginæ auersæ glutine commissæ cohærescerent, ne illæ ipsæ vacuæ deformitatem adferrent. Postea faginas formas plumbeis mutauit, has deinceps stanneas fecit, quò solidior minusque flexilis esset materia, durabiliorque: è quorum typorum reliquijs quæ superfuerant conflata œnophorum vetustiora adhuc hodie visuntur in Laurentianis illis, quas dixi, ædibus in forum prospectantibus, habitatis postea à suo pronepote Gerardo Thoma, quem honoris caussa nomino, ciue claro, ante paucos hos annos vita defuncto sene. Fauentibus, vt fit, inuento nouo studijs hominum, quum noua merx, nunquam antea visa, emptores vndique exciret cum hubcrrimo quæstu, creuit simul artis amor, creuit ministerium, additi familiæ operarum ministri, prima mali labes, quos inter Ioannes quidam, siue is (vt fert suspicio) Faustus fuerit ominoso cognomine, hero suo infidus & infaustus, siue alius eo nomine, non magnopere laboro (!), quòd silentum vmbras inquietare nolim, contagione co(n)scientiæ quondam dum viuerent tactas. Is ad operas excusorias sacramento dictus, postquam artem iungendorum characterum, fusilium typorum peritiam, quæque alia cum ad rem spectant, percalluisse sibi visus est, captato opportuno tempore, qui non potuit magis idoneum inueniri, ipsa nocte quae Christi natalitijs solennis est, qua cuncti promiscuè lustralibus sacris operari solent, choragium omne typorum inuolnt, instrumentorum herilium ei artificio comparatorum supellectilem conuasat, deinde cum fure domo se proripit, Amstelodamum principiò adit, inde Coloniam Agrippinam, donec Magonticum peruentum est, ceu ad asyli aram, vbi quasi extra telorum iactum (quod dicitur) positus tutò degeret, suorumque furtorum aperta officina fructum huberem meteret. Nimirum ex ea, intra vertentis anni spacium, ad annum à nato Christo 1442. ijs ipsis typis, quibus Harlemi Laurentius fuerat vsus, prodisse in lucem certu(m) est Alexandri Galli doctrinale, quae Grammatica celeberrimo tunc in vsu erat, cum Petri Hispani tractatibus, prima fœtura. Ista sunt fermè

ardini),⁵ Scriverius, Koning, Schaab, Wetter, Bernard,⁶ Berjeau,⁷ Pacile.⁸ We quae à senibus annosis fide dignis, & qui tradita de manu in manum quasi ardentem tædam in decursu acceperant, olim intellexi, & alios eadem referentes attestantesq. comperi. Memini narrasse mihi Nicolaum Galium, pueritiae meæ formatorem, hominem ferrea memoria & longa canitie venerabilem, quòd puer non semel audierit Cornelium quendam bibliopegum ac senio grauem, nec octogenario minorem (qui in eadem officina subministrum egerat) tanta animi contentione ac feruore commemorantem rem gestae seriem, inuenti (vt ab hero acceperat) rationem, rudis artis polituram & incrementum, aliaque id genus vt inuito quoque præ rei indignitate lachrymæ erumperent, quoties de plagio inciderat mentio: tum verò ob ereptam furto gloriam sic ira exardescere solere canebat, vt etiam lictoris exemplum eum fuisse editurum in plagiarium appareret, si vita illi superfuisset : tum deuouere consueuisse diris vltricibus sacrilegum caput, noctesque illas damnare atque execrari, quas vnâ cum scelere illo, communi in cubili per aliquot menses exegisset. Quae non dissonant à verbis Quirini Talesij Cos. eadem ferè ex ore librarij eiusdem se olim accepisse mihi confessi. Ista dictare me compulit cupiditas & studium defendendæ veritatis, quamuis illa odium sui plœrunque parere soleat : in qua tuenda potiùs quàm vt deserere vadimonium velim, ad suscipiendum odium paratior sim ac promptior. Nam istud facilè ponent, qui rem ipsam sincerè ac candidè indagabu(n)t & expende(n)t, tanquam in Critolai bilance appensam : at Veritatis, quæ Dei imago quædam est, qui non libenter patrocinium suscipiat, vix hominis appellationem mereri existimo, cuius cura atque amore nihil cuiquam vel sanctius vel antiquius esse debet. Tuendo veritatem & constabit suus vrbi nostræ honos, in cuius ereptam innocentis pulcherrimae gloriam recuperatumæ, & cadet eorum arrogantia, quos falsam alienæ gloriæ hæreditatem cernere non puduit, & quasi deiectis de ponte sexagenarijs alieni iuris possessionem superbè vsurparunt. At vereor vt surdis ista auribus canantur : vtcunque tamen erit, iuuabit me & memoriae inuentoris & gloriæ vrbis pro virili consuluisse, dum apud leues & veri incuriosos animos plus valet præiudicium opinionis (quod antea quoque testatus sum) quàm cum ratione auctoritas. Quæ iniuria mussitanda est & deuora(n)da parum lubentibus. Quanquam dolendum minùs foret eam laudem in clarissimam Germaniæ vrbem, velut aliam in familiam, transisse. si non plagio, sed recta ratione factum id fuisset. Verùm arbitror fatis volentibus hanc viam commodissimam visam, vti citissimè ad nitorem suum ac perfectionis culmen perueniret inuentum illud, orbi sale (quod dicitur) & sole magis necessarium in maiore luce hominu(m), per studia, magnatu(m) præmia, & honores (quibus artes aluntur) faciliùs emersurum, vti accidisse res docuit, quàm in extremo orbis terrarum secessu quodam & recondito angulo, inter hominum priuatorum sordes.

² Beschrijvinge vande Ghemuyrde ende Onghemuyrde Steden ende Vlecken van Holland ende West-Vriesland. In't Latijn door D. Adrianum Junium. Ende Verduytscht door Godefr. Boot. Delf. 1609. 4to.

³ La grande chroniqve anciene et moderne, de Hollande, Zelande, &c., jusques à la fin de l'An 1600. Recteillee tant des histoires desdites Provinces, que de divers autres Auteurs, par Jean François le Petit. Tome Premier. 1601. Dordrecht. Folio.—The text on the Haarlem legend is a curious mixture of Guicciardini, Junius, and Vergilius :—

"En ce temps [1453!] l'Art d'Imprimerie & la faco(n) de soudre les lettres & caractères pour imprimer en fetüille, ainsi qu'a present on use par tout l'Europe fut inventée en la ville de Harlem en Hollande, comme ceux de la ville s'en vantent, & quelques Autheurs en font mention. Mais l'Inventeur venant à Mourir avant que l'art fut en sa perfection, son serviteur (ainsi qu'on dit) s'en alla demourer à Mayence : où mettant c'este science nesessaire en public & lumiere fut receuüe ioyeusement, & la mettant en oeuvre avec diligence, on luy donna telle & si entiere perfection pour la cognossance qu'en travaillant ils en acquirent, que depuis on l'a estimé, & le bruit à couru par tout, que ce fut à Mayence que ceux de Harlem en afferment."

Thus far Le Petit translates Guicciardini literally : but after this he puts the fable of Junius between the text :—

"Il y avoit en la ville de Harlem un honorable Citoyen nommé Laurent Janson, dit le Coustre (qui estoit lors un honorable & profitable office hereditaire à sa famille), cestuy cy demouroit en une belle maison à l'opposite du Palais Royal (dont la structure en fait encore foy pour le iourdhuy). Vn iour Laurent estant au bois ioighant la ville se pourmenant apres soupper (comme c'estoit lors la coustume des bo(n)s bourgeois menans vie oyeuse) print de l'escorce de faulx de laquelle il s'amusa à tailler quelques lettres, lesquelles renversees il prenoit plaisir de presser sur du papier, & voyant que cela marquoit à droit, il continua d'en tailler en ceste façon tant qu'il en fit pour un vers entier, lesquels voyant avoir ainsi prins marque, pour en laisser quelques memoire à la posterité de ses enfans (!), comme chose nouvelle, il plongea lesdits caracteres en de l'encre l'un devant l'autre apres & ainsi les imprimoit sur le papier : puis pour le faire commodement lioit des mots tous entiers ensamble : ce que voyant ainsi succeder & que l'encre co(m)mune estant par trop fluide maculoit le papier ; ayde de son gendre Thomas Pietersz lequel eut espose d'une autre fils lesquels ont tous esté Bourgmaistres de la ville de Harlem (pour monstrer qu'une si noble science n'a point este inventee par des esprits serviles, & mechaniques) ils inventerent une autre sorte d'encre plus espoisse, & glueuse puis continuerent si bien leur invention (comme l'ouvrage apprend l'ouverir) qu'ils trouverent moyen de iondre de tels caracteres l'un parmy l'autre iusques à une Page entiere, qu'ils imprimoyent seulement d'un costé. & dont s'en voyent encore les impressio(n)s en ladicte ville de Harlem qui ont esté curieusement gardees en la maison (!) dudit Laurent par les arrierere nepveux de Thomas Pieterse(n) so(n) gendre.

"Apres qu'ils eurent cognu que cest art etoit seur en bois, ils en firent de plomb puis d'estain, & finalement trouve la science d'imprimer à deux costez (!) comme on fait encore : tenant leur art secrette : & comme chose si nouvelle, & si noble plaisoit à tout le monde que chacun en vouloit avoir, & que ce qu'ils avoyent co(m)mencé par plaisir croissoit en proufit, il leur covint avoir ces serviteur pour les aydes, & servir, soubs serment de n'en rien apprendre ny reveler à personne. Mais le malheur leur advint, qu'e(n)tre ces serviteurs un Iean (qu'aucuns disent auoir este ce Faustus) comme l'arron perivre, & desloyal aya(n) aprins tout ce qu'il eut sceu appre(n)dre en c'est art, espiant le semps la veille de Noel, que chacun estoit à l'Eglise, desrobba l'instrumens, & la science (!) de son Maistre, & senfuyt à Amsterdam, de la à Cologne puis à Mayence, ou se sentant estre en seureté, il mit finalement à en faire profession & à

need, of course, not trouble ourselves about the obsolete capucinade (translated, for

tenir boutique ouverte, Messire Adric(n) le icune Medecin renommé de la ville de Home en West-Frise, dit en son livre, *De Bataria*, avoir veu en langue vulgaire de ces premieres i(m)pressions d'un costé en la ville de Harlem. Dit outre avoir oüy dire de son Maistre d'Escole nommé Nicolas Galle, homme de gra(n)de memoire, & d'une venerable vielesse, que quand ledit Galle etoit encore icune, il auroit entendu d'un certain Cornille Imprimeur (!) à l'imprimerie dudit Laurent Ianson Inventeur : comment cest art avoir esté premierement trouvée (comme nous avons dit), depuis pollie, & decorée, & prins son accroissement, ce qu'il disoit avec telle ardeur que quand il faisoit mention du Larron, il ploureroit, & se tourmentoit par telle façon qu'il souhaittoit de pouvoir estre bourreau pour le prendre s'il estoit à recouvrer, se maugreant, & Despitant d'avoir iamais demeuré en un même seruice, avec luy, & couche en une mesme chambre."

Thus far from Junius. Ludicrous is now the quotation from Guicciardini which follows immediately afterwards:—

"Or ic ne veux ny ne peux temerairement iuger de la verite de ceste chose, me suffisant d'avoir escrit ce que dessus pour ne faire tort à la ville de Harlem ny au Pays de Hollande si ic suprimoye une chose qu'ils afferment : se plaignans du tort qu'on leur fait de le vouloir attribuer à autruy, pour les priver d'un tel honneur, qu'ils maintiennent leur estre premiereme(n)t deu. Touteffois, voyons ce qu'en dit Polidore Vergile en son livre des, *Inventeurs des Choses.* Iean de Guttenbergh (dit il) gentilhomme Alleman, & honoré du titre de Chevalier (ainsi que l'avons entendu de ceux de son Pays) fut le premier qui en la Cite de Mayence trouva, & inventa l'art D'imprimer les livres, & auant tout autre exerca ceste science : & lequel avec non moindre esprit, & industrie (ainsi qu'on dit) fut inventeur de l'encre de laquelle on use à imprimer. Ces mots de Polidore ne sont pas encore assez bastands pour demonster que Guttenberch en ayt esté tout le premier inventeur. Mais est à presupposer que le Larron Iean fauste (!) ne l'ozant de soy mesme manifester, craignant que son larcin ne fut descouvert, & luy puny selon son merite, l'auroit enseigne à Guttenberch, qui par ces grands moyens l'auroit fait valoir, & tout à coup abondamment mis en lumiere.

"Mais ceux de Royaume de China Disent que ces art est tiree de leur Inventio(n) premiere, pour quelqu'un qu'ils adorent co(m)me un deleurs dieux. Et que leurs ancestres traficquans avec les Roxolaves (qui sont Russes) & Moschonites, & cherchans les haures, & ports commodes de l'Europa, aucuns Allemans (mais plustost Hollandois lesquels comme nous avons dit plusieurs fois cy devant, ont esté souvent nommez Allemans, & qui sont aussi plus familiers de la mer & de longs voyages que nuls autres Allemans) les ayans suivy par la mer Erithrée, & par l'Arrabie estre venu en China, en auroy eut emporté quelques livres imprimez, lesquels seroyent tombez es mains de Gutenberch ou plustost que Laurens Janson luy mesme auroit fait ce voiage (!), & rapporté lesdicts livres (sans neautmoins scavoir comment ils auroyent esté faicts) pour une nouveauté, dont depuis il en auroit puise & tire l'art comme nous avons dit : car apparemment il pouvoit remarquer si ceste impressio(n) estoit taillée sur une planche entiere, ou bien si elle estoit imprimée par pièces (!), qui l'auroit fait penser à un si petit commencement d'espreuve comme nous avons dit, que depuis est tombe ez mains de Gutte(n)berch par le moyen dudit Larron. Ce que si ainsi comme les Chinois le descrive(n)t en leurs histoires : il s'ensuyt necessairement que l'art d'imprimer est parvenu d'eux iusqs à nous : de ta(n)t plus que ceux qui ont haute au Pays de China (dont y à plusieurs Hollandois) & en ont descrit leur voyage & particularité, tesmoignent y avoir veu des livres imprimez plus de cinq cents ans (si on doit croire les Chinois) devant que l'invention fut iamais cogniue ez Pays de pardeca. Quoy qu'il en soy ie m'en rapporte à la verite."

This childish rhapsody, for Costerian purposes usually cited by extracts only, ought to be known in full, to understand at once its scientific worthlessness. De Vries, who perused the book of Le Petit, and in 1823 even derived "four workmen of Koster" from it, was in 1843 bold enough to tell Europe: "De sorte que quand l'ancienne tradition (!) généralement répendue nous represente Coster, recevant la première idée de son invention pendant une promenade qu'il faisait dans le Bois avec ses petit-fils, qu'il amusait et qu'il exerceit à épeler en imprimant sur le sable (!, des lettres de bois détachées, puis les induisant d'encre pour les reporter sur le papier, — elle s'accorde parfaitement avec les paroles mêmes de Junius (!) et sert à les confirmer (!). Et le récit de Petitræus ou le Petit, contemporain de Junius et qui avait sûrement puisé dans d'autres sources la mention de l'invention de l'imprimerie de Coster (!!), met l'affaire entièrement hors de doute (!!!)."

⁴ *Commentarien ofte Memorien Van den Nederlandtschen Staat, Handel, Oorloghen, etc. Beschreven door Emanvel van Meteren. Ghedruckt op Schotlandt buyten Danswijck, by Hermes van Loven.* Voor den Autheur. Folio. The Haarlem legend was not yet inserted by Van Meteren in the Latin edition (Amsterdam, 1597), nor in the first Dutch ed. (Delft, 1599) ; but it appears in the edition of 1608. Van Meteren, a relative of the geographer Abr. Ortelius, died at London in 1612. His version of Junius' account shows a remarkable falsification : "The invention of printing is justly ascribed to Haarlem, which is perfectly proved by many signs and evidences, viz., that c. 1440, now about 160 years ago, there lived at Haarlem an honest man, named Laurents de Coster, who, often taking a walk in the Haarlem wood and meditating, cut some bark of beeches, on which he cut the figures of some letters reversely, in order to print them in the right way on paper, which letters he put together, first to a word, then to a verse, and so printed a number of lines for the benefit of his friends and descendants. But, as this was done so handsomely, he began to pay more attention to it, and invented, together with his son-in-law Thomas Pietersz., who left four sons, who have nearly all been burgomasters of Haarlem, a thicker, more sticky black ink, and having cut a sufficient quantity of letters, printed now some things, and also a Dutch book, ent. ' den Spieghel onser salicheyt,' which we have seen ourselves, and is still to be seen at Jacob Cool's, heir of Abrah. Ertelius, who possessed it for a long time. They had then no idea of printing a leaf on both sides, but on one side, and pasted the leaves together, as we may see in this book. Afterwards they cast letters of lead, thereupon of tin, to make them stronger, of which the tools and instruments (!) are still to be seen at Haarlem, in the house of the aforesaid Laurents de Coster, in the Market Place. As this invention began to be profitable to the inventers, they kept many servants, to enjoy in secret the profits of this invention, among whom one named Jan Faustus, who, after he had seen the art, and learned

instance, by Paoilo), with which Junius begins his story; we have never seen that the strongest assertions by all that is sacred, in whatever language they are put, are really the strongest proofs of any one's love for truth. He who swears, Calvin says, does not prove that he is right, but what he dares to do.

composition and the manufacture of letters, unfaithfully packed up, on a Christmas night, the type and the chief tools, and went with them to Amsterdam, hence to Cologne, and so to Mentz, where he got settled and printed, in 1442, with the letters of Laurents de Coster, a little book, called Doctrinale Alexandri Galli, and a treatise of Petrus Hispanus. From that time others exercised and improved this art, especially a certain Johan Tuthenbergius (?), of knightly origin, and was further propagated. . . As an evidence of the truth, Hadrianus Junius writes in his Batavia, that his schoolmaster Nicolaus Gallus, an old man, told him that he had often talked with a certain Cornelis, a bookseller, more than eighty years of age, who had been himself a servant and workman in the house of Laurents de Coster, and slept with the thief in one room and bed at the time when this Johan Faustus robbed him of the type and tools."

Van Meteren has perused, besides Junius, also Le Petit, according to the quotation from Vergilius. He confuses the "winepots" of Gerrit Thomasz. with "tools." He has computed the year 1440 rightly enough; but the workman Cornelis was, at the time of the theft, not yet or hardly born.

[5] Belgium dat is: Nederlandt, ofte Beschrijvinghe derselviger provincien ende steden. Eerst in 't licht gegeven door M. Lowys Gvicciardyn. Ende nu weder met veel byvoegselen, schoone Land-Caerten, &c., vermeerderd. Amstelodami. 1648. Folio.

[6] De l'origine et des débuts de l'imprimerie, par Aug. Bernard. Paris. 1853. 8vo. II.

With the revolution, caused in bibliography by the removal of Costerianism, the unproved arguments of Bernard, in the first vol. of his work, fall to the ground. For instance, at the commencement: "Depuis bien longtemps déjà l'on disserte sur l'origine de l'imprimerie, sans qu'on ait pu s'entendre encore ni sur l'époque précise de cette invention, ni même sur la nation à laquelle en doit revenir l'honneur: c'est qu'en réalité ce n'est ni à une année ni à un peuple qu'elle appartient; elle est due aux progrès de la civilisation, et toutes les générations ont rapporté successivement leur contingent à la réalisation de cette précieuse industrie, devenue au XVe siècle une véritable nécessité, et, par conséquent, l'objet des recherches directes de beaucoup de personnes. . . . Plusieurs tentatives eurent lieu dans ce but: il n'y eut pas un seul inventeur de l'imprimerie, il y en eut cent peut-être, si l'on compte tous les arts divers qui contribuèrent à réaliser le grand œuvre, la véritable pierre philosophale. Aussi trouva-t-on presque vers le même temps trois genres d'impression différents: la xylographie ou impression sur planches de bois; la chalcographie ou impressions sur planches de métal, soit au moyen de la figure en relief, comme pour la xylographie, soit au moyen de la gravure en creux ou taille-douce; et la typographie ou impression au moyen de types mobiles, c'est-à-dire l'imprimerie proprement dite."

But what B. says of the art of printing in general does not concern typography, and he ought not to mix up "imprimerie" and "typographie" together at the outset, to cause confusion in the minds of his readers, for the sake of Costerian prejudices. For it is indubitable that Bernard himself knew how to discern the case. For instance, he expresses himself clearly as to the art of printing (but no typography!) of the Chinese—even at present nothing more than block-printing—in opposition to: Documents sur l'art d'imprimer à l'aide de planches en bois, de planches en pierre, et de types mobiles (?), inventé en Chine bien longtemps avant que l'Europa en fît usage. Par M. Stanislas Julien, dans le Journal asiatique, no. 12 de 1847.

Obsolete are, in the book of Bernard, 1. Philery de figursnider t'Antwerpen, instead of Vvillem de figuersnider Tantwerpen; 2. the aprioristic, purely arbitrary reasoning on the antiquity of the Speculum (Ce livre, Speculum humanæ salvationis. va nous donner le moyen de démontrer que la typographie est plus ancienne qu'on ne le croit généralement); 3. that his pretended "Laurent de Coster de Haarlem" was born about 1370; for Coster would then have left the town at the age of 113 (1483).

Really new, however, in the work of Bernard, is a genealogical particular, in the relation Fust-Schöffer, but which I am unable to reconcile with what we know from other quarters. A document, namely, of 14th Jan., 1468, mentions Conradus Fust (the same who, in 1475, occurs in the letter of patent of Louis XI. as Conrad Hanequis = son of John), not only as partner of Peter Schöffer, but says distinctly: Conradus Fust, civis Magunt . . . et Petrus *qui habet filiam suam*. We may compare, about this secondary point, Bernard I. 256—268; Schaab I. 443, 445, 63, 73—77, 109, 115, 118, 119; Köhler (Ehren-Rettung) 100. Johan Fust himself, in the later imprints, calls Peter Schöffer "puer;" Peter Schöffer called himself his "gener" to Trithemius (Petrus Opilio, tunc famulus, postea gener, sicut diximus, inventoris primi, Johannes Fust); Johan Schöffer finally called Johan Fust his "avus maternus," Christina "filia," Peter Schöffer " filius adoptivus," himself "nepos" of Johan Fust.

How little reliable the accounts of the family Schöffer may have been with regard to the history of typography, because they, for the sake of ambition, falsified it, yet it appears to me improbable that even their degree of relationship with the money-lender of Gutenberg would be a falsehood. Peter Schöffer ought to have known who was his *wife*; Johan Schöffer who was his *mother*. Bernard ought not to have given this document *abridged* (I. 258) to conceal from his readers, that, if his translation of "Nachvare" is to be right, the word "vare" gets all at once three contradictory meanings. It is not here the place to treat this matter fully, else a genealogical dispute would not be difficult with one who, for instance, first writes (II. p. 293): "Mansion avait écrit pour ce Seigneur (Louis de Bruges) qui avait daigné tenir *un de ses enfants* sur les fonts baptismaux, un livre in-folio intitulé la Penitance Adam, dont il était aussi le traducteur." And then (only two pages afterwards !) says: "On ignore si Colart Mansion *a eu des enfants*." But it is not unlikely that the words in his document, filiam suam, may be regarded as a mistake for sororem suam; for I disbelieve that Peter Schöffer was married with a daughter of Conrad Fust, *son* of Johan Fust. The English-French logic (Inglis—Ottley—Bernard), which takes the Catholicon away from Gutenberg in order to ascribe it to Bechtermüntze, is also of weak

K

X.

1440.

LET us now examine the "Batavia," as those did who got the book in 1588, "on approval," from their bookseller, and who have, therefore, never read anything about the pretended Haarlem invention of the art of printing, except the three pages of Coornhert, and know nothing about it but the report originated from that account. For the boasting pedigree of Gherryt made us only smile, and not think of an investigation. But the literature in general, concerning the invention, we know *perfectly* until 1588; and we read, therefore, not only with surprise, but we go and see whether these things are really so. Before we analyse Junius' story, I desire my readers to forget for a moment all what they have read before about Coster. For without this abstraction their view is clouded, and a clear eye is indispensably necessary for an analytical examination. In the second place, we must not forget that the Netherlands took no exception whatever to the testimony of the 15th century in favour of Mentz. The calm resignation of the Magnum Chronicon Belgicum (1474), of the Chronicle printed at Gouda (1478), and of the Annales of Eloïsius de Roya (1479), harmonises perfectly with the silence of the Netherland typographers in face of the clamorous imprints of Mentz, although even some natives of Haarlem printed in other countries. Among others we find Claes Pietersz in 1476 at Padua, in 1477 at Vicenza; Hendrick of Haarlem in 1482 at Bologna, in 1483 at Venice, in 1488 at Siëna, in 1491 at Lucca; Gerrit of Haarlem in 1498 at Florence. But we find nowhere a single vestige of praise of their town, for the very obvious reason, that these contemporaries of the chandler Lourens Coster had nothing to say. This only concerning the argumentum e silentio. Whenever they speak, however, in the Netherlands, of the invention, it does not disturb the harmony of history. In the " Oratio querulosa contra Inuasores Sacerdotum," printed about 1495 by Chr. Snellaert, at " Delf, in Hollandia," we read : " constat . . . nostris nun temporibus Chalcographiam hoc est impressoriam artem in nobilissima germanic vrbe Maguncia fuisse repertam." The " Chronyk der landen van Overmaas . . . written by an inhabitant of Beek, near Maastricht," in the 15th century, says : " The printed books, or the art of printing, was invented at Mentz anno 1440; but afterwards it came everywhere in many towns in the years '60, '63, and '68. So in the time or year aforesaid, '64 and '65, and '66 and '67, began the very able and subtle art of printing to spread, that they began to print the books, and the books and Holy Writ became known everywhere and very cheap, so that a very well printed Bible valued " three golden overlans rynscher gulden," and even less. . In this way all the Scriptures were produced in German and in Latin, whereby every man who loved the Scriptures could learn and study."[1]

The " Chronycke van Hollandt, Zeelandt ende Vrieslandt" (Leyden, 1517,

---

alloy; for it does not follow. from the act of Dr. Humery. *which* types of Gutenberg's were his property. Bernard does not deserve refutation on this point, before he has refuted himself the better arguments of the German bibliographers. For to pick out, in such a cardinal question, La Serna Santander as an antagonist, is a little too easy. How far, moreover, Bernard was prevailed upon in his opinions by his unscientific antipathy against Mentz, is evident from a gross mistake, discovered by the authors of the "Collectio Weigeliana."

[7] Speculum Humanae Salvationis: le plus ancien monument de la xylographie et de la typographie réunies. Reproduit en facsimile, avec introduction historique et bibliographique, par I. Ph. Berjeau. Londres: C. J. Stewart. 1861. 4to.

[8] Kritiesch onderzoek naar de uitvinding der boekdrukkunst. Geschiedenis der vinding, &c.; oorspronkelijk in het fransch bewerkt door Ch. Paelle, nu in het nederlandsch overgebracht door I. H. Rutjes. Amsterdam. 1867. 8vo.

[1] Publications de la Société Historique et Archéologique dans le Duché de Limbourg. Ruremonde. 1870. 8vo.

Div. xxix.): "In the first year of the Emperor Frederick the Third, therefore, in the year 1440, the profitable art of printing books was first invented and formed." In an unpublished continuation of the chronicle of Jan Gerbrantsz., of Leiden, which was probably written about 1520 by some one who lived in the neighbourhood of Haarlem, we find: "Anno domini 1440 ars imprimendi libros Maguncia ortum habuit et Johannes Fust eiusdem artis primus omnium indubitatus inventor fuit."[1] Adriaen van Baerland (Liber Historiarum, 1532) and Christ. Massaeus (Chronicon utriusque testamenti, 1540), both Netherlanders, wrote that the invention took place at Mentz in 1440. Joh. van Reygersbergen also says, in his Chronicle of Zealand (Antw., 1551): "In the year 1452 Johannes Faustius invented, first of all, the art of printing books, at Mentz, in High-Germany."[2] Nay, still in 1597, Valcooch, schoolmaster at Barsingerhorn, writes in his "Regel der Duytsche schoolmeesters," published at Amsterdam: "A certain Peter of Germany invented first printing, whereby a thousand things are revealed which were first obscure and concealed, especially the seven arts which they teach in the schools." M. Alberdingk Thym, when he published a new edition of this pedagogical rhimework (Dietsche Warande, 1856), added this note to it:—"Valcooch gives no honour to Coster; he does not seem to know him. One may easily guess who this Peter of Germany is. This passage is in any case good evidence that the tradition (!) about Coster crept on very slowly and imperceptibly until Junius, else our vigilant Barsingherhorner would not have failed to mention it, either in order to support the account, or to contradict it." For such surprise however we have at present no longer any reasonable cause. Let us now hear what Junius says:—

"There lived more than 128 years ago at Haarlem, in the market-place, opposite the Royal palace [townhall], in a tolerably respectable house (as may be seen, because the building is still in existence in its entirety), a certain *Lourens Jan* (*szoon*), with the surname of *Coster* or *Sacristan* (which office, at that time very profitable and honourable, this family, celebrated under this name, possessed by hereditary right)."

Reading this in 1588, our first question is of course: *When* did Junius write this? The Batavia was published by Petrus Junius and Janus Dousa the elder, with the (prohibited) dedication to the States of Holland and a preface, both dated from Leiden and Delft 1575. If we now deduct from this date the 128 years, we get 1447, but—the thief prints already in 1442 at Mentz, and the story gives nonsense. Foreigners have afterwards been blamed for deducting the 128 years of the story from that date. Unreasonable; for we cannot ask that any one, in order to understand an author well, should first go and consult the resolutions of the States of Holland and the two manuscripts of the Batavia at the Hague and at Haarlem. Both the editors "have no doubt the most prudent care with respect to the accurate printing of the work, regarded and taken to heart as a sacred duty towards the beloved and highly esteemed deceased." At least they ought to have done so, and there was plenty of time for it in thirteen years, but they have neglected *one* of their most sacred duties, to regulate the chronology of the Batavia (although "the author's own son had copied fair his father's work under his own supervision"). The reader must be careful how he may clear up himself all the irregular dates in a book which was finished, according to the signatures crossed out in MS., in Jan. 1570, but in which additions have been made under the years 1572, 1573, and 1574, as for instance, a few meagre informations about the siege of Haarlem and Leiden. The author speaks of a heavy fire at Rotterdam and begins with the words: "annus ab hinc nonus agitur;" this would give

---

[1] De Navorscher. XVI. p. 129. XVII. p. 257. XVIII.

[2] In a later ed., Middleburg, 1634, this text was *falsified* by the interpolation: "With the letters, with which first the Speculum Humanae Salutis was printed at Haarlem." A second falsification was committed by the introduction, at another place, of the following words: "In the year 1428 the art of printing books was first invented in the renowned town of Haarlem, in Holland, by a distinguished citizen Laurens Janssen Coster." The zealous Costerian who perpetrated this fraud was properly chastised by his fellow-believer Boxhorn, in the following edition, Middleburg, 1644. II., 217.

to a superficial reader, who pays only attention to the titlepage, 1579 ; to a careful reader who has seen the preface, 1566. When did the fire take place, in 1566 or in 1579 ? Oh no—in 1563! We know this from another quarter, and we are now left to compute that Junius wrote this in 1572, although this passage is found in the text of the MS. and written by his own hand ; it is no *addition*, the fairly copied text runs on. "This may be explained by the fact that Junius could get no money from the States, if he did not produce work. He has therefore, after the dedication, gone through his work, augmented and improved it." Therefore not even the date of the preface of the MS. is a safe guide, and the edition of the Batavia, however long it may have been prepared, is uncritical, and it is left to us to look for a chronological guide. From the *place* where our story appears in the MS. of the Batavia, preserved in the Royal library at the Hague, it was inferred that 1568 ought to be the year in which Junius wrote the account, or, in order to be in harmony with the year in which the sheriff Louwerys Janszoon died, discovered only in 1823,—1567. There was nothing absurd in this approximation ; but it surprises me, that they went so far from home to find that which was so near at hand. The history of the theft, of which Junius produces the formal evidence of a witness, and which has to explain *how the art of printing went from Haarlem to Mentz*, is his chief object. Now, he says that within a year after this event (intra vertentis anni spatium), and in 1442 (so it is in the MS. too, and therefore no misprint as Ebert thought!), the thief printed at Mentz his first books with the stolen Haarlem types. Whether we now make the year begin with Easter (old style) or with New Year's-day (new style), the theft took place at Christmas 1441. The very well argued approximation therefore becomes a certainty, and perfectly agrees with an annotation of Scriverius, who had both the MSS. of the Batavia (that of Haarlem and that of the Hague) : "Junius wrote this about 1568." He began to write in 1566 and had the first volume ready at the end of 1569 ; the passage on Haarlem must have been written in the course of 1568, hence 1568 — 128 = 1440 becomes the positive date for the invention of printing at Haarlem, 1441 for the theft of Faust, 1442 for the commencement of printing at Mentz. When Alctophilus objected in 1823 to the chimerical year of the invention, 1423, fixed upon by a Haarlem committee, this synod enjoined him :—"If he will read the account of Junius again carefully, and not forsake out of his blind prejudice all common sense, he will plainly see himself and be obliged to acknowledge, that Junius said not a single word about the time of the invention." Now, however unpleasant it may be to forsake all common sense, it is neither advisable to discard all rules of sound hermeneutics to arbitrate that "habitavit" is euphemism for "obiit" (there *died* instead of there *lived* at Haarlem), as they wished (but only after 1823!). The question is not what they might wish that Junius *had* said, but what he really *has* said.

As to the name, Junius indulges here again in his etymological amusement, of which I have given already a few specimens, and which even caused him to write a whole chapter (cap. xxiii.) : "De significatione nominum et impositione veteribus usitata, tam gentium, quam Principum et personarum." In this case however he was so uncertain of his wisdom, that the words " in or by hereditary right (haereditario jure)" were first not in his MS., afterwards placed between the lines, thereupon crossed out again, but finally inserted in the printing.[2] Characteristic, indeed ! Could the man have known what troubles and ghosts he has called up by his chimera of a hereditary Coster-ship (sacristanship) he would for humanity's sake have restrained for once his mania for interpretation and simply mentioned the name of his hero, without anything more. Innumerable

---

[1] F. A. Ebert. Neue Prüfung der holländ. Ansprüche auf die Erfindung der Buchdruckerkunst (Hermes, 1823. iv. N. 2, pp. 3—85). How entirely obsolete the unfortunate "Prüfung" of Ebert is, is sufficiently evident from this citation : Deutsche Drucker trugen die neue Kunst in alle Lande. In Frankreich, in Italien, in Spanien, in Polen, selbst in den Niederlanden, war durch sie den Ruhm des Deutschen Namens verbreitet worden : nur in Holland findet sich während des ganzen xv. Jahrhunderts *auch nicht die leiseste Spur eines Deutschen* (!)

[2] Beschrijving van het in de koninkl. bibliotheek te 's Gravenhage berustende handschrift der Batavia, uit de nagelaten schriften van M. Gerard van Lennep. Met Fac-similés. 's Gravenh. 1840, 8vo.

nights would have been passed less sleeplessly, less historical injustices would have been committed, if Junius, mindful of his friend Martinus Costerus, had merely written: Habitavit ante annos 128 ad annum 1440 Harlemi ... *Laurentius Joannis Costerus.* In any case the real meaning of his words, when they are freed from the unnecessary verboseness of interpretation, is simply this: In the year 1440 lived at Haarlem *Lourens Janszoon Coster.*

The name, which Junius has first of all the courage to put in print, enables us to discover at once the warp across which our Haarlem scholar is going to weave his embroidery: *the pedigree of Gerrit Thomasz.* The inventor, Junius says, lived in the house in the market-place, "in which afterwards lived *his great-grandson Gerrit Thomasz.*, a distinguished citizen, who died only a few years ago in very advanced age, *and mentioned here for honour's sake.*" I understand! "Until this day (1568)" Junius says, "*winepots* are to be seen there, although very old (how is it possible!), *made of what was left of the tin types*"—after Coster had been totally plundered by Faust. Very striking, O Junius! But yet—was there not something else to be seen at the house of that distinguished citizen, descending from a burgomaster-family, which was much more convincing than those *winepots*? Had he not in his possession a *pedigree*, on which the hero of "deerste print" is mentioned, by the side of his son-in-law *Thomas Pietersz*, the burgomaster-grandsons, and the proprietor of those typographical winepots himself? Nay, what is more, on which the year of the "first print" was distinctly expressed? Ah yes, but just a man so "read" as Junius, can impossibly make use of that fatal year 1446! So many bookmakers before him had, in imitation of the Cologne chronicle, fixed already the date of the *invention at Mentz* in the year 1440, that it was *impossible* to assign to the fiction a *later* date than that year. And this happened, we saw it already before, even in Netherland books, consequently—the pedigree, Junius' *only* authority, was too dangerous a document to refer to it openly!

Now, just as Junius falsifies the year of Gerrit Thomasz., so he makes immediately afterwards a blunder against history, by making *Faust* (Fust) print at Mentz in—1442. We shall not waste a single word on this question, but only point out, in addition to those we have mentioned already, some predecessors of the learned author, who compelled him to antedate the year of "deerste print."

Matthias Palmerius (born 1423): "Namque a Joanne Guttemberg zum Jungen, equite, Moguntiae Rheni, solerti ingenio, librorum imprimendorum ratio anno 1440, inventa," &c. The same is found in the Nuremberg chronicle of 1493.

Jac. Wimpheling (1502): "Anno Christi 1440. Friderico III. Romanorum Imperatore regente, magnum quoddam, ac pene divinum beneficium collatum est universo terrarum orbi a Joanne Gutenberg, Argentinensi, novo scribendi genere reperto." Something to the same effect is found in the Chronographia of J. Nauclerus (Tub. 1500).

Michael Eysenhard (1517): "Circa annum Domini 1440, ars impressoria librorum apud Moguntiam Germaniae urbem reperta est, non minus utilissima, quam ingeniosissima."

Henricus Pantaleon (1565): "Typographiae primi auctores fuerunt Joannes Faustus et Ivo (!) Schefferus anno 1440." We might have quoted more of this author, but this passage is sufficient.

It was therefore *necessary* to antedate the year of Gerrit Thomasz. to 1440. Junius did do so. But he had also found the year 1442 as that in which there was first printing at Mentz, namely, by Polydorus Vergilius (De inventoribus rerum, 1499, 1517, and later). He could read there: "Itaque Johannes Guthenbergius, natione Teutonicus, equestri vir dignitate, ut ab eius civibus accepimus, primus omnium in oppido Germaniae, quam Moguntiam vocant, hanc imprimendarum literarum artem excogitavit, primumque ibi eam exerceri cœpit, non minore industria reperto ab eodem, prout ferunt, autore novo atramenti genere, quo nunc impressores tantum utuntur. (This atramentum shows also that Junius consulted Vergilius, for he writes of Coster: ... *primumque omnium atramenti* scriptorii genus glutinosius

tenaciusque, quod vulgare lituras trahere experiretur . . . *excogitauit*.) Decimo sexto deinde anno, qui fuit salutis humanae 1458 = 1442) quidem, nomine Conradus, homo itidem Germanus, Romam primo in Italiam attulit," &c.
The year 1442 was also given in the Lexicon Juris (Argent. 1541) sub voce Librarii: "Librarios item nunc recepta voce appellant librorum excusores. Cuius artis inventum Elsatiis nostris ante alias nationes donatum, apud Argentoratum Joanni Mentelino, prototypographo, Schotorum familiae proavo (the publisher of the work was Joh. Schott!), sub anno Christi 1442, licet eius publicatio, sed haud absque ingenio, Moguntiacis tribuatur." The Spaniard Petrus Mexia followed in 1542 the account of Vergilius, and wrote 1442. We shall see by what means Junius has linked his two dates 1440 and 1442. Everything is finished by him within these *two* years: the invention, the printing of the Speculum, the flight of Johan Faust to Mentz, and the establishment of typography there. Neither was this period of two years strange to earlier writers: Aventinus († 1534) represents Johan Faust, a citizen of Mentz, as having invented the art in 1450 and completed it in two years. The source of these *two years* is the imprint of Joh. Schöffer (1515), in which he says that his grandfather Joh. Faust first invented the art of printing in 1450, but made it serviceable for printing books in 1452. With Junius, however, everything goes so quickly that *every* thing lies between the walk of the inventor in 1440 and the flight of a certain Johannes in December, 1441: the invention of xylotypography, printing ink, the publication of the Speculum (of which he, unfortunately, did not know the *four* editions), the change into metallotypography, the crowding of curious people for buying printed books, the removal of the invention to Mentz, immediately followed by absolute oblivion of the whole event at Haarlem; notwithstanding the inventor survived the dismal Christmas of 1441 many years, notwithstanding his son-in-law-ink-inventor lived till 1492, notwithstanding three burgomaster-grandsons, who were instructed by their grandfather's typographical beech-bark-product. Fabula fabularum! Lambinet has not unreasonably remarked: "Junius montre quelques principes dans son roman, on y remarque la règle des trois unités, comme dans les drames; unité d'action, de temps et de lieu. L'art typographique exécuté à Haarlem dans les 24 heures."

The year of the genealogy, however, *compelled* him to remain within the year 1440, for the original 1446 could by no falsification whatever be reduced to an earlier date than 1440. If there had stood by accident 1456, the Costerians would have supplied us with the year 1436.

At Haarlem the year fabricated by Junius remained settled till 1628. We may consult Samuel Ampzing's "Beschryvinge ende lof der stad Haarlem in Holland," published that same year by Adriaen Rooman. An engraving representing a printing-office, is headed thus: Boeckdruckerye te Haerlem gevonden omtrent het Jaer 1440, (*Printing-office. Invented at Haarlem about the year* 1440), with a poem underneath of which the two last lines run: O noble, wise town, which invented first this art! Why does Mentz sneer? Thief, keep your tongue!

On the last page we read: "*Secundum Junium* inventa Harlemi Typographia circa annum 1440." Stronger: Scriverius gives at the beginning of his "Laure-Crans," in which he entirely revolutionised the first fable, a portrait, with the inscription, "Lavrentivs Costervs Harlemensis. Primus Artis Typographicae Inventor circa Annum 1440." Decisive: by the "Magistracy and citizens of Haarlem in everlasting memory of the event and the man" a public monument was placed, in front of his house, "de gulde Druyf" (golden bunch of grapes), in honour of Laurens Janszen Koster, namely, a large picture in oils, with the following inscription in golden letters:—

M. S.
TYPOGRAPHIA,
ARS, ARTIUM OMNIUM
CONSERVATRIX,
HIC PRIMUM INVENTA
CIRCA ANNUM CIƆƆCCCXL.

Seiz published for this reason in 1740, at Haarlem, his "third jubilee of the invented art of printing," and they placed the year 1440 on the silver medals, as the year of the Haarlem invention.[1]

Besides the *names* of the genealogy, Junius mentions also the *house* of Gerrit Thomasz. (Lourens Janszoon Coster). "Habitavit Harlemi in aedibus satis splendidis (ut documento esse potest fabrica, quae in hunc usque diem perstat integra) foro imminentibus e regione Palatii Regalis." Here we catch him at once either in his usual exaggeration, his inclination to bombast, or in a contradiction of the Haarlem stories, for the Coster-house was, according to the fragment of Van Zuren, already mentioned and written before Junius, decaying (quamquam ruinosi). Scriverius tells us in 1628, that in his time the house was "changed and divided among three masters." That part, which they still took to have been Coster's house, was called "*De gulden Druif*" (the golden bunch of grapes); when John Bagford saw it in 1706, it was a cheese-shop; until c. 1761 Mozes van Hulkenroy, printer in the market-place, in [the house of] Laurens Koster, inventor of the art of printing, lived there, but the other parts had formed already before the inn, "*Het gulden Vlies*" (the golden fleece). The so-called Coster's house, too, became about 1813 a public-house, "*Het Bossche Koffyhuis*" (the Bosch coffeehouse), and fell to ruin 13th of May, 1818.[2] When we now observe all those names of the Coster-house, it is perfectly clear that the building has been a tavern since old times. Taverns placed in a good position (in this case on the market-place, in the centre of the town) used to retain their first destination from generation to generation. And—we know now from the archives *Lourens Janszoon Coster* as inn-keeper; his (pretended) *grandson Pieter Thomaszoon* as inn-keeper too; while old tin winepots were to be seen at *Gerrit Thomaszoon's* in the Coster-house, cast of the letters of the inventor. When we put all these circumstances together, the result is that the innkeeper Lourens Coster lived till 1483 in that house in the market-place, was succeeded in his business by his son-in-law (not his grandson) Pieter Thomasz († 1492), and afterwards by one of the nephews of this last, Gerrit Thomasz. († cc. 1563). The house and the old winepots are now perfectly intelligible.

Before we further dissolve the real component parts of Junius's fiction, we have to point out what great use he made of his reading. For did he not use for the Batavia alone more than three hundred books? And has his great "reading" not been lauded in his original epitaph? Now, for such a "well-read" man, every thing that he required for the literary dress of his town-story was already printed: a German inventor (Joh. Faust); a son-in-law who improves the invention (Peter Schöffer); indications of the house of the inventor (in domo zum Jungen, in domo Boni Montis); sworn workmen. Lucye Coster and Thomas Pietersz. of the pedigree afforded a magnificent parallel for Christina (Dyne) Faust and her husband. Just as Faust was raised by his grandson to inventor, so Thomas Pietersz. is raised by Junius to adinventor. The track followed by Junius is visible in little *traits*. I give a few quotations from his story by the side of citations from his predecessors:—

Junius.

Immo haec, in viridi nuper quae *cortice fagi* | Carmina descripsi, & modulans alterna notavi, | Experiar.
Virgilius, Elogia quinta 13–15.

Coepit *faginos cortices* principo in literarum typos conformare, quibus inuersa ratione *sigillatim* charta impressis versiculum &c.

Annulus in digitis erat illi occasio prima, | Palladium ut caelo sollicitaret opus. | Illum tentabat molli committere cerae, | Redderet ut nomen littera sculpta suum.

Mr. Singer has (Researches on the history of Playing-Cards), both in a lively and successful manner, shewu the probability at least of Junius having borrowed this ambulatory story from the frolicksome dialogue of Anton-Francesco Doni, in his Mondi, of the date of 1552.

---

[1] Het derde jubeljaer der uitgevondene Boekdrukkonst, Behelzende een beknopt Hist. Verhaal van de Uitvinding der edele Boekdrukkonst .... Door Johann Christiaan Seiz, Franco-Germannus. Haerlem. 1740. 8vo. A Latin translation was published in 1741. Cf.:
Lof der drukkunste, te Haerlem uitgevonden door Laurens Janszoon Koster, omtrent het jaer 1440 ... door Jakob Kortebrant .... Delft. 1740. 4to.
[2] [Dr. A. de Vries] Lotgevallen van Coster's woning. Haarlem. 1851. 8vo.

Ex *levi ligno* sculpunt hi grammata prima, . . .
  Bergellanus, Encomion chalcographicæ (1541) 57—61, 118.

Joannes Fust, civis Moguntinus, avus maternus Joaunis Schœffer, primus excogitavit imprimendi artem typis œreis, *quos deinde plumbeos inrenit; multaque ad artem poliendam addidit ejus filius* Petrus Schœffer. Accursius, circa 1530.

Antea nec tales vidit binomis Ister | *Merces*, nec Rhenus Cornibus ipse tulit.
  Bergellanus l. c. 157, 158.

Quos genuit *ambos* urbs moguntina *Joannes* | Librorum insignes protocaragmaticos.
  Peter Schöffer, Institutt. Just. 1468.
Faustus, Germanis munera *fausta* ferens.
  Bergellanus l. c. 116.
Stemmate præstabat; vicit virtvde sed illud;—
Dicitur *hinc veræ nobilitatis Eques*.
  Bergellanus l. c. 55, 56.

Opera tamen ac multis necessariis adinventionibus Petre Schœffer, ministri suique *filii adoptivi*, cui etiam suam Christinam fustin prodigna laborum multarumque adinventionibus renumeratione nuptui dedit. Retinuerunt autem hi duo ita prenouninati Joannes fust et Petrus Schœffer hanc artem in *secreto*, (*omnibus ministris et familiaribus eorum, ne illam quoque modo manifestarent, iurejurando astricto*) &c.
Per Jo. Schœffer. *nepotem* quondam honesti viri Joannis fust civis Moguntini, artis impressoriæ primarii auctoris &c.

Dibdin, Bibliographical Decameron, p. 362. This partisan of Haarlem says very light-heartedly of the whole Coster-story: "for my own part, I disbelieve it altogether."
Postea faginas formas plumbeis mutauit, deinceps stanneas fecit.

. . . . quum noua *merx*, *nunquam antea visa*.

. . . . quos inter *Joannes* quidam, siue is (vt fert suspicio) *Faustus* fuerit ominoso cognomine, hero suo infidus & *infaustus*, siue alius eo nomine &c.

. . . . *cum genero suo* Thoma Petro qui quaternos liberos reliquit omnes fermè consulari dignitate functos (quod eò dico vt artem *in familia honesta* & ingenua, *haud seruili*, natam intelligant omnes) &c.

. . . . creuit simul amor, creuit ministerium, *additi familiæ operarum ministri* . . . Is ad operas excusorias *sacramento dictus* &c.
. . . . à suo *pronepote* Gerardo Thoma, quem honoris causso nomino, ciue claro, &c.

XI.

A BEECH IN "DEN HOUT."

THE able typefounder and printer Johannes Enschedé at Haarlem, wrote, about the year 1770:

"I have exercised printing for about fifty years and wood-engraving for about forty-five years, and I have cut letters and figures for my father's and my own printing-office in wood of palm, pear, and medlar-trees; I have now been a typefounder for upwards of thirty years; but to do such things as those learned gentlemen [Junius and Meerman] pretend that Laurens Koster and his heirs have done, neither I nor Papillon (the most clever wood-engraver of France) are able to understand, nor the artists Albrecht Durer, de Bray, and Iz. van der Vinne either; but such learned men, who dream about wooden, moveable letters, make Laurens Janszoon Coster use witchcraft, for the hands of men are not able to do it. To print a book with capitals of the size of a thumb, as on placards: *House and ground*, which are cut in wood, and which I have cut myself by hundreds, would be ridiculous; to do it with wooden letters of the size of a pin's head is impossible. I have made experiments with a few of a somewhat larger size. I made a wooden slip of Text Corpus, and figured the letters on the wood or slip; thereupon I cut the letters; I had left a space of about the size of a saw between each letter on purpose, and I had no want of fine and good tools; the only question now was to saw the letters mathematically square off the slip. I used a very fine little saw, made of a very thin spring of English steel, so cleverly made, that I doubt whether our Laurens Janszoon had a saw half as good; I did all I could to saw the letters straight and parallel, but it was impossible: there was not a single letter which could stand the test of being mathematically square. What now to do? it was impossible to polish or to file them; I tried it, but it could not be done by our type-founder's whetstones, as it would have injured the letters. In short, I saw no chance, and I feel sure that no engraver is able to cut separate letters in wood, in such a manner that they retain their quadrature (for that is the main thing of the line in type-casting). If, however, I wished to give my trouble and time to it, I should be able to execute the three words, 'Spiegel onzer Behoudenis' better than the Rotterdam artist has done in the Latin work of M. Meerman; but it is impossible, ridiculous, and merely chimerical, to print books in this manner."

We cannot wish for a more decisive and competent criticism of the story of Junius than this, given by a Haarlemer and a Costerian; for Junius represents Coster as having printed the Speculum in Dutch with wooden types; he makes him, in other words, do something impossible, ridiculous, and chimerical. It is true that the wooden types have been patronized until our time; that Camus has given a specimen of printing with wooden types of two lines, Wetter of one column, Schinkel[1] of half a page; that we are able to do much more with the means of the nineteenth than with those of the fifteenth century; but none of those specimens have proved what they should have proved: the practicability of printing a book with moveable wooden letters, *i.e.* to distribute the forms, to clean the ink from the letters, to submit them to frequent strong pressing, and to retain the usefulness of the letters employed, and without the aid of modern apparatus. They have only proved what men are willing to do for a favourite opinion, for a prejudice, which they *insist*, for once and all, ought to be *true*. This prejudice prevails on both sides: the Gutenbergians as well as the Costerians have, without any historical ground, made a xylographer of the inventor, who, they said, first made experiments with block-printing, afterwards anatomized the blocks, and so on. It is high time for criticism to make a fire of these imaginary wooden letters.

We have seen already that Gutenberg was no xylographer at all: the polishing of stones, the fabrication of metal looking-glasses, the use of lead, the goldsmith

---

[1] In a brochure entitled "Tweetal Bijdragen," Schinkel gives some "experiments" of his foreman, H. le Blansch, namely, seven lines, printed with types of palm-wood. The xylotypographic text runs: "That the first Dutch *Spiegel onzer Behoudenis* was printed with CAST types, is not to be doubted. Is it possible to print a book of some extension with *moveable* letters cut of wood?—YES. Le Blansch *sculp*." This YES is an unproved dictum, the contrary of which is evident already from the dancing lines of the experiment. Let a *book* be produced printed with moveable wooden letters, instead of all those experiments which signify nothing. It is just as with the ridiculous argument of Mr. H. Noël Humphreys in his book: A History of the art of printing, its invention and progress to the middle of the sixteenth century. London: B. Quaritch. 1868. (Extracts of this work have been translated into Dutch by H. Gerlings Cz. in the "Haarlemsche Bijdragen." Haarlem. Erven F. Bohn. 1869. 8vo.). Humphreys argues the possibility of Junius's beech-bark invention with the words: "I have myself, while writing this passage, cut out some letters in thin pasteboard about the thickness of birch-bark, and after reversing them, and sticking them on to a piece of paper to keep them in their proper places, have obtained impressions from them by dabbing them carefully with common ink stiffened with gum, and then rubbing the paper placed over them with the thumb-nail."

Will this idle talk prove now perhaps that *books* may be printed with letters of *pasteboard*, and that our *thumb* is a fit *printing-*press?!

But apart from all this Costerian talk, the question may not be put as Schinkel did, but simply: Were ever books printed with moveable wooden letters? No.

Regarding this point the opinion of Bernard is of value, because he speaks, just as M. Enschedé, in his capacity as typographer: "Le bois ne pourrait jamais, quoi qu'on fasse, donner cette régularité de foulage, cet alignement des lettres. Meerman, qui croyait les Speculum exécutés avec des caractères mobiles de bois, a prouvé, sans s'en douter, le peu de fondement de son opinion, en imprimant trois mots seulement de cette sorte dans son livre. Malgré tout le soin qui a été apporté à la confection de ces quelques lettres, et quoiqu'elles fussent maintenues par des interlignes au-dessus et au-dessous, elles offrent un specimen des plus grotesques, et elles dansent de la manière la plus ébouriffante. Que serait-ce s'il fallait faire tout un livre de cette manière. M. Wetter donne aussi un spécimen de caractères en bois; mais quoiqu'ils soient très-gros et interlignés, ils n'en dansent pas moins d'une façon très-grotesque, ce qui enlève toute valeur à sa prétendue démonstration. On en peut dire à peu près autant d'un autre essai de caractères en bois fait à la Haye, par M. Schinkel, alors imprimeur, dans une brochure hollandaise, intitulée: Tweetal bijdragen betrekkelijk de boekdrukkunst ('s Gravenhage, 1844. 8vo.) Au reste, M. Schinkel, que je vis lors de mon voyage en Hollande, est convenu avec moi que c'était là un tour de force *qui ne prouvait rien dans l'espèce*. M. Léon de Laborde a cru longtemps aussi à la possibilité d'imprimer avec des caractères mobiles en bois: il en a même donné un specimen dans son livre intitulé: Débuts de l'imprimerie à Strasbourg (Paris, in-8vo. 1840); mais les difficultés qu'il a éprouvées pour cet essai et pour d'autres qu'il a tentés depuis l'ont fait, je crois, changer d'opinion." [Origine de l'imprim. I. 33, &c.]

L

Dunne, the melting of the forms, all this points towards another branch of industry. The exact moment of the sudden thought of typography, of the making of moveable types, can of course never be determined without Gutenberg's memoirs. This moment, however, falls after the year 1440; since that time all that belonged to the art was investigated, and they were *ready* with the invention in 1450. Already then the plan existed of applying the new invention to the printing of the Bible. This account is in harmony with the agreement between Gutenberg and Fust about an advance by the last for the erection of a printing-office. The evidence of Zell, therefore, is totally free from any influence of the later Fust-Schöfferian boasts, by which they arrogate something to themselves at the cost of Gutenberg. Zell, although a disciple of Fust's and Schöffer's printing-office, mentions neither of them in connexion with the invention, however elaborate his account may be. Excellent! for neither of them invented *anything*: Fust became Gutenberg's money-lender only in 1450; Schöffer was about that time still calligrapher at Paris, and by his talents improved typography only afterwards. But the invention itself, the essence of typography, was ready in 1450. And this was not too difficult to be executed within a few years, after Gutenberg's mind had been led to think, and had been impregnated by a xylographic schoolbook, or something else, with the idea of moveable types. For the elements of execution existed already: the art of engraving in different kinds of metal, and the art of casting; to get stamps and matrices was therefore only a question of experiment. We know nothing of those experiments between 1440 and 1450, but we do know their result; it is clear to every thoughtful man, who does not encumber his mind with different citations of later date, that the inventor of the idea, while struggling to give effect to the thought conceived, of obtaining serviceable, durable, loose letters, had to think of some solid metal, not of brittle, unmanageable wood. But in order not to contest one prejudice by another, we simply ask again: What does the century of the invention tell us?

Ars imprimendi, ars impressoria, is the oldest term (1457) applied to the new invention, which signifies in general art of printing; but it is at the same time called ars caracterizandi, from character, letter (cf. the Grammatica rythmica of 1466). Schöffer calls the two Johanneses of Mentz, Gutenberg and Fust, whom he surpasses in the art of cutting letters, protocaragmatici. These terms point to χαράσσειν, to cut into, to engrave, and make us at once think of metal, of metal stamps, patrices. This notion of cutting, engraving, artistically of more importance to the fabrication of types than the mechanical casting, was so prevalent, that the oldest terms gave rise to the colossal error, that for a long time each letter had been cut separately, and that afterwards they got the idea of casting them. Even the able lettercutter Jenson calls himself metaphorically (Luctus Christianorum, Ven. 1471) a cutter of books, librorum exsculptorem. Sensenschmid in the same spirit says that the Codex Just. (1475) is cut (insculptus), and that he has cut (sculpsit) the work of Lombardus in Psalterium. The typographer Husner at Strasburg says in the imprint of the Speculum Durandi, 1473, that it is printed with letters cut of metal ("exsculptis ære litteris"), and of the Præceptorum Nideri, 1476, that it is printed "litteris exsculptis artificiali certo conatu ex ære. The goldsmith and printer Cennini at Florence speaks already in 1471, at the end of the preface to Vergilius, of the cutting in metal and the casting of the letters: "Bernardus Cenninus aurifex omnium judicio præstantissimus et Dominicus ejus filius expressis ante Calybe characteribus et deinde fusis literis volumen hoc primum impresserunt." Jenson (Breviarium August. Ven. 1485) says equally plainly that this work had been printed with letters, cut and cast by a divine art, "litteris divine sculptis ac conflatis." Just as the books are said to have been cut, so Schöffer speaks metaphorically about casting. He makes the "Grammatica vetus rythmica" of 1466 say: "At Moguntia sum fusus in urbe libellus" (I this book) am cast at Mentz). The first typographers were stamp-cutters themselves, they made their matrices and cast their types: hence the general phrase "sculpere;" hence also, by great difference of talent and practice, the difference which their work presents, and the reason why the later date of a book does not always include better printing. The earlier printer might have been a master, the later one a bungler. The conviction that the art of printing is metallotypography, not xylotypography, remained prevalent during the 15th century. Nauclerus (Tub. 1500) still tells us: "About the year 1440 the art of printing books with *tin* types commenced at Mentz." Celtes (Norimb. 1502): "You, oh broad-waved Rhine, wind your way already to the town of Mentz, which printed first with *metal* types." Erasmus speaks of "the almost divine invention of printing books with *tin* types" (stanneis typis). The epitaph of the inventor, written by Ivo Wittig, 1507, agrees perfectly with all this:—" To the honour of Johan Gutenberg at Mentz, who first invented the metal letters for printing and by this art deserved well of the whole world, Ivo Wittig has placed this stone to a memorial, 1507." Finally, it is clear from all this, why the words typographia and chalcographia had already begun to be used promiscuously during the 15th century, which was oftener repeated in the 16th.

But in the 16th century, when they were so much farther from the invention, the wooden letters make their appearance, as a fruit of the confusion between xylography and typography. The Germans have their Junius too, namely the abbot Trithemius, also a man of great reading, but with as little judgment, and they used *his work* just as uncritically as the Netherlanders that of Junius. With respect to Trithemius, also, the wrong method has been followed of putting his account of the invention of the art of printing as a kind of text before the investigation (Schaab and Wetter), and *then* looking for the first and authentic sources. Everything now which did not fit into this account was sophistically distorted, as if Trithemius had been inspired, instead of coming to the more reasonable conclusion of accommodating Trithemius to the facts. Here is the place for exposing the abbot.

Trithemius is said to have his account from the mouth of Peter Schöffer, who does, however, not deserve at all to be believed upon his word. For the man, who enters the service of Gutenberg and Fust at Mentz after 1450, when the invention was *completed*, and has yet the courage to declare in 1468, that he, Petrus, entered first of all the sanctuary of the art,—is, notwithstanding all his technical ability as typographer, a bragger, against whose information we ought to be on our guard.

His account to Trithemius is put c. 1484. What now does the abbot write after *that* year? We give his informations in chronological order. In 1486 he says: The " ars impressoria" was invented in our days (nostris diebus) at Mentz; 1506, 24 June, he writes the same in a letter to his brother Jacob. Nostris diebus: when is that? On the 16th Aug. 1507 he writes the same to Jacob Tymolan, but as to the date he adds: "tempore infantiæ meæ," while he was born 1 February 1462! In the chronicle of his convent, Spanheim (1506), his information is more accurate; he says: 1. that the art of printing with moveable types was invented about 1450 by a Mentz citizen (?), who was called Johan Gutenberg; 2. that he completed the work, after he had spent on it all he had, with the advice and assistance of good people, Johan Fust and others; 3. that Peter Schöffer of Gernsheim was the first propagator (dilatator) of the art, and printed many books during his lifetime; 4. that Gutenberg lived at Mentz in the house zum Jungen, still called at present after the new art. Every one initiated sees that this information is inferior to that of Zell; that all these informations are very meagre, by one, who is said to have been informed in 1484 about the invention by Schöffer. But a more complete account, written about 1514 and printed in 1690, will perhaps indemnify for this poverty. It says in substance :—

1. The art, unknown before, of printing books with moveable types, was invented (inventa et excogitata, read: excogitata et inventa) in 1450 by a Mentz citizen, Johan Gutenberg; 2. Who spent almost all he had on the invention, and was already on the point of giving the matter up (?) in despair, when he completed it, assisted by advice and money of Johan Fust; 3. First they printed with wooden blocks, on which the letters were cut (caracteribus litterarum in tabulis ligneis per ordinem scriptis), and composed forms (formisque compositis), the vocabulary called Catholicon; 4. They

could, however, print nothing else with these blocks, because the letters were cut in them and therefore immoveable; 5. After these inventions (!) they went on to finer ones, and invented a manner of casting forms of all the letters of the Latin alphabet, which they called matrices and in which they cast metal types, which they had formerly cut with their hands (!); 6. Trithemius indeed heard, about thirty years ago (c. 1484, he being therefore twenty-two years of age), from P. Schöffer of Gernsheim, son-in-law of the first inventor (!), that this art caused much trouble at the commencement of its invention. For when they printed the bible, they had spent more than four thousand guilders (an assertion contrary to the sum mentioned in the official law-suit!) before they had finished the third quaternion; 7. But Peter Schöffer, homo ingeniosus et prudens, invented a more easy way of casting types and brought the art to its present perfection; 8. These three kept the art of printing secret for a long time, until it was spread by the workmen, and first of all to Strasburg; 9. The three first inventors lived at Mentz in the house zum Jungen, called at present the printing-office (impressoria). (Contrary to his information of 1506: "Morabatur autem præfatus Joannes Gutenberg Moguntiæ in domo, dicta zum Jungen, quæ domus usque in præsentem diem illius novæ artis nomine dignoscitur insignita.")

Ergo: Gutenberg squandered first his money on *xylography*, which no longer wanted to be invented; invents, but together with Fust, for the sake of convenience, as those wooden blocks could be used but once, *typography*, and this art would have perished without the assistance of Fust and Schöffer. Notwithstanding our good, superstitious abbot has spoken with Peter Schöffer, and even if St. Peter had been present, he tells nonsense or has been a dupe.

Is it critical to allow ourselves to be guided by such thoughtless compilations, full of contradiction and untruths? The meaning of the account, namely to reduce Gutenberg's invention to nothing, to give Fust a share in the invention of moveable types, and to raise Schöffer to *the* great man, is so evident that the tendency sufficiently explains the untruths it contains. The explanation-tricks played with respect to that xylographic (!) vocabulary, Catholicon, prove sufficiently that we should be wrong in trying to learn from Trithemius' history; in his ignorance he has done, with the typographical Catholicon, what Junius did afterwards with the Speculum.

We find just as much traditional corruption in the Latin occasional poem of J. A. Bergellanus, in praise of the art of printing, published at Mentz in 1541. He came there in 1540, and made inquiries about the origin of typography, but that which he learned from aged citizens of Mentz does historically prove nothing; it only proves what was tradition at *that* time at Mentz. The main thing, according to him, also, is that Gutenberg, after having exhausted his own resources, assisted by the friendly advice and aid of Fust, began to cut the first letters—of light wood. The Fust-Schöfferian impudence, however, reached its acme in an account of the 17th century, of Joh. Fr. Faust of Aschaffenburg. The father of this arch-liar had written frankly and in accordance with truth: " Joh. Faust (Fust) war Mitverleger der Buchdruckerei in der Stadt Mentze; etliche wollen wider seiner Dank ihn zu einem Inventorem haben und machen, so aber nur mit seinem Vermögen und guten Rath in der That geholfen." (Joh. Faust was partner in the printing-office at Mentz; some persons would make an inventor of him against his own wish; he really helped only with his money and good advice.) But the son, with the act of the notary Helmasperger in his hands, draws up an account of the invention to this effect:—

1. The inventor, Joh. Faust (!) cut first an alphabet in relief. 2. He invented a black, substantial ink, and printed thereupon this alphabet and a Donatus. 3. But yet, thinks Fust, moveable letters would be preferable. 4. Therefore he cuts the blocks asunder and prints with the pieces. 5. His servant Schöffer cut letters on stamps and casts them. 6. Schöffer cuts secretly an alphabet, shows it to Faust, and gets as a reward his daughter as wife. 7. They invent also better material for the types. 8. Thereupon father-in-law and son put their workmen under an oath. 9. They conceal the wooden forms and string together the several wooden letters, which they now and then show to good friends. 10. Their neighbour Johan Gutenberg,

who had spiced everything, becomes their money-lender—but enough of this scandal of fiction.

From these foul springs bubbled up the wooden types of which the 15th century knew nothing. Just those who speak of wooden letters are the fabulists of the question: Bibliander in 1548, Specklin c. 1580. Angelo Rocca says (1591) that he saw them at Venice (namely, xylographic initials!); H. L. Spiegel composed a rhyme on them, Hert-Spiegel (1614); Paulus Pater (1710) and Bodmann (1781) have seen them at Mentz in worm-eaten condition. And where are those wooden types gone to? They have disappeared in a very simple way: namely, at Mentz, they used to give one of those wooden types of Gutenberg to every printer's apprentice who had finished his apprenticeship. Fancy such a distribution of relics! It is as if somewhere, in a church, pieces of the holy cross are distributed among the catechists on the occasion of their confirmation! These wooden corporation-letters at Mentz have just as much to do with Gutenberg as the little wooden corporation-ships in the cathedral at Haarlem with the capture of Damiate. With respect to all these fine accounts of later date, concealed among the bushy shrubs of tradition, science may proceed to the order of the day. One evidence, however, deserves our attention, as it substantially explains that of Zell, and has been wrongly interpreted by Wetter.

Johan Trechsel printed at Lyons from 1488—99. He published there, without date:—Expositio Georgii super summulis Magistri Petri Hispani, in 4to., with the following imprint:—

    Sic prima in buxo concisa elementa premendi
    Parva quidem scribe damna tulere bono;
    At ubi divisas Germania fudit in ere,
    Inciditque notas iisque ter usa fuit,
    Extemplo inventis cesserunt artibus omnes,
    Quas solers potuit scribere dextra notas.
    Sic prius in pretio mendicat dextra, donec
    Calluit impressos docta ligare libros,
    Principioque rudem nunc artem hanc ipse Joannes
    Trechsel eo duxit, quo nihil ulterius.

That is to say, the first elements of printing, cut in wood of a beech, caused very little loss to the able writers. But when Germany cut *separated*, loose letters in metal, and cast them and used them, the writing of the dexterous hand had to give way to the newly-invented art . . . The art, crude at first, was brought by Joh. Trechsel to an unsurpassable perfection.—Trechsel, therefore, is also one of those perfectors, as the history of typography shows us so many, and at whose head Peter Schöffer stands. But it is especially the beginning of the imprint which deserves our attention: it is not said that typography began with letters of beech-wood, but that *xylography* caused little loss to the writers of manuscripts.

That printing with engraved wooden blocks is meant, appears from the contrast to the invention of *loose*, metal types, *i.e. typography*. Just as in the account of Zell, two different modes of printing are given here: with immoveable *wooden* and with *moveable metal* types. Xylography is here also already the rival of the art of printing, and, therefore, the fabricator of little books (Abecedariums, Doctrinales, Donatuses); but neither here nor in Zell have we a difference between block-printing and typography only in *degree*, but in *kind*,—the moveable cast letters, the masterly, *subtile* manner of Zell; the "ars *subtilissima* caracterizandi seu imprimendi" of Jacob Meydenbach, Mentz, 1491; the "very quick art which has become more *subtile*" of Johan Veldener, Utrecht, 1480.

However, it was thought necessary to find the wooden letters of the imagination, and hence bibliography presents the dismal spectacle that almost all monuments of the excellent invention, that fruit of a vigorous mind, of a simple, but ample and grand idea, have been declared by would-be connoisseurs one by one to be xylographic. This caused the double trouble of first making out, with much verbosity and an air of perspicuity, incontrovertibly typographical masterpieces to be wood, and then afterwards putting aside this pedantry and returning to the simple truth. The origin of typography presents nowhere anything narrow-minded, worthless, or trifling, for it belongs to the *grand* facts of history,—but trifling minds have soiled it with their own littleness. The gigantic bible (of 42 lines) of Gutenberg—wood; the magnificent psalter of 1457—wood; the large bible (of 36 lines) of Pfister at Bamberg—wood; nay, even the Theuerdank, a typographically splendid work of 1517—wood; every thing wood, until at last, after much cavilling and trouble, they saw themselves compelled by degrees to acknowledge as monuments in metal that which they had reduced to wooden dolls. If all those transformations and metamorphoses were not so annoying they would be comical. One example: Gotthelf Fischer discovers in 1800 a fragment of a Donatus, in small folio, of 35 lines. No doubt this Donatus was not only printed with wooden types, no, it was even block-printing. In 1801 he discovered a second leaf, but fancies now to recognize in the types (!) those of Gutenberg's bible, in the initials those of the Psalter of 1457. Ergo: the Donatus is typographically printed, and—Gutenberg has also made the initials of the psalteria! Schöffer lost, therefore, his only merit. But Wyttenbach at Treves discovers in 1808 again two leaves of a Donatus, with the imprint: "Explicit donatus. Arte nova imprimendi seu caracterizandi, per Petrum de Gernsheim in urbe Moguntina cum suis capitalibus absque calami exaratione effigiatus." Ergo: the Donatus was not only no xylography, not only no product of Gutenberg, but not printed even before 1466, for Fust was, according to the imprint, already dead. This, however, did by no means prevent Lambinet from building a system on these two leaves, and simply this: Gutenberg did *not* print the bible of 42 lines; *Schöffer* invented patrices, matrices, and moulds, *i.e.* the real typography. The superficial Dibdin adds to this, in his Bibliographical Decameron, that this Donatus was perhaps the first experiment of printing with metal types, just as Schweynheym and Pannartz at Rome opened their printing-office with the publication of a Donatus. Such rigmarole deserves no answer.

Now, is it irony, or naïveté, when De Laborde writes on the difficulty of distinguishing wooden letters? He argues: "La difficulté, qu'on trouve à distinguer une impression sur lettres mobiles de bois d'une impression sur lettres mobiles de font doit l'excuser (Fournier), et les discussions, qui se sont élevées et qui s'élèvent encore au sujet des lettres d'indulgence de 1454, du Psautier de 1457, et du Theuerdanck de 1517 rendront chacun réservé dans son opinion." I believe unconditionally in the difficulty of distinguishing things which do not exist. In the present state of the question, however, all works on our subject, which rebaptize the inventor of typography as xylographer, must be regarded as scientifically obsolete.

Berjeau especially has tried, in his reproductions of the Canticum, Ars moriendi, and Speculum, to put this dying prejudice on foot again. He does, however, not produce one historical proof, but heaps mountains of hypotheses one upon another, which, notwithstanding their great multitude, never change their nature: $0 + 0 + 0 + 0$, although for ever continued, remains always $=0$. He says simply: "Si l'imprimerie a réellement été inventée par un xylographe plus intelligent que ses confrères, cet inventeur a dû commencer par scier des images avec leurs inscriptions pour les employer dans un autre ouvrage du même genre. Il a dû ensuite scier dans sa planche un certain nombre de mots et de syllabes, qu'il était facile d'utiliser dans une autre composition." Certainly, *if* such *had* been the case, it would have *really* been the case, for nothing is more logical than the formula $A = A$. But facts, which we only have to consult, do neither appear nor disappear with *if* and *perhaps*.

Those fatal, unhistorical wooden types! Wetter spent really the amount of ten shillings on having a number of letters made of the wood of a pear-tree, only to please Trithemius, Bergellanus, and Faust of Aschaffenburg, the first two falsifiers of history in good, the last in bad, faith. His letters, although tied with string, did not remain in the line, but made naughty caprioles. The supposition —that by those few dancing lines the possibility is demonstrated of printing with 40,000 wooden letters, necessary to the printing of a quaternion, a whole folio book— is dreadfully silly. The demonstrating facsimile demonstrates already the contrary.

Wetter's letters not only declined to have themselves regularly printed, but they also retained their pear-tree-wood-like impatience afterwards. He says, "I have deposited the wooden types with their forms in the town-library, where they may be seen at any time." Nothing is more liberal. But let us now see what Bernard says: "Lors de mon passage à Mayence, en 1850, je priai M. Wetter de me faire voir les caractères de bois qu'il a fait graver pour son livre ; il eut l'obligeance de me conduire chez son imprimeur, dans l'atelier duquel il les avait laissés ; mais le prote nous apprit qu'ils avaient été volés. Peut-être un jour quelque naïf Allemand, les trouvant parmi les reliques du voleur, nous les donnera pour les caractères de Gutenberg. Voilà comment s'établissent trop souvent les traditions." I say, with Bernard: "je nie positivement qu'il existe aujourd'hui des livres imprimés en caractères mobiles de bois ;" but I do not only deny that they exist at present—I deny that they ever have existed.

I also deny that I have deviated from the text; this review has shown to which class of authors Junius belongs, when he writes, in 1568, that Lourens Janszoon Coster began to print in 1440 with types of the bark of a beech. Or else does any one feel inclined to show me this invention done by another chandler, on a walk (sumpto cibo aut festis diebus), in the Haarlem or in the Hague wood? I allow them to make use not only of good tools, but even of a wood-engraver; I allow them to choose any kind of cortex: oak, beech, chestnut, lime-tree, &c. And the lines they would make a trial with (versiculum vnum atque alterum) are not even required to be alexandrines, nor is it necessary to let Thomas Pietersz. look first for printing-ink. I only ask for the art with the egg, *long* after the death of Columbus.

But *is* it after all really certain that Junius speaks of *loose* wooden letters? The more I have learned to place myself in the course of his thoughts, and in the notions of his time, the more improbable this seems to me. The pieces of beech-*bark* would make us think of some extension: the "sigillatim" indicates only inverted printing; Coster proceeds from small to great things, from little lines to figure-books with accompanying text. After these little lines he "undertook greater things." We might suppose that Junius shared—and after all this is most probable—the error of his time, nay, of even the laymen of our own time, which confounds the common art of printing with typography. This opinion, moreover, agrees better with "deerste print" of Thomasz., and the "crude manner" of Coornhert. It is true, that Junius's change of the wooden "formas" into tin ones, seems contrary to this supposition ; but that transformation is not quite coherent with his story. The tin forms made their appearance suddenly afterwards, when he speaks of the theft, because they could not be entirely wanting, as Junius had read too much of the metal letters of Mentz. And as for *clear* notions on the connexion of xylography and typography, no one must expect them in our bookish scholar. When even in 1815, professor Tydeman thinks the question decided in favour of Haarlem, if only there has been printing there, no matter of what description, even if merely with engraved blocks, then it would not be strange, when Junius is content in 1568 with xylographic printing. I for one am convinced that Junius regarded the Speculum as a purely *xylographic* work. But I am not able to *prove* it from his contradictory text, and have therefore not thought fit to omit my argument against the fictitious wooden letters of the 15th century.[1]

---

[1] How the etymology may have suggested to Junius the idea of bark, is evident from the "Wörterbuch" of Jacob and Wilh. Grimm:—

Buch, boek, althd. puoh, mhd. bnoch, goth. bôka, alts. buok, ags. bôc, eng. book, alth. bók, schw. bok, dän. bóg. Dies Wort führt unmittelbar in die heidnische zeit, wie den Griechen βύβλος, βίβλος bast, rinde und dann, weil sie bemahlt, beschrieben wurde, schrift, brief und buch, den Römern *liber* bast und buch bedeutete; so gieng unser vorfahren, die ihre schrift auf steine und zum gewöhnlichen gebrauch auf buchene breter ritzten, die vorstellung des eingeritzten über auf buche, den namen des baums, aus dessen holz breter und tafeln am leichtesten geschnitten werden konnten ; noch im heutigen buchstab weist stab auf den hölzernen deutlich hin, nicht anders bezeichnete auch codex und tabula sowol das beschriebene holz als hernach des buch.

Buchstab, althd. puohstap, ags. bôcstäf, altn. bókstafr, schw. bokstaf, dän. bogstav. bei den Gothen darf man bókstabs pl. bókstabôs vermuten.

Buchstab ... bestätigt zusehends die von buch gegebne deutung, wenn uns die bóka, d. i. die buche,

XII.

SPECULUM NOSTRÆ SALUTIS.

There was a time when people declared fossils, as well as the whole animal process of destruction and digestion, to be a "freak of nature." What this method of explanation has been for geology, the uncritical learning of Junius has been for the knowledge of books. His description of the Dutch Speculum, which has no other value but as a curiosity, runs thus: The Speculum is printed in 1440 by Laurens Janszoon Coster, at Haarlem; it was the *first* book printed by this inventor with *wooden* forms or letters, and on one side, on account of the infancy of the new invention; but in order to conceal the unsightliness of this process, the blank backs of the leaves were pasted on each other. After the change of the wooden letters into leaden and tin ones, Johan Faust (for I rid the insinuative phrase of Junius from its hypocritical dress) absconded with them in 1441 from Haarlem to Mentz, and printed there with these letters in 1442, for a *certainty* (certum est) the Doctrinale of Alexander Gallus.— *Not one word is true of all these informations:* the Specula were *not* printed xylo-, but typographically; the Dutch editions are not the earliest, but the latest editions, printed when the types had become worn by use; the Speculum was *not* anopisthographic on account of the ignorance of the printer, but because the engravings are worked by the *frotton*, an impediment to opisthographic printing; the unprinted pages were *not* pasted one upon another, although this was accidentally done in the copy which Junius used for his novel; the Doctrinale, in the types of the Speculum, was printed, and afterwards discovered, in the Netherlands, not in Germany. Johan Fust did not dream of printing at Mentz in 1442; Gutenberg did decidedly not return from Strasburg before 1445, and contracted with Johan Fust only in 1450. *Such* is the history of the 15th century, which we cannot allow to be reconstrued by a few strokes of the pen of an incompetent person in 1568. The work of Petrus Hispanus, too, printed at Mentz in 1442, has been trumped up by Junius from his "reading." It is evident from every word he wrote that his bibliographical knowledge, and consequently his bibliographical authority, is equal to 0.

It would therefore be unnecessary to pause one moment longer upon the Speculum, if the Costerians had not played greater tricks with it afterwards. Their Bosco, Jacobus Koning, was a real expert in this work, and he proceeded thus: Given a prize essay to make the Coster-fable true; given a copy of an illustrated book, entitled: Spieghel onser behoudenisse, without indication of place, printer, and year,—Koning puts some pairs of spectacles on (*not* all of glass), makes an awful connoisseur's-face, and begins to peruse, to look, to stare, to gaze, and then again to

---

den gehalt der schrift überhaupt darstellt, so sind die bokstabós alle einzelnen vom baum geschnittenen tafeln und reiser. auf die büchnen stäbe wurden die zûge geritzt und später gemahlt. bei Ulfilas erscheint uns stabs nur in der abstraction von στοιχεῖον, element, wie die buchstaben element sind aller schrift, und rede; unter dem worte stab soll dessen zusammenhang mit staun κρίσις und stôjan κρίνειν entfaltet werden, der richter hält den stab und das urtheil erfolgt, gleich der schrift, durch stäbe. anklage hiesz unserer vorzeit rugstab, eid eidstab, verurtheilung harmstab und dem altn. feiknastabr, dirae, imprecatio würden ags. faenstaf, ahd. feichanstap zur seite stehen, dem altn. helstafr die hellirunen, todesrunen, den auch verwünschungen pflegten mit runen eingeritzt zu sein. an der nahen berührung von runstab und buchstab kann niemand zweifeln. bruder Bertholds rede von gezierten, geflorierten buchstaben (Kling s. 305. 306) erscheint sinniger, wenn men die nachhallende eigentliche wortbedeutung hinzunimmt und selbst in handschriften des mittelalters lîszt die laubverzierung ausgemahlter buchstaben sich noch darauf beziehen. im Tristan 362, 30 werden spâne 'in lange wis' aus reiseru, um ein T und I zu bilden, geschnitten; das ganze alterthum unserer runen und loszo hängt mit den gebrauch solcher buchstaben genau und vielfach zusammen, wie neuere untersuchungen dargelegt haben. die längst unverstandne benennung wurde in allen deutschen sprachen bis auf heute fortgeführt.

gaze, to stare, to look, to peruse, until he finds himself again gazing, and—really there he sees from the *book*, from nothing else but the BOOK : 1. that the punch used for the matrix, was cut in wood; 2. that the matrices were made of lead; 3. that the mould was defective; 4. that the material used for the letters consisted simply of lead or tin; 5. that the printer used only an ordinary house- or hand-press; 6. that round the pages they used a wooden chase; 7. that no composing-stick was used; 8. that they had no different kinds of spaces; 9. that the imperfect state of the printing-balls was the cause of the book being printed on *one* side; 10. that Coster had a little spot on the left side of his nose. We see, Koning was as clever as the sleeping lady, who is able to explain the whole course of a disease only from the tassel of a nightcap.

Let us place, by the side of the decisions of this clairvoyant, with his imagined "artistic" eye, simply the account of a connoisseur, also a Netherlander and temporary Costerian. Mr. Holtrop writes on the same book: " Les défauts des caractères consistent exclusivement dans des défectuosités : à la lettre E *manque* la partie supérieure ; la lettre M a le jambage du milieu coupé en deux par un trait blanc, lequel trait blanc est produit par *l'absence* d'une partie du jambage. Maintenant pourquoi attribuer à une nouvelle fonte des défauts qui en réalité prendraient leur origine dans l'emploi de caractères usés et cassés ? Si Koning, dans ses observations, au lieu de se borner aux lettres capitales de cette édition hollandaise à une fonte, les eût étendues aussi aux minuscules, il y aurait rencontré des défauts semblables. Quant à moi, j'avoue qu'au premier abord le caractère de cette édition semble différent de celui des autres, mais examiné de près il est le même, seulement plus usé et surtout très-mal imprimé. Si cela est vrai, comme je le crois, l'édition hollandaise à une fonte aurait été imprimé la dernière." And so it is, indeed, for other reasons too: the edition which was according to Koning's fancy the *first*, the sandy foundation of his whole system, is the *last*, of reality.[1]

That the grammatical foundation of his system is by no means firmer than his typographical, is at once clear from the following comparison. The printed edition is an abbreviation of the MS. :—

1464. Manuscript.	First Dutch edition.
HIer beghint dat spieghel der menscheliker behoudenisse.[1] O/ec mach hi daer in sien dat hy mits vyants bedroch v'doemt is. En*de* hoe hi ou'mits d'bermherticheit gods weder v'soent si	(H)Ier beghint dat speghel der menscheliker behoudenisse. O/ec mach hi daer in sien dat hy mits viants bedroch verdoemt is. En*de* hoe hi ou'mits d'bermherticheit gods weder v'soent si

[1] In welken openbaer wert die valle d'menschen En*de* die manier d'wedermakinghe. In desen spieghel so mach j man merken om wat saken wil scepper alre dinghen den mensch ghescapen heeft.

---

[1] An inquiry concerning the invention of printing, in which the systems of Meerman, Heineken, &c., are reviewed . . . by the late Will. Young Ottley, with an introd. by J. Ph. Berjeau. London. 1863. 4to.

Ottley explains the irregularity of the types of the Specula by the fact that they might have been cast in forms of clay, or plaster, just as Bernard says: "Suivant moi, les caractères du Speculum ont été fondus dans le sable, comme les petits colifichets destinés aujourd'hui à servir d'epingle de chemise, de breloque de montre, &c." But typography is not the only branch of industry which has suffered from economy and pursuit of gain. The hypotheses of Ottley and Bernard, however, alter the main question, the fact that the Speculum was printed with cast types, not a bit, and an elaborate criticism would, therefore, not reward the trouble.

I must not leave Ottley's book without having pointed out that the (Costerian!) author exposes one of the many literary dishonesties of Koning. In an elaborate discussion of the French translation of his work, he says:—" A short 'Supplement' closes the volume. Mr. Koning therein tells us, that in the year 1816, a work of mine, entitled 'An Inquiry into the Origin and Early History of Engraving upon Copper and in Wood; with an account of engravers and their works, from the invention of chalcography by Maso Finiguerra to the time of Marc Antonio Raimondi. London, 1816, 4to.,' had fallen into his hands; and that he had read it with the more pleasure, as it contained some things corroborative of his own opinions, and favourable to the pretensions of Haerlem. He observes, that I have there proved, by certain deficiencies in some of the lines of the vignettes in the Latin edition of the Speculum, which Heinecken and Santander consider as the most ancient, that, when that edition was printed, the engraved blocks had suffered various fractures, the marks of which do not show themselves in the vignettes of the edition commonly called the second Dutch; and that, consequently the edition last mentioned was certainly printed before the other. This is quite true; and it proves that

Edition with worn type.	1483. Veldenaar's edition.
En*de* ghine tot den wiue alleen wesende sonder den man, want die viant lichteliker bedrieghet die alleen is dan die ghesellen heeft.² Die ma*n* is van god in den paradise overgheset en*de* dat wyf is ghescape*n* van der ribbe*n* des slapende*n* mans.³	Ende ghinc tot den wiue alleen wesende sonder den man. Want die viant lichteliker bedrieghet die alleen is dan die ghesellen heft. Die man is van god in den paradise overgheset ende dat wyf is ghescapen van der ribben des slapenden mans.
(H)Ier begint die spieghel der menschliker behoudenisse. O!ec machi daer in sien dat hi mits viants bedroch v'doem*t* is. En*de* hoe si ou'mits d' bermher*t*icheit gods weder v'sont si	Hier beghint die spieghel der menscheliker behoudenisse. Oeck soe mach hi daer in sien dat hi mits des vyants bedroch verdoemt is. Ende hoe si ouer mits der barmherticheyt goods weder versoent si.
En*de* ghine totte*n* wiue allee*n* wesende so*n*d' den man. Want die viant lichteliker bedrieget die allee*n* is d*an* die ghesellen heeft. Die ma*n* is van god in den paradise overgeset en*de* dat wyf is gescape*n* van d'ribben des slape*n*de ma*n*s.	Ende ghinc totten wiue daer si allene was sonder den man. Want die vyant lichteliker bedriecht een die alleen is dan die ghesellen heeft. Die ma*n* is van god in de*n* paradise overgheset ende dat wyf is ghescapen van der ribben des slapenden mans.

² Aldus dan so heeft die viant enam onse moeder v'scalct. Dat menschelike geslachte leydende tot d' wreder doet. Daer om is dat die man ghescapen is in den acker van damascho ende dat wyf is ghemaect in den paradise.

³ God heeft volma dat wyf bouen den man geeert want hi se in d' stat d' wellusten ghemaect heeft. Niet en heeft hise ghemaect van den slime d' eerde. alse den man. Mer van den been ende van den vleische des slapende mans. ende edelen op dat si van den voet ghemaect wesende. van den man niet en soude versmaet wesen. Noch van den hoefde. op dat si bouen den man gheen heerlicheit hebben en soude.

We may, therefore, say of the Dutch Speculum what was remarked by M. Campbell in Schinkel's catalogue about a MS. copy of the "Byenboeck" (Book of bees) of 1461 (printed at Zwolle, by P. van Os, 1488): "Il est très-remarquable qu'il y a divers passages dans cette traduction, qui ne se trouvent pas dans les exemplaires imprimés." It appears, further, that there can be by no means any question of change of dialect during the publication of the Dutch editions; that the MS. with the grammatical mistake *dat* (neuter) Spiegel (fem.), comes nearest to the Latin Speculum; that the first Dutch edition still followed this mistake, but that in the second the neuter pronoun to the word Spiegel was corrected. Koning in this point, however, wished to prove how distinctly we can see some things with closed eyes. He "compared" the above extracts from word to word, and it "appeared" to him, not only that both the undated editions had preceded the MS., and were therefore older, but that also his imagined first edition (with old type) "was really and indeed published first of all." Exactly: the types gradually improved by use, as the worn-out horse in Dickens, which remained upright by means of its harness, but went on spontaneously "as soon as the carriage moved on." Koning, moreover, asked the advice of professor A. Ypey at Groningen, who "tested" the "two-fold opinion" of Koning "with all possible accuracy, not only from word to word, but as it were from letter to letter, and found it so wellfounded, that he did not doubt any longer." Now, the professor entirely concurs with Koning in the following points: I. That the copy of the Spiegel, which is considered (by Koning) to be (but typographically, *i.e.* infallibly, is *not*) the oldest, is *really* the earliest edition; that it was followed by the second; that the MS. of 1464 was preceded by these two editions, and that the edition of Veldenaar of 1483 appears to be the last. II. That the language of these three editions and the MS. of the Spiegel, is not the Flemish or Belgian, but the pure Batavian-Dutch language, just as it was spoken in the 15th century [exactly, in the 15th century] in the provinces of Holland proper and Utrecht." How useful, sometimes, to consult a professor! This one assures us, in the present case, that a book which he had never seen, much less read, before, looks exactly as it is described to him in a letter; that the first edition was

---

Mr. Koning had been right in giving priority to this Dutch edition. But, it is also proved by me, in the same manner, that the other Latin edition is the most ancient of all; and that the pretended first Dutch edition was the last printed of the four; and upon this, although Mr. Koning had the opportunity of examining and comparing these two editions as often as he pleased, he preserved a profound silence. Surely, as the proof is the same in all these cases, it would have been wiser in Koning not to refer to it in the one case, unless he was prepared to do it in the other."

followed by the second (which is an unusual case!); that the last edition is really the last; and, finally, that when it appears that the book is written in the French language, it is no German. I wished, for the sake of the author of the "Geschiedenis der Nederlandsche tale" (History of the Dutch language), that he had made a fool of his client; but I am afraid that, notwithstanding his ridiculous advice, he wrote the letter without laughing. It was necessary to speak also of this misère, on account of the fuss Pacile made of this so-called examination of Ypey of the language of the Spiegel. It is only equalled by the decision of Koning: "Let every one who is in favour of Mentz come to Haarlem, compare there the two Latin and the second Dutch Specula with the first Dutch edition, of which the only copy is preserved there, and *if there be but the least lore of truth in his bosom*, he will feel compelled to acknowledge frankly the anteriority of the last to all the others."

And notwithstanding . . . . .

The study of these so-called "first productions" of typography, to which we are constantly referred, is not bad; provided that we do not naively suppose that they fell like meteors from the sky just a little while ago, and ought now to be chemically examined for the first time; provided also that we understand what study is. Armed, like Koning, "with a knowledge of the mechanism of the art," which we may obtain in a couple of hours in every printing-office, with a box by your side full of unsifted citations, arrived on the four winds,—to stare yourself blind on one single book, that is no study, but fantastical biology. Uninterrupted looking at one point makes you magnetical: sparks begin to skip over such a book, over such a Koran descended from heaven; the sparks become flashes, those flashes torches, and at last the condition of the man, who fancies that he is still studying, becomes visionary. What he writes is no science, it is the process of a disease. Comparative, universal examination alone begets science and produces results. This comparative study has been acknowledged—how long already?—as the only true one for mythology, psychology, for linguistic, and a number of other subjects, and has produced results which renew mankind. Let us not stick here to a decidedly obsolete prejudice. The Spiegel ought to be thrown into the full stream of all the typographical productions of the 15th century. So many incunabula are then floating before, behind, and by the side of it, that it cuts no strange figure at all between 1470 and 1480; while, on the other hand, it appears *before* 1440 as a *deus ex machinâ*. Just as the mysteries of all the capitals of Europe formed a separate popular literature in the second quarter of our century, so the Speculum flourished during the last quarter of the 15th century. The literature is always a fruit and mirror of the prevailing spirit of the time; its chief productions constitute the ebb and flow of human life. A (very imperfect) list of productions of the period of the Speculum will prove what we adduce. Besides the undated works:—Speculum humanae salvationis, cum Speculo S. Mariae Virginis, latine et germanice; Spegel der mynschliken Behaltnisse; Speculum artis bene moriendi; Der frawen Spiegel; Der Beichtspiegel; Speculum sacerdotum; Speculum salvatoris; Speculum sapientiae; Speculum bte marie virginis;—the following were published with a date: Speculum salvationis humanae, Parisiis 1498; Spiegel onser behoudenisse, Culemborg 1483; Le mirouer de la redemption de l'humaine lignaige, Lyons 1479, '82 en '88; Spiegel der menschen behültuiss (separate or "mit den evangelien und epistelen"), Basle 1476; Augsburg 1476, '89, '92, '97, 1500; Reutlingen 1492; Speculum conversionis peccatorum, Alost 1473; Speculum vitae humanae, of Ulrich Zell at Cologne and Ulrich Gering at Paris; Rome 1468, '73; Augsburg 1471; Munster in Argan 1472 en '73; Paris 1475; Lyons 1477 &c.; Spiegel des menschlichen Lebens (Augsburg, Günther Zainer), 1479, 1488; Le Miroir de la vie humaine, Lyons 1477, '79; Specio de la vide humana, 1491; Speculum aureum animae peccatricis, Paris 1480, '82, '99; Antwerp 1487; Leipzig 1494; Ulm 1496. Speculum artis bene moriendi, Sterfboeck, Zwolle 1491; Landshut 1520; Speculum exemplorum, Deventer 1481; Cologne 1485; Strasburg 1487, '95, '97; Speculum christiani; Speculum stultorum, London cc. 1480 en '84; Speculum rosarium Jhesu & Mariae, Antwerp 1489; Speculum sermonum super salvatione angelica, Antw. 1487; Spiegel der armen sündigen sele, Ulm 1484, '87; Spiegel des Sünders, Augsburg 1480, '82, '97; Spegel der Dogede, Lubeck 1485; Spoygel der Sachtmödigheit, Lubeck 1487; Speculum saxonicum; Sachsenspiegel, Basle 1474; Der menschen spiegel, Augsburg 1476; Spieghel der simpelre menschen; Spiegel der volcomenheyt, Antwerp; Spyeghel der kersten ghelouc, Antwerp 1482; Spyeghel der ionghers, Antwerp 1500; Spiegel der Sitten, Metz 1500.

This speculum-literature did, of course, not disappear at once in the 16th century. Besides undated works (e.g. Speculum intellectuale felicitatis humanæ, Sp. phlebotomiæ), there were published also Speculum dom. nostri, Nuremb. 1570; Sp. vitæ beati Francisci 1509; Sp. Romanæ magnificentiæ 1575; Spiegel der Gerechtigkeit dorch den hilligen Geist, dorch H(enric) N(iclaes) 1580. But it begins to disappear in the century of the reformation to make room for the sermons and exegeses of protestantism.

The apparently dry list of the editions of the Speculum published while this literature was at its height, which was more especially in the last quarter of the 15th century, is to any historical mind a speculum in itself, which reflects the spirit of the time. Now, I ask any one who thinks, do the Dutch "Spiegels der behoudenis" belong in that broad stream or out of it? Can we, apart even from the positive facts of history, imagine a more unphilosophical theory than the isolation of these books, their removal to 1440, 1430, 1420? And this especially in the Holland of the first half of the 15th century, which did not go then at the head of civilization! At that time the Southern Netherlands were the vanguard of Europe; not before we began to fight as the advance-guard of European liberty, awakened our energy, united with the best elements of Flanders, which were now removed to the North; not before then did we grow from a tribe into a nation.

Just as untenable are Koning's other criteria of the great antiquity of the Speculum. He mentions first the resemblance of the type with the Dutch writing. But all the incunabula present this tendency to imitate the characteristic letter of the indigenous manuscripts; the Italian, French, German, English incunabula reflect the characters of Italian, French, German, and English manuscripts. Tber Hoorne says at the end of his Fasciculus temporum, printed at Cologne 1474, that he imitated the handwriting of the author so accurately, as if it had been written with his own hand. So Nicolaus Jenson cut his types at Venice after the model of the beautiful Italian manuscripts; Colard Mansion at Bruges, after the so-called "Grosse Bâtarde" of the Burgundian-Flemish manuscripts; Antoine Vérard at Paris, after the model of the French, and William Caxton, at Westminster, after the Anglo-Saxon and British codices.[1]

---

[1] "The first printer, when he set about forming his alphabet, was never troubled as to the shape he should give his letters. The form which would naturally present itself to him would be that to which he and the people, to whom he hoped to sell his productions, had been accustomed. It is not at all wonderful, therefore, that the types used in the first printed books closely resemble the written characters of the period; nor that this imitation should be extended to all those combinations of letters which were then in use by the scribes. Thus the Psalters and Bibles which appeared in Germany, among the first productions of the press, were printed in the characters used by the scribes for ecclesiastical servicebooks, while more general literature was printed in the common ba-tard-roman. When Schweinheim and Pannartz, emigrating from Germany, took up their abode at the famous monastery of Subiaco, near Rome, they cut the punches for their new types in imitation of the Roman letters indigenous to the country, although the Gothic tendency still shows itself. In the dominions of the Duke of Burgundy, where the vocation of the scribes had been so extensively encouraged, we find the same plan pursued. Colard Mansion, the first printer at Bruges, was also a celebrated calligrapher, and the resemblance between his printed books and the best written manuscripts of his time, is very marked. The same character of writing was also in use in England; and Caxton's types bear the closest resemblance to the handwriting in the Mercers' books, and to the volumes of that era in the Archives of Guildhall."—The life and typography of William Caxton, England's first printer, with evidence of his typographical connection with Colard Mansion, the printer at Bruges. Compiled from original sources by William Blades. London. Joseph Lilly. 1861. 4to.

The archives of Utrecht contribute something to the life of Caxton which was unknown to Mr. Blades. C. 1462 Caxton established himself at Bruges "in the important position of Governor of the English nation in the Low Countries. The Governor was a sort of king over his countrymen, with almost unlimited authority." As such Caxton makes his appearance in the Utrecht Buurspraeck-boeck (pub-

Koning very elaborately treated of the paper-marks, which occur in the editions of the Speculum. This point may be settled too.

Knowledge of the paper-marks of the middle ages has become an indispensable part of bibliology, a study which was almost neglected by diplomatists. It was, on the other hand, of the greatest interest to bibliography to determine the time, in which the undated editions of the 15th century were produced; and it began, especially in our century, to look for a criterion in the water-marks of the paper on which the incunabula have been printed. For that purpose, De la Serna Santander (Supplément au Catalogue, &c. 1803) gave representations of 147 water-marks; Jansen (Essai sur l'origine de la gravure en bois, 1808) 208; Koning (1816 and 1818) 26; Dr. C. Hermans (Handelingen van het provinciaal genootschap—Transactions of the provincial society in Noordbraband, 1847) 77; Sotheby entered into great details on the water-marks in his "Typography of the Fifteenth Century" (London, 1845), while the third volume of his "Principia Typographica," London (1858), is entirely devoted to the "Paper-marks." In the splendid work of Weigel, mentioned before, 90 water-marks are figured at the end of the second volume. We may add to this literature the work of M. De Stoppelaar, which was published in Holland and gives on sixteen folding plates no less than 260 paper-marks found in the archives of Zealand.[1] Circles and angles, horns, mermaids, scales, keys, dragons, the lamb of God, bunches of grapes, castles, stars, hearts, bulls'-heads, anchors, deer, dolphins, serpents, unicorns, goats, figured letters, hands, mugs, shields of arms are represented most of all. The chronological order shows that these purely industrial figures have also gone through their history: that the manufacturer of paper progressed from the bending of his copper or silver wires, from the original single lines, angles, and circles, to the compound figures

---

lished in de Archief voor kerkelijke en wereldsche geschiedenissen, inzonderheid van Utrecht . . . door J. J. Dodt van Flensburg. V. Utrecht. 1846. 4to. :—

1464. Des Saterdaechs na Clementis. Die raet, out ende nywe, gheven gheleide den eersamen, wysen, Willem Caxtoin, gouvernor, ende den coepluden vander nacien van Engelant, mit horen liven, goeden ende coepmanscappen, alhier te moghen comen, wesen ende bliven, ende weder van hier te gaen mit horen comanscappen, alsoe dicke alst hem ghelieven sal, &c.

1465. Des Saterdaechs na Victoris. Die rade gheven gheleide den eersamen, wysen, Willem Caxtoin, goevernor, ende den coepluden vande nacien van Enghelant, &c.

1467. Op Alresielen dach, Willem Caxtoin gheleide.—In the years 1408, 1441, and 1445 Claes Ketelaer is mentioned, in 1433 Henric Henricxsz., the "verlichter," and in 1466 Peter Dircxsz., the "boeldedrucker." A beacon to sail towards Utrecht! For here a *prenter* really appears: perhaps the printer of the plates of the Speculum.

Noordzick, in his "Oproeping aan Nederland," 1847, tried to make the temporary residence of Caxton at Utrecht, as protector of the commercial interests of England, serviceable to the Coster fable, by calling him "Factor of the Dutch merchants at London." Van Westreenen drew attention to this distortion and called Caxton, not altogether correctly either, "Head of a compagny of Englishmen at Utrecht." He thinks this all the more important on account of the confirmation it gives to the supposition of the relation between the earliest printers of Utrecht, Haarlem, and the first English printing-office. De Vries, after having defended Noordzick against this attack, by arguing that Noordzick knew quite well that Caxton was an Englishman, and that the head of a company of English at Utrecht could have been just as well Factor of Dutch merchants at London, makes the following naive confession: "M. Noordzick called Caxton, by preference, Factor of the Dutch merchants in England, and not of English merchants in Holland, in order to point out more distinctly the close relation of Caxton to the Dutch, and thereby the probability of the history that the art of printing was brought by him to England *from Holland*." Delightful logic! in order to make it more probable that Caxton brought the art of printing to England from Holland, Noordzick places him rather in London than in Utrecht! But, Noordzick soon observed his mistake, for in 1848 he changed the ridiculous title given to Caxton into a better one: Factor of English merchants at Utrecht.

Caxton, he who had resided also some years in Bruges, when Colard Mansion printed there, and who had been in Cologne and Utrecht, and had introduced typography into England, writes himself, in 1482 (Policronicon, Liber ultimus), while describing the events of 1450: "Also about this tyme the crafte of Enpryntyng was fyrst founde in magounce in Almayne, whiche crafte is multiplyed thurgh the world in many places, & bookes ben had grete chepe and in grete nombre by cause of the same crafte." Blades adds to this quotation the words: "We have here Caxton's account of the popular (?) belief of his age, and it is undoubtedly the true one." The author ought to have stopped here and not ventured into Costerian sophisms, beneath the dignity and character of his book. They have prevented me from following him.

[1] Het papier in de Nederlanden gedurende de middeleeuwen, inzonderheid in Zeeland, door mr. J. H. de Stoppelaar, pp. 1—125 of vol. VII.: Archief. Vroegere en latere mededeelingen voornamelijk in betrekking tot Zeeland, uitgegeven door het Zeeuwsche Genootschap der Wetenschappen. Middelburg. 1869. 8vo.

which began to resemble drawings. And, although the marks (for common paper) have disappeared, the remembrance of a mark generally used in a favoured kind of paper, still lives in the language: the hunting-horn was gradually transformed into a *post*-horn, and, although it is no longer found in our vellum-post, it is still said that we write our letters on post-paper.

The only true method to be followed by this inquiry also, is to examine paper-marks and dates, without troubling ourselves with pedant suppositions. All cavilling, as long as all the materials are not together, is loss of time, and drowns the questions long before they are ripe for decision. To collect indefatigably building-materials, and to pass sentence only when the documents of the process are complete, is demanded by science from the self-denial and perseverance of its priests. The results of the examination of the paper-marks are for the present mostly negative to bibliography, but removal is as indispensable as building. Meerman already argued, in accordance with De Boze, Clement, and Fournier, the invalidity of the paper-arguments (Manca sunt igitur omnia, quae ex singulis chartaceis petuntur argumenta); and Fisher commenced his essay: "Die Papierzeichen als Kennzeichen des Alterthumskunde anzuwenden," with an argument to the same effect. Koning, on the other hand, raised the water-marks of the four editions of the Speculum to one of the chief pillars of his system, in which this illustrated book had a Haarlem origin in the period between 1420 and '40. Although his pretences were already amply refuted by Lehne,[1] Schaab, and Wetter, many continued to value these fantastic air-balls. The work of De Stoppelaar contributes, in spite of itself, to give to that of Koning the finishing blow on this point also. As for the main point, this author has distinctly shown the invalidity of Koning's supposition that the letters in the paper of the 15th century (in our case the P and the Y) were royal initials. Moreover, this unprincipled system condemned itself by the palpable anachronisms and perilous tumblings to which the projector of this supposition saw himself compelled in his explanations.

As paper-marks of the "Speculum" and the "Spiegel," Koning gave six different bulls'-heads, the lily (this figure is no lily, but an anchor), two unicorns, a double key, a hand, three different shields of arms, a bow, two dolphins, the letters M A in a circle and six variations of the letter P, of which the three last obviously represent the Y. The bull's-head, which is found in different variations since 1301, with bar and cross from 1370–1523, was such a general paper-mark, that Koning himself acknowledges that it proves nothing by itself, and could, consequently, be left out of the discussion.[2] The anchor (Koning's lily) which originated already in the 14th century, became in the 15th century the greatest rival of the bull's-head. This sheet-anchor of Koning occurs in incunabula of Ulrich Zell at Cologne, of Ulrich Gering at Paris, and it was "generally" used by the Netherland printers of Utrecht, Gouda, Delft, Louvain and Deventer. A third mark, the unicorn (1398–1620), was so generally used that it appears "nearly throughout" in the first works published at Deventer, Delft, Utrecht, Alost and Louvain. De Stoppelaar says of it: "We meet henceforth (from the beginning of the 15th century) in the

---

[1] Einige Bemerkungen über das Unternehmen der gelehrten Gesellschaft zu Harlem, ihrer Stadt die Ehre der Erfindung der Buchdruckerkunst zu ertrotzen. Von F. Lehne. Maintz. 1823. 8vo.
Vier brieven, gewisseld tusschen Mr. Jac. Scheltema en Jac. Koning, over de laatste tegenspraak van het regt van Haarlem op de uitvinding der drukkunst (!) Haarlem. 1823. 8vo.
Nieuw onderzoek naar de aanspraak van Holland op de uitvinding der boekdrukkunst, door Prof. Ebert te Wolfenbuttel; en Brief wegens het geschrift van prof. Friedrich Lehne. Met eene voorrede en eenige aanmerkingen van Jac. Koning. Haarlem, 1825. 8vo.
Historisch-critische Prüfung der Ansprüche, welche die Stadt Harlem auf den Ruhm der Erfindung der Buchdruckerkunst macht, durch Beleuchtung der Ansichten ihrer Vertheidiger, des Herrn Ebert und des Herrn Koning. Von Friedrich Lehne. Mainz. 1827. 8vo.

[2] Representations of the bull's-head are found already on the tables of Schwarz, de Orig. Typog. diss. III., and by Sardini, Esame sui principi della Francese ed Italiana Typographia (Lucca, 1798). One of Koning's variations is found in the Utrecht works printed by Ketelaer and de Leempt. I found a variation of the P in the Spiegel in the paper of a Haarlem Sheriff-register of 1496, another even in the treasury-accounts of 1539.

ost every year this mark, which, not made by all paper manufac-
are and skill, looks sometimes graceful, and sometimes deformed.
ever, have in general so much similarity, that we can hardly
: distance of time, any difference in shape. On that account
twenty years, a few of them at random, and among those which
st of all, or deviated mostly from the ordinary form." The
ad unicorn, therefore, may also be regarded, as far as Koning's
id 1420—1440 is concerned, as finished with. De Stoppelaar
th mark: "The keys which are standing back to back, belong
15th century;" and he notices that they occur at Middelburg
s Hertogenbosch in 1463. They appear afterwards in Cologne
urs as paper-mark throughout the whole of the 15th and 16th
udented wheel, De Stoppelaar gives a representation of the years
g, however, has made the greatest abuse of the initials which
i. Without thinking of the name of the manufacturer or of the
manufactured, these paper-marks are raised by him to a dynastic
paper-fabricator conceals, from the very outset, a royal betrothal
ial P. stands for Philip, and just for that Philip whom Koning
t; the Y. is Ysabella of Portugal, the wife of Philip the Good,
ot married before 10th March, 1430; and the imagined initial of
cady at 's Hertogenbosch 1395, and occurs at the Hague till
guese princess had been dead already a long time. After the
iod M. A. becomes Margaret, although her daughter Jacoba
: to find also Charles the Bold, is explained by Carolus Bur-
Carolus (!), and C. I. by Carolus Imperator. We see that the
observed even the most delicate political distinctions, and took
Charles, king of the Romans, with Charles, the emperor. As
ved the greatest part in this arbitrary game, they are fittest of
g it for good and all.
hough Koning did not discover it before 1428, appears already
ts of the counts of Holland at the Hague. A variation of this
a (Koning's) second Dutch and Latin editions of the Speculum.
oppelaar, "the greatest part of the books, published after
ries in the course of the 15th century, have *the same* mark as
1 De Leempt at Utrecht, of Richard Paffroed at Deventer, or
, of Martens at Antwerp and Alost, of the Fratres communis
[ohn de Westphalia and Conrad Braem at Louvain. Editions
ve the same mark too." Very true. But he adds: "On the
was ever printed on paper with this mark at Mentz; neither
ters it afterwards. Only at Cologne we find now and then the
ce or four editions, all of them, however [N.B.!] of the latter
itury." Untrue. Koning's criterion is found in the Mammo-
ntz by Peter Schöffer in 1470, in the Scrutinium scripturarum
78; the Mammotractus of Koelhof, Cologne, 1479, has the P.
e first is still found in Boëtius, De philosophiæ consolatione,
at Nuremberg in 1486; Libellus Juris, Strasburg, 1490;
501. Facts which were pointed out already before 1830, may
ok for truth, be ignored in '69. In all these editions, in all
these years, the P. had as much connexion with duke Philip
:. It is remarkable how the often-repeated assertion that one
er-marks of the so-called Haarlem editions does *not* occur at
arliest Netherland and Cologne books, proves just the contrary
prove—the priority of the Mentz to the Dutch incunabula, the
g the Speculum from the second to the third and fourth quarters
Instead, therefore, of the paper-marks adding weight to Koning's
a trap, dangerous to this argument, concealed in these marks.

He had the recklessness of ignorance to put this hazardous alternative: the cause of Haarlem depends upon the examination of the Speculum, and must stand or fall with it. We take him at his word. Before the face of this honest examination of the Speculum the cause of Haarlem " is fallen."

The archæological and artistical examination of the engravings of the Spiegel, for which we might have a support in the xylographic alphabet discovered at Basle, of the same school and with the date 1464,—may remain out of the question. For as woodcuts, copies of drawings, whose birth we cannot determine within a quarter of a century, they are an unlawful criterion, which has only caused confusion. As result of the discussions on this subject of Heinecke, Santander, Douce, Ottley, Chatto, Sotheby, Humphrey, Guichard, Renouvier, De Laborde, Passavant, Lacroix, Ruelens, Berjeau, Sotzmann, Waagen, Harzen, Weigel, &c., we only know that it is impossible to determine the age of the engravings of the Speculum within ten or twenty years. The fact is simply, that the pure North-Netherland, common Low-German character of the xylography of the Speculum, places the book historically in the second half of the 15th century, and—in connexion with the whole current of the Netherland-German development of wood-engraving, with the positive dates of all the discovered typographic and xylographic illustrated works (mostly from c. 1470 till the 16th century) far in the third quarter of that century, and so on till 1500. I may add to this that Holtrop, the best judge of Netherland incunabula, during a long discussion on the Specula, made the following confession to me : " When you ask me on my conscience, I must say : *these books are not so old.*"[1]

---

[1] When I had written this, the long-protracted illness of Mr. Holtrop terminated with his death. By this loss I am at liberty to sketch, without any reserve, the relation of this most competent judge to the Coster-question. His death before the completion of my work is very painful to me ; the public expression of his final decision would have been of inestimable value to me. The many afternoons, during the years 1867 and '68, on which Holtrop never got tired of talking the question over with me, either in connexion with his Monuments, which would soon be completed, or with the account of Junius, which we had examined already a hundred times, before us—these hours, as so many fruitful lectures, will not only never be forgotten by me, but they enable me to state precisely what Holtrop thought of the question. He was a man too talented, too well versed in the literature of the question, too well acquainted with the Netherland incunabula, to put up with the charlatanry of Koning and Paeile, with the conceited language of the jacks which were used, about 1848, to get up the case of the statue. He never concealed for a moment his contempt for all that had been written on this question. He was nothing but a Costerian "in expectation." After having worked for years on the careful collection and publication of materials necessary for a history of the Netherland incunabula of the XVth century, it could not be demanded from him, at his advanced age and with his health undermined, to open the discussion again ; he transferred that to younger and fresher strength, and repeatedly encouraged me to continue my investigations, when I became wearied with the struggle against that ocean of books with which this question has been inundated in the course of three centuries. "I feel bound," said Holtrop, "with regard to my arrangement of the Monuments typographiques, to keep to Junius's account; I cannot let it precede by a book, to build a deviation on it ; that is now the work of another, that is now *your* work." He said this because I was more prepared than is generally the case in this matter, as I had agreed, already some years before, with Dr. A. de Vries, by whom I, as well as all others, had been morally intimidated, to make of all his writings on this subject, one work in German. During my study for that task, doubts made themselves master of my mind, for I found mistakes everywhere ; my bibliographical conversation with Holtrop gave another direction to my researches; the investigation itself of all that belonged to the question gave me certainty. I *know* that Holtrop would have agreed with the results—with the decisive results of that investigation ; for he was, I repeat it, nothing more than a Costerian of the statu quo, in an objective, truly scientific sense.

One moment, however, his fancy seems to have led his opinion astray.

Mattijs van der Goes, who printed at Antwerp from 1482—91, used, in a work of 1487 (Sermones quatuor novissimorum) two xylographic vignettes, one of which represented a savage, the other a ship, both represented in the Monuments (pl. 101). Of the last-mentioned wood-cut, Mr. Holtrop gave the following description :—

"La seconde vignette représente un grand navire, à trois mâts, vu de babord, comme on en rencontre dans les manuscrits du XVe siècle ; il est amarré ; ses voiles sont pliées ; chaque mât est surmonté d'une cage ou corbeille. Au sommet du grand mât flottent deux pavillons, l'un aux armes du Saint-Empire, l'autre aux armes de la ville d'Anvers. Le mât de l'avant porte un pavillon avec une marque dont j'ignore la signification ; peut-être est-ce le chiffre de l'imprimeur. Le château d'arrière porte un pavillon au monogramme de l'imprimeur (un M. surmonté d'une double croix). Le bastingage est orné de neuf écussons. Les trois du milieu, en suivant l'ordre de gauche à droite, représentent : le premier les armes de l'Evêché d'Utrecht, le second la Croix de Bourgogne, le troisième les armes d'Autriche. Les écussons du château d'avant représentent, dans le même ordre, la Province de Hollande, la ville de Harlem et la Province de Zélande. ceux enfin du château d'arrière, les armoiries de la famille d'Ursel, celles de la

XIII.

JOANNES FAUSTUS.

Junius was, with all his contemporaries, dupe of the Faust-legend. He was therefore compelled to graft his Coster-legend, not on history, but on the untruths of the grandson of Fust. The Haarlem false prophet had no other hero at his disposal but Johan Schöffer's fictitious inventor, Johan Fust of Mentz. Armed with this knowledge, Junius, well read, in the active and passive sense of the word, baptizes Coorn-

---

famille de Ranst et un écusson représentant une oie, armes de la ville de Goes ou van der Goes, en Zélande.

"Il me paraît assez probable que van der Goes a voulu donner ici plus que sa marque typographique, et qu'en choisissant pour sa vignette la forme d'un navire, ce n'était pas simplement pour faire allusion à la ville d'Anvers, alors déjà célèbre par son commerce. Je crois qu'il a voulu rendre une idée sous la forme symbolique d'un navire. Ce genre de symbole se rencontre plusieurs fois. C'est ainsi que lorsque le Duc Philippe le Bon a célébré, à Lille en 1453, la fête de la Toison d'Or, un des entremets du magnifique banquet donné à cette occasion, avait la forme d'un navire (caraque) ancré. Dans la 'Pompe funèbre, faite à Bruxelles, par ordre de Philippe II, pour l'Empereur Charles V, en 1558,' figure un navire magnifique, pavoisé aux armes de l'Empereur, orné d'écussons et de sculptures emblématiques. Ce navire était le porteur des hommages rendus à l'Empereur.

"Ici l'imprimeur a choisi un superbe navire pour indiquer, d'une manière symbolique et chronographique, l'époque, à laquelle il exerçait son art. Je soumets l'explication suivante de sa vignette au jugement de mes lecteurs.

"Sous le règne du Duc de *Bourgogne* Philippe le Bel, qui gouvernait les Pays-Bas sous la tutelle de son père, Maximilien *d'Autriche*; lorsque David de Bourgogne, son grand-oncle, occupait le siège épiscopal *d'Utrecht*:—*Matthias*, natif de la ville de *Goes* ou *van der Goes*, dans la Province de *Zélande*, exerçait l'art de l'imprimerie à *Anvers*. ville du Margraviat du *Saint-Empire*, lorsque Jean *de Ranst*, Seigneur de Morsele et de Canticrode, était Marquis d'Anvers, et lorsque Lancelot *d'Ursel* était Amman de la ville d'Anvers.

"La dignité d'Amman était conférée à vie. et comme Lancelot d'Ursel succéda en cette qualité à Jean de Dintre en l'an 1483, il s'ensuit que cette vignette n'a pu être gravée qu'après cette année. Elle paraît ici, en 1487, déjà passablement fatiguée et cassée, ce qui me porte à croire qu'elle date de quelques années auparavant.

"Restent alors les deux écussons de la Province de *Hollande* et de la ville de *Harlem*. Elles s'expliqueraient comme celles de la Zélande et de Goes, savoir: *Harlem*, ville de *la Hollande*.

"Mais dans quel but l'artiste fait-il figurer ici cette ville? S'il avait voulu faire allusion à une ville quelconque des Pays-Bas, où l'on exerçait l'imprimerie avant lui, il aurait pu choisir Utrecht, Alost, Louvain ou Bruxelles, villes où l'imprimerie était introduite depuis les années 1473, 1474, 1476; tandis que l'on ne connaît de livre imprimé, dans la ville de *Harlem*, avec date certaine, que du 10 Décembre de l'an 1483.

"Van der Goes doit avoir eu une raison bien particulière d'orner la proue de son navire symbolique des armes de *Harlem*. Serait-ce peut-être que l'artiste ait voulu indiquer la ville de *Harlem* comme le berceau de l'imprimerie? Dans ce cas sa vignette serait le plus ancien document en faveur de la cause de Harlem."

Against this interpretation of the Antwerp ship we must put the axiom that the knowledge of a Haarlem invention of typography among the Netherland printers of the fifteenth century, without their having mentioned it with a single word in all their imprints, is historically *impossible*. If Matthijs van der Goes, who printed for instance in 1482 the "Spieghel des gheloefs," had had the same opinion of the "Spieghel der menscheliker behoudenisse" as Junius, he would not have concealed it in a typographic charade, which, in ingenuity, surpasses a rebus in an illustration.

But the supposition of Holtrop is too ingenious to put it off with an axiom.

In the first place, as for the symbolic character of the ship, Junius relates in the Batavia also something of ships as emblems, and that just Haarlem ones. After having related the capture of Damiate by the Haarlemers, he says: "Cuius rei memoriæ sempiternæ institutum reor, moreruque per manus in hunc vsque diem traditum observat Harlemæa pubes, vt Calend. Jannarijs (quæ an huiusce stratagematis testes fuerint clam me est) nauiculas serratas proris instructas imaginesque victoriæ argumenta, bacillis suffixas, in publicis supplicationibus circum ferat." Nothing, therefore, prevents me from reading the arms on Van der Goes' woodcut as Holtrop did, and then to add: And just now, as the town of Haarlem in Holland has a ship as emblem on account of its heroic deed, I, Matthijs, of Goes in Zealand, have a ship, &c.

But I really don't know whether the custom, as related by Junius, existed already at Haarlem a century earlier, and find, moreover, the interpretation too affected. It is as unreal as that of Holtrop.

Are we allowed to regard the three boards in the middle of the ship as three shields of arms? And if the first were to signify episcopal Utrecht, why is it then placed next to the Burgundian cross, a

bert's "unfaithful servant" as Johan Fust. But he performs the sacrament with trembling hand. Thus he speaks: "Among the workmen was a certain Johannes; I will not anxiously inquire (!) whether it was he (*as is supposed*) who bore the ominous name of Faustus, but was unfaithful and unfortunate to his master: or really another Johannes. For I have no wish to annoy the dead, as they must have suffered enough during their lifetime from the pangs of their conscience." Junius, it is true, upsets a moment afterwards this story with his own hand, by elaborately describing the passion of the bookbinder Cornelis, who slept for some months with this "villain" Joannes (ut fert suspicio), and must therefore have known his name; but this is no obstacle to an orthodox Costerian mind; let us listen to Jacobus Koning: "One can understand that this villanous servant, brooding over such an awful project, concealed his real name, and presented himself only by the name of Johan (so common among the Germans)." Of course, Jacobus, one "can understand." As soon as in 1440 the Speculum had been advertized in the "Börsenblatt" at Leipzig, the rich Fust of Mentz made a trip to Haarlem as "Wanderbursche," learned on his journey beforehand the way which he should have to return over Amsterdam and Cologne, went into the service of Laurens Janszoon Coster, chandler-typographer in the market-place (who could get no longer men enough at Haarlem), slept some months with our darling Cornelis, who lay just then in his cradle (the sharper thought, du lieber Kleine, bei dir ist's sicher ruhen, du wirst mir allerdings nichts anhaben, wenn's dazu komt!), learned quickly the moulding of candles and composing, and took himself off already, 25th Dec. 1441, as a thief, not only with the printing-machinery, but also with the brains of Lourens Coster, Thomas Pietersz., and the other workmen; for these had not only lost their *types* after the theft, but they had so entirely forgotten all about the *typography*, that only a century afterwards people began to remember it. All this may "be understood," namely, by weak brains, as history; by sound brains, as farce. And what does the poor fellow dare to add to his miserable explanation? To have furnished so many proofs of the theft that "no unprejudiced, impartial reader will doubt it a moment longer. For those who, animated by blind prejudice, *are incapable of being convinced at all*, we (Koning, for this class of people insist upon writing in plurali eminentiæ), have not taken up the pen." Now, I must acknowledge that Koning has supplied spick and-

---

sign, no arms? Why is mention made of Utrecht? What connexion has Utrecht with the rest? Why is the third shield of arms, the bar sinister, to signify Austria? Because Maximilian, already king of the Romans, is archduke of Austria and guardian of Philip? This is very far-fetched, and resembles Koning's dynastic paper-marks.

Some observations, also, with respect to the other shields of arms. The first (from the left to the right), the lion, may signify Holland, Braband, and five-and-twenty countries and towns, especially *Zierikzee*. The second seems to be that of Haarlem, but it may also be that of Tholen, and it resembles much that of Alost. The third may stand for Zealand, but the fourth and fifth hardly for Ursel and Ranst: at least, according to a representation of the genuine arms of these families, which I received some time ago from Belgium. The sixth, although Smallegange and d'Ablaing give it in a different way, may be Goes (gans, Engl. goose).

The nine arms of the ship-board, read from the left to the right, are, according to Holtrop: I. (prow) 1. Holland, 2. Haarlem, 3. Zealand; II. (middle) 4. Episcopacy of Utrecht. 5. Burgundy, 6. Austria; III. (stern) 7. Van Ursel, 8. De Ranst, 9. Goes. But they may also be read in this way: 1. Zierikzee (Halmale), 2. Haarlem (Tholen, Alost), 3. Zealand, 4. Zwolle, 5. ?, 6. Louvain (Schevenisse, Borselen in Zealand), 7. Van Ursel ?, 8. Gouda (Kruiningen in Zealand), 9. Goes. If we assume, therefore, that the wood-cut was engraved after 1483, and worn already somewhat in 1487, a very rational, unaffected sense arises for that period from the idea that the arms may signify a series of towns where printing-offices were established at that time. And look—in the middle we find *Zwolle, Louvain*; higher up, *Haarlem*; after that, perhaps *Gouda*. But I don't know what to do with the others. I put, therefore, conjecture against conjecture, and reason thus: I, *Matthijs*, of *Goes*, disciple of Jacob Bellaert, of *Zierikzee*, printer at *Haarlem*, have established myself at *Antwerp*, free town, &c.

With our Haarlem claims to the honour of the invention of printing, we have successively relied upon an imagined, and afterwards falsified, pedigree of an unknown Haarlem citizen; on a story which represent the art of printing as having been invented, propagated, stolen, and lost, in Holland within two years; on a fictitious date of 1428; on a Haarlem sheriff-innkeeper, who died already before the fictitious invention had taken place; on a complication of historical distortions, logical mistakes, wilful mystifications; heaven forbid that we should now base the fable on a charade, on an Antwerp wood-cut! For on this turning earth a wrongly interpreted wood-engraving is not capable of upholding a statue.

span new proofs of the theft of the invention of the art of printing, simply *revealed* by Junius in 1568 (1588), as having been committed on Christmas-eve, 1441, by Johan (ut fert suspicio) Faust.—Namely, that theft of Johan in 1441 was, according to Koning, committed on Christmas-eve, 1439, by the Mentz knight Friele Gensfleisch, brother of Johan Gensfleisch Gutenberg!

And the evidence for this unscientific scandal is to be found in the fact, that in a Latin edition of the Speculum twenty xylographic leaves, and in a Dutch edition of the same work two leaves, printed with a smaller type, occur, from which it appears —*that Friele Gensfleisch took with him some printed leaves of these two editions*, probably in order to get the more unobserved and quicker out of the gate of Haarlem.

The second evidence is found in the treasury-accounts of Haarlem. "There we find noticed every year the sums paid to messengers, for journeys they made in behalf of the town, among them now and then to the bailiff or the constabulary of Amsterdam. But it is remarkable that in the accounts, from St. Mark (25th April) 1439, to St. Mark, 1440, the despatch of one of the town-messengers to the bailiff or the constabulary of the aforesaid town, is mentioned no less than nine times; and still more remarkable, that the first item is entered on the last holy day of Christmas, while, finally, we find that an interview took place between the bailiff Jan Heynenzoon and Dirk van Wormer, in behalf of the town of Amsterdam, and the constabulary of Haarlem. It is true that the subject of this busy correspondence is not named;" but that is of course of no consequence to Koning; one must be "totally blind," "entirely incapable of conviction," "deprived of all common sense," "addicted to miserable fault-finding;" in short, be a tissue of anti-Costerian unrighteousness, not to see plainly that there *is* to be read, not what I, for instance, read there this moment, but the intelligent Koning. We find in the treasury-accounts of 1439, p. 168ᵇ:—

"Item some of the constabulary had a meeting with Jan heynen soen and Dirc van wormer, who came on behalf of the town of Amsterdam with certain messages to Haarlem, at the house of florijs aelbrechtssoen and spent there," &c.¹

Who does not perceive that Jan and Dirc came, in behalf of Amsterdam, to inquire about Friele Gensfleisch, the German robber-knight, who, laden with Louwerys Janssoen's printing-office, as Samson with the gates of Gaza, was making a journey from Haarlem to Mentz? Koning even omitted stronger evidences, for the same account says: "Item on St. Louren's-day despatched Hubert (the town-messenger) to Muden, and afterwards to Ouderkerc, to Jan Heynensoon, and was absent iij. days."² Thus, the magistrates of Haarlem made inquiries after Friele Gensfleisch at Muiden and Ouderkerk too, and, with a kind attention, on the name-day of Louwerys Janssoen! But Koning was really not so silly as he appeared here. He *knew* more than he pleased to tell us. I am obliged to prove his dishonesty. He prints in his Essay: "We assure our readers that nowhere in these accounts such a repeated dispatch occurs, and this circumstance incontrovertibly deserves particular attention." Exactly. And while now in public writing the reason for this "repeated dispatch" is said to be the pursuit of the mythic thief of an *invention*, the true reason is put down in his manuscript.³ There prevailed in that year a contagious

---

¹ "Item soe saten sommige van den gerechte mit Jan heynen soen en*de* Dirc van wormer, die van der stede wege van aemstelredam mit zekeren boetschappen tot hairlem gecomen waren tot florijs aelbrechtssoens huze en*de* verteerden aldair mits cost en*de* XXVI mengelen wijns en*de* costen illic mengele II stuver fc. III lb ix s IIII d."

² Item op sinte lourijs dich hubert (der stede messelgier) gesent tot muden ende voirt ter ouderkerc an Jan Heynensoen, en*de* was wt iij. daghen.

³ This curious MS. is a folio volume, wholly written by Koning himself, with a neat and small handwriting; it contains 332 pages, is provided with an index of 14 leaves, and has on its vellum-back the following title: *Thesauriers Rekeningen der stad Haarlem* ('Treasury-accounts of the town of Haarlem). It is evident from the contents that Koning studied with microscopic punctuality the municipal accountbooks of Haarlem, from 1417 to 1475; that he read every item, scrutinized every page, counted the letters, spied into the commas and full-stops, and investigated the water-marks. As a proof that I wish to be understood literally, I give one annotation which we find on p 115 (year 1448):

"Looking over this book, my attention was for the first time attracted to the fact that here on the top

disease at Haarlem, which caused great mortality, on account of which many members of the government left the town. On page 89[b], it is said : " Some of the constabulary were summoned to the Hague, who were not at home on account of the mortality;" page 105[a] "Sent Hubert, xxii Oct., to the bailiff of Uitgeest and afterwards to Alkmaar, to our constabulary who stayed there on account of the mortality;" page 105[b] "Sent Hubert, xviii Nov., to Wyk-op-zee to Jan van bakensteyne, burgomaster, who stayed there on account of the mortality;" page 187[b] (from the recto of which I quote, by-the-way, as a curiosity, that twenty-four pence was paid for a barrel of beer, drank by men who came to ring the large bell against a heavy thunderstorm, which seems to indicate a profane competition with the thunder), "Item the Sunday after our Lady-day ysbrand van schote(n), burgomaster, is summoned to Haarlem from Alkmaar, where he stayed on account of the mortality;" page 138[a] "Item Ysbrand van Schote(n), burgomaster, and florijs willemssoen are summoned to Haarlem from Alkmaar, where they were staying on account of the mortality, and they had to speak about business of the town;" page 164[a] "Paid at herman pollen's house, where the constabulary, clerks, and messengers who were at Haarlem during the mortality had met; spent at Willem van Zaenden's house, where they met during the mortality, about matters of the town;" page 164[b] "Paid at the house of Jan Dirk tymanssoen, where some of the constabulary made expenses during the mortality;" page 165[b] "Item the Friday after St. Pontian's the constabulary gave a dinner to Lord Van Oestervaut . . . . at the house of the bailiff, where was offered to Lord Van Oestervant," &c. Koning, therefore, could *not* help seeing the reason of the uncommon bustle in the year 1439, and he did see it; he put it down on the very

---

of the letter i no dot (i) is placed, but an oblique line (í). The same possibly takes place in earlier Treasury-accounts (this to be investigated, in so far as they are still in my hands).—In the fac-simile of the Spiegel [speculum] by Meerman, we see on many of the i's the same line instead of a dot.—This shows again that the printer of that Spiegel imitated the manuscripts of his time, and [affords] also (in addition to the other observations) reason to suppose that this work belongs to Haarlem (!) "

We see what was the object of Koning's investigation, and that he not even disdained arguments so trifling as that line on the i, as fine and as strong as cobweb. At the same time he copied everything from the Treasury-books which appeared to him of some importance, even if it stood in no connexion whatever with his answer to the prize-essay of the " Hollandsche Mantschappy der Wetenschappen te Haarlem" (Dutch Society of Sciences at Haarlem). A few examples will make this plain :—

1429. Item van twe waghens dair onse goede lude mede voeren van brugghe tot ghent, also onse genadige he(re) hue bourg[ne] en(de) onse genadige vrouwe alle die wagens op dede houden tot hoirre behoeft en(de) men an gheen waghens come(n) en conde dan om den meesten pe(n)ninc. te samen geg. VI. lb. VIII. s. (Item for two carriages with which our people went from Bruges to Ghent, as our gracious Lord of Burgundy and our gracious Lady took all the carriages for their own use, and none were to be had but for the highest price . . .)

Item opte(n) XXIIIste(n) dach in meye so hier tydinghe gecome(n) was dat die zerouers die die schepe(n) op zuderzee ghenome hadde(n) weder becraftcint ware(n) van die van enchusen so wordt pieter symonsz van der stede weghen tot enchusen gesent om twaer dair aff te verneme(n). . . (Item on the 23rd of May, as the tidings arrived that the pirates who had taken the vessels on the Zuiderzee, had been captured by the people of Enkhuizen, Pieter Symonsz was sent to Enkhuizen to learn the truth about this affair.)

This much will suffice to prove the copiousness of Koning's extracts. After his death the MS. came into the possession of Dr. A. de Vries, from whose left property it was bought by me in 1864. After having finished this essay, I have given it a permanent place in the Royal library (at the Hague), whereby every one is able to judge of my sentence on Koning.

Koning, until 1475, omitted not a single annotation, which M. Enschedé thought afterwards worth while to take a note of, including even the items which regard the chandler Louwerys Janszoon Coster, and which have been used with inconceivable rashness by M. J. A. Alberdingk Thym. The Treasury-accounts of Haarlem, therefore, contain no more items which could throw light on the momentous question, which is being discussed again, since a year or two, in Holland and elsewhere. I have the necessary documents in my room. Let every one make a distinction between Jacobus Koning, author of the prize-essay, and Jacobus Koning, author of this manuscript. For his over-complete collection of materials for his work is one thing, the incomplete use which he has made of them in his public plea is another. No one, who does not wish to see a favourite idea confirmed by a sophism, but desires only truth in this purely historical question, can any longer put up with this defence. The same may be said of the argumentation of Dr. de Vries, although it is in every respect, even in dexterity and daring, superior to that of Koning. The unwearied champion of the claims of Haarlem made a deep impression on many, also on myself, by his perseverance, acuteness, and the ability with which he contrived to conceal the gaps in the legend. He had for more than half a century studied the Haarlem system, identified himself with it; and when, to the triumph he had gained, and to the acknowledgment of his talent, a natural respect for an uncommonly advanced age, coupled with a still clear mind, added itself, every one lost even the courage of doubt.

page on which he built his theory, which I quoted. He was, therefore, not stupid, but wary, when he wrote on page 185 of his Essay, that the numerous dispatches of 1489 "incontrovertibly deserved a particular attention," for he himself had transcribed the true reason. But stupid was he, nevertheless, for he forgot what he had let out on page 150: "In the latter half of the year 1439, there prevailed at Haarlem an awful, highly dangerous disease (probably the plague, not unreasonably inferred by Koning from the dearness of 1489, followed by want and bad feeding), which increased to such a height that the members of the government left the town and resided elsewhere, at Alkmaar, at Wyk-op-Zee, &c., being consulted in those places of retreat on the cases which presented themselves, and summoned to Haarlem only in the greatest necessity. Whether Laurens Janszoon has been one of the victims of this disease cannot be determined." Herewith Koning's beautiful demonstration of the theft may be regarded as buried with the victims of the epidemic of 1439 and 1440.

Just as officious as people were at all times to alter the year of the invention, according to the better use they could make of it, of equally chameleon-like nature, the Joannes (*ut fert suspicio*) Faustus of Junius proved soon to be. With Petrus Bertius (Tabulae Geographicae, 1600) Faust *is* already a threefold villain (trifurcifer). Scriverius rhymed still, it is true, on "Hans Fuyst," but at the same time in "memory of Hans Gutenberg" as thief. On two opposite pages in the Lauwerkrans, we read:

> Thou, Haarlem, art robbed of thy noble printing-office,
> Which arrived at Mentz and directly all over the country;
> How has Hans done this? how has he managed it?
> He put his hand out, grasped, and closed his fist.
>
> Ah! rascal! ah! are you there? is it you, Hans Gutenbergher?
> Why, does this name become you? Yes, twofold rascal, and worse!
> Notorious by theft, oh shameless man!
> This word is still too mild for your villany.
>
> Because you concealed Laurens' good and carried it away,
> And stole it falsely: so hear we now speak
> Of Goedenberghers praise; however they disguise it,
> By the Goeden-berg they betray the Guyten (rogue)-berg.

In this punning fits the conclusion:

> But in order that you may have something as a reward,
> Be exposed to view as a thief in this picture.

By so much plebeian insolence we had a right to be astonished at the indignation of the Mentz people. And on what foundation does Scriverius base his imputation? He merely says: "The books of Mentz cause me to think whether Johan Gutenbergher is not the man who, with bag and baggage, ran away from his master Laurens Jansz. Coster and offered the art to others in Germany and sold it."

For that reason he fearlessly addresses Hans Guytenberg thus:

> "Shameless rogue, who robbed us of this treasury!"

The impudence of Scriverius was imitated by Seiz, whose silly history I will quote afterwards. But some years later, in 1752, Faust played a part again as thief. In some verses (Harlemi typis Mosis van Hulkenroy, ad Forum in Laurentio Costero, primo Typographiae Inventore) it is asked, with reference to the stone statue of 1722: "Why not erected a monument of metal, and Faust, his servant, exposed, chained by his feet, to atone with humiliation for this robbery of letters?"

Meerman knows, in 1765, still better who was the thief: he says, "after I have considered everything, it is beyond doubt (extra dubium), that the unfaithful servant is Johan Gensfleisch the elder, born at Mentz."

Kluit, a clergyman of the isle of Zuidbeierland, where he probably had preached very orthodox sermons on the ninth Commandment, wrote two years later:

"If Gensfleisch had not robbed his master, we should not have been obliged to wander so long about: now, the dispute is finished, as Meerman has shown that

Haarlem may boast alone of the honor. Mentz, pull your hairs out, now you, with your own eyes, see your villanous theft so well rewarded."[1]

The thieves remained Johans in any case. But in our century even that was no longer necessary. Koning makes his appearance with Friele (Frederick) Gensfleisch, Gutenberg's elder brother. Scheltema, who felt it necessary to drown this question, too, in his literary wash, the moment he saw that Schaab had discovered that the "brief-printer *Henne* Cruse lived in 1440 at Mentz," threw out insinuations against this innocent man also.[2] The "Gids" of 1849, contained an Essay of Dr. Doedes, afterwards approved by Noordziek, in which we find : "According to all probability we may suppose that while at Strasburg, Gutenberg had received already from his relation in Holland, who was employed in Coster's printing-office, some hints as to the art of printing; possibly also that Donatus, whereby he was led to print something similar himself with loose types, and for that purpose probably associated himself with Mentel (!). Now he hears, in the midst of his typographical experiments, of Johan's return from Haarlem, an intelligence which was sure to make a man like Gutenberg hasten to Mentz." I don't understand why Noordziek did not publish, with notes, this correspondence of Gensfleisch the elder at Haarlem with Gensfleisch the younger at Strasburg, which is, no doubt, preserved in his "Coster archives"! it would have thrown *much* light on the Mentz conspiracy. Berjeau at least became a little more cautious : he speaks only of *Jean de Harlem*. Rutjes, the Dutch translator of the thoroughly dishonest book of Paeile, knows in 1867 that it was *Hans*. And these horrors are not yet over. Constanter threw, some time ago, by means of the "Navorscher," an inconvenient quotation from a Kennemer chronicle into the discussion, and M. J. A. Alb. Thym writes instantly : "As for me—as long as the contrary has not been proved, I take the continuator of Jan Gerbrantzen to be a descendant of, or to have been bribed by, Johan Fust; it was his interest, merely to put aside the claims of Haarlem, which, since the secret had been revealed [ah ? !] by Coster's heirs, were proclaimed louder every day [to outvoice silent Haarlem ?], although he, probably, dared not to flatter himself that, three centuries afterwards, such an importance would still have been attached to his unguaranteed assertion." M. Thym's aversion from "unguaranteed assertions" is gratifying ; but his tactics with respect to the continuator of Gerbrandsz. are not noble. The most simple notions of common sense and honest polemics seem to get infected by the cancer of Costerianism. The negative of his assertion *can* not, but the positive *ought* to be proved. A asserts that B is a thief. What has B to do ? He is *not* able to prove that he is *no* thief. Neither is it his task at all ; it is the duty of A to substantiate his accusation, and his proofs alone may afford a point of investigation and discussion. It is not allowed to make any assertion at random, and to exclaim, triumphantly : prove only that it is *not* true! On the contrary, the asserter has to prove that *his* assertion is *true;* else his courageous statement deserves no answer when it concerns science, contempt when it concerns morals. "As for me," says Thym, "*as long as the contrary has not been proved*, X is a bribed man." I answer, as long as M. Thym does not substantiate this imputation, X is *not*. How would he like, for instance, this assertion : As long as the contrary is not proved, I take M. Thym to be an impostor ? I must be able to say: J. A. Alb. Thym is, on account of this, and that, and something besides, an impostor ; but as long as I have no shadow of reason or of evidence, it would be base to sully him with such talk. So the arch-stupid or very crafty charlatan Paeile has dared to whisper of Gutenberg's "alibi"! yes, alibi; as if ever an atom of *evidence* had been produced of a Mentz theft! There has been nonsensical gossip in abundance ; but neither substance nor shadow of serious evidence has been found in any Costerian book. For the story which a man

---

[1] Uitvinding der boekdrukkunst, getrokken uit het latynsch werk van Gerard Meerman, met eene voorrede van Henrik Gockinga. Amsterdam, 1767. 4to.

[2] Bericht und Beurtheilung des Werkes von Dr. C. A. Schaab, betitelt : Die Geschichte der Erfindung der Buchdruckerkunst, von Jac. Scheltema. Amsterdam, 1833. 8vo.

without judgment is pleased to serve up in 1568, about a so-called fact of 25 Dec. 1441, and which has been distorted ever so many times, will not be called, I think, evidence. The looking for the name of the thief, and for the year of the theft, destroy already this fine evidence. Otherwise, the circle which the metamorphosis of the thief has described is comical enough. He was, became, and is at present: c. 1560, a *foreigner;* in 1561, an *unfaithful servant;* in 1568, *Johan Fust;* in 1628, *Johan Gutenberg;* in 1765, *Johan Gensfleisch der Alte;* in 1816, *Friele Gensfleisch;* in 1833, *Henne Cruse;* in 1861, *Jean de Harlem;* the Ahasuerus of the Coster-legend, who commenced his career as *foreigner,* finished it as *Haarlemer.*

Pater Antonio Cambruzzi, who in the Memorie istoriche de Feltre, in the middle of the 17th century, invented a story in order to make an Italian invention of typography, makes Fust act at least a decent part. According to him, the real inventor of the idea of moveable letters, was the learned poet Pamfilo Castaldi. He imparted his discovery to Fust, who resided at Feltre to study the Italian language. The pater represents it as having happened in 1456, because, when he wrote, 1457 was the earliest typographic date known; if he had been aware of the letter of indulgence of 1454, he would have written 1453. Faust thereupon took the idea with him to Germany, applied it, and thereby got from some the title of first inventor, although others ascribe the invention to Gutenberg, the German. But the true first inventor was Pamfilo Castaldi. Padre Antonio, addio! No, an Italian pater is not so easily to be got rid of; guided by ignoramuses and sophists, his countrymen have erected, on this farce, a statue to Castaldi!

A contemporary of Cambruzzi, Richard Atkyns, was involved in a long and expensive process with the Stationers' Company at London, in consequence of which he died poor in prison. To defray the expenses of this law-suit, Atkyns fabricated a history of the invention of the art of printing, and published it at London in 1664, referring for authority of his history to some manuscript.[1] In this work he endeavoured to prove that the right of exercising typography was a royal prerogative, and that it did not begin at London (Westminster), but at Oxford. He made of the Cornelis of Junius, *Corsellis,* one of the workmen of Harleim, where John Gutenberg (!) had invented it; this Corsellis was, at the expenses of the king, bribed with great difficulty by Caxton ("for the town Harlem was very jealous, having emprisoned and apprehended divers persons, who came from other parts for the same purpose"), and printed the first book at Oxford in 1468. So the press of Oxford precedes all others, "except the city of Mentz, which claims seniority as to printing, even of Harleim itself, calling her city Urbem Moguntinam artis typographicae inventricem primam, though it is known to be otherwise; that city gaining the art by the brother of one of the workmen of Harleim, who had learned it at home of his brother, and after set up for himself at Mentz." This story of a man, who wished to recall the days of Elizabeth and James, because there were then more books burnt in ten years than could be printed in twenty, was considered by Seiz, Meerman, De Bruyn,[2] Koning, Pacile, good enough to support Junius' account of the theft. We, as Hollanders, ought to be ashamed that Europe has got Meerman's defence of such absurdities in good Latin. Finally, it is here the place to mention the Strasburg story of the chronicle of Daniel Specklin (1536—89), edited by Gebwiler and Schott, and published at Strasburg in 1640 by J. A. Schrag:—

"Anno 1440 . . . the magnificent and very useful art of printing was first brought to light and invented here at Strasburg, by *Joan Mentelin* (!), who lived "am Fronhoff zum Thiergarten." He had a servant named Hans Genszfleisch (!), born at Mentz, whom he trusted with his invention, because he found him very dexterous and

---

[1] The original and growth of printing. Wherein is also demonstrated, that printing appertaineth to the prerogative royal ... collected out of history, and the records of this kingdome by Richard Atkyns. Whitehall, April the 25th, 1664. London. 4to.

[2] De stad Haarlem en hare geschiedenissen ... door G. W. van Oosten de Bruin. Haarlem, 1765. Folio.

intelligent, and hoped to get further on through him. He was, however, shamefully deceived by him, for this Gensztleisch made the acquaintance of Johann Gutemberg (!) who was a distinguished and rich man, and knew already something of Mentelin's art. To him he revealed all secrets, and as they expected to gain much money and goods by this art, but could not do much at Strasburg in the presence of Mentelin, they resolved to go to Mentz. But God, who leaves no faithlessness unpunished, visited at last Genszfleisch, so that he was deprived of his sight." "The press and types of this first invention," says the editor of this story, "were still in existence within man's memory (as Daniel Specklin testifies in his MS. chronicle, *who had seen them*), and they were made thus: the letters were of wood, also whole words and syllables, and they were provided with a hole, in order to bind them together with string; the press also was of wood."

Where are the men of the Haarlem legend? Here speaks a contemporary of Junius, a Strasburg architect; he, too, assigns 1440 as the year of the invention; he also mentions the name of the inventor, and distinctly points out his house; he gives him a Hans as servant; his inventor, too, is shamefully deceived by Hans, who also fled to Mentz. Junius and Specklin agree literally in all these circumstances. Only one particular is wanting in the Haarlem legend to make it perfectly like that of Strasburg: the pierced wooden letters. Fortunately, neither these remained wanting. H. L. Spiegel († 1612), a friend of Coornhert, wrote in his Hert-Spieghel:—

> " O great mind of Haarlem, your praise will always sparkle,
> Although the glory of Mentz has entirely obscured your fame.
> You have fitted little staves of wood together,
> And afterwards put them together (like writing) with string."

But Specklin's story wins it from that of Junius in the strength of its proofs; he has no doubt as to *which* Hans deceived the inventor Mentelin, he positively knows his name: it is Hans Gensfleisch, born at Mentz. The deceiver is even visited by God with blindness: *i.e.* God Himself argues in favour of Mentelin. Specklin does not refer, as Junius comically enough does, to old wine-pots, but to the most unexceptionable evidence which a man who is satisfied with tradition can wish for—to the *press* and the *types* of the inventor, which he has seen himself. Finally, the account of Specklin is, in the main, infinitely more rational than that of Junius; it does not represent Hans as running away with the *types* and the tools, but with the *art*. In the face of this fine stroke of the Strasburg story, that of Haarlem dwindles to nothing; for he who wishes to reveal the secret of typography does not want, when he understands the art, to load himself with anything; for, as the Greek philosopher after the shipwreck, he carries his riches always with him.

XIV.

THE BOOKBINDER CORNELIS.

" I REMEMBER," relates Junius, "that Claes Gael, the instructor of my infancy, a man of powerful memory, and venerable on account of his grey hair, told me that he as a child often listened to the account of a certain bookbinder, Cornelis, a greybeard of more than eighty years of age, who had been servant (subminister) in the printing-office of Loureus. The old man related the whole course of the affair, as he had heard it from his master: the process of the invention, the improvement and development of the crude art, besides many other things, and got then always, on account of the infamy of the theft, in such a passion and emotion, that he, in spite of himself, burst into tears as soon as he had come to the account of the theft; yes, the old man got into such a rage at the loss of so great a fame, simply by a theft, that he would act the part of executioner of the thief, if he had been still alive; he cursed the villain in the most fearful way, and regretted that he had slept for months in the same bed with such a scoundrel." Or, according to the pithy translation of Scriverius: "And the old man was so perplexed and so enraged, that it seemed as if he could have torn the thief to pieces if he had been alive; he uttered imprecations against the base scoundrel, and cursed and damned the nights which he had passed with this villain in one bed-room for months."

Let us endeavour to master our emotions, and when Cornelis, "on whom (as Koning justly remarks) the whole account of Junius is especially based," has calmed down, analyze without any passion this gist of the account, this main evidence of Junius, without allowing our judgment to be bribed by the tears, the fury, or the imprecations of the bookbinder.

We have here a chain of tradition, of which apparently not one link is wanting: Junius, Gael, Cornelis, Lourens Janszoon Coster. It was necessary to stretch and wring this chain by the ordinary interpretation, until it could enclose the *sheriff Louwerijs Janszoen*, when it presented the following formula: Cornelis + Gael + Junius = subminister + puer + puer = boy + boy + boy; going backwards: Junius the author + Gael the tutor + Cornelis the man of at least 80 years = greyhead + greyhead + greyhead. It required many tricks before they could get to this elasticity. They explained the story in this way. Junius hears the account of Gael in his infancy, youth, pueritia; Gael listens as boy, youth, puer, to Cornelis; Cornelis learns as servant (apprentice) the history of the invention from Louwerijs Janszoen. Let us put this pueritia of Junius c. 1525 (for it ought at all events to come after the death of Cornelis), and the venerable old age of Gael in his sixtieth year; Cornelis is then born about (1525—60 = 1465 + 15 =1480—80 =) 1400, ergo—122 years of age; he then even binds books in his 115th year. If we allow, however, Cornelis the human age of eighty years, he was then a contemporary of Louwerijs Janszoen, in so far that he was hardly being rocked in his cradle when L. J. was laid in his coffin.

Now, according to the point of starting by the computation, they would find the man either impossibly old or impossibly young. Had Louwerijs Janszoen himself (who administered an oath to his men, did he not?) told the whole history of the invention to a *child?* Had they put a *child* in the bed of a thief? If not, then Cornelis reached an old-testament, antediluvian age, of which we know nothing in history; and thoughtful Costerians felt the objection, and were inclined to administer simple tonic remedies to the exegesis. Meerman was forced to the conclusion that Cornelis, at the death of his sheriff-printer-subsacristan, had been only ten or twelve years of age, *i.e.* he concluded nonsense.

Ottley therefore proposed something which he considered "more reasonable." He was right in calling Meerman's conclusion "a conclusion little calculated to give weight to Cornelis's testimony." It was indeed! But what then? Well, let us cut the Cornelis of Junius into two, and dissolve him into an old and young Cornelis bookbinder. In this way we get really a useful quantity of years for distribution. "If my hypothesis as to the two Corneliscs be admitted, every objection to the chronology in the text that I am aware of, ceases." We ought not to be too stingy towards a man who reasons so conclusively. He may have as many Corneliscs as he likes, on condition that he will leave us in peace for the future.[1] De Vries invented another escape. In order to delay Gael's account to Junius, he tries to let him study "medicine" from Gael. But Junius did not study his profession in his pueritia at Haarlem, but at Louvain, at Bologna, and at Paris. However, this unreal bungling

---

[1] In his later work (1863), Ottley proposed another sophism. "It may be proper here to remind the reader, that although Cornelius, according to Junius, used to speak of the history of the invention, and of the gradual improvements made in it, as he had heard them described by *his master*, he does not appear to have expressly said that that master was Lawrence Coster" (!) Again a desperate effort to conceal the folly of a story, in which all the authorities hear the principal facts in their infancy, but only communicate it to others in their second childhood.

o

need not occupy us any longer, now the sheriff-innkeeper, Louwerijs Janszoen (about whom we shall speak hereafter), who died in 1439, has irrevocably been pulled down as inventor of the art of printing. By the explanation of the date in Junius' story, by the correction of the date in Thomasz.'s document, the extracts from the Haarlem archives, the exposure of the chandler L. J. Coster in 1870, the hero of the stone memorials, of silver and bronze medals and of sheriff-documents, still exhibited day by day to the public, is defeated, never to rise again from his grave. May he henceforth rest in peace!

We collect in this case also first what the archives contain. I have found several members of the family of Gael. In 1486 the sheriff Claes Pieterz. Gael; in 1495 Florijs Claesz. Gael; in 1498 Jan Claesz. and Lottijn Pieterz. Gael. The last was probably the father of Junius' tutor and authority, *Dr. Claes Lottynsz. Gael*, sheriff of Haarlem in the years 1533 and 1535, and who was really a contemporary of Cornelis. Junius calls him formatorem pueritiæ meæ; but from this description does not necessarily follow that he gave Junius the account while he held this position. The man who was sheriff in 1535 *cannot* have been a man of very advanced age already in Junius' infancy. In the second place, it is a mere composition of Junius, that his tutor listened, as a *child*, to Cornelis; for when Cornelis died in 1522 Gael was no longer a boy at all. Junius *delays* here the chronology. Finally, Gael did not want a powerful memory " to recollect a man who was still alive when Junius was already at the Latin grammar-school at Haarlem. The ornamentation is here obvious to everybody. Why, however, does Junius refer to Gael? I presume that Gael was somewhat addicted to family pride, to feed that of Gerrit Thomasz., the man of the pedigree. At least I found in the registers of the sheriffs, Oct. 1484, this item:

"Ysbrant Gael, induced by certain circumstances, sells to his two daughters, Geertruyt and *Ermgaert*, all goods, houses with ground, furniture, money, silverwork, gems, clocks, and jewels, and further all other goods, effects, nothing excepted, which he possesses at present, and properly belong to him."[1]

We have seen that *Ermingaert* (no common name) appears on the pedigree with her arms, by the side of the chief person, Gerrit Thomasz. What, if she had been the daughter of Ysbrand Gael? But on the pedigree she is called Ermingaert Jansdochter.

Let us now look for Cornelis the bookbinder. We find in the ledgers of the cathedral, first:

1474. In this year is paid for the first time to "Cornelis the bookbinder" six florins on account of the binding of books. Similar items occur in 1485, '87, '96, 1508, 1510, '12, and '15. In 1507, 1508, and 1510, payments to him are entered for the colouring of the capitals on the "bulls of the indulgences," on the letters of indulgences, spoken of in the 5th chapter. After 1515 his name appears no longer as binder or illuminator, probably on account of his age; at least, in and after 1517 another bookbinder occurs. These dates were known. They may be supplied by the following items, extracted from the treasury-accounts of Haarlem: 1487, Cornelis the bookbinder pays xv pence for taxes. 1492, Cornelis the bookbinder is registrar of the Smee- and Cruysstraat, and he pays 12 pence. So also in 1493. We have not looked so carefully in the registers of the sixteenth century, but it is of no value at all whether we have a few pence for taxes more or less of our hero.

Junius calls Cornelis not only bibliopegus, but also librarius; he has been that also. In 1823 was exhibited at Haarlem a copy (already known to Seiz in 1740) of Bartholomeüs, the Englishman, "Van den propriëteiten der dingen," printed by Jakob Bellaert at Haarlem in 1485, on the last leaf of which we find this annotation:

"Item bought at Haerlem in die Cruysstraet at Cornelis the bookbinder's, in

---

[1] "Ysbrant *Gael* vercoept geertruyt ende *ermgaert*, zijne twee dochteren, om sonderlinge saken hem daertoe permoveerende, alle alsulke goederen, tzy huysingen met haerl. erven, imboel, huysraet, gelt, silverwerck, cleynoden, clocken ende juwelen, en voirt alle and' goeden, renten ende geen uytgesondert als hij nu tertyt heeft ende hem eygelic toebehoeren."

May, 1492, when the people of Alcmaer and their countrymen entered with their banners, etc., by me, Anthonys de Minor."[1]

We are so fortunate as to know also the years in which Cornelis and his wife died. The register of the church of 1522 contains: "Item Cornelijs the bookbinder was buried in the church, for the making of his grave, xx pence."[2] That of 1525: "Item, Cornelijs, the bookbinder's widow, was buried in the church, the making of her grave xx pence; on account of her poverty not paid more than x pence."[3] "We may infer from this fact," says Koning, in an attack of great acuteness, "that these people were not in easy circumstances." As to the question of Cornelis, who was able to work till 1515, we may explain it in this way: the full-grown age of Junius' tutor, still sheriff at Haarlem in 1585, falls in the 16th, his youth in the 15th century. He knew Cornelis until the old age of the binder; we have to take Gael's advanced age for a definition of the dignity of the witness to whom Junius refers, and, without applying this advanced age literally to the years in which Gael instructed the Hoorn boy, take him in general for what he was during his lifetime: a venerable old man with a strong memory. Talesius, says Junius, also heard the account of Cornelis, and imparted it to him; now this Talesius was only born in 1505 (1506), and therefore not more than seventeen years of age at the death of Cornelis. The determination of the bookbinder's age, when Gael heard him more than once give the account as a man of at least eighty years, must therefore refer to the real old age of Cornelis, *i.e.* the binder reached the age of eighty or somewhat more.

There are insoluble objections to the evidence of that bookbinder. First, a number of very troublesome observations may be made. What did Cornelis learn as assistant at his master's, the inventor of the art of printing, that is to say, in the sense of Junius, wood-engraver and type-founder? Of all this nothing; of those new, profitable inventions, which attracted purchasers from every quarter, nothing; but he did learn the innocent sewing of books. And yet that bookbinder knew the secret *art;* his master had told him the whole course of its invention; and now, the *tools* could indeed have been stolen from the shop of the master, but the *art*, the invention, this pearl of great value, this knowledge, *could* not be robbed from the brain of the servant. Neither was this servant too doting not to discern the value of the case. Oh no! How bitterly could he begin to cry when he mentioned the theft, which took so much honour away from his master! That servant swears, cries, curses the villain who so effectually ran away with the whole of the *invention* of typography at Haarlem, that no mortal hears a syllable more of it in history for more than a century. Did Cornelis only swear about it during the days of his second childhood, or already since his youth? We trust, from his sensitive, affectionate, dog-like disposition, that he already swore and raved as man in the prime of his life, still possessed of a clear voice and mind proper to that stage of life. Oh guardian angels of superstition, come to the rescue of your people! A raging, crying, cursing bookbinder, consequently a man who must have been pretty well audible to the public: such a witness, it is said, was at Haarlem from 1470—1522 (till 1483 simultaneously with his master, till 1492 with the son-in-law-adinventor!) and—the death-like silence is not disturbed; we have to wait till 1568 before that pithy evidence of the Haarlem invention is recorded, till 1588 before it is printed. Were then the people at Haarlem petrified? Were then the Haarlemers who printed in foreign countries, devoid of all human feeling, and could nothing induce them to allude in their imprints to the grand fact of the Haarlem invention, related to them by their crying fellow-townsman? Is Jacob Bellaert occupied from 1483—86 at Haarlem with printing, and so little a servile repeater of

---

[1] Item gecoft te Haerlem in die Cruysstraet tot Cornelis Boecbinder in 't jaar MCCCC ende LXXXXII in meije, doe die van Alcmaer mit hoer landluden daer in quamen mit hoer banieren etcetra, van mi Anthonys de minor.

[2] It. Cornelijs die bunckebynner is begraven in die kerck, dat opdoen van zijn graf xx st.

[3] It. Cornelijs die buekebijnners wedu is begraven in die kerk, dat opdoen van haer graf xx st. om over myts haer armoed nijet meer betaelt dan x st.

another's words that he boldly prints in the text of Bartholomeüs, the Englishman, when he meets with too great absurdities: "I, master Jacob, do not believe this;" or, "I, Jacob, think that this is wrong" (dit werdt door mi meester Jacob niet gelooft; or, mer ick Jacop meyn dat het verkeert is)—did this critical printer of Zierikzee remain for three years deaf to Cornelis, in the birthplace of his craft, where he, with a single word in his imprints, would have wreathed a laurel, not only for Haarlem, but also for himself? By his business of binder and bookseller, Cornelis came in connexion exactly with those people who could understand the matter, and save it from oblivion. And those obdurate burgomaster-grandsons of the inventor, how cynical is their calm silence in contrast with Cornelis's excitement! But even Dr. Gael knows nothing better to do with the affecting complaints of the old man than to tell them, the gods know when, to a former pupil. Just as it often happens, Junius schemed in this excited bookbinder an ornament, with which he destroys his own fiction.

It will undoubtedly be superfluous now to analyze, not only historically, but also psychologically, that crying and swearing of a servant, circa sixty, seventy, or eighty years after his master had been robbed, for the folly is not worthy of the seriousness of philosophy. He who is of another opinion may write a drama—The faithful bookbinder or the imprecatory evidence of two centuries.

Cornelis knew the first printing-offices of Jacob Bellaert and Jan Andrieszoon at Haarlem; from 1483—86 he was certainly in the prime of life, his business was sure to bring him in connexion with printers, and we know that he sold in 1492, to M. Anthonys, a copy of the first and only Haarlem work provided with a complete imprint. If we assume that the crying and swearing witness (as pia fraus) is not altogether fictitious, and that Cornelis has really told something, then, in the mind of the ignorant man, the first printing-office at Haarlem has grown into the first printing-office on earth. Or did, perhaps, some theft take place, either at Bellaert's or at Andrieszoon's, by one of the servants; and did these matters afterwards get mixed up in the head of the old man, or hashed up together, consciously or unconsciously, by the Haarlem talk in the second half of the sixteenth century? For, *Lourens Janszoon Coster*, a contemporary of Cornelis, left Haarlem in 1483, before the earliest typographic date there, before 10th December, 1483. Or did the people at the printing-office take Cornelis in with a story, accepted by him for current coin? All this may be asked, all this is historically possible, and the germs of a legend are found in these data; but I don't think that we require *one* of these conjectures, or even have a right to make them. Cornelis *could not* sleep in 1441, as servant of Lourens Coster, with Johan Faust, or have any recollection of that year; consequently he was *not able* to tell his contemporaries anything, much less to swear so vehemently about it. Neither *could* he invent those Mentz editions of 1442. We have, therefore, no right to involve the homely man in the fable of Junius, who perfectly well knew that it would not do to send his story into the world without at least some apparent evidence, and so looked, without thorough study, for a so-called eye-witness of the robbery-story. As a schoolboy he may have known the old bookbinder, or at least may have heard from him, or have got him from the inscription in the book of Bellaert. But he puts him some years back, just as the date on the pedigree. The *old* Gael ought to have heard as a lad the trick of that villanous thief from the decrepit Cornelis. Strange, the old *Gael*, who still lives between 1530 and 1540, should in his *youth* have known Cornelis. But *Gerrit Thomasz.*, who is alive even between 1560 and 1570, who died in advanced age, who *must* have known the bookbinder of 1522, who is said to have been great-grandson of the inventor, the master of Cornelis, who could not often enough remember, with reasonable family pride, the oaths and the crying of the old faithful man—*this* man is *not* referred to with regard to Cornelis. But *Gael* knew him as a child, oh yes; Talesius, who left Haarlem already when still a lad, *he* recollected him very well—yes, certainly. But the man of the wine-pots would not have said a single word about him to Junius? He who feels inclined to take Cornelis as an accomplice in this tissue of falsehoods, may follow up his desire; as for me, I look upon Junius as the only man.

XV.

QUIRIJN DIRKSZ.

"This account (of the theft) agrees with the words of the burgomaster Quirinus Talesius, who told me that he formerly heard nearly the same from the mouth of the bookseller (Cornelis)."

Next to Claes Lottijnsz. Gael, Junius' second authority is Quirijn Dirkszoon, from 1567—70—therefore, during the time that Junius was writing the Batavia—presiding burgomaster at Haarlem. It is worth while to look into the career of this witness. We are enabled to do so by his contemporary and biographer, Pieter van Opmeer, born at Amsterdam in 1526. Opmeer studied, as Junius, at Louvain, and settled afterwards at Delft, where he studied Greek, medicine, law, and later, out of zeal for Roman Catholicism, theology. He applied himself, moreover, to painting, engraving, and architecture. During the siege of Leiden he was appointed, by Valdez, secretary of the Spanish military council. He resided at Amsterdam till 1578, but quitted that town when it joined the revolution. He died the 4th of November, 1594. Opmeer, therefore, was Junius' contemporary and fellow-believer, and of the same profession. He knew Van Zuren, at whose press he published in 1561 (the year of Coornhert's dedication of the Officia), against the Protestants : "a very good book for the antiquity and truth of the common Christian faith, against the wicked innovations of all heresies, described a thousand years ago by V. L. G., and now translated from the Latin into Dutch."[1] He left, moreover, a history of the world, continued by him to the year 1569, and continued after his death by Laurentius Beyerlinck, canonist at Antwerp, and published in 1611 in folio, under the title of : Opus chronographicum orbis universi a mundi exordio usque ad annum 1611, Antverpiae. Under the year 1451 this book gives an ugly wood-cut of Joannes Favstvs Calcogr., with the words : Etenim hocce anno Moguntiae à Joanne Favsto ars imprimendi exerceri cœpta est. Fuerat is annus Joannis Scoeferi Chalcographi nostrae aetatis, vir dignus vt celebretur. At the end of the work is a "Historia martyrum Batavicorum," published separately, as Catholic martyr-book, in Dutch.[2] In this book Talesius makes his appearance as martyr of the Roman Catholic religion. The murder committed on him at the time of the siege of Haarlem is described in detail, but at the same time a review is given of his earlier life, from which I gather the following particulars. (Let no one omit to notice that Opmeer knew Talesius as well as Junius did ; that Van Zuren at Haarlem printed for him in the same year when he opened his printing-office with the famous book of Coornhert ; that he obtained his informations about Talesius mainly through Van Zuren). Quirijn was born 12th January, 1505 (1506) at Haarlem ; his parents were Dirk van Lispen and Maria Jansdochter. He was educated at the Berg Gymnasium at Cologne, where he, as an excellent disciple, obtained a laurel. This education at Cologne is explained by a document in the archives of Haarlem, of 1st April, 1509, whereby the magistracy of this town bind themselves "to pay every year four valid keurfurstl. florins for the *bursa montis* at Cologne, for the support of needy students ; and promise

---

[1] Een seer schoon boecxken voor de outheyt ende waerheyt des gemeenen christen gheloofs, teghens die Godloose niewicheyden alder ketteryen, beschreven over duysent jaren door Vincentium Livinensem Gallum, ende nv wt den Latyne in onse Nederduytsche sprake overghesct. 12mo.

[2] Martelaars-boek, ofte Historie der Hollandse Martelaren, welke om de Christen Catholyke Godsdienst, van de Hervormde Nieuwgesinden seer wreed sijn omgebragt : Beschreven door d'Heer Petrus Opmeer, Amsterdammer. Antwerpen, 1700, 1702. 8vo.

to make, as much as possible, the inhabitants of Haarlem study there."[1] At the age of sixteen or seventeen he went to Basle, where he entered the service of Erasmus, and just as Nic. Cannius (afterwards tutor of Opmeer at Amsterdam) was employed by Erasmus in copying Greek, so Quirinus in copying Latin works. He received his surname Talesius from his learned master. This connexion lasted seven years, and it appears that the two countrymen lived with each other on the best footing. In 1527 Erasmus entrusted his confidant with a delicate mission to England; at least, he writes to Richard Pacæus that he has sent his Quirinus to England for some business, for two particular reasons—1. in order that he (Erasmus) might put a stop to the robbery of a villanous impostor; 2. that he may consult the friends, whether it would be easy to listen to the desire of the king and the archbishop of Canterbury to come over to England.[2]

On this occasion Erasmus recommends the young man of 22, not as a servant, but as a dear son. He wrote to Thomas Morus: "You will hear of my sad circumstances more in detail from my Quirinus, a young man of tried faith, whom I resolved to send to England beforehand, because he knows all my circumstances, and in order that I may consult, through him, with my friends what were best to be done, or to be omitted." Erasmus' feelings towards his Quirinus are most plainly expressed in his testimonial, that nobody had ever served him with more love (quo nemo alius mihi servivit amantius). When Talesius returned to his native country he received from Erasmus this testimonial: "I, Erasmus of Rotterdam, have presented to my former servant, Quirinus Talesius, for his faithful service rendered unto me, 150 crowns, to do with them whatsoever he likes. In acknowledgment hereof I have written this with my own hand, and confirmed with my device. Given at Basle, 10th March, 1529." The seal in red wax, contained on one side the symbol Cedo nulli, on the other the words Donatio Erasmi. In a letter of recommendation to Maximilian of Burgundy, dated Friburg Brisgoæ, 23rd July, 1529, Erasmus praises him as a modest, faithful, good-natured young man, more learned in Greek and Latin than he seemed; that there was more in him than his outward appearance promised; who seemed to be of steel as regards study, and on that account used to be called, by Hubertus Barlandus, the Marian mule. After Talesius had settled again in his birthplace, he kept up a correspondence with Erasmus. Erasmus congratulated him, for instance, 7th May, 1532, with the pensionaryship of Haarlem in a letter which is now probably lost, but has been mentioned by Petrus Opmeer. The works of Erasmus (Lugd. Bat., 1703, fol. III., p. 1456) contain a letter dated 31st October, 1532, with the address: "Erasmus, Roterod. eruditissimo viro Quirino Talesio, inclytæ civitatis Harlemensis Pensionario, S.P." Talesius brought with him from Germany a portrait of Erasmus of life-size, painted by Holbein. "I still remember," writes Opmeer, "that I have often seen this portrait in his house at Haarlem, valued by the best painters at 200 crowns." It is also said that Talesius corrected the Colloquia, omitting that which could offend the pious, or what had been added by the author more in order to take revenge than to instruct. It was further alleged that Erasmus bequeathed him in his last will 400 crowns.

At Haarlem Talesius had friendly intercourse with Junius, for he is consulted by him in a love-affair (the "charming description" of which is found in Junii Epistolis, p. 108, and in Vita Junii in Obss. Misc. Nov. v. iv., p. xii., p. 401). Junius calls him Dodonæum quoddam isthic (Harlemi) oraculum.[3] These are the particulars which we know of the connexion of Talesius with Erasmus and Junius. Only a few words more about his further career.

Burgomaster Quirijn married a widow Haasje Dirks; opened, like his father, a drapery, by which he came much in contact with boatmen and merchants; made his

---

[1] Inventaris van het Archief der stad Haarlem, opgemaakt door Mr. A. J. Enschedé. Haarlem, 1866. 8vo. I., 75.

[2] Desiderii Erasmi Opera Omnia. Lvgd. Batav. 1703. Folio. III.

[3] Hadriani Junii Epistolæ selectæ nunc primum editæ. Editionem curavit P. Scheltema. Amstelodami, 1839. 8vo.

fellow-citizens "pay him handsomely;" remained faithful to the Roman Catholic religion; was taken prisoner during the siege of Haarlem, and murdered (being suspected probably, on account of his opinions, of connivance with the enemy) 27th May, 1573, with wife and daughter.[1] This sad end is amply described in the work of Opmeer mentioned before: the martyrdom and death of Quirinus Talesius.

Therefore Talesius had personal intercourse with Erasmus for seven years, and the two men kept up their intercourse by letters afterwards. This important fact deserves all our attention.

Talesius was born 1505, went to a gymnasium at Cologne, and is from 1522—29 at Basle in the service of Erasmus. In the same year 1522 we saw that Cornelis the bookbinder died, from whom Talesius may have heard the Coster-story. But Talesius had not even spent his youth at Haarlem! At what age do they wish to let the boy go to the Cologne school? Did the boys have often holidays at that time? Or has Talesius been at home before his departure for Basle—say, for instance, in 1520, and did he call, *en passant*, on Cornelis to have a book bound? It is unlikely that he was still binding at that time; but he was, no doubt, still ready to swear against Jan. Let us for one moment assume an impossibility, and say that Quirijn, as Haarlem boy, has really heard and understood that story of Cornelis; but then the remembrance of it would have been much more lively in the young man of between 17 and 24 than in the man of maturer age, who, between 1566 and 1570, communicated the story to Junius, to Erasmus II. And this young man conversed all those years with Erasmus, and we saw on what intimate footing. Now, come, under these circumstances, he *could not* have failed to tell Erasmus I. what he knew! But this first Erasmus—the friend of the celebrated South-Netherland printer Martens, whose epitaph, it is said, he wrote; the guest and corrector of the no less celebrated printer Froben; 38 years older than his Haarlem amanuensis, and somewhat better acquainted with the Netherlands than he who left them already as a boy; scholar, famous all over the world, who always worked for the press, and understood its unspeakably high importance; who ascribes in 1519 and 1529 the invention of printing to Mentz—this first Erasmus knows *nothing* of a Haarlem invention; and—if Talesius heard anything at all from Cornelis and had told him—then it is clear that Erasmus believed *nothing* of this gossip; for in his annotation on the letters of St. Jerome (in Epist. IX.), edited by him at Basle in 1524, by Crespin at Lyons in 1528, at Paris in 1533 (therefore during and after the long continued intercourse with Talesius), he speaks thus: "All those who apply themselves to the sciences are under no small obligations towards the celebrated town of Mentz, on account of the excellent and almost divine invention of printing books with tin letters, which, as they assure us, was born there." This testimonial in favour of Mentz does not signify more than a hundred others, but against Haarlem its strength is all-powerful, destructive in connexion with what we have said before. I produce here not a single new date; that which I sketched above was known to the Costerians, at least to Koning and De Vries, for we consulted the same authorities. Their proceedings with that quotation are a specimen of thoroughly false tactics. In the first place, it is argued that Erasmus did not yet know Talesius when he gave his vote to Mentz, and his verdict of 1528 and later is calmly put in 1516, by means of confusing the Opus epistolarum with the edition of the Opera Hieronymi of Erasmus, published by Joh. Froben at Basle in 1516, although editions were also published by Gryphius at Lyons in 1526, '29, '30, at Paris in 1534. Of course in this manner they easily got rid of the period of 1522—29. In the second place the year of his birth is concealed (which, however, was not even thought necessary by the innocent Koning), and thereupon De Vries reasons thus: "Quirinus Talesius, or M. Quirijn Dirkszoon (in the town-registers, and in the minutes of the town council, never mentioned, according to the habits of that time, just as our Koster, by his family-name [? read: by the surname given him by Erasmus]) . . . the celebrated

---

[1] (Pierre Sterlincx d'Anuers:) Een Corte waerachtighe Beschrijvinghe, van alle Gheschiedenissen, Aenslaghen, etc., voor de stadt Haarlem gheschiet . . . Anno M.D.LXXIII. Ghedruckt tot Delft, 1574, 4to.

friend and agent of Erasmus, for whom he transacted already in 1527 a very important mission to England in a delicate affair, and with whom he must have been connected a considerable time before; wherefore [wherefore!?] it is beyond doubt that he had been able to speak often with Cornelis the bookbinder (who died only five years before) when he as a *youthful scholar* wanted to make use of his services."

Good gracious! . . . . !

Yes, a youthful scholar, indeed, who left Haarlem already at the age of ten or twelve years, and who was, at the death of Cornelis, only sixteen or seventeen years old. It must have been an affecting sight, when the youthful scholar had put away his hoop and marbles, and the not very youthful bookbinder his tools, and both commenced to lament, in the "Kruisstraat," the robbery of Haarlem's honour, in the year of our Lord 1441. The trouble which Cornelis, while still in his swaddling-clothes, must have felt, when that Mentz knight, armed with harness, helmet, and sword, came at night and rudely disturbed him on his little bed, explains sufficiently the aversion which was impressed on the bookbinder's memory till his last gasp. Now, the honour of their country was worth a small sin, else our dear Quirijn ran greatly the risk of becoming addicted to swearing.

The hearing of the witnesses is finished, and we are now enabled to pass sentence with a full knowledge of all documents of the process. We have found *nothing* whatever which resembles in any way an historical proof for the claims of the Netherlands in general, and Haarlem in particular, to the honour of the invention of the art of printing. And now we have brought to light all documents regarding the question in their genuine condition, now the literary apparition even of the ordinary imaginary evidence has gone the way of all ghosts, as soon as they are subjected to criticism. We have discovered a phantom, but no reality. The trouble of the investigation is rewarded by the fact that a simple review of the course of the story exempts us for the future from the labour of a positive refutation. For, the opinion that, *apart* from the Haarlem story, undated Dutch incunabula of the 15th century may afford matter of dispute between Haarlem and Mentz, is a gigantic petitio principii, a scientific heresy, which leads to everlasting fire. He who, armed with this unhistorical, arbitrary, aprioristic, entirely obsolete, principle, might feel inclined to come forward as the life-guard of Coster (Gerrit Thomaszoon), prepares himself a defeat, of which the remembrance will last for ever.

Our earliest authority is Gerrit Thomaszoon, who in the middle of the 16th century caused to write on vellum that Lourens Janszoon Coster brought "doerste print" into the world in 1446. On this foundation-stone the Haarlem castle in the air is built. That single "print" of the year 1446 was already considerably extended by Van Zuren; he tells us: "In this town the art of printing was born; here it first saw daylight. Here its parts were shaped and developed so far, that it was fortunately able to grow further. Indeed, here it has been diligently and carefully treated, nursed, exercised and formed, for a *long time*, as we use to do with children. It has been kept enclosed within the walls of a private house for *many years*. Here it was educated. Here it was *long* cultivated, supported, and brought up; indeed, much too parsimoniously and straitened, until it, despising the narrow circumference and humble aspect of its simple home, became the companion of a certain foreigner, and having put off the rags with which it had, for the greatest part, had to put up in its paternal house, made its appearance *at last*, in the greatest splendour, in accordance with its rank and value, at Mentz, before the eyes of every one." In the report of the committee at Haarlem, formed (8th Aug. 1822) to determine the date of the invention, it is said : "From these repeated expressions of Van Zuren of *long time* and *many years* (diuerte, diu, multosque annos), it seems to us, that we may reasonably conclude, that from the time of the birth of printing until its transmission to Mentz, about twenty years must have elapsed." With pleasure: we then get $1446 + 20 = 1466$!

---

[1] Rapport van de commissie, benoemd door den Raad der stad Haarlem, tot het onderzoek naar het jaar van de uitvinding der boekdrukkunst, &c. Gedaan aan Heeren Burgemeester en Raden der stad Haarlem, den 8 Augustus, 1822. Haarlem, 1822, 8vo.

We have seen that Van Zuren doubted whether it were not better to leave the subject undiscussed, as people were not likely to submit to seeing those of Mentz deprived of the honour of the invention. It is easy to understand why he, after further consideration, gave up the idea, and was not dishonest enough to come forward as the first public Costerian. Neither does Coornhert tell us anything more than "that the useful art of printing was invented first of all at Haarlem, although in a very crude way" (= "deerste print"), but without name of the inventor or year of discovery. "Afterwards" (when?) the art was brought to Mentz by an "unfaithful" servant. We have therefore reached the year 1561, without hearing anything more than a mere assertion which everybody had been able to make anywhere. Guicciardini was told, that the (unmentioned) Haarlem inventor *died before he had brought the art to perfection*, and that his servant went to live at Mentz, where he revealed the art and was very gladly received. "I am neither able nor willing," says Guicciardini, "to express an opinion as to the truth of this account." We see that already in this account, printed in 1567, there is no room for the theft, and no question of an *unfaithful* servant, for the death of the master left him perfectly free to depart. The short accounts of the contemporaries Van Zuren, Coornhert, and Guicciardini, totally destroy each other. Van Zuren represents the art as having been many years exercised at Haarlem and developed in all its parts, so that it could prosperously grow on; according to Guicciardini, it was left imperfect by the inventor. If these stories had been left to themselves, they would have died their natural death and soon fallen into oblivion. But Junius assisted them with his learning, and so the legend, supported by the means which we have learned by degrees, obtained historical appearance.

Gerrit Thomasz. now, and the father of lies, may account for our innkeeper's inclination to descend from the man of the first "print" on earth; I was not present when the pedigree was ordered and paid for. It is enough that we now *know* how the story was "brought into the world"; it is sufficient that we are able to understand how the Haarlem citizens got to read that thing; how it was discussed; how more sensible people began to oppose Mentz to their fellow-townsmen; how they, as a matter of course, began to cry: Then the art was stolen from us; how the one advanced this, another that, to explain how the matter *could* have happened; how Van Zuren stepped forward to put the case into some clothes, but abandoned it, overcome by doubts and his better self; how Coornhert did not think it improper to open, in 1561, the new printing-office of Van Zuren with a book in which we find: "the useful art of printing books, invented first of all at Haarlem"; how Guicciardini could speak, in 1565 or '66, of memorials, namely: the fine vellum document of Gerrit Thomasz. and his wine-pots, which probably originated from the innkeeper Lourens Janszoon Coster; how, at that time, however, the question had not been solved, and the art of printing was represented as having been brought by a servant from Haarlem to Mentz, *after the death of his master;* how, at last, Junius,—he, the historian of the country, and functionary of Haarlem, who particularly wished to please the town in which he lived,—thought the moment had come to give to the town-gossip an appearance of credibility.

There prevails a popular prejudice *that all traditions have a nucleus of truth in them*. Decidedly untrue. Only this is true: all traditions have a cause, a reason, a *nucleus;* but that that *nucleus* must necessarily be a *truth*, is a foolish supposition of ignorance. The nucleus of the Loosduin miracle was a monkish joke; that of the St. Pancras miracle at Leiden, the striking similarity between a stone and a loaf;[1] that of Junius's

---

[1] I have quoted already the excellent evidences referred to by Guicciardini for the Haarlem merman (circa 1520). His authorities are so much superior to the Cornelis of Junius, that this evidence may not be compared with theirs. Berjeau writes on this case : " Quand Guicciardini et George Bruin, à leur article de Haarlem. nous parlent d'une syrène trouvée dans la lagune, qui, de leur temps, couvrait de campagnes aujourd'hui fertiles, dans les environs de cette ville, nous sommes disposés à douter de la rectitude de leur jugement : nous pensons qu'ils ont eu tort de croire sans examen un récit de pêcheurs ignorants, qui ont pris un phoque pour un homme, ou confondu un esquimaux, jetté par la tempête sur les côtes de l'Europe (!) avec un monstre fabuleux de l'antiquité. Si Junius, dans sa Batavia, eut rapporté beaucoup de faits semblables

imaginary town Verona, near Alkmaar, a grammatical error. And so on with innumerable other legends. The cause is not only not always a truth, but very often a fabrication, sometimes an error; but it is certain that without some help these children never come into the world.

The history of typography abounds with examples which confirm this assertion. Dr. Johan Cube of Frankfort wrote a Hortus sanitatis in German, which was printed (1485) by Peter Schöffer. The author says in his preface: "I left this work unfinished, until I went to the Holy Sepulchre to obtain grace and absolution."[1] Würdtwein (Bibl. Mog. 123) brings these words uncritically in connexion with the imprint (Moguntiæ per Petrum Schoyffer de Gernsheim), and the story is at once ready that Peter Schöffer made, during the last years of the fifteenth century, a pilgrimage to Palestine. To atone for the theft of his father-in-law or grandfather Johan Fust?

A manuscript on the coins of France says of Louis XI. (De Boze, Mém de l'Acad. des Inscript. XIV. 236):—" Qu'ayant sçu qu'il y avoit à Mayence gens adroits à la taille des poinçoins et caractéres, au moyen desquels se pouvoient multiplier par impression les plus rares Manuscrits, le Roy curieux de toutes telles choses et autres, manda aux Généraux de ses Monnoyes y dépecher personnes entendues à ladite taille, pour s'informer sécrétement de l'art, et *en enlever* subtilement l'invention; et y fut envoyé Nicolas Jenson, garçon saige, et l'un des bons Graveurs de la Monnoye de Paris." Jenson's ability as cutter of stamps is the only real nucleus of this story, in which, this time, for an agreeable change, the robbery of the typography is not placed at Haarlem or at Strasburg, but at Mentz.

Jacob Cromberger, a German, printed in 1526, at Sevilla : Visiones deleitables por Don Alfonso de la Torre. In the imprint the printer gives a brief account of the invention, under almost the same heading as the celebrated chapter in the Chronicle of Cologne : En donde y por quien fue inventada la arte de imprimir libros, y en que anno se divulgò. It runs thus : " The art was invented in Germany, in a town called Mentz, situated on a large river, the Rhine, the capital of an archbishopric. A noble, very rich citizen of this town, called *Peter* (!) *Fust*, invented it. This art spread in the year of our Lord 1425 (divulgò se la dicha arte en el anno del Sennor de mill y quatrocientos y veynte cinco annos). Afterwards in the year 1431 (en el anno de mill y quatrocientos y xxxi) a quarrel arose between two archbishops; he who had no

---

il eut mérité peut-être une partie des injures que lui ont prodiguées La Serna Santander, Schaab, Wetter, Umbreit et tant d'autres; mais il semble que ses adversaires, n'ont connu de la Batavia, que l'extrait qu'on en trouve dans tous les livres de Bibliographie ; car aucun d'eux n'a relevé la moindre erreur dans le reste de son ouvrage." It appears from this that neither Berjeau, himself, has read the Batavia, else he would have found there " beaucoup de faits semblables," for instance, in the description of Leiden, where Junius relates : " Porro ciuitas magnificis nobilium ædificijs pulchrè exornata est, habet terna Parochialia templa ; in quorum) vno, cui Custodem dicarunt D. Pancratium, Canonicorum collegium : in altero, quod Apostolorum Principi sacrum, ostenditur panis in saxum induratus, qui capsulæ ferreis cancellis præmunitæ inclusus, ad testandam posteris prodigij memoriam, asseruatur. Id ita habet. Anno suprà millesimum 316. in summâ annonæ difficultate, sororem opulentam altera egentissima in sobole numerosâ, flagitarat panis subsidium, ne fame interirent liberi ; illa inficiatur se habere, sancteq. deierans Deum obtestatur, vt si quid panis domi habeat, id omne lapidescat. Quid multa? preces secuta dicitur certa ostenti fides miraculo conculo confirmata."

That I have appreciated the exact value of Guicciardini's account is still more evident from another curious place in the introduction, where Mentz has the preference to Haarlem. " Attribuiscesi gloria particulare alla Belgica, d'essere stata inuentrice di piu cose memorabili, & *prima elle hauere trouato nella citta di Maganza*, benche alcuni voglino (come piu auanti si dice) fusse nella citta d'Haerlem, la stampa, cio è il modo di stampare i libri, & altro in carta : inuentione tanto diuina. che se li nostri piu antichi l'hanessero ritrouata, il tempo ne la barbaria de gli huomini, non ci poteuan' priuare di innumerabili libri, & d'altre memorie uenerande in tutte le scienze, composte da huomini egregij.—The time of the composition of the Descrittione lies between 1560, the date of the commencement, and 1566, the date of the preface to the reader : (Essendo io dimorato lungo tempo in questi paësi Bassi di Fiandra, parte principale della Gallica Belgica, & hauendo in diuersi tempi, & varie occasioni vedute, vdite, lette, annotate, & con cura, & diligentia molte cose cotidinianimente osseruate, truouo questa Prouincia tanto illustre, & vn' membro tanto importante dell' Europa, ch 'io ho deliberato di farne a vtilità comune, vn' ampia descrittione nel grado & forma che in fino a tutto l'anno M.D. LX. si ritruoua).

[1] " Deshalben ich solichs angefangen Werk unfolkommen und in den feddern hangen lies, so lang bis ich zu erwerben Gnade und Ablas mich fertight *zu ziehen zu dem heiligen Grabe*."

possession of the town, had connivance with certain citizens of the aforesaid town, who opened him the gates in the night of St. Simon and Judas; he pushed with his people into the town and killed nearly all the inhabitants. The slaughter was so great, that the blood flowed in the streets like the water when it is raining. By this occasion that remarkable man, Peter Fust, was killed," cuya anima aya gloria con todos los passados. We see how microscopically small the nucleus of truth is in this chronology too: namely, that the first spread of typography took place six years before the capture of Mentz by Adolph (1462—6=1456, *i.e.* after the law-suit between the inventor and his money-lender.)

The fabrication of Atkyns of the fictitious Haarlem printer at Oxford, Frederic Corsellis, is simply founded on a misprint in the date of an Oxford edition of 1478 (Expositio St. Hieronymi), where the omission of an X was the cause of the year 1468 being found in the imprint. This invention of Atkyns was made use of in several ways. On Deventer and Cologne incunabula artificial imprints were made, as if they were Oxford editions of F. Corsellis of 1469, '70, and '72, and so dexterously, that such a connoisseur as Joh. Enschedé became the dupe of the fraud, at an auction at Amsterdam in 1757, and for a long time considered such a copy to be genuine. Encouraged by this success, however, they went too far. For on one of the fly-leaves of a fictitious early edition they made even a signature of Jan Corsellis, brother of the fictitious Frederic Corsellis, with a note in an impossible dialect, in which Jan Corsellis says: "This book I have received from my brother in England, as a remembrancer, because it is the third book which my brother Frederic Corsellis printed in that country. My brother says that he is not allowed to come over from England, and that if he dared to leave it 'lurens jaan soen kooster' would kill him, because he had left him—Haarlem Jan. A.D. 1471 i: Korselles." (zoo sol lurens jaan soen kooster hem ome levene bringen om dat hi hum haatte verlaacten-haarlem january dueto ano domi 1471 i: korselles). Another very clever falsification, represented an F. C. and H. interwoven, and, underneath: "Fredricus Corcellus haerlem 1472," with an explanation of the mark by Wynkyn de Worde: "this mark means F. Fredrik, C. Corcellus, and H. Haarlem, because he came from Haarlem in the year 1465, to print books in England, and was our first printer."

As a last example we may give a story, published for the first time in 1604 at Strasburg by Walch (Decas fabul. fab. 9, 178, 181), which he tells on the authority of a Netherland "old man," Hendrik Schoor, who is said to have it in his turn from other " old people." According to this story Fust went, shortly after he had finished the bible of Gutenberg, to Paris with the copies, and, declaring them to be manuscripts, sold them first for 60, afterwards for 50, and later even for 30 crowns, while the scriptores charged 500 crowns for one copy of the bible. The low price, however, besides the circumstance that Fust could supply fresh copies at any time, and that they were all exactly alike, drew the attention of the purchasers to the fraud. They began to understand that these bibles could not have been written, and that Fust was a sorcerer. They instituted a law-suit against him, examined his house, seized the remaining copies of the bible, and Fust, if he wished to save himself from the stake, was compelled to reveal the new art to Parliament. It is clear what elements this fable is composed of: we know that Fust went, indeed, as head of his business with Schöffer to Paris, and died there in 1466; that Schöffer after this year instituted there a law-suit for the recovery of some books which had been confiscated for the benefit of the French crown; that the first bible is undated; that printing caused the prices of manuscripts to fall greatly; that the first letter-stamps were cut, from the nature of the case, after the model of the written characters of that time. This story now, respecting Junius' thief, Johan Faust (afterwards mistaken also for Doctor Faust, the wizard of the magic history), was regarded by the Costerians as good enough to be applied to their hero Lourens Coster. Boxhorn is the first who in 1632, in *direct contradiction with the account of Junius*, under the heading: "Great fraud discovered in the first of the printing-offices," by means of this childish story explains away the Mentz imprints of the fifteenth century; he naively expresses himself thus : " To this we may easily answer, that we grant that the first printing-office was nothing but a deception ; because the booksellers sold the printed books as written by hand, for the sake of profit."[1] And so the trick was played by which the decisive objection that the contemporary Netherlands had *never* heard *anything* of their inventor, Lourens Janszoon Coster, was evaded. The elaborate fable regarding Fust of Mentz is only in the 17th century applied in a modified form to Coster of Haarlem ; and on this childish talk Meerman, Koning, De Vries, and Noordziek go on chattering, with a facility which would lay the morality of these gentlemen open to suspicion. Or would they, perhaps, have no moral objection whatever to giving us the fac-simile Speculum of Berjeau for a *typographic*, the reproduction of the Beichtspiegel, by Holtrop, for a *xylographic* work ? They chattered on the swindling of their inventor and his son-in-law as if there were question of the most natural, most honest and most unquestionable matter of the world, and they must therefore submit with patience to some surprise at their moral standpoint. If we, moreover, observe the *kind* of books in question, as for instance the Speculum (on paper, without coloured initials, with generally well-known wood-cuts), the explanatory trick excites not only aversion, but deep pity.

Harzen observed already in 1856 : " This scandalous anecdote does not only want all historical foundation and probability, but is in direct contradiction with Junius' own words. Junius says : the new merchandize, never before seen, was in great demand, and produced great profits (nova merx nunquam antea visa, emptores undique exciret cum huberrimo quæstu). It is clear enough from these words, that the publisher did nowise try to sell his printed books, as it were stealthily, through the medium of trustworthy agents, in the old covers, as manuscripts. If that had been the case, they could never have been taken for a new merchandize, which had never been seen before. But he, as an honest man, sold them for what they really were : new, never before seen productions of his own invention and industry ; and in this way only we may explain the great demand and the material profits which arose from it. What pitiful attempts were made to make it plausible that Coster, and no other, printed the Speculum ! For the sake of such an object they did not hesitate falsely to accuse Coster and his son-in-law, Pietersz., both respectable, wealthy persons and distinguished magistrates of the town of Haarlem, of having, for the sake of gain, systematically exercised, for a number of years, a trade founded on dishonesty and deception. And without taking offence at such an undignified part, they merely descant on the profits produced by this fraud : really too great a sacrifice brought to the defence of a favourite theory."[2]

Quite now in harmony with the above examples, the Haarlem legend has a nucleus : the *first* forgotten printing-office at Haarlem of 1483—86, made serviceable, sixty or eighty years afterwards, to the vanity of Gerrit Thomaszoon.

Meanwhile the negatived prejudice, that all legends are based on truth, was the cause of uncritical foreign antagonists of the Haarlem legend consenting, without a shadow of historical ground, that a certain entirely unknown Haarlem sexton, L. J. Coster, had been a brief-printer, a xylographer. But the man has been *nothing*, which stands in [any connexion with printing, either xylography or typography ; he was an honest chandler, only a little restless, for he changed his line of business, set up an inn, and tried it even in his old days, in 1483, in another place. Instead of having invented typography, he ran away from it when it arrived at Haarlem. Or did he receive his wine from Germany, hear something from a Highlander about the invention at Mentz since 1460, and work now and then in " den Hout" by way of pastime ? We know *nothing* about it. Or did he pilfer, in 1483, the printing-office of Master Jakob Bellaert, who

---

[1] Toneel ofte beschryvinge der steden van Hollandt . . . int Latyn beschreven by M. Z. Boxhornius. Int Nederlandts ouergeset . . . door Geeraerdt Baerdeloos. Amstelredam (1634). 4to obl.

[2] Ueber Alter und Ursprung der frühesten Ausgaben des Heilspiegels oder des Speculum humanæ salvationis. Von E. Harzen. (Archiv für die zeichnende Künste . . . herausgegeben von Dr. Robert Naumann. Leipzig. 8vo, 1855 & 1856.)

settled at Haarlem in that year? I deny the Costerian thief-inventors the right of taking offence at this question for a single second. Our chandler is no more inviolable than Gutenberg. If Matthijs van der Goes had printed at Antwerp with the types of Bellaert, we might have thought that Lourens Janszoon arrived there in 1484, and that his master had stuck, out of mere pleasure, the arms of Haarlem on board of the xylographic ship; that Bellaert's people had abused the thief, in presence of Cornelis the bookbinder, who worked for this *first* Haarlem press; that Cornelis had slept once or twice in the inn at the market-place, the house of the thief; that Cornelis became doting after 1520, and began to confound the history of the theft committed by Koster; that he began to rave, especially when he had prepared himself, by means of a pint or two, for crying. This little history would have been forged after the method of Costerianism: take paper, take ink, take a pen, and don't trouble yourself about anything further, only—write! Put down what comes into your mind, and never mind on the second page what you wrote on the first; go on as if never anything had been written in other countries against the fable; repeat for ever the thousand times refuted cavillings, until the public, from sheer exhaustion, submits to them; but, especially—be impudent, and go through thick and thin: your reward will be a decoration, the stupid amazement of the plebeians, and the contempt of posterity.

After this historical and literary criticism of Junius' story, a philosophical one is superfluous. Otherwise it may be given in a few remarks. The invention of printing is, according to him, the fruit of mere chance; there is no trace of a social, psychical, and technical predisposition of his inventor; no seeking, no struggling, no ebb and flow of failure and success; nothing but a single *name*, a public walk, and all things are ready. In the worthless philosophy of the Costerians they skirmish busily with the part which accident plays in inventions, but they generally forget a few little things. "Archimedes discovered by chance the rules of the balance of solid bodies." Oh yes, but it was Archimedes who took a bath, you know; bathing, by itself, we might do everlastingly without discovering anything but the degrees of the agreeableness of the towels. "It is by chance that Galilei, shut up in the cathedral of Pisa, discovered the laws of the pendulum, while he observed the regular movement of the lamp, which hung from the arch." Exactly, Galilei "observed." Do you know Galilei? "It is by chance that Newton, sitting under an apple-tree at his country-seat, Woolstropp, discovered, by the falling of an apple, the laws of general gravitation." Very accidentally, and the gardener's nose put out of joint! Ingenious historian, your understanding suffers from fits and swoons, but in all you tell us there is not an atom of "chance" concealed—nothing, nothing at all.

Just as according to Junius typography originates from *nothing*, so no sooner is it invented than it dwindles again *into nothing*: the family of the inventor, the workmen, the purchasers, all are aware of the grand fact, but it sinks into the grave of oblivion. Three Haarlem burgomasters, grandsons of the inventor—yes, even his son-in-law—see a printing-office at work at Haarlem for three years, but the deathlike silence about the world-event in their family is not interrupted.

The inventor lost with his *tools* the *invention* also. Deprive an artist of his pencils, and you wrap at the same time his talent in your paper; will he never be able to paint again? Or would you still know languages, if the hobgoblins had flown away with your dictionaries?

It is perfectly clear from Junius's words (suppellectilem instrumentorum herilium ei artificio comparatorum) that the thief took *all* the tools away. He must have been glad when he safely reached home with his load.

The thief left behind him in the office not even so much that Coster and his son-in-law could save at least the *honour*, for it was just this circumstance which put Cornelis in such a rage in his old days, that Coster by this theft had been robbed of *the honour of the invention* (ob ereptam furto gloriam sic ira exardescere solere senem). And *yet* Gerrit Thomasz. had wine-pots made of the remaining type-metal!

We may easily imagine to ourselves the temper of inventor and son-in-law-fellow-inventor on the day after Christmas. I fancy to hear them speak in the empty workplace.

Lourens Janszoon Coster (to the surprised men): "How are you looking so perplexed?"

Claes Claeszoon (the foreman): "Looking? I see no press; all the letter-boxes are gone; everything seems to have been put away; we can therefore do nothing. Are we going to move? It is strange that that foreign fellow alone was privileged to know it, for he has not come yet."

Coster: "What moving? What foreign fellow? Don't dish me up any folly. Bring me up the things!"

The men stare at each other in dumb amazement and mutual suspicion, whether they had passed the Christmas days soberly. At last they come to an explanation. They send for Jan, but Jan is gone. They examine the Laurentian house, but nothing is found. Cornelis is placed, sitting in his baby-chair, in the midst of the indignant workmen, but his crying makes the matter not a bit clearer. Thomas Pietersz. arrives to correct the proof-sheets of a guide for Coster's fellow-members of the corporation (the clean and economical tallow-chandler, with wood-cuts), and proposes, in the first excitement of indignation, to send a telegram to Amsterdam, Utrecht, Delft, Urk. But his father-in-law, less hot-headed than the foolhardy youth, has tolerably quieted down already. He answers:—

"I've had enough of this d——d invention, and will have no more of it. Send a telegram? No, thanks. I remain simply what I am—a chandler. Change is not always an improvement: we see this again here. Peter, when people call for printed books, do as if you know nothing about it; the rage will wear out very soon. And you, men, do just as I: return to your old business. Don't trouble yourself about the art of printing, for that is a very uncertain livelihood—you see that by your master; but remember your oath, never to tell anybody about it; keep your tongues, you know. For I feel not the least inclination to see people laugh at me. But when you want to buy candles, oil, soap, and other things, you know how to find your way. Remember, for that stupid novelty has cost me many a penny. I will ask my sister Madge to make the shop a little tidy, and then efface the thing from my mind. The fun has been too short to be long sad about it."

Gerrit Loefsz. (who cared no longer for his old work): "But might we not have another printing-office ready in a week or two? We are now too nicely on the way to give it up."

The inventor of typography (with majesty): "Go to the devil with your printing-office!"

This first strike of typographers, therefore, came from the master and not from the compositors. Never was a strike so well founded, and never lasted a strike longer. And so the Haarlem invention of printing, anno 1440, was totally put aside on 27th Dec. 1441, before the clock struck twelve.

XVI.

THE REVELATIONS OF SCRIVERIUS.

IN the year 1440, the chandler, Lourens Janszoon *Coster*, walked once in the Haarlem Hout, cut letters out of the bark of a beech, printed them reverse (sigillatim) on paper, and *typography* was invented. *Xylography* was not invented so prosaically in 1428 by the sheriff-innkeeper Louwerijs Janszoon, also on a walk in the Haarlem Hout. The wind had blown very violently a moment before. The walking sheriff takes up a branch which had fallen to the ground, but this time not of a beech but of an oak, cuts three or four letters "in relief in the wood," and wraps them in paper. He is overtaken by sleep. He rests peaceably in the charming wood, where the amorous Pan played the whole day, the voluptuous Galathea could never satisfy her lust, satyrs and fauns thronged, the Naiads of the "Sparen" (the river of Haarlem) met with the Hamadryads. A soft rain is descending while Louwerijs sleeps. The paper cover of the concealed oaken branch, gets suddenly a coloured impression of the cut letters, either by the dampness of the ground or by the rain. Thunder-claps awaken the sleeping innkeeper, he looks at his soaked paper —xylography is invented! This striking event of 1428 is revealed to us two hundred years afterwards at Haarlem by Petrus Scriverius in rhyme. But, alas! no sooner have we, full of admiration, heard what great things happened to an unknown countryman, than our feelings are deeply shocked again by the tiding that a good-for-nothing servant packed up, on a Christmas-night, all that belonged to the art, slipped out of the gate, and disappeared with bag and baggage.

Three letters (Jan, or Fur, trium literarum homo. Scriverius) his name. No more of this villain. For I should not like him to retain a name.

After this sad Christmas the inventor (can we be surprised?) had no longer any pleasure in the matter:

"He disliked the thing; it disturbed his senses,
To begin the work of printing directly again,
He had lost his tools; and the man also had
Sufficient to live; it was of no consequence (!)."

Yet when, in 1442, a Doctrinale was printed at Mentz, he got a little out of temper though.

He said: "Son-in-law (Thomas Pietersz., Scriverius) see, we are done for. Are we to put up with this calmly? Oh, would my head were water! . . .

There lies the Haarlem child, with its clever father,
And you, perjurer, are still alive. Oh, you live, traitor!
Oh hypocrite, oh thief! you eat the bread of your master . . . ."

Man, however, does not advance by lamentations. Neither does he need confine himself to these; the Muses do not rule in vain.

"Ah, author, take courage: write against Germany,
And taunt her freely with her villany,
But what is this? The language of untruth curtailed
Dares yet to open its mouth: it dares to sneer.
Well, let us withstand it, prohibit Mentz from lying
And deceiving others by her errors and lies.
You are not in want of matter; it is done as soon as it is begun,
And all the glory of the Germans goes up in smoke."

Let us place ourselves at the feet of this author. Through him the innkeeper Louwerijs Janszoen became inventor of xylography and typography; through him an unambitious sheriff got a shop with blockbooks, innumerable portraits (even those of the inquisitor Ruard Tapper, and of Erasmus), two stone statues, silver and bronze medals, a monument in the Haarlem Hout, prize essays, decorated apostles, a German martyr (Ebert), biographies, fac-simile signatures, the descent from a count. And all this with such an overpowering force of proof, that Scriverius even declares the rejection of the portrait in the "Lauwerkrans," which no one knows where he took it from, to be atheism: "Dissimulare virum hunc, dissimulare Deum est."

" אמר יוסף הכהן : נראה כי כבר נמצא הדפוס בימים ההם: ואני ראיתי ספר נדפס בויניציאה בשנת שמנה ועשרים ארבע מאות ואלף "

i.e. Joseph the priest says: It appears that printing was invented already in these days; for I have seen a book *printed at Venice* in the year eight-and-twenty, four hundred and thousand (1428).—With these lines from a Hebrew chronicle, which especially treats of France, Italy, the Ottoman dynasty, and is continued till 1553, we will endeavour to arm ourselves against the above anathema. The author, Joseph ben Meir ben J'huda ben J'hoschua ben J'huda ben David ben Moscheh, who descended from the priests ha S'fardi, was born 10th Dec. 1496, at Avignon, from Spanish parents, and died as Jewish physician, in or shortly after 1575, in Italy. The original text of his chronicle was printed in 1554 at Sabionetta, by Cornelius Adelkind. A copy of this rare first edition is preserved in the British Museum at London. As there had not been printed at Venice before 1468, and as it was *impossible* to print in 1428, many years before the invention of the art of printing, it is clear that the author was very much mistaken with his annotation on the Jewish year 5188. Which book, perhaps undated and provided with a written note or a wrong date, may have been the cause of his error, cannot be decided. But the author, when he wrote these two lines of his chronicle, could never have supposed that he was chiselling at that moment the pedestal on which, in 1722, a statue would be erected at Haarlem in honour of the Haarlem citizen *Louwerijs Janszoon*. For Scriverius made himself master of this quotation, in a way beneath all criticism, even of the 17th century, and without understanding it; he mutilated the Haarlem tradition, and gave it that direction, in which it has moved until our time.[1] We must be on the look-out, when the "true laurel for Laurens Koster" is wreathed by him.

"Although Hadrianus Junius, on account of the valuable protests and confirmations of old, respectable, and distinguished magistrates, who related what they had received from their forefathers from mouth to mouth, ought to find belief with every one, as being no relation to the dead Laurens Jansz. Koster . . . And yet it pleased the Germans and others since (!), misled either by misunderstanding or jealousy, to ascribe the invention of printing to Mentz, which is a great injury to our dear town of Haarlem. I could therefore not remain idle and connive at such a thing. The assurance I have of it is too great, and the reasons are too important. If I remained silent and did not destroy the settled opinion, where I had an opportunity of doing so, really my fellow-citizens and all sensible people would justly think this negligence and this purpose to be an everlasting shame to me. I will therefore dutifully and carefully consider, according to my little knowledge, and following the above-named Junius, the honour of the town and my own. The first blow was struck by Junius and by P. Bertius, who followed him (in Contractis Tabulis Geographicis)."

We have tested the strength of that "first blow"; the second blow, which Scriverius is now going "to strike," does not deserve a word of explanation. "I will here briefly and honestly expose all I know about the case, besides what is related by Junius and others, *who had not yet such a perfect knowledge of it*. We are all deceived by an innate weakness and imprudence; and we ourselves deceive others by our sinful nature—knowing better. Such is, I firmly believe, the case with the question of printing (!) It must therefore surprise nobody *that only at present the naked truth, which had hitherto been lost in a deep pit, is discovered and brought to light.*

"It is my opinion that the art was first invented ten or twelve years before the year of our Lord MCCCCXL. (in which the most reliable authors agree) in Holland, at Haarlem. Junius has told its beginning and progress before us. And although he discovered some particulars about the invention, yet he has (I may be allowed to say it without disturbing his ashes) his errors, and may not be pronounced free from inadvertence. I give this caution beforehand, and submit it to the judgment of

---

[1] The more recent abuse of the words of Joseph ha-Kohen was committed by Dr. B. Tideman, who, making it even more easy to him than Scriverius in 1628, wrote in the Nederl. Spectator of 1868, p. 317: "A Hebrew chronicle continued till 1553 . . . . in which the author . . . . assures us that he has seen at Venice, anno 1428, a book printed *with the invention of Coster at Haarlem!*"

the sensible reader, who will compare my discourse with that of Junius. What malevolent and obstinate people will answer, neither concerns my heart nor troubles my mind, feeling sure of, and relying on, the good cause which I have before me, and the plain truth, which, like a heavenly sunbeam, neither night nor darkness, however thick it may be, can obscure." One proof immediately follows, and makes it as clear as the sunlight that—nobody must ever care for such big words.

"To-day (A.D. 1628) it is just full two centuries ago that the excellent and valuable art of printing made its appearance (A.D. 1428). Not in the manner as it is used now, with letters cast of lead and tin . . . No, it did not go on like that; *but a book was cut leaf for leaf on wooden blocks.*

"A certain Jew, named Rabbi Joseph Sacerdos, mentions, in his chronicle under the year of the Jewish era 5188 (*i.e.* 1428), a book printed *at Venice and seen by him* (although born in 1496!), without, however, giving the title; but he says it was an original book, and that the art of printing first commenced with it (!) Really I hope that Mentz will not be so bold as to appropriate to itself also this work; *still less Venice* [where exactly the unmentioned book had been printed, according to Rabbi Joseph] where at that time, and long afterwards, no printing-office had been found. Nay, there is no other town in whole Europe but Haarlem which dares to claim the honour of the art so early [*i.e.* even Haarlem had, until the moment Scriverius wrote this sentence, not dared to ascribe to itself the honour of the art one minute earlier than 1440!]. This book, which was shewn to the Jew at Venice, as something strange and peculiar, was, according to what I can find and suggest, such an one as still exist, and I possess myself . . . That the Jew does not give the title of the book, is no wonder, as it has no name. It was printed in folio, and contains certain figures, to the number of forty, of the Old and New Testament." Here follows the description of a xylographic Biblia pauperum. "In the manner of the preceding book," Scriverius goes on, "I have seen another printed book, named in Latin Canticum. Again, I have seen a book in Latin, printed with rude and clumsy letters, entitled Temptationes Dæmonis; careless workmanship, but in which the first principles and experiments of the art, and of the new invented printing-ink, could not only be observed with the eyes, but also felt with the hand. The forms of all the aforesaid works have been cut in wood. The art was undoubtedly commenced in this way. The Donatus also has been cut on wooden blocks, of which book Mariangelus Accursius and the author of the Cologne chronicle gave an exceedingly complimentary, and, for us, highly honourable account. The noble lady Veronica Lodronia, the grandmother of Josephus Scaliger, had also a little book of "Ghetydgebeden" printed, as it seemed, from wooden blocks. It is evident from Accursius' excellent account that Jan Faust conceived and got the idea of the art from a Dutch Donatus, printed from engraved wooden blocks. And this is confirmed by the distinguished and excellent author of the Cologne chronicle.[1] According to what Junius and others tell us, the letters of the book called 'De Spieghel onser behoudenisse' were cut in, or every letter made separately of, wood. Laurens had cut so many letters from the bark of a beech, put and closed together, that he was able to print something with them, and also a Dutch book entitled 'Den Spieghel onzer Salighéydt.' But I doubt very much whether this so-called 'Spieghel' be the right Peter, and I believe that it was the book which I mentioned (namely, the Biblia pauperum). That the letters (of the Spieghel) were cast, and not cut, is as evident and clear as the sun at mid-day. So that, if we should wish to say more about it, it would seem as if we lit a candle in full daylight. No, printing was executed first

---

[1] It is highly necessary to point out this unprejudiced interpretation of the Cologne chronicle. Accursius, Bertius, Scriverius, Boxhorn, on their standpoint of equality between xylography and typography, did not feel the want, like the later Costerians, of distorting the text of the Chronicle, and have herefore accidentally understood its meaning. In 1861 Berjeau was compelled to acknowledge: "Nous nanquerions cependant à notre profession de foi (!) d'impartialité, si nous ne disions pas tout de suite: l. que les témoignages d'Ulrich Zell et d'Accorso se confondent et peuvent fort bien ne s'appliquer qu'aux Donats xylographiques." &c.

thus: a whole leaf, the figures as well as the accompanying text
and printed. But we must not think that every letter was cut
and that these letters were collected and put together to a line,
of lines to an example for learning and reading. And Ju
paid more attention to this fact, if he has seen the Spieghel h
he must have been misinformed. Our acute Laurens first cut th
close to each other, in the manner of writing, on wood or tin;
he was so successful [O sancta logica, ora pro nobis!], he
working, and, having invented the matrices, cast his letters.

"I will not say further how the noble art of engraving and
is connected with the invention of printing, which arose after
branch also belongs to the laurel of our citizen. Indeed, a
which was to be mentioned especially, as we hear speak of th
publishers of prints, and their praise is spread. But just a
Fuyst imitated the appropriate art of printing, so the excellent
and drawers who . . . also handled the artistic chisel and knife,
and publish their engravings, cut after the printing of the Haar
have been instructed by, and got their first experience from ou
Laurens Koster. This honour belongs (I say it again) to his lau
able that our fellow-citizen be acknowledged in this without d
nivance. *Which, although it has not been done hitherto, I hope*
place after this my advice and disclosure."

I have amply quoted from the "Laurecrans" of 1628,
less method of Costerianism presents itself here in full fl
nakedness. I know no literature more paltry than that which
was got up to dress a fable. He who is *willing* to see, must
the air of the Haarlem invention is built up. 1. An insignifica
in a Hebrew chronicle of the 16th century mentions a boc
in 1428. 2. This inaccurate passage is made serviceable
Although the impossible book of 1428 is not mentioned in it, ye
xylographic Biblia pauperum in it. 4. On account of this Je
antodated Haarlem date, 1440, is again changed into 1428,
the inscription of the so-called Coster-house *falsified*. 5. Scri
enough to put the imaginary invention at Haarlem in 1428, an
that same year printed books could have been found already a
it is *said* in 1568 (1588) that Laurens Janszoon Coster invente
printing, so it is *said*, not before 1628, that he is the inventor
story of 1588 could at least refer to a Haarlem pedigree, and a
from it, but we *see* the story of 1628 got up by Scriverius, before
NOTHING. And this *nothing* is the real foundation on which the
erected.

Boxhorn, in his turn, pushed with firm hand the invention
having given one quotation, we may dismiss him also for eve
1420 the first foundations of the noble art of printing began to b
Laurentius Costerius. That this art was first begun in the year
and not thirty or forty, as is the most common opinion, *has*
Joseph (!), who says in his chronicle that the earliest (!) book w
in the year of the Jews 5188, of the Christians 1428. I have
that book of Josephus, although I have long been looking for it.'

For about two centuries long we were kept tacking about be
But a date was wanted for the fourth jubilee at Haarlem. The c
the council of Haarlem with the task of fixing that date, fortune
the Haarlem wood was destroyed in 1426, during the siege c
Jacqueline, and the committee were now of opinion that the
veniently be divided between the two extreme terms of 1420
huckster-agreement, the year 1423 is fixed upon as the time o

Coster, but of *Louwerijs Janszoen*. For, by the removal of the traditional date they could no longer make any use of the Lourens Janszoon Coster of Junius with 1440 (1446); the sheriff who died in 1439 fitted better in the second fable than a person of the second half of the XV. century, just as the chandler would have been more suitable to the earlier story. And in the same paltry manner in which the Haarlem inventor of typography is created by Scriverius also the inventor of xylography, so he was, until the time of Koning, charged with the sacristanship and all possible blockbooks which they discovered, either of Netherland or German origin. Every one knows henceforth the value of Costerian waste paper.

Indeed, I know that in the diary of the Coster fêtes of 1856 (Gedenkboek der Costerfeesten), we are assured in a haughty tone that the opinion as if Lourens Janszoon had been a sacristan and a xylographer is "a system of *the past century*, set aside by us (De Vries and Noordziek) for good and all," but I know also that a Costerian cannot be trusted, especially when he uses strong expressions. The system which makes of Lourens Janszoon a sacristan and an engraver, is *not* a system of the past century; it was positively that of Koning and Scheltema; the sacristanship was set aside by De Vries not before 1841, the xylography (temporarily) in the same year. I will bring a few things of that system of "the past century" under the notice of M. Noordziek. In the "Konst & Letterbode" of 1823 he may read a letter of "the learned" Jac. Koning, which contains "new evidences of the legitimacy of the claim of Haarlem to the honour of the invention of printing." Among them we find the important discovery, made by Koning a few weeks before, about the "figures of two picture-books made by L. J. Koster—namely, the 'Ars moriendi' and 'Biblia pauperum,' of which last book the blocks—just as those of the 'Spiegel onzer behoudenis'—had remained in the Northern Provinces of the Netherlands.'" Besides Noordzick's "Gedenkboek" of 1856, there exists also "Gedenkschriften wegens het vierde eeuwgetijde.... van stadswege gevierd te Haarlem, 1823, byeenverzameld door Vincent Loosjes" [Memorials of the 4th jubilee celebrated by the town of Haarlem, 1823, collected by Vincent Loosjes]. The addenda E contains a "Brief description of the books printed by L. J. Koster at Haarlem, between 1420 and 1440 ... exhibited on the occasion of the fourth jubilee of the art of printing." And here the reader finds quietly announced as printing work of Coster: 1. The (German) Apocalypsis; 2. The Biblia pauperum; 3. The Ars moriendi; 4. The Canticum; while this list is preceded by the following inconceivably stupid explanation—at least, I am hardly able to believe my eyes while I copy the nonsense—"Lourens Janszoon Koster, a distinguished citizen and inhabitant of Haarlem—where he often held the offices of treasurer, sheriff, &c.—was born in or about the year 1370. On a certain day (why was the date not given?) in summer-time (in summer-time!), walking in the wood [the "Hout,"] situated near the town (situated near the town, oh Haarlemers!), he cut for pastime (for pastime!) some letters out of the bark of a beech-tree. Having got thereby (!) the idea that such letters cut reversely (such letters cut reversely!) were fit for printing, he tried it first with a line or two, as examples for the children of his son-in-law. Succeeding in this, and having invented a more solid and less blotting ink than the common writing ink, he undertook more important works. He made a much greater number of moveable letters cut of wood, and put them together. But now he found out that this manner of printing was not fit for larger work, and was only serviceable for a few lines or verses, and not for any work of greater extent, as the loose wooden letters were too weak and too flexible to be joined together properly and to stand the pressure of the press used by him for printing. To meet these inconveniences, and to give more firmness to his letters, he tried to print with fixed letters or wooden blocks, in the manner of the printers of cards (!) He engraved whole figures on wood, accompanied by more or less elaborate explanations, and among them the Apocalypse of St. John, &c. Although succeeding in this work, he soon perceived that these wooden blocks could serve no other purpose, and he had, therefore, to make new blocks for every other book, which required much time and trouble. He now thought of improving his former—in this respect (!) much more preferable—

way of printing, and, instead of moveable wooden letters, to devise, if possible, a more solid sort of letters," &c. In *this* fable, typography (= bark-printing), discovered, by way of pastime, on a walk in summer-time, begets xylography, and the inconvenience of xylography leads to metallo-typography. This is the greatest nonsense ever spoken on the subject. And in the face of all this, people talk of an "abolished system of the past century"! No; notwithstanding the bold untruth of the "Gedenkboek," it is clear that they were in 1823 not one step from the folly and impudence of Scriverius. Neither was Noordziek himself free from the Haarlem sheriff, Lourens Janszoon, as the inventor of the art of engraving, and of that of printing with moveable types—altogether mere inventions of Scriverius. Let us restrain, however, our surprise at such proceedings, for worse things than these must be disclosed.

XVII.

LOUWERIJS JANSZOEN.

VERDICTS given by the counts of Holland at Haarlem in 1380 and 1408, during the civil broils of the Hooks and Kabeljaws, make mention of Jan Louwerijszoen and Louwerijs Janszoen. The fact that they belonged to the same party, the distance of 28 years which lies between them, the ancient custom of transmitting the name from the father to the son, &c. &c., make it probable that these two persons were father and son.[1] However this may be, it is certain that in the *first* half of the fifteenth century a person lived at Haarlem whose name was Louwerijs Janszoen. He was there winemerchant, innkeeper, councillor, sheriff, treasurer, and governor of the hospital, and he died in 1439. His seal (arms) and signature are preserved in the town-hall at Haarlem, where we have of the sheriff *Louwerijs Janszoen, in originali:* two testimonials (1422 and '29), a receipt (1425), four orders (1422, '28, and '31), a receipt (1431), and a declaration signed by him as governor or regent of St. Elizabeth Hospital.

Louwerijs Janszoen went as councillor to Dordrecht in 1417, to Gouda in 1418, as treasurer to Leiden in 1426. As sheriff he was sent to the diet at Delft, where, on the 3rd July, 1428, the reconciliation took place between Philip and Jacoba (Jacqueline). This absence lasted twenty-five days. In the same year, at the end of July, he attended the assembly at Leiden to deliberate on the grand requisition (bede) demanded by Philip. He returned to Haarlem as one of the negotiators, and took, with four other functionaries, a sum of 1,500 schilds to the duke at Leiden. The latter journey lasted twenty-one days. In 1430, six Haarlem deputies made a journey to the Hague, in order to negotiate on the prolongation of the peace between Holland and Friesland; among them was Louwerijs Janszoen.[2] It is equally clear that he possessed an annuity from the town, for we find that from 1418 down to 1435 payments are made to him for interests, in 1418, xi. lb. xii. s., which amount was reduced in 1435 from eleven to three pounds. The several items have been given already by Koning in his "Verhandeling." Besides the items for the wine which was fetched from, or drunk

---

[1] Cf. the "Groot Charterboek van Holland en Zeeland door F. van Mieris. III, p 365 en IV. p. 111. Jan Louwerijszoon and Louwerijs Janszoon belonged to the Hooks. The last was, 26th Sept. 1408, sentenced to pay a fine of 60 nobles, because he had taken part in the emotions of 1405. The treasury-accounts of Holland, Zealand, and Friseland, in the archives of the Hague, mention, under 18th June, 1408 —1st Oct. 1409, the receipt of this fine:—Item noch ontfaen, bi hande van Dirc Offus, van Louris Jansz.' LX. Noble.

[2] All these data have been printed already in extenso, and historically enlarged upon in the "Bijdragen" of Koning.

at, his house, and of which we have to speak hereafter, I find only two more, which tell us that Louwerijs Janszoen received payment from the town—namely, in 1417, at the time that fighting was going on at Gorinchem, he was among twenty-five armed citizens, who were away for ten days, and each of whom received fourpence a-day; and in 1429, when the Haarlem Hout, destroyed during the siege (by Jacqueline of Bavaria) of 1426, was being replanted. At least, among the payments made for that work we find: Item. *louwerijs Janssoen*, for four days' wages while he worked in the wood, for 3s. a-day, makes xii. s.[1]

In 1434 Laurens Janszoen appeared still (just as in 1420, '21, '26, '30, and '34) as one of the " Six " (treasurers). His name is not mentioned the two following years, and of the account of 1438 only a fragment has been preserved. But as the accounts since 1435 have not been verified and approved before 1445, nothing is to be learned, since that year, from the names of those who signed them.

This rapid view of particulars, already published, is sufficient. The evidence, however, for the innkeepership of Louwerijs Janszoen, has to be given in a more elaborate manner, for although the proofs of this circumstance have already been published before, the fact has been systematically denied. We will give the documents chronologically.

" 1422. Item zat tgerecht tot *louwerijs Janssoens* om der stede maten te verhueren. aldair verdroncken xxviii. d." (The court held a session at the house of L. J., to lend out the measures of the town; spent there in drinking xxviii. d.) In 1426, the Wednesday after Lady-day, the burgomaster, Jan van Bakenesse, and a few others of the constabulary, with Willem van Egmond and Heynric van Wassenaer, spent iiij lb. xi. s. at L. J.'s.—The Tuesday after St. Agatha, three "boyersche guldens (à 22½ st.)" are paid to L. J., as having been spent at his house by some of the constabulary, with W. van Egmond, Jelijs van Cralinghe, and Joost van Steenhout.—Also, when the grating of the font was made by contract, vii. s. iiij. d. were spent in drinking at *Louwerijs Janszoen's*. We find, in 1426, eleven more items of the same kind. At one time the expenses were at his house; at another time the wine was fetched by a messenger of the town, and drunk, as was the custom at that time, by the members of the council in the town-hall, *e.g.*:—

" tot zinen huize ghehaelt en op den huze ghedroncken zijn v menghelen wijns " (fetched from his house and drunk at the hall v mengels (a measure of two pints) of wine).

" by brandetge messelgier [bode] opten huze ghehailt i mynghel" (fetched and brought to the hall by Brandetge messelgier [messenger] i mengel [of wine]).

" by boudyn Koc ghehaelt ende den hoer van lichtevelde ghesceynt ij cannen " (fetched by Boudyn Koc and sent to the Lord van Lichtenvelde ij litres).

" by dirc Janszoen de bode tot *louwerijs* voorser ghehaelt en opten huze ghedroncken" (fetched by Dirc Janszoen, the messenger at [the house of] the said Louwerijs, and drunk at the hall).

" by Jan Zeelander tot *louweriis* Janszoen ghehaelt" (fetched by Jan Zeelander at Louweriis Janszoen's).

Expenses were made at his house " when the harness was taken to the hall"; when the treasurers " settled with the labourers, carpenters, smiths and porters." In 1428 money was spent at his house by some of the constabulary, when they "had been about to injure the brewer who had not paid them their beer-money" (omme gheweest hadden omme den brouwer te beschadigen, die hoir drincke bier gelt niet betaalt hadde).

---

[1] I give this item exactly as I find it. As it was not suitable to Koning's system, he had very calmly printed (Bijdragen I. 32) : " When we meet in the Haarlem registers, now and then, with a name which would, in most respects, wholly or partly be the same as that of our Laurens Janszoon, we have to distinguish carefully, by one or other addition, this person from the one with whom we are concerned." And, as a proof, we find, for instance, quoted : " Louwerijs Janssoen, *workman*, (account of 1429)." In the same manner L. J. was promoted in his " Verhandeling " (p. 147) to " officer of the Civic Guard," by means of concealing the *equal* wages of the twenty-five armed citizens. The work in the wood stood, no doubt, in connexion with the replanting, with which a sheriff or municipal treasurer would have something to do.

We find twice positively mentioned a sum paid to *Louwerijs Janszoen* for expenses at his house, by some good people from the country. And in 1429 the "constabulary of the nupoert" were treated to two litres of wine which were "fetched from *louwerijs Janssoens*." The following year some of the constabulary make expenses at the house of *louwerh. Jansz.*, when Claes Gerbrantsz. "brought secret tidings regarding the beer of Amersfoort."

With all these items the following, respecting the supply of wine by *Louwerijs Janszoen* to the parish church of St. Bavo (the cathedral of Haarlem), agree remarkably well.

In 1421 the church received xi litres of wine from him—In 1423 xxviij litres of wine for the singers—In 1426 we find among the expenses for wine for the whole year the following items: "*lourens Jansz.* [for] xlv pints [of] an 'oude Tuyn,' and xiii pints [of] a 'cromstert', and for easter-wine "Item *lourens jansz.* 54½ stop."

That there is here only question of expenses for the church, is evident, both from the quantity of wine, and other items found in this account: "It. van nuw was ghecoft 43 pond was. It. 4 outer kersen [het] stic 4 lb. was. It. pascaers 16 lb. was. (Item bought again 43 pounds of wax. Item 4 altar candles 4 lb of wax apiece. Item an easter-candle, 16 lb of wax).

In 1428: "Dit is van den wiin die alt jaer ghehaelt is, elc pint een cromstert... It. *Louris Jansz.* 28 p. en 4 luven" (This is for the wine which has been bought this whole year, each pint a cromstert... Item L. J. 23 p. and 4 luven); 1431: "Betaelt van saugwyn *louwerijs Jansz.* ix cromstaert" (paid for wine for the singers, l. J.); 1432: "Item van wijn die ghehaelt is van heyligen cruysdagh tot Sinte Geerden dagh, als men den excyns verhuyrt, *Louwerijs Janssoen*, gehaelt cxlj¾ pint" (Item for wine fetched, from holy cross-day to St. Marg. day, when the taxes were farmed, L. J. fetched cxlj¾ pints).

In 1433 the church receives from *Louwe Janszoen* " Lii Johannes-tuyn, die hij onder [hem] ghehadt heeft ii jaer lane van rike griet" (Lii Johanues-tuyn, which he had taken care of for two years for rich Margaret), and he supplies moreover xvii½ pints of wine.

With these items the innkeepership of Louwerijs Janszoen may be considered as proved. The objections which could probably be made to the identity of Louwerijs Janszoen who sells wine to the church and to the town-hall, and at whose house expenses are made, with Louwerijs Janszoen who, in the capacity of councillor or sheriff, makes journeys to Dordrecht, Gouda, Delft, Leiden, the Hague, and, as treasurer or as councillor, settles municipal accounts, fall to the ground, when we know that we have had many burgomasters, who were at the same time brewers, coopers, smiths, innkeepers, and the like.[1]

---

[1] That Meerman did not make, from the items for wine in the registers of the church, the inference, so ready at hand, with regard to the social position of Louwerijs Janszoon, was caused by his making him, misled by Junius's etymology, the impossible Koster (sacristan) of the church, whose duty it was to "fetch" the wine (Laurentinm ædituum ad iuferiorem classem rejicere necessum erit). Koning went on with this monstrous sacristanship of the Haarlem sheriff, and soothes himself in his MS., as if he did not understand the old signification of the preposition "by" (per), with this awkward observation: "N.B. This wine was fetched *at* Boudyn Koc's. Hence it is evident for once and all, that the wine had not been supplied by L. J., but had probably been drunk at his house, or had been paid by him in his quality. This is to be observed continually." Clever! As if the wine had not been fetched *by* the messenger *at* L. J's. That De Vries, who disputed intentionally and effectually this Kostership of Louwerijs Janszoon, did not come to the right conclusion, is more critical. He even says (in his treatise: on the name Coster and L. J. C.'s pretended Kostership, p. 13): "Concerning these items (for wine fetched), it is, in my opinion, not possible [!] to decide in what relation the name of Lourens Janszoon makes its appearance." He then simply makes "presents" of them given *by* the church! One may judge, however, from the following account:

1426. Wtgheuen van wijn van alt jaer. (Payments for wine for the whole year.)
It. dirk ghysbrechtz LVI pint. i oude tuyn ende xv pint. i cromstert.
It. coen xxiiij½, van i oude tuyn . . . ende LV pint van i cromstert.
It. dirk spiker LVI½ pint. van i oude tuyn ende xii pint van i cr.
It. lourens Jansz. XLV pinten i oude tuyn ende xii pint i cromstert.
It. Jan van berkenrode XL pint + 10 pint. And so on, while under the paswijn (easter-wine) three of the above-mentioned merchants occur again, thus:

The item of his funeral in the church of St. Bavo is well-known. We find in the memorandum of 1439 : Item *lou Janss.* breet ii. gra. cloc en graf. (By this interpretation the arguments in the "Gedenkschriften" (Haarlem, 1824, p. 338), fall to the ground; there is no question of two florins, but of two graves.)

Surely this must be the same man. At least after 1439, Louwerijs Janszoon appears no longer among the sellers of wine to the church, and after 1439 the town-annuity of three pounds is entered in the treasury accounts under the name of *Vrouwe louwerijs Janssoens weduwe* (widow), who is mentioned from 1440—52. We stand, therefore, with our *Louwerijs Janszoen* on the solid ground of history. There lived, in the first half of the 15th century, until the end of 1439, some one of that name at Haarlem, who has been an innkeeper, councillor, sheriff, treasurer, and governor of an hospital.[1] There is nothing in the career of this man which deserves our attention. And yet, *he has a statue at Haarlem.*

After the mutilation of Junius's fabrication, Scriverius began, in his own way, with his head full of prejudices and bibliographical errors, and completely fanaticized against Mentz, to look for the Haarlem inventor, and in an earlier period, of course, as he abandoned the year 1440. And, lo ! he finds in a sheriff-document of 1431, that there lived at that time at Haarlem a man, whose names accidentally agreed with the christian names of *Coster*—our sheriff *Louwerijs Janszoon.* Scriverius was at once ready with the premature and false conclusion that the sheriff was identical with Junius's inventor of the art of printing, and he wrote in the Laurecrans : "Be it known that I find that our *Laurens* has been a sheriff, and that he sealed letters here in the year 1431." This mustard-seed of error, this unreasonable confusion of persons, produced a tree, a thorn-bush, which flowered until this day, and was only burnt this year. The pedantic, etymological quibble of Junius on the origin of the name Coster, begot the *Koster* (sacristan) -legend, that monster which annoyed already, in 1639, Mallinckrodt, who accepted this quibble as current coin, and combined it with Scriverius's discovery (Nihil dicam de Ædituo in primaria & patritia Laurentii istius familia hæreditario munere, quamvis *instar monstri* habere possit consularis hic Junii ædituus).

It. lourens jansz. 54½ stop (of) 5 gr. 1 stop.
It. Jan van Berkenroed 26 stop.
It. coen op die beke 24½ stop.

The municipal payments to L. J. for wine are explained by "meetings, deliberations" of the government, which took place in his house, instead of at the Town-hall. The pretence deserves no refutation in the face of a circumstance communicated in one breath, that the Haarlem municipality "had its own wine-cellar underneath the Town-hall," bought in 1388 from the Dominican friars. It is natural that the payments took place mostly on behalf of members of the town government, for those only could abuse in this manner the revenues of the town ; a citizen did not enjoy "free wine" at the expense of the town. That especially the constabulary made so often expenses at Louwerijs Janszoen's may be explained from the charter of Maximilian of Austria, 1480, in which it is decided that the bailiffs, superintendents of the dikes, &c., are thenceforth not allowed to give verdicts within towns or villages, but in a public court, on the road, or in a house *where no drinks or eatables* are sold. It is incorrect to say that there existed no inns yet in Holland in the 15th century.

[1] A burgomastership of Louwerijs Janszoen appears nowhere ; but, it would be of not the least consequence with respect to his social position. The post of honour of burgomaster, as well as that of koster (sacristan), has been gradually 'screwed up in the apologies of Junius to a degree of importance, which it nowise obtained during the 15th century; it was considered at that time a privilege to be relieved of magisterial duties as soon as possible. They were unremunerated posts of honour (= burdens). This unhistorical varnishing has, no doubt, contributed to Koning's and De Vries' antipathy to an innkeeper-sheriff, although they could know better, and the first recorded himself the innkeepership of Pieter Thomaszoon at Haarlem, in 1472 and '89, in his manuscript. This Pieter Thomasz., supposed grand-child of Lourens Coster, supplies, just as his grandfather, the town with wine (1471 and '73), hires "the wind-lass" (1473), and farms the taxes of the wine and beer (1474 and '75). We find, 1454 : Item gheschenet mynen heer den stedehouder een maeltyd tot pieter thomassoens dair die van den gerechte en meer anderen by waren, zou costen mit wyn ende bier ende mits vier stede kannen wyns die hem in syn herberghe gheschenet worden xxiij lb. 5 s. iiij d. (Item presented to my lord the Stadtholder a dinner at [the house of] pieter thomassoen, which the constabulary and others attended, would cost with wine, beer, and 4 litres of wine of the town, which were given to him in his inn, . . .). Similar payments take place to the same person in 1455 and 1457. We find, in 1473 : Item on St. Marc-day (when the oath was administered to the new burgomasters) paid for two mengels of sweet wine, fetched at pieter thomassoen's, for each mengel iii pence, and one penny for bread. Koning, of course, does not see which way the wind blows, but by the dinner of the count Van Oostervant at the house of Lourens Coster (1454), quoted already, he notices : " We might infer from this that the house of this *Lou Coster* was a public inn." Of course !

However, this round triangle was defended by Meerman, maintained by Koning, and only destroyed in 1841 by De Vries. But it was not destroyed before the insignificant office of sacristan was declared, without any historical precedent, to be *hereditary*; not without the sacristan-ship having been embellished, contrary to the most plain charters, with a thousand-and-one visions. All this arose from a single pedantic parenthesis. By the side of this Koster (sacristan)-legend, and interwoven with it, runs, since Scriverius, the *Sheriff*-legend, which originated from nothing but the above quotation. The rippling, caused by the throwing of this stone in the stream of tradition, became wider and wider; the stream overflowed its banks; it drowned the old tradition; it washed the original Lourens Janszoon *Coster* away for ever, and threw another upon the bank, who had thought of typography (xylography) as little as the chandler, and whom the Haarlemers of the 16th century had never thought of either! Researches of Van Oosten de Bruyn, and Meerman, about 1765, brought more sheriff-letters with the seal of *Louwerijs Janszoon* to light, and lo! it appeared from this seal that he had a lion rampant with the label of a younger branch and the bar-sinister. And, although they still clung in 1740 to the vellum pedigree, to *Coster* and the *dore*, yet afterwards all this is not mentioned any more, but—the inventor of the art of printing is a bastard of the house of Brederode! It was now necessary to find *Costers* as bastards of that family—and Meerman simply degrades, without a single valid reason, the legitimate family of the Van der Duins to bastards. And while large clouds of dust of useless learning are driven upwards, these great genealogists think not a moment of the most simple elements of heraldry—of the first question which they ought, in any case, to have asked, before they looked for an answer and pronounced an ancient family illegitimate—namely, the question of the *colour* of their sheriff-arms. A lion rampant signifies nothing by itself, for we were already very fond of lions in the middle ages. Why is only Holland meant by a lion without colour, on a field without colour? Why was Lourens Janszoon not a younger son of a bastard of Heemskerk, Berkenrode, Van Nispen, Bouwens, Van Eck, and so many others who all bore a lion in their coats-of-arms? Let every one consult the heraldic charts. On that of Leiden we see at once, as the arms of Willem Jacob Willemsz., a lion with label, red on gold. But, especially those of Haarlem exhibit a whole menagerie of lions rampant: Van Loo (silver on blue), Verbeek (blue on silver), Damast (red on silver), Schatter (black on silver), and so also Boeckhorst, Alkemade, Doortoge, Van den Berg, Bronkhorst, Langerak, Van der Leek and others. Indeed M. Alberdingk Thijm, the writer of the preface and commentator (in the Dutch translation) of Paeile's uninterrupted sophism, in which the Haarlem sheriff Louwerijs Janszoon is changed into a Brederode, was right when he wrote the other day, in the periodical *Nederland*, that "(divers) dolls of straw had been dressed in a livery of Brederode, which existed nowhere but in a fertile imagination, and on the patient paper of fabricators of pedigrees." But what then was the object of this heraldic charlatanry? By the side of the noble Gutenberg they placed a chimerical descendant of a count.

The sheriff Louwerijs Janszoon (van Brederode) was now allowed to be a sacristan, even a sexton, and to fetch wine for the church; but a wine-merchant, an *innkeeper?* heaven forbid! The documents which prove this fact incontrovertibly, were cruelly mutilated.

And so they went on, inquiring and arguing on a false basis, until the date-committee of 1822 discovered the year of the death of the sheriff Lourens Janszoon, 1439. And the *Lourens*-legend of Scriverius had already taken so deeply root, *so* far were people already distanced from the *Coster*-legend of Junius, that they took without any perplexity the man who died in 1439 for identical with the man, who, according to Junius, invents printing in 1440, and is robbed by his German servant in 1441! In short, the rash mixing up of persons by Scriverius in 1628, led to the event, full of bitter irony, that in 1856, at Haarlem, a metal statue was inaugurated in honour of a sheriff-innkeeper, who had neither anything to do with the typography invented after his death, nor with the so-called tradition recorded by Coornhert and

Junius. That statue is rejected not only by the historical criticism of our time, and the more perfect knowledge of our century; no, if the witnesses in this suit could rise again, Hadrianus Junius would protest against this distortion of his account, confirmed by the most solemn affirmations; he would protest against the rejection of his Ædituus Custosve, so learnedly explained by him. Nay, more, the honest Louwerijs Janszoen, who was a conservative sheriff, would oppose such a revolutionary tradition; he, the sound Roman-Catholic, would oppose the anabaptism of his Calvinistic townsman of two centuries later, for he was neither *Coster* nor was called so. The only point of contact between him and Lourens Coster, Thomas Pieterszoon, and Gerrit Thomaszoon, was a congeniality in their innkeepership.

There is, therefore, before 1628, not the slightest trace at Haarlem of an earlier date than 1440 as the year of the fictitious invention. Not earlier than the first-mentioned year does Scriverius place himself, by a salto morale, beyond the Batavia, and fabricates an absurd history from his own head, which has no foundation but his own brains. Boxhorn afterwards goes back to 1420, Cogan decides upon 1422, but later upon 1428 or 1430. Koning makes an end of all this uncertainty in 1822. He had succeeded in "discovering a new and more solid foundation, which *proves* (Koning says he no longer hesitates to use this word) that the year 1422 ought to be regarded and fixed upon as the first period of Koster's (!) invention."

Now, he produced a proof, compared with which mathematics is only childish play, and, to fill the cup of wit, he declares that everything he alleges " *is evident from an original pedigree, written on vellum, and in his possession,*" i.e. the document, now published, with 1446 as the date of the first "print!" Let every one first look on that pedigree, and afterwards on the following argumentation, to be found in the "Konst- and Letterbode" of 1822:—

1370. Koster (!) born.
1392. ,, at the age of 22, marries (the *not* mentioned!) Catrina Andriesdochter.
1393. Lucia Laurensdaughter born (!).
1415. ,, ,, at the age of 22, married to Thomas Pieterszoon.
1416. Pieter Thomaszoon born.
1417—1422. One or more children born from this last marriage.
1438. Pieter Thomaszoon, at the age of 22, marries Margriet Jan Florisdaughter.
1439. Thomas Pieterszoon born.
1440. Margriet Pietersdaughter born.

No press has here enough signs of exclamation: at the age of 22, at the age of 22, at the age of 22—really the art of printing was invented in 1422! Here is Koning's reasoning: "We might antedate or postdate the year of marriage or birth, of the one or the other; but, however we may cipher, we will come to no other conclusion but that: the grandchildren of Koster, born from his daughter Lucy, must have reached, in 1422, the age of between *two and seven years*, and were therefore just in that youthful age in which a few lines as examples of their grandfather could be of service, and would have been received by them with childish pleasure."

Dear me! yes, that childish pleasure, especially in their *second* year! How do we see them stretch forth their hands, crowing, when grandfather comes home again from the wood with wooden letters! And when he had printed with their father Thomas a Pater noster or an Ave salus mundi, for the sake of clearness and convenience in Latin, the little Thomases split their faces with laughter from childish pleasure! But no, no jokes by so much disgusting quackery. The contemptible noodle speaks of all those marriages, all at the age of 22, as if he had been at the wedding-party; he makes dates unscrupulously, and builds on them the proof that typography was invented at Haarlem in 1422.[1] A public which accepted these bubbles for

---

[1] It is here the place to explain Koning's blunders respecting his researches in the Haarlem archives, of which we have mentioned already a few. In the first place, as to the alleged rarity of the name of *Lourens* (Koning, Bijdr. I. 32), the following (incomplete) list is nowise a proof of it. I find in

realities, was ripe for the jugglers' committee, which decided that it happened in

the registers of Haarlem :—1420 Jan Louwenszoen weduwe, Lourijs Jan nieuwe Janszoen ; 1422 ('26 en '27) Louwerijs Janszoen van Stryen ; 1426 Jan Louwerijszoen ; 1427 Jan oudenzoen en Louwerijs sin soen, Knth. louwers' die roden weduw ; 1428 Louwerijs Jan Ouwensoen ; 1430 Jan Louwensoen ; 1433, '34 Louwerijs Jan Ouden soens soen; 1434 Jan Louwerijssoen die cleyboer; 1439 Jan Louwensoen te Sparendam ; 1440 Heer Jan, Pieter, Vrank, and Willem louryssoen. (As all these sons of Louwerijs appear in 1440, after the death of L. J., besides the widow Ymme, and pay borrowed money to the town, they are perhaps his descendants. At least we find by them question of "inheritance"); 1448 Louwe, basket-maker; Louwe Janssoen, coffin-maker; 1451 Lourijs Jan Oudensz., Louris wed. in de leest ; 1453 Louwe Janssoen, the shoemaker; 1470 Louris Jansz., carpenter ; 1476 Jan Louriszoon ; 1481 Lauken, the sexton; 1483 Louris Janszoon Blankert ; 1487 Louris Janszoon, mason ; 1488 Pieter and Anthonis Louriszoon ; 1492 Lou Jan Louwensoensz., Cornelis Louriszoon, Jan Lou, shipwright; 1493 Louris Janszoon, carpenter ; Louris, stone-cutter, and Louris Janszoen, shoemaker.—In the memorandums of the church: 1422 Bauc Lourens wid., Willem Lourensz. 1423 Grote lourijs wid. 1439 It. Jacop Jansz. van grote louwijs sijn oems graff geg. liii. phs. scild. 1445 Louwerijs, the joiner. 1447 Pieter Louwerijs wid. 1450 Louwerijs Janszoen bi die cleine houtpoort iii pont (for the making of a testament) ; Louwen Janszoen kint cloc. 1452 Pieter Louwerisz. XLII pinten zoetwyns, LXXVII p. malvezey ix gl iii gr. ii stuvers; CXXVIII p. malvezey ellec pint i braspennim. 1453 Jan Louwesoen die timmerman siin zoen cloc. 1455 Willem Louwerijssoens dochter cloc salvator (See on the clocks mentioned here : De Vries, Eclaircissemens sur l'histoire de l'invent. de l'imprimerie, trad. de Noordzick. 8vo. La Haye, 1843, p. 182,) ; Katrin Willem Louwerijssoens wijf id. ; Jan Louwerijsz. the stone-cutter ; 1461 Lontgen, chest-maker, een legerstede, cloc salvator, testament ii. nobel ; 1464 Louwerijs Jan Ouwenszoen ; Jan Louwerijssoon, the mason's wife cloc ; Jan Lou. the smith op die oude graft testament. 1465 Gherit lou wyff cloc salv. en graff. It. gheertruut pieter louwenzoens wyf, wonende tot Delf, heeft die kerc betnalt van hoer mans wegen vi stuvers. It. Aleyt louwen dochter, pieter louwenzoens zuster, living on the bakenesser graft (canal), she lives there with eylert, and also owes the church vi d. ; 1467 Ghertruut lou chestm. wid. ; 1473 Louwerijs Jansz. testament, Jan Louwes-zoon cloc salvator. 1475 Lou op die burgwal. 1478 Louwerijs the carpenter, it. the mason, it. the stone-cutter. 1495 Pieter Louriszoon, shipwright, all the clocks and the making of a grave 8¼ rns. fl. Really, the Lourenses were exceedingly rare at Haarlem ! During my later researches in the archives I was struck by the abundance, especially in the 16th century, of Lourenses Janszoons ; this name occurs as frequently, during the 15th and 16th century, at Haarlem, as Müller, Meier, Smith, and Brown at present in Germany and England; a circumstance very convenient for a local legend. It is obvious how dishonest Koning's proceedings were with respect to this number of Lourenses Janszoon, especially in connexion with the carefully concealed vellum pedigree, and what an amount of bad faith was required to dare to write on "the care with which they were accustomed to distinguish the sheriff (-innkeeper) from the few others of similar names in the town registers. They never distinguished anything with respect to this sheriff!

But what is of more importance : What discoveries did Koning make with respect to *Costers*? Some have taken pains to prove " that a family of the name of Coster lived in Holland during the 14th century," and it appears from the Necrologium Egmondanum, amongst other things, that Willem, dictus Coster, was buried in the church of Egmond in 1302. Here we have to observe, by the way, that also in this form, the name of Coster is frequently mentioned, just as is the case with the " Laurentius Johannis cognomento Ædituus Custosve" of Junius, while the sheriff never had this name in the original documents, however often the opportunity may have presented itself for giving him the name. There was, therefore, material enough in the archives of the XVth century to prove that there were Costers at Haarlem. Koning mentioned already (Verhandel, p. 142 note), 1418, '20, and '22 Jan Coster; 1426, Baertout Coster, Wouter Dirc Costerszoon, Heinric Coster Galenszoon, but this significantly economical enumeration could be somewhat increased from his MS. Jan Coster appears there four times in 1420 in connexion with the corn-taxes. He died in 1436. Further, are mentioned : 1447, l'onwels Costersz. ; 1451, Item betaelt lou' coster ii menghelen wyn . . . 1454 Item count van Oostervant viii daighe in Octobri anno Liii tot *lou coster's* een maeltyt gheschenct wert, so bleef men denselven lou coster dair af sculdich xvii guld. 1456 It. meester Koster een legerste en testament 7 gl. Ghertuut Jan Coster's dochter test. l ryns. gl. cloc salvator. 1462 † Ymme pieter Coster ter lied. 1463 † Aelbrecht costers zuster. 1464 † Pieter Coster van der lied. 1468 *Louris Coster* and other citizens are summoned to the Hague. 1471 Pieter Jansz. Coster. 1473 † Aecht pieter Costersdochter. 1478 † Pieter Coster. 1487 Margriet Jan Costers wid., Dirick and Pieter Jansz. Coster. 1492 Ymme and Machteld Coster Pieter, Claes and Jacob Dircksz. Coster. There were, therefore, neither Costers nor Lourenses wanting at Haarlem. In his preface to the translation of Paciле's Essai hist. et crit. sur l'invention de l'imprimerie, M. Alb. Thijm published for the first time, five items concerning the Haarlem chandler Lourens Janszoon Coster, communicated to him by M. A. J. Enschedé. This rash, at least, very uncritically used, communication, is already famous in other countries. It was translated into French by M. C. Ruelens (Bibliophile Belge, 1868) in German by Dr. Emil Weller (Serapeum, Intelligenz-Blatt, 31 Aug. 1869) under the ironical heading of : die von Prof. A. J. Enschedé zu Harlem entdeckten kostbaren Documente, auf deren Grund die Holländer neuestens beweisen wollen, dass der Lichterzieher L. Coster die beweglichen Lettern erfand und der arme Gutenberg ein reiner Dieb war.

What, however, no one hitherto knew is that Koning also had copied the items respecting Lourens Janszoen Coster, the chandler, in his MS. ; but he understood so well that that person did not suit his argument, that he preserves in his works the profoundest silence about him, and not even mentious his name among the Costers quoted by him as examples. I find in the index to his MS. : "1441, Louwerijs Jansson—paid to him the candles, which have been burnt this year.—As this is the only [!] time that we meet with this name in this book and in all the accounts after 1435 [!], *this* Louwerijs Janszoon may have been a chandler, or one who supplied candles." This is said by the very man who says

1428.[1]
Let us cover this scandal with something comical. More than a century later than Scriverius, in 1740, Seiz had discovered the secret of the invention at Haarlem in the 15th century so far, that he devises, in all earnestness, the following ludicrous chronology (Lourens Janszoon is here, for variation, melted together with Lourens Coster):—

Anno 1428. Lourens Koster, walking in the Haarlem Hout, cut, by way of pastime, some letters in the bark of a tree, &c.

1429. Having been occupied with this work for about a year, and getting more and more experienced, he begins (therefore as *xylographer* by accident)

1430. to cut whole figures in wood, with some words added as text, and so

1431. printed the *Temptationes Dæmonis*,

1432. the figures, representing some *histories of the Old and New Testament* [the Biblia pauperum],

1433. those of the *Canticum Canticorum*,

1434. those of the *Apocalypse* [a *German* block-book!]

1435. He begins to cut a *Donatus* on wooden blocks and to print it; but seeing that he could not make use of those blocks and letters for any other book, he cuts

1436. a few separate letters of lead, in order to be able to make, by putting them together, words and lines.

1437. Seeing that this work took so much time and trouble, and that it gave but little satisfaction, he invented

1438. a means of casting letters of lead; and having cast as many as were sufficient for two pages, he begins

1439. to print, as well as he could, a *Donatus* and the Dutch "*Spiegel der Behoudenisse*."

About this time *Gutenberg*, induced (!) by the report of the *Haarlem invention*, had come to Haarlem, entered the service of *Koster*, and prints for him, whence Gutenberg got the name of the *Book-printer of Haarlem*.

1440. Gutenberg absconded; he was able to *cut*, but not to *cast*, letters.

1441. He establishes a printing-office at Mentz, and

1442. prints an *A B C* book, *Alexandri Galli Doctrinale*, and *Petri Hispani Tractatus Logici*. Koster, meanwhile, having cast new and better letters of tin, instead of those of lead, which Gutenberg had stolen from him, and having made new furniture, printed

1443. The *Spiegel der Behoudenisse* for the second time, and

1444. The Latin *Speculum Humanæ Salvationis*. The magistrate of Haarlem, seeing the success of this art, and induced by the escape of Gutenberg,

1445. makes a law, that none of the men working in Koster's printing-office should leave Haarlem for another place, &c. (Gutenberg meanwhile communicates something of the art to Mentelin at Strasburg, and persuades *Gensfleisch* (!), called

---

already under the year 1442 (*one* page further): " Lourijs Coster repairs the lanterns for Our Lady in the tower, p. 150; Lourijs Coster supplies the candles burnt by the guards in the townhall, p. 150vso." Besides the member of the order of St. John, Jacob iansz. Coster, extracted by Koning from his MS. (at present in the Royal library at the Hague) " Liber Memoriarum Domus Hospitalis S. Joannis Hierosol. in Haarlem," the following names, which belong to the present class, occur in it: Pieternel lourys ian zoons wyf soror, lourijs ian zoon frater hoer man, Katrijn Willem lourijszoon wijf, Jan Louris zoon. Here neither appears any one "dictus" Coster.

[1] I say jugglers'-committee; remembering the well-known and true "ex ungue leonem," we may observe this sample of the argumentation of their spokesman: " When, in consequence of a long investigation (!), the year 1423 had been fixed upon as the most proper for the time of a jubilee, we (Dr. De Vries) were surprised to find in a German book, ent.: Gemeinnützige Nachrichten für die Provinz Ostfriesland, Aurich, 1805, the following words: 'Bekanntlich wurde die Kunst, mit unbeweglichen hölzernen Lettern zu drucken, im Jahr 1423 von Jansson zu Harlem, und mit beweglichen hölzernen (!) und bleiernen von Johann Guttenberg und Faust, in den Jahren 1439 und 1440 zu Strasburg und Maintz zuerst erfunden.' A slip of the pen or a misprint, probably caused this accidental agreement, and the author meant, perhaps, in imitation of Scriverius, the year 1428."

"We were surprised"—by a *misprint* of the year 1805!

afterwards *Faust* (!), and *Medinbach*, two well-to-do citizens of Mentz, &c., and these resolve

1446. to compose and print a *Latin Bible*, &c.)

1450. Koster seems to have printed about this time *Historia Alexandri Magni* [an edition of Ketelaer and De Leempt at Utrecht].

1456. Koster, having by his experience very much improved his art and having zealously printed books, the report of his art, and probably of some of his works, is brought into England, and comes to the ear of the then Archbishop of Canterbury, Thomas Bourchier, who, surprised at this, tells King Henry VI. about it, and persuades him

1457. to try and get the art, at any cost, from Holland to England, where it was known by this time, that *Gutenberg* had been *the first Book-printer* at Haarlem, and whom people believed to be still in that town.

1458. King Henry VI. having consulted with others on this affair, they found that, on account of the great jealousy of Haarlem and the rigorous prohibition of the magistrate there with regard to this art, they would not succeed in their object but by much money, secret negotiations, and able negotiators (Robert Turnour and William Caxton were entrusted with this kidnapping).

1459. Turnour and Caxton conceal themselves first in Amsterdam, afterwards in Leiden. Two bribed Dutchmen debauch at last one of the workmen of Koster, called *Frederik Corsellis* [the *Cornelis* of Junius]; on a certain night he ran away from Haarlem in disguise and went to Leiden to Turnour and Caxton, who had prepared a ship, and now went to England with the said Corsellis, where he, under an escort to prevent his escape, was taken to Oxford, in which town he was not ready with his printing-office before 1468.

After the death of Laurens Koster at Haarlem, which probably took place about the same time with that of Gutenberg and Faust, anno 1467, his printing-office ceased to exist, and the workmen established printing-offices in other Netherland towns; we find, for instance, the wood-cuts of the *Spiegel der Behoudenisse* in the hands of a certain Johann Veldenaer, who, anno 1483, printed at Kuilenburg the same book in 4to., with the identical wood-cuts, cut in two.

Here the fable runs riot. Even our "forefathers' rash negligence" of Coornhert and Junius's "socordia avita" are completely forgotten by this ludicrous spinning of a legendary cobweb.

The reason why I could not spare the reader this chronology, is the calmness with which Seiz allows his hero to live until c. 1467, many years after the theft. This fact stands in connexion with one of the many sad phenomena of this history: it was *known* afterwards at Haarlem that the chandler Lourens Janszoon *Coster*, the man with the name in the vellum pedigree and of Junius, appears much later in the archives than the *sheriff*, who is mentioned there seventy-six times, but *never* with the name of *Coster*. It was thought necessary, however, to conceal this discovery.[1]

Before we bid farewell to Scriverius, we may safely say that the results obtained

---

[1] All later authors were henceforth caught by the mixing up the persons of the *sheriff* Laurens Janszoon and the Lourens Janszoon *Coster* of Junius. Cf. :—

De boekdrukkunst en dezelver uitvinder Laurens Jansz. Koster. Door P. J. V. Duseau. Amsterdam, M. Westerman & Zoon. 1839, 8vo.

Lorenzo Coster. Notizia intorno alla sua vita ed alla invenzione della tipografia in Olanda. Per Domenico Carutti. Torino, Stamperia Reale. 1868. 4to.

Who was the first printer? (*Saint Pauls*. A magazine edited by Anthony Trollope. London, 1868, pp. 706 e. v.) 8vo.

The double-man of 1370—1483 and later was, therefore, much more exclusively a stage-hero than was imagined in the compilation of :—

A. Loosjes Pz.: Laurens Coster. Tooneelstuk met zang., Haarlem, 1809. 8vo.

L'Imagier de Harlem, ou la découverte de l'imprimerie. Drame-légende à grand spectacle en cinq actes et dix tableaux. Et prose et en vers, de MM. Méry, Gérard de Narval et Bernard Lopez . . . . Représenté pour la première fois, à Paris, sur le théâtre de la Porte-Saint-Martin, le 27 Déc. 1851. 8vo.

N. Destanberg : Laurens Coster. Drama in dry bedryven. Antwerpen, 1855, 8vo.

are: the earliest Haarlem story of the 16th century originated the belief that *Lourens Janszoon Coster* had invented there in 1440 the art of printing; in the 17th century *another* person takes his place, who is *not* the man of the earliest fable; the other person, substituted by Scriverius, is the sheriff-innkeeper Lourens Janszoon, since worshipped by the defenders of the Haarlem myth. The erection of a statue in honour of that sheriff was, even with regard to the pretended tradition, a *mistake;* the metal innkeeper in the market-place at Haarlem is the Nepomuk of our national vanity, canonized in ignorance and deceit.[1]

---

[1] This logical conclusion, after I had expressed it in the Nederl. Spectator, was the cause of the following public correspondence:

To Dr. A. Van der Linde, the Hague:

I am compelled to oppose emphatically the conclusion expressed at the end of your last article on the invention of printing. Namely, in the year 1856, *no* metal statue was erected in honour of the sheriff Lourens Janszoon. The case stands thus:

My uncle, M. Joh. Enschedé, had already, some twenty years after the Koster-fêtes of 1823, come to the conviction that the inventor of the art of printing was not the sheriff Lourens Janszoon, who died in 1439, but a Lourens Janszoon Coster, who was still alive in 1447.

He was desirous of communicating this conviction to M. de Vries, but the violent emotion which mastered him [De Vries] at the mere thought of doubt of what he thought he had so incontestably proved (of which emotion you had some experience yourself), made my uncle resolve not to publish what led him to his conviction, as long as his friend. M. de Vries, was alive.

When it was, however, intended to erect a new statue in honour of the inventor at Haarlem, he thought it to be his duty to prevent, if possible, its erection in honour of the sheriff, and he succeeded in averting any mention being made on the pedestal of his office and his arms.

As the description of the Costerian documents [at Haarlem] was made by M. de Vries (1862), it was impossible to omit those which only concerned the sheriff and not the chandler. I only got the knowledge of a statue having been erected here for the chandler, when I occupied myself with making notes from the Haarlem archives about Haarlem painters, and made at the same time a note of all I found respecting Lourens Janszoon and Lourens Janszoon Coster. As soon as I had communicated to my uncle what I had found about the chandler, he told me that he had known it already for a long time, and at the same time the reason why he had kept the secret.

At present, this reason for secrecy no longer existing, I only wish to state that in 1856 a statue was erected not for the sheriff, but for a man who was really called Louweriis Janssoen *Coster*.

I have the honour, &c.

Haarlem, March 14, 1870.   A. J. ENSCHEDÉ.

To Dr. A. J. Enschedé, Archivist of Haarlem:

Although I appreciate the consideration which induced M. Joh. Enschedé to spare Dr. de Vries, I cannot help thinking that it would have been better this time to let one man die for the people. For—before scientific Europe the new statue of the Haarlem inventor is based on:—

Meerman's Origines typographicae,
The French translation of Koning's work,
Scheltema's German review of Schaab,
The Eclaircissements and Arguments of De Vries;

and all these works refer to the sheriff Louweriis Janssoen, who died in 1439. Before the public of Holland the new statue is based on:

Van Oosten de Bruyn's Description of Haarlem,
Gockinga's abridged translation of Meerman,
Koning's Prize Essay,
The Memorials of the Coster-fêtes of 1823,
The Dutch works of Dr. A. de Vries,
The "Geschilstuk" of Noordziek,

all works which also move round the *sheriff*. Before 1867 the public had never heard anything of the Haarlem *chandler* Lourens Janszoon Coster. But I may not reproach you with the, according to my opinion, too great indulgence of M. Joh. Enschedé. Meanwhile your information confirms the correctness of my explanation of the account of Junius by a strictly scientific method, &c.

VAN DER LINDE.

XVIII.

COSTERIANISM.

ALL men of scientific education and honesty are at present able to judge of the value of the foundations of the Haarlem tradition. A fiction of the 16th century, formulated and finished by Junius, published in 1588 in his Batavia; a second fiction of Scriverius in the *Laurecrans* of 1628; they prove *nothing*, they contain neither substance nor shadow of fact; they annihilate each other, and each comes to destruction by internal contradiction and untruth. But although they constitute no historical evidence, yet, or perhaps just by reason of this circumstance, they have brought a sect into existence, and have been the cause of an unhistorical tenet, which, on account of the myth of its creed, ought to be baptized as *Costerianism*. The task which remains to me after my criticism of the origin of the fable, is to give a sketch of the progress of the sect until it succeeded in making its error national and canonizing its hero.

Dogmatic belief sets up simply a supernatural world, a metacosmos, which transcends the categories of thought and knowledge, is inaccessible to all criticism, and unaware itself whether there exists a metaphysical reality or not, which corresponds with this phantasy. The purely subjective, chimerical character of this belief, makes it inaccessible to objective argumentation, averse from science and investigation. Every one is undoubtedly free to people the ghost-world of his imagination as he likes, whether he feeds his imagination from Schuking, Veda, Zend-Avesta, Thora, Bible, decrees of a council, Koran, Book of Mormon, or Medium. But as soon as any believer wishes to realize his dream, science has a right, and it is its duty, to oppose. I may prohibit no one from dreaming, or attaching value to his dream; but no one may command me to dream *with* him, to acknowledge *with* him a chimera as a fact. As belief is sentimental in its nature, it is, like every visionary condition, peevish, troublesome, intolerant, touchy. It makes up for the want of proofs by dicta, sophisms, sentiment. It looks for no connexion between belief and proof, between facts and argument, but—because it excludes all argument and proof itself—between belief and character, between vision and condition of the mind. And how will it be when this condition makes itself master of history? As long as belief has only to do with the gods and goddesses, sub-gods, and other inferior deities of its own creation, it may remain, as individual opinion, within the limits of its dominion; the measure of luxuriance of every one's fancy cannot be regulated. But when the belief throws itself upon purely historical questions, it goes beyond its legitimate bounds, and the abuse of imagination becomes, scientifically, a crime. Nobody has a right to *believe* when and where Erasmus was born; when, where, and by whom the naval battle of four days was fought. We *know*, or we do *not* know it. And yet, Costerianism has sinned against this simple truth for three centuries; that, which is, and ought to be, nothing but a purely *historical* question—an inquiry into the invention of typography—has been treated by Costerianism as a *dogma*, an article of faith, to be accepted under forfeiture of national salvation. And the phenomena which have characterised the existence of all sects, ever since our history exists, have not been wanting among this sect, so long as it found adherents: to derive facts from the imagination, instead of reality; to falsify the questions in the very formulæ in which they are proposed; never to ask for truth, but for the appearance of truth; to conceal the want of real strength in verbosity; to spare no means for the sake of the sacred object; to repeat apparent evidences and to give no heed to refutation; in short, applying the conservative, *theological* method.

Our eye is now prepared for the diagnosis; we are able to discriminate the disease of Costerianism. Facts were drawn from the imagination, and not from reality. I have given, in the course of my work, so many examples of this forging and inventing that further proofs are almost superfluous; but in order to show the deception, which public opinion has been driven into, they require to be augmented.

To the category of the pedigree described before, belong in the first place the MS. notes, mostly of Haarlem origin, found in xylographic and typographic incunabula, *fathered*, after the example of Junius and Scriverius, upon Coster.

I. Koning says of the (German) Apocalypse: "It is remarkable, that in front of the copy at Berlin, just as in that of Haarlem, the *inscription* and *portrait* of Koster is bound."

II. De Vries says, in his description of a copy of the same work at Haarlem: "To the work was afterwards added the beautiful engraving representing Coster at full length, in the ordinary dress of a Dutch magistrate of the 15th [read 16th] century, with a letter in his hand, engraved after the model of P. Saenredam, by A. Rooman."

III. In the 17th century the following title was printed for the copy of the Canticum preserved at Haarlem: Liber tabularum ligno incisarum a Laurentio Costero Harlemensi circa annum salutis humanae MCCCCXXX.—It is followed by the wood-cut representing Coster at full length, holding a board with the inscription: "Figures and blocks cut in wood, printed by Lourens Jansz. Coster of Haarlem about the year MCCCCXXX." (Figuren ende Taefelen in hout gesneden, by Lourens Jansz. Coster van Haarlem ghedruckt omtrent den jaere MCCCCXXX.)

IV. In front of the Ars moriendi at Haarlem is bound the same printed title, but representing in the middle the arms of the town instead of Coster's likeness. At the foot of the first page of the preface is written, in an old hand: "This is a work of the first printer, at the time when the first press was invented or commenced at Haarlem."

V. In a copy of an edition of Ketelaer and De Leempt of Utrecht (Liber Alexandri Magni), preserved at Haarlem, is written above the title: Heindrick Dirricx Mes has given this book to Willem Janss. Verwer as a remembrancer, 1586¼. In dexterâ virtus." (H. D. Mes heeft dit boeck W. J. Verwer ghegeve(n) tot een memorie 1586¼.) And on the fly-leaf: "He who gave me this book told me that it was printed at Haarlem, for such was the manner of printing formerly." (Die my dit boeck gheschoncken heeft, heeft my geseyt, dat het binnen Haerlem ghedruckt is, want dus plach men van ouds te drucken). In front of this work a copy of the "Spieghel onser behoudenisse" had been bound up formerly.

VI. The Speculum at Haarlem has, besides a portrait of Coster engraved by J. Visser after J. van Campen, a modern printed title: "Liber cujus nomen est, Speculum humanae salutis Harlemi ex officina Laurentii Joannis Costeri Ao. 1440." Underneath are the arms of Haarlem.

VII. On a separate leaf of the Spiegel, in the museum Meermanno-Westrenianum at the Hague, is written in the latter part of the 16th century: "This belongs to the first rare incunabula printed in Holland, by Laurens Coster at Haarlem" (dit is van de eerste drucken die in Holland gedruckt syn, en raer van Laurens Coster te Haerlem).

VIII. The copy of the first edition of the Speculum preserved at Haarlem bears the following title on the binding: Dat Spiegel | onser behoudenisse | gedrukt | te Haerlem | bij Lourens Coster | MccccxLIII. (The "Spiegel onser behoudenisse" printed at Haerlem by L. C. 1443.) This title was to harmonize with the words: Uyt de | bibliotheek | van | Mr. Gr. Meerman | advocaat | MDCCXLIII. (From the library of M. G. Meerman, barrister, 1743.) On the other hand, we find written on the binding of the copy of the last Dutch edition at Lille, in a hand of the 16th century: "The Spieghel der behoudenis, being the first book of Louris Coster, inventor of printing, printed at Haarlem about 1440." (De Spieghel der behoudenis, sijnde het eerste boeck van L. C., vinder der druckerij gedruckt binnen Haerlem omtrent Ao. 1440).

In this copy is also put the portrait of Coster, which occurs in the "Laure-crans." The original inscription of the 16th century (Item dit boec hoert toe den susteren van Sinte marien Convent woenende tot hoern) was in the 17th century crossed out and renewed, in order to be able to change *Hoorn* into *Haerlem*.

IX. Dibdin mentions a Missal in 8vo., of which the types, he says, belong to those of the Speculum, with the written date: "Geprent tot Haerlem bij mij Laurens Janszoon Coster, 1450." (Printed at Haarlem by me, L. J. C., 1450).

X. Finally, in 1768, a fac-simile of the Abecedarium was made by Joh. Enschedé, with the inscription: "Representation of the A.B.C., Pater Noster, &c., printed with moveable letters by Laurens Janszoon at Haarlem, for the use of his daughter's children, certainly the earliest remains of the first press."

It clears our view to look over this propaganda all at once. None of these super- and sub-scriptions are any better than the deceptions concerning the fictitious Haarlemer Frederick Corsellis, printer at Oxford.

By the side of the fictitious first Haarlem xylographer-typographer, Laurens Janszoon Coster, a *second* fictitious Haarlem printing-office was opened gradually under the firm: *Heirs of Coster*, and it was said to have existed till 1470. Did no one conceive that the second printing-office *destroyed* the first, and *buried*, with the heirs of Coster, the founder of the firm? For, a Haarlem invention of typography, and that followed by a Haarlem printing-office from 1440—1470, therefore together from 1420—70, without a single human being having ever heard about them, is more impossible than impossible. Now and then, in moments when the inexorable logic startled them, the Costerians shut that shop of the heirs of Coster; but then those books, with their equally impudent dates, made their appearance again, and the shop had to be re-opened. Is there a more biting satire on the Coster-fable conceivable? In order not to appear more cruel than I really am, I prefer to have it written by Costerians.

Seiz, in 1740.

"Koster had hardly finished the first edition of his 'Spiegel der Behoudenis,' when one of his servants, a German by birth . . . . went, on Christmas night of the year 1440, when all the people had finished working and gone to church, to the printing-office, put some tools and some types in a bag, and absconded . . . . Koster was not a little perplexed and annoyed that his servant had played him such a trick, had robbed and ruined his press, and had transferred his art to somewhere else, where he practised it now himself, as his own invention. But he could do nothing but re-establish his press. He again cast other types, not of lead, but of tin, which succeeded better than the first, and printed with them a second edition of the Spiegel. and afterwards an edition of the same book in Latin. We have no information as to what happened further with Laurens Koster and his printing-office."

Meerman, in 1765.

"We cannot think that the heirs of Lourens, after he had died, and the theft had been committed shortly afterwards (!), would have lost courage and no longer exercised such a profitable art. For his three sons Pieter, Andries, and Thomas were still alive . . . . Besides that Cornelis and other clever servants, whom Lourens had employed, were still at hand, after Gutenberg had escaped. We might wish that Scriverius and others had not erred so greatly as to assert that Lourens was so perplexed by the theft that he exercised the art no longer, because it is certain that it was continued after his death. The industrious heirs published two editions of the 'Spiegel.' Since they printed the Spiegels, they published, in other type: Historia Alexandri Magni, Regis Macedoniæ de Præliis; Vegetii Epitoma; B. Hieronymi de viris illustribus; Thomæ à Kempis Opera varia." (N.B.—All these incunabula are editions of Ketelaer and De Leempt at Utrecht.)

Gockinga, in 1767.

"M. Meerman has clearly shown that this Donatus (*i.e.* the Cornelis-fragment of 1474!) was printed with moveable types, but he reasonably remarks that we are not indebted for it to Laurens but to his heirs, which is evident from the fact that we find here not only the *full-stop* (punctum), but also the *semicolon* (duo puncta). The accurate author is of opinion that this book was published a little later than the second (Dutch) Spiegel, between the years 1460 and 1470."

Koning, in 1816.

"Nothing, forsooth, has tended more to lessen the value of the work of M. Meerman in the opinion of foreigners, than that part of it in which books are ascribed to the descendants of Koster, which were never printed by them." After Koning in his turn had fathered the "Faccie morales Laur. Vallæ," and the "Singularia juris," upon them, he says: "All this ought to confirm us in our opinion, that the first Haarlem printing-office was continued for some time after the death of the first inventor, till about the year 1470, by his descendants or successors."

De Vries, in 1823.

It will be remembered that G. Braun, in his map of Haarlem, inserted a translation of the words of Guicciardini; and that this proves *nothing* but copying, is evident from what he writes under Mentz: Huic urbi typographicæ artis debetur inventio. In Guicciardini (= Braun) we read at the end of the popular story, which was simply related as a curiosity: "But, before the inventor could perfect his art and bring it to light himself, it is said that he died, and that for that reason his servant went to Mentz and practised there the art for the use of the general public," &c. With this quotation from Braun, "confirming (read, copying), the evidence of Guicciardini" was linked, in 1823, the following: "The surviving relatives of our Koster *took*, directly after the discovery of the theft (of which G. does *not* speak), *all necessary measures* to overtake the thief, but were not successful in their efforts. *They resolved, nevertheless, to keep the robbed press a-going*, and to recover the loss as soon as possible: not so much on account of the profit, as out of interest in the art (?) and esteem for the deceased, by whom the whole work, from the first beginning, had been devised and executed, and whose favoured doll it had been for many years. The son-in-law of Koster, Thomas Pieterszoon, who, as successor of his father-in-law, would manage the business, was a man of wealth and distinction, whom no direct aim at profit, and a more moderate ambition (where is the just this moment invented "interest in the art" gone to?) than the father, moved to feel concerned for the art. The simultaneous loss of the talented and industrious man, who had been the inventor and manager of everything, of the most practised servant, and of a great part of the most important tools, was not so easily to be replaced."

De Vries, in 1814.

"Coster's son-in-law can have had neither much inclination nor occasion to continue his secret art energetically, nor to invent and make new and better tools, but made, no doubt, a shift with what was still serviceable. And when at last, by the import of foreign books which were provided with imprints, the secret of the existence of the art, so long concealed, became known also in our country, and as that foreign work surpassed his in beauty, he lost, no doubt, all inclination to go on any longer with a trade which would have to contend with so much emulation, and promised so very little profit for the future. Wherefore he at last resolved to get rid of his printing-office and book trade: sold his printing tools and all what belonged to them, and had only one or two pots (which De Vries, in 1850, provided even with an "appropriate inscription !") made of a quantity of worn and useless tin types, as a remembrancer of the paternal invention, to be preserved among his posterity. That such indeed must have been the case; that there was, after Coster's death until about 1470, an *uninterrupted, carefully concealed, practice of printing*; and that there existed in our country for many years an entire seminary of practisers of the art, is confirmed by many and strong evidences (!)"

"The son-in-law and heir of Coster, Thomasz., although wealthy, had a numerous family, of at least seven children, four sons and three daughters. He cannot have slighted and neglected the press which his father-in-law had left behind, and which had been so dear to the beloved deceased, and had cost him so much. A prudent Dutchman does not so easily neglect things which yield good profits."

Let us now see what follows! "We are not at liberty to decide positively which remains of early printing are the productions of Coster's press, except those distinctly mentioned by Zell (Zell on Coster!) and Junius, ... nor may we build reasonings and conclusions on vague suppositions as to the condition, the time of working, and the productions of Coster's press after his death, *about which history has said nothing at all*." Who says this? De Vries, in 1841! Three years afterwards, however, he thought proper to re-open the printing-office about which history had said "nothing at all," in order not to leave Renouard in embarrassment with his copy of the Saliceto. For the sake of this work it was again "very probable that the successor of Coster, on a familiar footing (!) with one of the Haarlem knights of St. John, had seen with him a manuscript (of the Saliceto), and had been enabled, through his intervention, to print (this work), and to sell the copies for manuscripts." This last trick especially is invaluable: to sell the Saliceto for *manuscript:* and such a trick of the *wealthy* Thomas Pietersz., who had more regard for the *art* than for the *profit;* and all this could be done by a firm of which history has told us "*nothing at all.*" Certainly a St. John's knight, with whom Thomas was on "a familiar footing," was necessary in this novel.

Just as there is no longer any excuse for this bungling, so the days have also passed that we could skirmish with one or two Donatuses and *one* Doctrinale and *one* Abecedarium, as experiments of *one* printer. This was possible in former times; but since we have found not one fragment, but an every-day increasing literature of Donatuses and Doctrinales, this obscure Haarlem manufactory of Donatuses of the inventor becomes a childish play. Moreover, the dates, all after 1474, fit in history, but not in the fable. For, a small, cheap vellum school-book may safely be supposed to have fallen very soon, by a hundred accidents, into the hands of a bookbinder. This is more natural than that Cornelis preserves a piece of vellum printed *before* his birth, and deposits it after 1474, as a kind of providence, in the church of St. Bavo, in order to make its appearance as "witness" when the German boldness has got to a vexatious height. A "providence" which plays the Mentzers a trick in such a rascally manner, and which is so "clever," is a providence which is suitable to Coster, but not to the seriousness of truth. Cornelis is *an octogenarian*, according to Junius. Well, that octogenarian died in 1522, so that he was at least not born *before* 1440. Besides, therefore, that he could not have had a hand in the Speculum nostræ salutis of Junius, he could, infinitely less, have had anything to do with the Donatuses, which are fancied in 1420, 1430, &c. But at the age of thirty-five, in 1475, he could be a bookbinder for the cathedral, and also use Donatuses of 1470 and later.

As the Donatus question has continually moved in a circle, and the Costerians have also in this case indefatigably heaped the one logical sin upon the other, especially the sin which is called subreptio, it ought to be settled at once. The Costerians of the 17th century confused, from misunderstanding, *xylography* with the earliest typography. They did not, therefore, distort the words of the Cologne chronicle, but explained them just as Accursius. A fragment of a xylographic Donatus would have appeared to them a sufficient evidence against the pretensions of Mentz. Scriverius "sang"—

> Where are you hidden in a corner, Donatus? whither
> Do you command me to go? Where shall anybody find me
> Such a wished-for book: to Haarlem the dearest pledge,
> Which may help you in your honor, and be a shame to Mentz?
> What means are there? If I knew where to find it,
> I would travel to the farthest Indies:
> I would bear with patience the hottest sun,
> If I found there the desired Donatus.
> They might take me to the North Pole,
> If it were to be found there. What should I not stir?
> Heaven and Hell.

If Scriverius had got his wish, if at that time already one or other fragment of a *typographic* Donatus had been found, he would *not* have regarded it as the *admonitio* to the Mentz invention, alluded to in the Cologne chronicle. He would have reasoned thus: the chronicle speaks, just as Accursius, of Donatuses *cut on blocks*; this Donatus has been printed with cast types, like the Spiegel,—ergo, "this is *not* the right Peter." Later, when they began to define the invention in question better, the reasoning was reversed thus: this discovered fragment of Donatus (although printed c. 1490 in the convent Den Hem, near Schoonhoven!) is *typographic*, consequently the chronicle could not mean *xylographic* Donatuses. The origin of this mad logic is frankly described by Seiz, and I quote his description, because, by tracing the beginnings of false reasoning we save ourselves the fruitless reading of books which are based on them.

"Johannes Enschedé bought at a sale in Haarlem, July 16, 1740, a Duitse Psalter in small 8vo., printed at Delft, in Holland, by Heinrich Eckert van Homberch, anno 1498, bound in leather, as was the custom formerly; and he, observing two slips of vellum inserted in the binding of the book, printed in old-fashioned type, he loosened them, and found, to his great surprise, that they were the remains of *Grammatica Donati;* and after we had carefully examined and compared the types, it was obvious that they were of the same make, and had the same defects, as those of the first (read second) Dutch Speculum of L. Koster. There we have, we said, a proof of what the Cologne chronicle and Mariangelus Accursius have said of a Donatus printed in Holland [in tabula incisa!], before books were printed at Mentz. Any one may now see the aforesaid slips at Johannes Enschedé's, and compare them with the types of the Spiegel, and he will be convinced that they are really of one and the same making, and that consequently these slips are really the remainders of the Donatus printed by Koster at Haarlem between 1440 and '50. *Vicimus causa! We have triumphed over Mentz!*"

It was possible in 1740 to amuse oneself with such cheap victories; but he who would wish to celebrate them at present, would make himself ridiculous.

While Junius had confined himself to the mere *name* of the inventor, without knowing anything of his social sphere and position, Scriverius made him (by mistake) a sheriff, and (from misunderstanding) a practiser, even an inventor, of *xylography*. An unnamed biographer of the fictitious Haarlem printer, however, knew already in 1730 much more of him. He tells us in a: Life of Lourens Jansz. Koster, Haarlemer, first inventor of the art of printing: "Lourens Koster often used to take a walk after dinner in the Hout. From his infancy he had been an amateur of the art of engraving, *and he went often to the house of such an artist*, to spy from him the art in silence. While walking in the Hout he took now and then a piece of the bark of a tree, either a beech, an oak, or a lime-tree, cut some letters out of it with a knife, and put them, after having wrapped them in paper, in his pocket." And further:

"We need not think that, whoever (at that time) looked for a written book, had to go to the convents, to fetch it from the priests; but we may reasonably suppose that there were at that time shops in the town, where the priests brought the books which they had written, in order to sell them, and we do not hesitate to say that *Lourens Koster had such a book-shop*, where one could obtain pens, paper, and ink for money and kind words, as well as written books, just as we have known, and even at present, councillors and assessors, in some towns of Holland, who were not ashamed of keeping a shop, of which they derived great profits. Koster could sell his printed books much cheaper than those written by hand. And although he had to keep up the price, to avoid suspicion of the invented art, he seems to have sold them at a much lower price than the written ones, whereby he got many purchasers, whom he did not want to send empty away, or to wait, while he had an abundance of copies. But the multitude of buyers increasing from day to day, outside and inside Haarlem, the work so increased that Koster could not do it alone with his *brother-in-law*, Thomas Pietersz. He engaged amongst others a certain Jan Faustus, or Fust, by birth a German, of Mentz," &c.[1]

We know that Van Mander (born in 1548 in Flanders, but who had been a citizen of Haarlem for twenty years) published in 1604 a book on painters (Haerlem, 4to.). On page 200 we find the following words: "The very useful art of printing books, of which Haarlem claims, with sufficient evidence, the honour of the invention" (die seer nutte Const van Boeck-drucken, daer Haerlem met ghenoech bescheyt haer vermeet den roem van d'eerste vindinghe te hebben). In the edition of 1764 (Amsterdam, 8vo. I. p. 16), Jacobus de Jongh, who supplied the indefinite words of Van Mander (for the last wrote *before* the Batavia had been printed!), was obliged, by the name of "L. J. Koster, at Haarlem, member of the government, and several times sheriff," to acknowledge: "although people in Holland also disputed him and his native town the honour of this invention, trying even to argue that, *according to all appearance there never was a Laurens Koster* . . . ." This alarming fact, however, did not prevent the annotator continuing: "It would only be just to place and esteem Koster among the *painters*, at least among the *engravers*, because the amateurs of the prent-printing owe to him their amusement, as he was as well, nay rather, an inventor of the art of prenting than of the art of printing, and he cut and printed the first prents." Let no one fancy that such fictions were forged only in the 16th, 17th, and 18th century. The Costerians went indefatigably on. Let us listen attentively for one moment to Dr. Abraham De Vries.

(Junius, when relating the theft, draws two big lines between Haarlem and Mentz; he says that Johan (Faust) went to Mentz *viâ* Amsterdam and Cologne, without saying whether Johan kept up correspondence from those places with his former little bedfellow, Cornelis; without giving any reason why he did not take some rest also at Bonn and Coblentz; without saying whether Faust had embarked already at Cologne, with the stolen printing-office, and rowed straight on to his native place. Junius *mentions*

---

[1] Levensbeschrijving van beroemde en geleerde mannen. Second Part. No. VI. Amsteldam. 1730. 8vo. pp. 9—82: Leven van Lourens Jansz. Koster Haarlemmer, eerste vinder der Drukkunst.

only Amsterdam and Cologne, in his time the commercial route between Holland and Germany. But let us now hear what De Vries contrives to prepare out of these two names, according to the homiletic art of cooking words:—

Beloved brethren in Loureus! your religious attention will find my text in the Batavia of the holy prophet Junius, which I will read from the inspired original, trickling with spiritual richness and historical bliss. It runs thus: Amstelodamum principio adit, inde Coloniam Agrippinam.) "After he had committed the theft, says Junius, the thief went first to Amsterdam, afterwards to Cologne. This does not mean, as some, with inconceivable neglect of all sound exegesis, have understood the words, that the thief travelled by Amsterdam and Cologne; for what could be more indifferent to the reader than to know the route the thief took, and why only these two places were named? No, Junius would have us understand: that they traced the thief twice,—twice, first at Amsterdam, and afterwards at Cologne, they were on the point of catching him; but every time he perceived in time that he was watched, and succeeded in making his escape. That this must be the meaning is perfectly clear from the nature of the case, the whole connexion and the studied brevity and conciseness of the style of Junius, and is incontrovertibly proved by what immediately follows: that the thief, arriving at last at Mentz, found himself in safety, ceu ad asyli aram, ubi quasi extra telorum jactum (quod dicitur) positus, tuto degeret; that is to say, now for the first time sitting, as it were, by the altar of an inviolable asylum, where, shot-free from the arrows of his pursuers, he could live in safety for the future. The pursuit of a criminal who had once contrived to escape from the jurisdiction where the crime had been committed, was at that time a very difficult work, because every town, every village, every manor, possessing its own jurisdiction, formed a sort of separate state, where judicial inquiries in behalf of a neighbouring place could be made only after very troublesome negotiations. The thief, relying upon this circumstance, did not hesitate to stop for a considerable time at Amsterdam, and had probably already tried to establish himself there under another name. But Koster's relatives did not sit quietly down. M. Koning discovered in the treasury accounts notices of an extraordinary busy negotiation of the constabulary of Haarlem with that of Amsterdam. (Here follows the already exposed deception of Koning respecting the unusual mortality of 1489.) From this fact we may with much probability infer, that serious efforts were made at once to discover and pursue the thief, and that the inquiries at Amsterdam, where they had learned he had stopped for a considerable time, were continued for a long time before they discovered the place where he was concealed, whence, however, he had made his escape before they came to look for him.

"The fugitive understood, of course, that after this pursuit at Amsterdam, he could not be safe in the whole dominion of the Netherland State. He retreated therefore to Cologne, where he could not expect to be any longer in danger. But the son-in-law and other relations of Koster went on with their inquiries, and learned at last that the criminal had started for Cologne and now resided there. Between that town and Haarlem there existed at that time a busy trade, and an amicable relation between the magistracies of both these towns. It was therefore not difficult for the magistracy of Haarlem to persuade that of Cologne to give orders that the criminal who had fled thither should be traced and captured, but his cleverness threw them off the scent. Only after two fruitless efforts to conceal himself elsewhere, the thief arrived at Mentz. Departed from Haarlem in the very last days of 1489 (!), he has no doubt been staying in the beginning of the following year, 1440, for a considerable time at Amsterdam."

It would not be difficult, with such exegetic bungling, to publish the diary kept by the thief during his romantic tour. All the arguments of Dr. A. de Vries are of the same bad alloy.[1] Koning, on the other hand, was in the habit of first making one

---

[1] Eclaircissemens sur l'hist. de l'invention de l'imprimerie, cont.: Lettre à M. D. Schinkel, ou réponse à la notice de M. Guichard sur le Speculum humanæ salvationis;—dissert. sur le nom de Coster et sur sa

hypothesis, then a second, and *proving* this by the *unproved* first one. We advance much with such proceedings.

I have said already that the Coster-question has never been treated as an

---

prétendue charge de sacristain; recherches faites à l'occasion de la quatrième fête séculaire à Haarlem en 1823. Par A. de Vries. Trad. du Hollandais par J. J. F. Noordziek. La Haye. 1843. 8vo.

Bewijsgronden der duitschers voor hunne aanspraak op de uitvinding der boekdrukkunst, of beoordeeling van het werk van A. E. Umbreit: die Erfindung der Buchdruckerkunst. Door Abraham de Vries. s' Gravenhage. 1844. 8vo.

Argumens des Allemands en faveur de leur prétention à l'invention de l'Imprimerie, ou examen critique de l'ouvrage de Mr. Umbreit ... par A. de Vries. Traduit du Hollandais par J. J. F. Noordziek. La Haye. 1845. 8vo.

[Dr. A. de Vries:] Catalogus Bibliothecae Publicae Harlemensis. Harlemi. 1848. 8vo. Supplementum 1852.

[Dr. A. de Vries:] Hedendaagsche voorstelling van Coster en de uitvinding der boekdrukkunst, in Frankrijk. 's Gravenhage. 1853. 8vo.

All these works teem with those mistakes of method which had been overcome already in every other branch of scientific inquiries. Their chief fault is a reasoning à priori, which, arising from a shrewd system of suppositions, possibilities, prejudices, does not allow history to speak with incorruptible exactness, but makes of it a simple ornamentation, and a means of denying every one else a voice in the matter. Just as we have theological and philosophical dogmas, so we have also an historical dogma, that seeks to withdraw the most "critical" things from criticism, that monopolizes a sacred, unassailable doctrine (in our question the infallibility of Junius), and, in the worship of that dogma, bids farewell to strict impartiality, to logic, and all unwelcome facts. In this way the evidence of the authors of the 16th century on the origin of typography gradually degenerated into inspired texts, of which every syllable is capable of being expanded into a sermon, provided the text speaks in favour of, and not against, the favoured dogma. In this last case people fondle and distort the text, until, buried under a mountain of sophisms, it says just the contrary of what a sincere exegesis requires to read in it. We should have, for instance, abundant materials for a striking article on the martyrdom of the well-known words of Accursius (c. 1530, not only printed 1591) on xylographic Donatuses in Holland, the importance of which has been just as much extolled as their utter worthlessness was exposed, according to the way in which they were interpreted. Partiality is by such a method unavoidable, and De Vries metes in this respect freely with two measures; evidences for this opinion are to be found in plenty. I will give a few examples:—

1st. The character of the authors is extolled or abused, according to their relation to the claims of Haarlem. Erasmus, for instance, knows, notwithstanding his relation to Talesius, *nothing* about a Haarlem invention of printing, but ascribes it twice to Mentz. And in order to explain this troublesome fact, it is simply insinuated that Erasmus (the greatest scholar of his time, loaded with honour even of princes) was induced to give this evidence (*i.e.* if it has any signification against better knowledge) by a silver cup, which he received as a present from the elector of Mentz, and—out of respect for the printer Frobenius! (This insinuation concludes with changing the words of Erasmus into a "pretty clear evidence in favour of Haarlem.") The counter-arguments are repeatedly called "miserable cavillings," the argument of a Gutenbergian is always "sly," "crafty," "impudent," founded on a "pia fraus"; but on the other side the most insignificant author obtains by the most simple (welcome) observation the most honourable epithets (the learned, the judicious, the greatest judge, the honest, frank, truthful *x*). Now, all these vices and all those virtues are psychologically possible, but—only not all the last exclusively among the Costerians. Is Schoepflin in his defence for Strasburg capable of a pia fraus? the fanatical enthusiast for Haarlem is none the less guaranteed against it; is Erasmus liable to be influenced by a present?—Junius, the physician and curator of the Latin school at Haarlem, married there with a Haarlem woman, and, paid by government for being the historian of his country, is not accessible to any other but sacred influences; if the authority of Trithemius may be rejected because he shares the superstition of his time and class,—the same canon has to be applied also to Junius. The man who thinks himself mentally minor enough to ask the permission of a theologian for reading prohibited medical books; who in the spirit of his time makes mention of the Edam mermaid, and says that he will not reject the story, because the remembrance of it is still so fresh and—is handed down to posterity by the matrons (a mulierculis de manu ad manum tradita); who does not spare his readers the mawkish miracle of the "little woman of Loosduinen" (who produced 364 children alive at a birth, who were baptized by Bishop Guido, for the sake of convenience, all under the name of John and Betsy, whose little souls, with their mother, were with God, and whose little bodies " Sub hoc saxo requiescunt ")—when *he* relates something, this Hadrianus Junius stands as little above criticism as his fellow-believer Trithemius. One and the same man got sometimes two different characters, if he, with regard to Coster, —no, with regard to the invented portraits of Coster—became contaminated with heresy. Doubts had arisen in foreign countries whether M. van Westreenen really "believed" in Coster. The reply to this answer was: "M. V. W., who in his Essay (of 1809) has confessed a belief (!) so reverential and agreeing in every respect with the opinion of his relative (Meerman). he, the celebrated possessor of so many incunabula, the scholar, presented with many decorations, should secretly be an unbeliever (!) ... Who can believe anything so unchivalrous of the manifold knight, anything so contradictory to the Dutch character of the ancient-noble Hollander, who obtained so much honour by his writings in behalf of the honour of Holland?" Why? The decorated scholar, not only nobleman but a noble man, has written a good book and deserves respect. But—the baron, that awful radical, questions, years afterwards, not the Haarlem invention, but simply the genuineness of the representations which passed as portraits of Coster, and we may hear how now the same decorations tend to destroy

historical question, but as a dogma, as a *question of faith*. This also we are able to prove as clearly as the day. Coornhert is the first who tells us what was *believed* at Haarlem, and what he *believed* himself. Junius commences his story with a solemn oath as to his *credibility*, while afterwards the gist of every Coster-argument consisted of a verbose plea for the "credibility of Junius." In the arguments of Koning, Scheltema, and De Vries, we meet every moment with clerical terms of *faith*. And when at last Noordziek began to beat the drum to awaken the public, he made use of language, as if he were recruiting for the papal infallibility or for the corporeal assumption of Mary. I give one or two proofs of his drum-beating :¹ "The tone of contempt and ridicule with which foreigners (after the work of M. Meerman) spoke of our claims, became louder and louder, so that the Dutch themselves, who visited Germany, or read much German, were silenced by it. *Faith was made to waver.*" "We might reasonably have expected that the book of Koning ought to have brought the *unbelievers* among foreigners also to a better insight." "The additions published afterwards by M. Koning remained unknown in foreign countries. Hence the tone of *unbelief*, ridicule, and abuse, in which the Germans and French indulged with respect to the claims of Haarlem, continued as impudent as before." "M. Mortillaro was *converted* by reading the treatise of M. Tonelli, and the opinion that the honour of the invention is due to our countryman, is now common in Sicily." The Sicilians, that highly developed people, including the Princess of Belgiojosa, monks, fishermen, and bandits, are therefore all converted to the Coster-gospel. How refreshing is such an information to our patriotic heart! Betsy of Scheveningue also

---

him. "If M. Van Westreenen had not used tricks, to make himself, during his travels through foreign countries, agreeable to influential foreigners, how comes it, that he, who never has produced anything but little papers of very small value and signification, who never rendered any excellent service of public notoriety to his country or to science, sees himself nevertheless presented, in a manner wholly unprecedented, with *thirteen decorations*, and with such a great number of titles of honour from foreign courts and scientific societies?" And in another place the man "who obtained so much honour by his writings in behalf of the honour of Holland" is spoken of thus: "How foreigners think of the man and take him for a ridiculous fool is evident, amongst other things, from *Reiffenberg's Bulletin du Bibliophile Belge.*" What on earth does "the ridiculous fool" want to object against Coster-engravings, of which it has been *proved* that they were spurious. What has a "believer" to do with the genuineness or spuriousness of a relic?

2nd. The citations in favour of Haarlem were mutilated (clipped), those in favour of Mentz concealed, and the two kinds of citations weighed with false weight. Since Scriverius (1628), the important evidence of Ulric Zell was quoted, but always torn to pieces in a way which no ecclesiastical council could improve upon. The same took place with the quotation from Guicciardini. If we, like Dibdin, count for nothing the literary evidences in favour of Mentz, more than seventy in number, and reduce them to—two, then it may be permitted to take off a little from the Haarlem provision. Was Guicciardini, copied by others without investigation, for instance, an authority to whom we could refer conscientiously? His communication only proves that he, during the decisive decennium of the tradition, 1560—1570 (Van Zuren, Coornhert, Junins), learned something at Antwerp concerning the popular belief at Haarlem, perhaps by correspondence with Junius, who had been entrusted, on the part of the States of Holland, with a work of the same nature as that which Guicciardini finished in 1566. If we further observe that Guicciardini, while very briefly describing Hoorn, speaks with much praise of Junius (Dottore in medicina, ma dottissimo ancora in tutte le altre scienza, gran Poeta, & veramente Philosopho chiaro & celebre),—then is Junius the most probable source from which Guicciardini derived his indefinite information. But I have no intention to buckle on the harness in defence of this supposition. (Some evidences of a correspondence between Guicciardini and Junius could perhaps be found in the letters of Junius, which are preserved in the Library of the University of Utrecht, and belonged formerly to Burman. An exact comparison also of the *Batavia* with the Descrittione would perhaps explain their relations. But it would not reward the trouble.)

The true reason of Mentz being mentioned on the earliest incunabula was discovered by De Vries in 1823: it arose from a desire of the typographers for customers: an explanation which is as simple as we can wish for. But considering the silent typographers at Haarlem in 1483, '84, '85 and '86, and the silent Haarlemers who printed already since 1476 in Italy, a peculiar courage is required to be able to ask: Is there a stronger evidence for [for?!] a Haarlem origin of the art?

De Vries, however, tried one effort to fill up the menacing gap. He commented on the inscription: Nicolaus Petri de Harlemo de Hollandia Almanus (although of the same kind as that of Theodoricus de Rhijnsburg et Reinaldus de Noviomago Alamanni, Johannes Alamannus de Medemblik) thus: This circumstantial mention of Haarlem as birthplace seems to serve as recommendation, or as a desire of making a show with the name of Haarlem.

¹ Het geschilstuk betrekkelijk de uitvinding der boekdrukkunst, geschiedkundig uiteengezet door J. J. F. Noordziek. Haarlem. 1848. 8vo.

believes strongly, unshakeably, and devoutly, " in our countryman." At the inauguration of the statue, Pauwel Foreestier (Pseudonyme of M. Alberdingk Thijm) (Dietsche Warande, 1856, p. 454) gave vent to the following overstrained monkish ecstasy :—
"Forgive me, ghost of the virtuous Coster! forgive the offensive shudder! you have, you have existed indeed, a man of flesh and bone, in spite of me—of every one, of the most pronounced idealist. *I believe in you* ; I am convinced that you lived and worked in the year 1420 or 30 ; I press, with emotion, your pale, bony, and delicate right hand. I believe that you are the man of the Donatus, of the Spieghel onser behoudenisse . . . Why should I not believe in you ? *There* is the spot in the Hout, where you found [picked up] the noble art ; *there*, near that handsome monument. Yonder is the house, the Coster's house, on the market-place, where your cradle was rocked whilom. Noble sheriff, dilettante printer, you have been the dupe of that thief Guytenberg ; the dupe of those same Mentzers, who were known of old as great traitors. And why should we not believe in you ? Is there anything obscure in your history ? Have we not the grave-register, in which your name is inserted among those who mingled their ashes with our dear paternal ground ? Here are the letters of your name, one after another—it is not Laurens, but Lourens ; here are your arms, with the honourable ordinary bar through the lion. No, that bar is no emblem of the bar which runs through your history. No bar runs through it ; but that corrupted race, that brood of vipers, the reviewers, would make any one doubt everything. But in full earnest—if the man who was celebrated there at Haarlem, the 15th, 16th, and 17th of July, must be a myth, a shadow, an idea, a poësy, a painted curtain, where nothing is behind ; then I declare De Ruyter and Prince William I. and Rembrandt, nay, Prince Frederick, and all other admirals, painters, princes, and inventors of arts and sciences, to be myths as well. He who has been at Haarlem, and really has been there, *ought* to be convinced. Scholars and believers do not agree *so*, words here and silence there do not *so* harmonize, numerous corpora delicti do not come together in such striking order—when we have to do with a national prejudice, with an amusement, with the identity of a pot-sherd." Wittily argued, if it were to prove the Conceptio Immaculata. But such an exclamation would be *impossible* by the statues of De Ruyter, Cats, Rembrandt, Vondel, Tollens, Van Hogendorp. And we must not forget that Foreestier addressed so enthusiastically the *sheriff*-dilettante-printer, while *another* stood there, and the *tallow-chandler* gave a significant glance at M. Joh. Enschedé!

Fanaticism and heretic-hunting, inseparable from every creed, because the calmness of objectivity is wanting, betrayed themselves very soon among the Costerian sect. Scriverius was bold enough to add to his "Laurecrans" the portrait of some hypochondriac, which, without a word about its origin, had to pass as a likeness of L. J. Coster. He wrote under it :

> "Vana quid archetypos et præla Mogvntia jactas?
> Harlemi archetypos prælaque nata scias.
> Extulit hic, monstrante Deo, Lavrentivs artem.
> Dissimulare virum hunc, dissimulare Deum est."

Coster-denial was atheism. This magnificent beginning was a prelude to things which were yet to come. But because it is impossible to out-do this logic of Pieter Scriverius, we had better consider at once the evidences of the sectarian falsification of the question.

We have only to represent clearly to ourselves the course of the polemics. *The attack was not made before the end of the 16th century by Haarlem*, by the publication of the Batavia. In the year 1600 Bertius gave some notoriety to the (modified) fable of Junius, in consequence of which Nic. Serrarius defended, in 1604, the right of Mentz. In 1630, Junius was refuted by Naudé ; in 1689 by Mallinckrodt, who was, in his turn, opposed by Boxhorn in 1640. The quarrel had begun. This *historical* beginning, however, was immediately *falsified* by the Costerians. Instead of acknowledging that the Haarlem claims were made, after Mentz had been for more than a century in undisputed possession of the glory of the invention, the parts were reversed: the people at Haarlem hypocritically feigned to be attacked, while they represented Mentz as the attacking party, endeavouring to rob Haarlem of an old and generally acknowledged right. In this way they proceeded until our time, with all the obstinacy and rage of a bad conscience. Let us only hear what the first disputant asserts, what Scriverius dared to write against those whose attention had been first drawn to the pretension of Haarlem by Junius and Bertius. "Printing was invented at Haarlem, according to the explanation of Junius, Coornhert, Zurenus, and others. The Mentzers and others who *conspire* with them object to this, and I will give a brief sketch of what has been *bragged* and written lately, wide and far, in behalf of their defence. Serrarius *denies*, with immoveable countenance, that printing was first invented elsewhere but in Mentz." What "immoveable countenance" was necessary to doubt a story published in 1588, and concerning the year 1440, and which *nobody* outside Haarlem, nor even inside the town, for a whole century had ever heard of? Scriverius argues, with intolerable bluntness, that people ought simply to have complied with the story of Junius. "Although Hadrianus Junius—relating what old, respectable, and distinguished magistrates had heard from mouth to mouth from their forefathers, and which they confirmed with strong protests—ought to have been believed by every one, as he was no relation to the dead Laurens Jansz. Koster . . . Yet it pleased, *henceforth*, the Germans and others, having often lost their reason either by misunderstanding or anger, to ascribe the invention of printing to the town of Mentz, which was the highest injury to our dear town of Haarlem." And, addressing Serrarius, he says:—

"As you have read the book of Junius, who has proved his good faith sufficiently, who was a blameless man and free from deceit, why do you talk any more? In vain you wish to rob the art from the Haarlemers; in vain do the people of Mentz try to divide this honour. I pray you read my work, and, if you have any sense of shame, forbear, and abandon your false work." While on the Spiegel he wrote this beautiful line:—

"You have now caused Mentz to stink everywhere."

The second apologist proceeded in the same way. Boxhorn wrote in 1644: "As Laurens Coster sold the printed books for manuscripts, he has prejudiced himself and his honour. For that reason *ignorant* people ascribed the invention of printing to Mentz. I had given this opinion after M. Scriverius had wreathed that brilliant laurel round the head of our talented Haarlemer, thinking that this would have been sufficient, and would have shut the mouths of the Mentzers and the Germans who spoke in her favour. However, the Munster deacon, Bernard Mallinckrodt, opposed, some time ago, the *truth*. But we have shown, in an especial treatise, *how faint and lame* his pretended arguments were."

XIX.

GERARDUS MEERMAN.

IN 1760, the celebrated work of the Strasburg professor, Daniel Schoepflin, *Vindiciæ typographicæ*, was published. Although Meerman had formerly, in opposition to Wagenaar, declared the Coster-story to be a novel, and that he was convinced, for good reasons, of the priority of the Latin to the Dutch editions of the Speculum, yet his vanity urged him to publish also a book like that of Schoepflin. It should also be a quarto, and be provided with facsimilia, but it should be executed in a still more magnificent style. Without believing honestly in the Haarlem invention; without submitting to the text of Junius, and seeing no chance of attacking the right of Mentz, he devised a loophole, by dividing the claims of the towns Mentz, Strasburg, and Haarlem, which were at that time vieing with one another. To give it an appearance, he imagined two unknown and totally impossible modes of printing books with moveable *wooden*, and with brass types, each letter *cut* separately. Coster obtained as his part the invention of the wooden, Johan Geusfleisch (whom he distinguishes from Gutenberg) that of the cut metal, Schöffer that of the cast, types.

This nonsense has so often been exposed already that it is superfluous to do it again. The worst of all is, that Meerman was repeatedly and urgently cautioned by the experienced typographer Joh. Enschedé, that he was devising an impossible system. The learned fool was too conceited and too dishonest to listen to the Haarlem citizen, who far surpassed him in sagacity and competence with respect to the question. He commenced his work in 1760, and the following year he hastily published a "Conspectus originum typographicarum,"[1] while the work itself did not appear before 1765. I have to justify my disrespectful tone towards Meerman and his work. The perusal of forty autograph letters concerning the publication of the monument, which he intended to erect to *himself*, not to the sheriff Louwerijs, perfectly enables me to do so.

In the summer of 1760, immediately after having read the work of Schoepflin, and without a thorough study of the subject, he addressed Joh. Enschedé at Haarlem, proposing the publication of a "work on Typography," which was to be a quarto of c. 18 sheets, printed as handsomely as possible, at the expense of the author, with the promise of placing the name of Enschedé on the title when the work turned out well. It would take, however, "some two or three months before he could begin to print it." Meanwhile they could make a sketch of the first leaf of the Spiegel and Donatus; "but it would be better to do the Spiegel first, because then the vellum leaf of the Donatus could be stretched, *in order that the lines should agree exactly with those of the Spiegel*: else Fournier would criticize me terribly." Meerman often and anxiously alludes to this trick. For instance, in a letter of 23rd Feb. 1761: "I take Van Noorden to be a very clever man, and the drawing of the page of Donatus may safely be entrusted to him; but he ought to soak and stretch the vellum, that the length of the lines may agree with the leaf of the Spiegel drawn by him. Else we must expect remarks." Ex ungue leonem! But I find other, equally distinct, traits. With respect to the fable of Atkyns, defended in Meerman's book, he writes: "I have found a good expedient (!) to defend it, by saying (!) that Corsellis was the first printer in England with wooden letters, as Laurens Jansz. has been (which I will prove to be quite possible), and Caxton the first in metal letters, as in that sense Thierry Martens was the first printer in Holland." Exactly: Meerman found "expedients," and this is the whole secret of this plea of his vanity. On 8 Oct. 1760 he requested to have about ten lines figured of the first leaf of the *Historia Alexandri Magni* (printed at Utrecht); "for," he writes, "I think I shall be able to show that this was printed by the heirs of Laurens Jansz." And although afterwards (14 Jan. 1761) he feels obliged to acknowledge: "I begin to doubt very much whether the Thomas à Kempis, and consequently also the Hist. Alex. Magni, were really by the heirs of Laurens, for at the beginning of the work of Kempis it was said that he was already dead, and he died in 1471: ergo, not printed before A. 1472; at that time Thierry Martens had already arrived in the Netherlands, and who says . . . that the descendants of Laurens were still printing at that time?"—yet, notwithstanding this opinion of 1761, he told us in 1765 that the Historia Alex. Magni was printed at Haarlem by the heirs of Laurens! The honest doubts, however, of 14 Jan. 1761, were accompanied again by the remark: "I hope

---

[1] Conspectus originum typographicarum, a Meermanno proxime in lucem edendarum. In usum amicorum typis descriptus. 1761. (Hag. Comit.) 8vo.
Plan du traité des origines typographiques, par M. Meerman. Traduit du latin en français. Amsterdam (Paris) 1762. 8vo. By Claude Pierre Goujet.

that the engraver of the Donatus has soaked the vellum leaf; else the lines of this book would not agree with those of the first edition of the Speculum." He asked to borrow the edition of the Spiegel by Veldener, giving as his motive: "As I hope to draw a new argument, from the comparison of the different spelling of this and the two former editions, for the priority of the first edition, about which I shall consult competent people." I see that among the competent people consulted was even Fournier, who gave at that time the only true explanation, that the types of the so-called earliest Spiegel "were very worn." But the truth was no corn in Meerman's mill of expedients. Finally, as to the person of the fictitious inventor, Meerman, in a letter of 29 Aug. 1760, asks for a copy of the sheriff-arms of Louwerijs Janszoen, in order "to send it to some connoisseurs to investigate to what family he belonged. For I feel sure that he was not called *Coster*, but that he derived that name only from the office he held. And it is a mistake of Scriverius [Junius] to say that this office was hereditary in his family, the contrary of which appeared to me from an old charter." Thus speaks the publisher of the old pedigree, and thereupon, falsifying the text, calls his hobby-horse *Editnus*. Returning afterwards to the arms, he says: "On the ground of these arms I will try, on very probable reasons, to link Laurens with the family of Van der Duyn." Because, according to the arms, he was "evidently a nobleman." The poor nobleman-sheriff-innkeeper, martyr of probabilism, changed into a sexton-sheriff-woodengraver-printer!

Enough has been said on the value of Meerman's beautiful book. It cost him a great deal of money, for it was to surpass that of Schoepflin in everything. ("Fournier has ridiculed Schoepflin on account of the inexactness of his plates. I should not wish, for hundred ducats, that such remarks could be made on my plates.") The paper was to be of the finest, even if it cost 15 florins the ream; a number of engravers, "the greatest artists," were entrusted with the work, and afterwards dismissed as bunglers (Folkema, Lyonet, Van der Spijk). While Houbraken was good enough to engrave the portrait of Laurens Jansz., the chief person, the author had his own made in France. "My portrait is being engraved by Daullé at Paris, he being an artist of the first rank, in comparison with whom Houbraken is nothing. He makes the whole portrait himself, while Houbraken does only the head. I pay him 8,000 French livres, and I should have had it from Houbraken perhaps for 400 or less. But there is master above master. This will come in the beginning of my work." Now, you really look very satisfied, in the beginning of your work, oh advocate-apostle; while the Enkhuizen divine looks somewhat doubtful, because he does not know with what right he is exhibited *there*.

The mistakes of Meerman are, I repeat it, the more inexcusable, because he knew better. The able and frank Johannes Enschedé omitted no opportunity for many years to correct him. What was his reward? He tells it in a letter to M. J. Visser. "I have lent M. Meerman all my early editions, all what was rare, and all he asked was at his service; but when I asked him to lend me a book, I received not even an answer to my polite request, because I did not like to call *white black* and *black white*. It is a pity his laborious work is based on such false grounds. Gockinga, the echo of Meerman, has, by his translation, augmentation, and, as he thinks, explanation, obscured the truth still more."

The warning Joh. Enschedé fared no better than his warning descendant and namesake. Meerman was not inclined to give up his wooden types, his "expedient," for in that case he would not be able to do anything against the rights of Mentz. De Vries did not wish to abandon the sheriff, for with the chandler the Haarlem structure of lies falls immediately to pieces.

In such falsifications of history people not only obstinately persevered, but behaved as if the claims of Haarlem were gradually winning, those of Mentz losing, ground. I cite again Abraham De Vries.

"Not impudent enough to declare an account, so elaborate and circumstantial, and confirmed by such unexceptionable witnesses and evidences as that of Junius, as a mere fiction, and yet seeing no chance to contradict it with sufficient reason, the partisans of Mentz *tried to save* themselves through a *loophole*, and to *enforce* it as well on themselves as on others, namely: that Junius, however learned he may have been, had not the least knowledge of the proper nature of the art of printing.

"It is well known that for some time several German and French authors, *not able* to refute conclusively the *evidences* advanced for Haarlem's claim, and not willing to cede to foreigners the honour which they had hitherto appropriated entirely or partly to their country, have not hesitated to play the ungenerous trick of confusing, by a haughty, imperious, and sarcastic tone, the antagonists of their pretended rights, which they could not maintain any longer in a legitimate way; to represent them in the eyes of *ignorant* people as worthy of no attention, and so to silence them."[1]

Of Meerman's work De Vries says (we are now in 1823) truly: "The work of the learned, but not very judicious Meerman, has done more injury to Haarlem's cause than all its antagonists together." Very well! But what follows a few pages further? "The foreigners attacked the heavily-armed defender of Haarlem by airy assaults, and having, with great ease, beaten out of his hands and smashed a single weak piece of an unsuitable weapon, with which he in an evil moment had provided himself, they mocked at the rest of the real and uninjured armour of the unconquered—nay, not even in any tender part wounded—adversary, ventured themselves no further in such a combat, but tried, by setting up a loud shout of triumph, to give themselves the appearance of acknowledged victors . . . This vain tattle of thoughtless superficiality, accepted and echoed by numerous credulous people as the living language of well-founded conviction, had gradually perplexed and confused a great deal of the civilized world outside old Netherland . . . but—at last the 'Holland Society of Sciences' bestirred themselves for the violated honour of their meritorious countryman," and—"allowed themselves to be taken in by the literary rascal Jacobus Koning. Further: "The claims of Strasburg, beyond doubt, have even more appearance of truth than those of Mentz!"

"How would an author, who had dared to take such a liberty (the spinning of a legend), among a people so earnest and truth-loving as the Dutch, especially in Junius' time, necessarily have entailed upon himself the general hissing and ridicule, nay, the deepest contempt and detestation(!)" Especially in Junius' time! Here the expression of Lessing is of force: "He, who under certain circumstances does not loose his wits, has none." Further:

"It was by no means certain unknown old men. . . ., as the antagonists of Haarlem repeatedly echo one after another, from whose mouths Junius got his information." "*The so-called evidences* (of the Germans) are: First, some passages from

---

[1] These bombastic sentences contain, in reality, everything advanced by the Costerians against the troublesome objections in:—

(Karl Heinrich von Heinecken:) Nachrichten von Künstlern und Kunst-Sachen. Leipzig, 1769. 8vo. pp. 241—314: Anmerkungen über die Beweisthümer, welche die holländischen Scribenten anführen, dass Laurenz Janson Coster die Buchdruckerkunst erfunden habe. And from the same:

Idée générale d'une collection complète d'estampes. Avec une dissertation sur l'origine de la gravure et sur les premiers livres d'images. Leipzic et Vienne. 1771. 8vo.

Girolamo Tiraboschi: Dell' inventione della stampa (Prodromo della nuova Enciclopedia). Siena, Pazzini e Bindi. 1779. 4to.—Is a confutation of Meerman.

Dictionaire bibliographique choisi du XVe siècle. . . . précedé d'un essai historique sur l'origine de l'imprimerie par C. A. De La Serna Santander. Bruxelles, an XIII. 1805. 8vo.

Origine de l'imprimerie, d'après les titres authentiques, &c. Paris, 1810, 8vo. II. And since Koning:

A. A. Renouard: Note sur Laurent Coster à l'occasion d'un ancien livre imprimé dans les Pays-Bas (Catalogue de la Bibliothèque d'un amateur. II. pp. 152—58). Paris, 1819. 8vo.

Geschichte der Erfindung der Buchdruckerkunst zur Ehrenrettung Strasburgs und vollständiger Widerlegung der Sagen von Harlem dargestellt von J. F. Lichtenberger. Strassburg und Leipzig, 1825. 8vo. Also in French: Strasbourg, J. H. Heitz. 1825.

Notice sur le Speculum Humanæ Salvationis, par J. Marie Guichard. Paris, 1840. 8vo.

Kurzgefasste kritische Geschichte der Erfindung der Buchdruckerkunst . . . nebst Widerlegung der Ansprüche der Städte Strassburg und Harlem auf die Erfindung, und Abfertigung der neuesten Behauptung Gutenberg sey ein Böhme und geborener Kuttenberger. Wien, 1841. 8vo.

The best refutations, however, are those of Schaab and Wetter.

authors of the latter part of the 15th and the beginning of the 16th century... Secondly, some *bragging* imprints of printers anxious for customers... Thirdly, a very great number of passages from old chronicles and other books also of the latter part of the 15th century...." (Let us watch for a moment the dexterous fingers of this Costerian juggler!)

"The greatest part of those informations are nothing but *verbal* repetitions of some predecessor, so that this apparently formidable army, by which the student is as it were confused at first sight, shrinks, after a closer consideration and a more careful scrutiny, to a very small number of evidences of very little value." These words give an exact representation of the so-called evidence for Haarlem, quotations from Guicciardini (1567) as regards foreign countries, quotations from Junius (1588) as regards Holland. According to the measure applied by De Vries in bad faith (for he *knew* more than he wished to tell) to the Mentz evidences, he had no right to ascribe an atom of reality to his Haarlem non-evidences, NOTHING, NOTHING at all. And yet, even an oratorical diversion of Schiller in his 'Abfall der Niederlande,' even a failure of Henmann's memory, are good enough for him to throw dust in the eyes of the people. "Finally, in the fourth place: Some juridical documents, belonging to law-suits of the first printers, and from which it is clearly and incontrovertibly evident that these pretended inventors of printing, regarded from a moral side, *signified very little*." No Costerian is a competent judge of morality! "The well-deserved praise, which the talented Mentz and Strasburg artists had earned by the fortunate improvements they devised, by which they carried the imperfect art of printing to a high degree of perfection, would have come down to posterity more unsullied, *if the obstinate desire of maintaining a false pretence* had not been the cause of discovering juridical evidences of shameful law-suits, which are now everlasting monuments of their mutual discord, avarice, unreasonableness, and indelicacy in morals." Further: "The account of Trithemius is the sheet-anchor on which, properly speaking, the whole cause of Mentz depends."

M. Noordziek put the crown on this work of public fraud, when the long-continued deception had triumphed. "The attention has at last been called to the fact, that Holland, outvoiced by wild shouts, kept silent for a long time, but re-appeared always with dignity, declaring at the same time with energy, that it had been wronged, and was prepared to produce the most convincing evidences of the fact." "By bringing this point clearly before the world (by putting before the Germans undated Donatuses of the years 1470, 1480, 1490, and later!) the claim of Gutenberg to the invention of moveable letters (between 1440 and 1450!) *falls entirely to the ground*." "The dispute as to the question, in what country and by whom the invention was made, has been violent. That point is now, after great efforts (of De Vries, Schinkel, and Noordziek), and according to the opinion of experts (De Vries, Schinkel, and Noordziek) *settled*, and Holland has, without injuring in the least the honour of Gutenberg (for, Noordziek tells us, the man was merely assisted by a *thief*, by his *uncle*, Johan Gensfleisch!), *revindicated*, in the most energetic and *convincing* manner, the honour of the invention for L. J. Coster." "The invention, celebrated over all the civilized world, originated, as was so satisfactorily proved and acknowledged, in Holland; the inventor was almost everywhere believed to be a Hollander."[1] No wonder that Noordziek always speaks of the "conquered enemy." I am perfectly willing to enable him, if he chooses, to rejoice at the convulsions of that "conquered enemy." By the inauguration of the statue it was thought necessary that M. L. Metman should humbug the deceived people a little: "*Ignorance and prejudice alone* are able to pronounce against Holland. Be my witness, you who have examined what the acute and learned De Vries, assisted by his artist friend Schinkel, and by the untiring and persevering zeal of our Noordziek, has submitted to the judgment of his countrymen and the foreigner! The truth may remain concealed in darkness for a long

---

[1] **Gedenkboek der Costers-feesten** van 15, 16 en 17 Julij 1856. Door J. J. F. Noordziek. Haarlem, 1858, 8vo.

time; when it appears in the light it may be ignored and violently attacked: nay, its sacred cause may for a moment appear desperate; but its splendour breaks more and more through the clouds... and shines every time more clearly and irresistibly... The hordes of its enemies become thinner every day; the number of its followers becomes greater and more powerful, until even the last contradiction of *impudence* is silenced and the victory is accomplished."

When such bombast began to be accepted as current coin, nobody was restrained from doing what he liked. In the Arnhem Gazette, No. 108 of 1823, Alethophilus (M. G. van Lennep) took the liberty to make some objections to the year 1423, fixed upon at Haarlem on a sandy ground as the year of the invention. One of his remarks was, that "without the account of Junius, there was no safety for the cause of Haarlem, especially with regard to its citizen Laurens Janszoon Koster, who—we could not repeat it often enough—was mentioned *only* by Junius as the inventor of printing." The "Konst and Letterbode" of the same year inserted these remarks also, and added some malicious notes to it by way of apparent refutation. The note to the above-quoted remark runs: "This ridiculous and disgusting repetition has been answered before, remark c." Curious to know which author has mentioned L. J. Coster *before* Junius, we look for "remark c," and lo!—in that refutation of Alethophilus' "disgusting and ridiculous" argument we read: "Junius was the *first* who mentions the *name* of the inventor"; but this expression is immediately followed by the lie: "And many contemporaneous authors, who were able to draw also from other sources, have soon afterwards further explained and confirmed his accounts concerning the person of the inventor." This untruth explains the mean tactics of the Costerians, by which they put into the hands of ignorant people the three accounts of Zell, Guicciardini, and Junius, which mutually destroy each other, as a completion of that Haarlem legend, which they have composed from them. He who wishes to make of these accounts *one* history is a noodle, or an unscrupulous bungler. Yet the sect exhibited this pitiful spectacle. And here again the exegetic tricks of De Vries are most characteristic. "We have a right," he says, "on the authority of Braunius and Guicciardini (of whom the *first* copied the *second*!), to refer, concerning the principal facts of Junius' account, to witnesses, who must have lived very close to the time of the invention (!) And these so much older witnesses (who, at most *two* years before Junius, put an indefinite town-gossip on paper, *without* mentioning the inventor, *without* naming the time of the invention, *without* saying a single word of what had been printed!) deserve our particular attention and belief, because they not only perfectly agree with the account of Junius, but also mention, according to Braunius and Guicciardini, *one* very important fact, *omitted by Junius*, and whereby an obscurity in his account *is fully explained*. Namely, one of the greatest objections which the Germans and French made with so much fuss, is, that it was hardly conceivable how the theft of some stamps, matrices, and other printing tools could deprive the inventor of the art, at once of the fruits of his invention. If the inventor, who naturally must have felt a great interest in his own invention, and have taken great care to keep his art and the furniture belonging to it secret,—if he had suffered himself to be robbed and deceived, yet he would certainly have spared no pains to pursue the thief, and to get back all that had been stolen from him; and, if he had not succeeded in it, he would have repaired at once with the utmost zeal all he had lost —told the world of what infidelity he had been the dupe—published directly some work, signed with his name—thereby averted the danger of being deprived of the honour and profit of his invention—and, at the publication of the first product of the press of the fraudulons supplanter, have exposed, accused, and prosecuted him. Braunius (who ascribes the invention of typography to Mentz!!), confirming (read: copying) in this respect the evidence (!) of Guicciardini, makes this exaggerated objection totally disappear as a castle in the air. He tells us of these old, now lost memoirs (! Gerrit Thomasz., Van Zuren, Coornhert) what Junius had forgotten (?) to notice, and which was, however, necessary to a perfect understanding of the case, namely, that the departure of the servant of the inventor for Mentz, and the transmission of the art by him to that town, was *caused* by the death of the inventor, before he had been able to bring his invention to the desired perfection, and to appear with it in public. (Where remains the *new merchandize* of the fable of Junius, never before seen, which attracted purchasers from everywhere?!) And this circumstance, not recorded by Junius, but mentioned by much earlier (!) authors, clears up all that is obscure. The unfaithful servant was tempted by the favourable opportunity which the confusion, caused by his master's death, offered him. (Oh, holy church-going of Christmas, 1441, your violation is avenged!) The great profits produced in later times by the sale of work, which had turned out better and resembled as much as possible the handwriting of that time, and was therefore sold for manuscript, had animated for a long time the foreign adventurer with the wish of enriching himself by such a profitable trade. *By his master's death the press had to be left to his care and supervision for a long time.* On a certain (!) Christmas night (for 1441 does not suit the sheriff who died in 1439), when all the people of the house were gone to church to celebrate that high festival, and he alone was to watch over the house and printing-office, the temptation was too strong for him. He bundled a good deal (not *everything*, as Junius has revealed?) of the matrices and stamps (how *imperfect* was that invention!) and some types and printed sheets, which should serve as a guide (!) and example, together, and took to his heels."

De Vries knew quite well what he was about when he objected to the discovery of the chandler Lourens Janszoon Coster, of the years 1440 and 1450! He knew perfectly well that the Haarlem nonsense could only obtain an appearance of sense by tampering with a man who was dead *before* the German invention, *before* the fictitious robbery. He was too well acquainted with the polemic literature on the subject not to know that the Haarlem bubble would burst at once when the chandler was to hold a candle to the account of Junius. On the other hand, however, the hero of De Vries died before the year of the invention fixed upon by Junius, and therefore equally useless for an honest explanation of the account of the Batavia. The cause is irretrievably and irrevocably lost!

Or do I count, perhaps, too much without the " laymen in the question," who, concealed under the scientific rags of their " authorities", are bold enough to soil the question, which is no longer a question, with some lawyer's tricks?[1] No one is able to argue with such people, who are half-a-century behind in real development of

---

[1] While my first essays on this subject were being published in the " Nederl. Spectator," M. D. van Eck, lawyer at the Hague, without being competent to form an opinion in the matter, but like a second Meerman, coming forward with expedients, tried to divert attention from the main question, and to confuse the public anew, by inserting in the newspapers an: " Explanation of Ulr. Zell's account, by Dr. van der Linde." "Zell states," thus Dr. v. d. Linde reasons, " that Johan Gutenberg at Mentz was the first inventor of printing. If, therefore, he also said, according to the partizans of Haarlem, that the first inventor was found in Holland, he would have committed a great folly. Perfectly true, but the premise is inexact; for Zell never said that the art of printing was invented at Haarlem: the contrary is true; but (but?) he relates facts (!) which happened in Holland, and from those facts the partisans of Haarlem argue that he who has a right notion of the word *invention* must acknowledge that it took place in Holland. And if the argument of the friends of Laurens Janszoon (Coster) [sic] is well founded, it is a matter of course that Zell has given an improper (!) signification to the word invention, but not that he has committed a great folly."

His further sophisms may be found in my answer, which was inserted in one of the Dutch newspapers: " While my article on Ulr. Zell had made a deep impression on the most competent critics, the " layman " Van Eck declares that this was " not " the case with him, and he is open-hearted enough to tell us that his being so totally " a layman " in the matter of printing is the reason for this non-conviction. He pretends, even without knowing the question superficially, that the chronicle of Cologne speaks of *typographically* printed Donatuses; that the impulse to the devising of typography, of which it speaks, had already been given by moveable cast types; that, therefore, the invention of typography had been made before 1440, in Holland. And he has the courage to maintain this, although the Costeriana, Bertius, Scriverius, Boxhorn, of earlier times, Berjeau, and others of later time, all whose arguments he ignores, have found in the chronicle nothing but xylographic Donatuses; although I had pointed out the difference between xylography and typography which the whole context of the account indicated: and although finally those xylographic school-books nowise historically originated from Holland, but from Flanders. That " new manner," that " present manner," that " now-a-days manner," was, in the 15th and 16th century, a definition of typography, in contrast, not with a less beautiful typography, but with an impression from engraved forms. As Van Eck goes on struggling against this, the only rational explanation, I will give a 17th century quotation of an unsuspected author—Scriverius

judgment. It does not seem to enter their head that, even if we found in the Cologne chronicle what there is not, but what their unreasonable dexterity puts into it, they would not advance a single step nearer their aim. They don't seem to have the faintest idea that the history of the years 1440—50 cannot be re-construed in 1499 by mere *talk*, but by *proofs* unknown till that time. Even if a chronicle of 1499 had *said* that *typography* was invented in Holland before 1440, that assertion alone would not be an infallible oracle, but we should have to see whether it agreed with the well-proved documental history. And would any one desire at present, in 1870, *nearly four centuries later*, to put between the four lines of the Cologne chronicle, a hitherto unknown Haarlem *chandler-innkeeper*?!

The fancy of all orthodoxies, that they submit to the authority of sacred books, while they always explain that authority according to their own arbitrariness, is curiously evident among the Costerians. Just as many believing Christians abandon, piece by piece, every dogma of the Bible, from the Hebrew myth of the creation in Genesis down to the millennium of the Apocalypse, and yet pretend to be believers, so the Costerians play with their gospel according to the requirements of the moment. I have quoted already enough of these incongruities to consider myself free from producing other examples, although there would be material enough for a big volume. Only one or two more proofs from the warm but poor plea of Pacile.

In a totally deceptive explanation of the account of Junius, in which he heaps the one untruth upon the other, Pacile swears also by Hans, Cornelis, Galius; that theft *ought* to be true. Very well. But here we have two explanations of this orthodox Costerian by the side of each other :—

Pag. 88. "The circumstance of the theft is too curious that Cornelis, from whom Junius had his account directly (!) could have been mistaken; we must therefore assume that Guicciardini, Braun, and Eytzinger [3 times 1=1], who consider Coster's workman to have been no thief, but say that he brought the art to Mentz after the death of his master, *were imperfectly informed with respect to this point*."

Pag. 103. "It is true, Matthias Quadus makes no thief of the servant of Coster; but the circumstance of the theft is in reality an indifferent circumstance. It is indeed not necessary that the secret of the art should have been stolen; that the Mentzers are not the inventors of it (!) is sufficient to justify the claims of Holland; it is sufficient to know that this art was communicated to them, and Quadus increases the number of authors to settle the fact incontrovertibly (!) "

And here the sophist is in full strength on one and the same page (106) :

Pag. 106. "We had at first no intention to quote the evidence of Van Mander (Haarl. 1604), or

' Van Mander had lived for a long time at Haarlem. He was able to collect in that town the

himself. This Costerian enthusiast, says : "The... art of printing came to light, not in the manner as is usual at present, with letters cast of lead and tin... but a book was cut leaf for leaf on wooden blocks."

But let us assume for a moment that there is reference in the Cologne chronicle to typographic Donatuses, then the famous account of 1499 runs thus : 1st. Typography was invented first of all at Mentz between 1440 and '50. 2nd. Before that time, however, before that very first invention, typography was invented in Holland. 3rd. The first inventor was Johan Gutenberg at Mentz. Who feels inclined to quarrel about such talk of miserable Costerianism? and to argue with Van Eck, who says, " that word *yet* is of importance as a contrast," is too ludicrous.

Van Eck's other "expedient" about the signification of the words *inventor* and *primus inventor* is also for ignorant people. Apart from the old pleonastic style, which Van Eck does not seem to know, he ignores the question altogether. Trithemius, indeed, wrote nonsense, and it has been pointed out what made him do it; this point, too, has been settled more than a century ago. All that the 16th century accounts have asserted regarding *primi inventores* must not lead us to a distortion of their language, but ought to be historically explained from the well-known facts, which I need not repeat here for the 100th time for those who do not desire to learn. Only this : if people would have the courage to assert, after my translation of the Cologne account *in extenso*, that Zell indicates Gutenberg as the *improver* of typography, I then pity such logic.

M. van Eck has never seen Donatuses, else he would know that only a connoisseur is able to distinguish the xylographic from the typographic ones, and that it would be psychological nonsense to make any one invent independently typography by seeing a typographic copy. No one, who does not know the case beforehand, sees anything in a typographic Donatus which distinguishes it from a xylographic one. But who, with a clear conception, has a xylographic text, a book (for that is the main point) before him, may thereby, by comprehending the impracticability of xylography, the waste of time, and the unfitness of the wood-engravings to other purposes, come to meditate on another mode of printing. This, as Zell informs us, happened with Gutenberg.

rather his simple assertion, not confirmed by a single proof, but we wished to show how the Flemish idiom is understood by most people, who take the trouble to explain it."

materials from which Junius wrote, and to know the antiquity, correctness, and generality of the Dutch tradition. On that account he declares himself without hesitation for the right of Haarlem."

To my sorrow I have to be brief, but I trust that the required *proofs* have been produced. In general, the method of the Haarlem apologists may be thus defined: just as the ignorant layman promiscuously quotes from all the books of the Bible, and from all periods, as if he had to do with one work without the least gradation of credibility, so the Costerians cite all authors and all chronicles indiscriminately, even if centuries lie between them, without an atom of critical sifting, without any apprehension of the necessity of scientific preparation. And just as the believers respectfully make way for Strauss and Baur, and do as if they never existed, so none of the Costerians ever had the courage to venture upon the works of Schaab and Wetter. For the miserable scribbling of Scheltema against the first, and the two pedantic raids of Noordzick against the latter, are too far beneath criticism to deserve the least attention. The one essential point ever made by De Vries against them is confined to his witty refutation of the assertion that the sheriff Louwerijs Janszoen had been an innkeeper: the more funny now we know that the opinion was perfectly right.

"Nothing can, undoubtedly, be a more convincing evidence of the exorbitant ignorance of the Germans of our paternal morals and usages, than the silly inference, which a Schaab, Lehne, and Wetter have drawn from the annotations in the registers of the church and the treasury accounts, that our Lourens Janszoon was a winemerchant or an innkeeper; wherefore they gave him the nice names of landlord, tavernman, &c. But such ludicrous assertions, inspired by the desire of representing as ridiculous an account against which they are, to their sorrow, not able to advance any reasonable argument, deserve no serious refutation." But what to do with the items of wine supplied to the church? This question is capable of being very *musically* solved thus:

"From the notification: *Item for Singers'-wine*, we might suppose that Coster, who was perhaps a good singer and an adept in music, had the direction of the music on occasion of one of the high festivals, where the most talented and distinguished amateurs of the art of singing assisted in the solemn choral song, and had for that reason been treated to wine by the church."

While the sheriff-innkeeper is singing in the cathedral, let us skip over the Costerian bungling with the portraits of the chimerical inventor. I called already attention with a few words to the first Coster-portrait, as such imported in 1628 by Scriverius, the projector of the year 1428, and of the innocent sheriff Louwerijs Janszoen. This portrait, engraved by a contemporary of Scriverius after some family-portrait, perhaps of Gerrit Thomaszoon, in any case not older than the 16th century, is not, as was incorrectly asserted, *invented*; it is no "ideal" composed by Costerians, but, just as the undated Utrecht incunabula, baptized, after it existed already, with the name of L. J. Coster, and in order to make it suitable to the Laurecrans, armed in its right hand with the *Roman* (and not Gothic) letter A. The Costerians were content with putting under the engraving: "J. Van Campen, pinxit; J. Van de Velde, sculpsit." Soon after, in 1630, a portrait followed of Laurens Coster, at full length, by P. Saenredam, and published by A. Rooman ("excited by Scriverius' enthusiasm"), with the same Latin and Dutch verses as on the portrait in the Lavrecrans of 1628, and really an imitation of it. Boxhorn was so kind as to describe the publication of this engraving in his Theatrum Hollandiae (1632) thus: "Laudabile Magistratûs exemplum secutus est Civium nonnemo, qui publicam Laurentio Costero statuam cum honorificâ inscriptione erexit." Foreigners were therefore led to believe that a *statue* had already been erected at that time at Haarlem in honour of Coster. Later copies of this paper statue bear the address of P. Casteleyn. The portrait was afterwards painted again by Jacob Van Campen, after whose drawing it was engraved by Cornelis Koning, who published it at Haarlem again with the well-known Latin verses of Scriverius, and the Dutch translation of Ampzing. To later editions the words, "Hugo Allardt," were added. All the numerous Coster-portraits are more or less good, more or less free imitations of the ugly face in front of the Lavrecrans of 1628, besides the other substituted pieces of the 18th century.

The most amusing imitation was that of an amateur-artist of the last century, C. van den Berg, who wished to play the collector J. Marcus a trick. He engraved a small wood-cut, after the portrait of Van Campen, with the name Laur' Ja(n)ssoe(n), in old-fashioned style, underneath, gave the copies, with a little soot and dirt, an antique appearance, and made Marcus happy for a few weeks. The poet Langendijk, the typefounder Joh. Enschedé, and other amateurs, got each a copy, but Van den Berg was too honest to mean anything more than fun; he told afterwards Marcus himself the value of that antique wood-cut. Although every investigator could and ought to have known these things, yet Jac. Koning was bold enough, in the second nomenclature of his collection of rare books and manuscripts, to describe a copy of this portrait as: "PRINTED BY, or at the time of, Lourens Janszoon Koster"! In the sale catalogue of his books (1833) his sons inserted this childish and deceptive description literally. And even after all these circumstances were known and ascertained by the controversy between Van Westreenen and De Vries, the latter, echoed by Noordzick, was obstinate in maintaining the genuineness of some of the copies of this engraving!

The Haarlem painter, L. van der Vinne, in his youth, painted, in the beginning of the former century, a study, after the drawing of Van Campen. But, lo! in 1762 this picture is offered for sale by Van Damme at Amsterdam—the same who produced the false inscriptions respecting the imaginary *Corsellis* of Oxford—provided at the back with a very old inscription: *Lours Jans to Harlm*. MCCCCXXXIII., and a monogram A O, which was explained to mean "Albert van Ouwater." Excellent discovery! Here was a genuine, contemporaneous portrait by a painter of the fifteenth century! A trifle, however, was wanted to make the joy perfect. Albert van Oudewater, who had painted the "celebrated" inventor of printing in 1433, was born in 1444!—This history is full of despairing irony from beginning to end. Just as the sheriff Lourens Janszoon invents the art of printing *after his death;* just as Cornelis works at Donatuses *before his birth;* just as the chandler Lourens Janszoon Koster entirely forgets his invention *during his lifetime*, so the painter Albert van Oudewater becomes already a zealous Costerian *long before he was born*.[1]

It is, therefore, no wonder that in an imaginary conversation between Koster, Seneca, and Huss, the inventor himself says to the Roman philosopher: "In the year 1400, or about the end of the 14th, or the beginning of the 15th century, for I am not able to give the precise year, I was born at Haarlem, in Holland." And of the invention he knows only: "At one of my walks, sitting on a bench, I saw at my feet some branches and pieces of beech bark, which had been blown down. I took some of them up, and cut, by way of pastime, without having any particular object, some letters, which pleased me so that I wrapped them in a piece of paper. This pleasant occupation, my great delight, the beauty and calmness of the spot, the fatigue caused by the walk, and the soothing rustling of the trees, made me insensibly fall asleep. The paper containing the letters which I had cut fell on the wet ground before me, and the porous paper sucked the moisture like a sponge, making the sap of the beech-wood, which was brown by nature, more fluid. I cannot say to a certainty

---

[1] Iets over de afbeeldingen van Laurens Jansz. Koster, door den Baron Van Westreenen van Tiellandt. 's Gravenhage. Gebr. Van Cleef. 1847. 8vo.
[Dr. A. de Vries:] Bewijzen voor de echtheid en gelijkenis der oude afbeeldingen Coster. Ter wederlegging van het Iets van den heer Van Westreenen. Haarlem, A. C. Kruseman. 1847. 8vo.
De zoogenaamde "Bewijzen voor de echtheid en gelijkenis der oude afbeeldingen van Koster," wederlegd door den Baron Van Westreenen van Tiellandt. 's Gravenhage, J. L. van der Vliet. 1848. 8vo.
[Dr. A. de Vries:] Eenige losse aanmerkingen op de voorgaande zoogenaamde wederlegging van den Heer van Westreenen, of zijn Iets gebragt tot Niets. 8vo. Unpublished MS. at present in the Royal library at the Hague.

whether I put my foot unwittingly, in my sleep, on this paper with the letters, and thereby impressed them on the soaked paper, but it is probable. When I awoke and did not find my letters, I saw the paper lying at my feet. I took it up to see whether my letters were still there, but how great was my surprise to find them impressed, but reversely, on the paper!"[1] How attentively must this poor inventor of 1758 have listened afterwards, in the underworld, to Meerman, Koning, Scheltema, and De Vries, who, rather contradictorily, tried to make him understand what he had, unconsciously, done during his lifetime! The poor man seemed to have no idea whatever of the nature of typography. In this respect he was really painted "after life." Oh! result, when the ghost of M. Johannes Enschedé appeared, and, assisted by the chandler, delivered him from his quarrelling promoters!

In 1765, Van Oosten De Bruyn and Meerman produced another portrait. That of the former, who had also a sheriff-letter of Louwerijs Janszoon of 1422 engraved, had underneath the arms of the sheriff, and these words: "Laurens Janszoon, sheriff of the town of Haarlem, inventor of the noble art of printing. After an old picture, at present belonging to M. Joannes Enschedé, Jz., and bought by him from Willem Cornelisz. Croon, the last descendant of Laurens Janszoon, who died, unmarried, at Haarlem, in 1724." This was therefore the same Croon for whom the vellum pedigree was continued—a man who, just as Gerrit Thomaszoon, wished to descend from the inventor of the art of printing, no matter whether the sheriff-legend of his time killed his fictitious ancestor, Coster. The unnamed portrait in the possession of this Haarlemer, curiously resembles that of the inquisitor Ruard Tapper of Eukhuizen († 1559, cf. J. F. Foppens, Bibliotheca Belgica, 1739. II. 1084 and 807 ; Historie van Enkhuizen, by Geeraerdt Brandt, 1747, p. 196); according to Gockinga, it resembles that of Sir Thomas More. They tried to explain the great difference between this well-executed portrait and that of the misanthrope in Scriverius, by some talk about the difference of age and about "marks of death" in the face of the earliest portrait. De Vries made a dexterous use of this loophole. "It was justly remarked by the acute and judicious Enschedé the elder, that the portrait of Van Campen exhibits something obviously cadaverous, from which the talented man inferred that the original piece, after which Van Campen painted his, must have been the work of a contemporary of Coster, who painted the face of the remarkable man while he was laid on his death-bed. Who could look carefully at the engraving before the Laurecrans, without acknowledging this observation to be well-founded ? To whom would the distorted features not appear as something gloomy, like that of a corpse ? Who is able to represent to himself that well-known face in the numerous ordinary portraits of Coster, after Van Campen, or the features of the statue which disgraced the market-place at Haarlem, and which was made after that portrait, without calling to his mind at once a painfully distorted face, in which, although less than in the engraving, yet something death-like, something sad is visible ? And a man of such a delicate taste as Scriverius (!), and artists like Van Campen and Van de Velde, would have imagined such a sad and painful face, such unpleasant and inexpressive features, to be the face of the lively, energetic, and able inventor of the most admirable art! No—there must have existed a peculiar, very important, all-prevailing reason why Scriverius—a man who was able to find all the existing portraits of Coster, among his descendants who were still alive, to trace the time and the occasion of their making, to compare and value them—choose such an unpleasant portrait, and had it so exquisitely painted, and engraved with so much care by such celebrated artists. Now what may have been the reason for this ? Indeed, no other than that he, after careful examination, had come to the conviction that this portrait was faithfully painted after the man's own face, although already pale, discomposed, and distorted by death. No portrait, however beautiful and however well answering to the representation of an inventive genius, unless a true and genuine likeness,

---

[1] Maandelijksche berichten uit de andere waereld, of de spreekende dooden . . . Zeeven en dertigste Samenkomst, tusschen Laurens Janz. Koster, eerste uitvinder der Boekdrukkunst ; L. A. Seneca . . . en Johannes Hus. VII. i. Jan. 1758. Amst. 8vo.

could satisfy the truth-loving (!) Scriverius. The truth was to be well-founded, if he endorsed it (!). That cadaverous hue, and those marks of death, therefore, in Van Campen's picture, are strong evidences for the genuineness and faithfulness both of the original representation, and of Van Campen's copy." Baron Van Westreenen answered, very cleverly : " It is a pity that the learned author does not seem to have known the treatises written to show the resemblance of the Byzantine Madonna with that painted, as it is said, by the Evangelist Luke ! The arguments found in them would have, perhaps, been of some use to him to demonstrate exegetically the likeness of a portrait of a person who died two centuries ago." This correct remark explains the true character of the Costerian apologies; a Costerian should present himself only with the tonsure and monastic gown, for his creed is ultramontane in origin and history. M. Thijm, who wishes to dedicate the Haarlem statue to *philosophy*, means with this abused euphemism, nothing but the *legend*. Philosophy is the doctrine of science, of truth, and has nothing to do with all the frauds comprised in Costerianism. De Vries wrote against the incontrovertible remarks of his antagonist: " M. Westreenen contents himself with impudently calling the unmistakeable marks of death in the portrait of the Laurecrans a story, and calumniously ascribing its invention to mean motives of selfishness." How natural is this indignation in the theologist of Costerianism, who explains, *always* and *everywhere*, and in *every one*, EVERY anti-Costerian opinion or doubt from by-designs, from *other* reasons than conviction ! Umbreit was perfectly right when he remarked, in 1843 : "Really, the last Dutch defendants of Haarlem (Koning, Scheltema, De Vries) do not write as if they had a respectable public before them, but just as if it consisted of ignorant children, whom they, barefacedly, could make believe anything they wished.¹ Alas ! they made the public believe *everything!* So soundly did it fall asleep by the Haarlem lullaby, that the second class of the Royal Institute, in their report on the "Eclaircissements" (De Vries—Noordziek), dared to declare, with unsurpassed stupidity, that " they could not help remarking how much more sensible and dignified the attitude of Mentz and Germany would have been if they—*not envying Haarlem the feeble firstlings*, or leaving, at all events, the question about them undecided—had made of the celebration of a jubilee by Germans, a solemn remembrancer of the time in which the first printed bible, that invaluable monument of the art, issued forth from their printing-offices.

XX.

A HERALD OF LIES.

IN the "Diary of the Coster-fêtes," M. Noordziek says : " In May 1846 I made a plan of having a monument erected at Haarlem in honour of Lourens Janszoon Coster." In the preface to this Diary, dated 1857, he reflects with natural satisfaction on his Costerian career. "When I have finished this work I may consider I have contributed enough to a lasting maintenance of the fame of our ancestor. Since 1840, I have energetically co-operated, and neglected no occasion to establish his claims as the inventor of the art of printing ; since 1846 I have, in fulfilment of a vow made to myself, unceasingly strived for the realization of my favourite idea, crowned last year with such a brilliant success. In those sixteen years, the best part of my life, I have collected an " Archive" of the facts connected

---

¹ Die Erfindung der Buchdruckerkunst. Kritische Abhandlungen zur Orientirung auf dem jetzigen Standpunkte der Forschung von August Ernst Umbreit. Leipzig, Wilh. Engelmann, 1843. 8vo.

with Coster, which contains a great number of documents, printed as well as written: a collection of immeasurable value to me, as comprising the history of all that has been done in this respect for the maintenance of the glory of the Netherlands during a long period."

It is difficult to me, after having copied these words, to remain master of my feelings. There is so much cruelty in the irony of events, the destruction of illusions is so painful, and especially the idea that M. Noordziek's life-long perseverance was devoted to a chimera is dreadfully tragic! I know by experience what it means to waste the best energies of the mind on a nothing, and should I not have sympathy with a fellow-sufferer? But no! no weakness. M. Noordziek is so fortunate as to be able to make good the wrong he has done. Thinking to work for our honour, he has laboured for our shame. Let him now manfully oppose his own creation. Or is this asking too much of human self-denial? For common minds, yes. But not for the man who wrote himself about "a sort of antagonists, who, like M. Weigel, could and ought to know better; but who, once having declared themselves in another sense, are not to be persuaded to confess publicly their error, as they fear in that case to be considered no longer worthy of the high place which they occupy in the literary or scientific world. A narrow-minded idea," Noordziek exclaims, "which ought to be opposed with energy. The student of history, especially, ought to feel himself above this. The ideas and opinions on a subject ought to be modified as soon as the discovery of earlier data demands. *A refusal to alter one's conviction is equal to a denial of the truth.*"

This motto gives me courage. I will describe in outline how the bronze statue was erected.

In May, 1846, M. Noordziek sent to the government of Haarlem a "report" in which "the present state of the quarrel (also called "dispute" and "law-suit") was explained." He wished to wreathe a new laurel among the hairs of Haarlem's symbolic virgin, as a lasting remembrance of the fact, of which the world had resounded (well!?) and as a national homage to the man, who, by the wisdom (or craft) of Providence, had been destined to produce an art which was to lead humanity, by a securer way of development, to the state in which it is at present." Thereupon he gives the Government to understand, that the Royal Netherland Institute had declared, with respect to the "*Eclaircissements*" and the "*Arguments*," that the question, therein treated, was incontrovertibly decided; that the *loopholes* and *tricks* of Haarlem's and Coster's antagonists were *destroyed*; that the *credibility* of the advanced evidences was maintained to the utmost; that the. denial of the decisive value of our evidences "was judged, convinced, and made powerless, in a manner satisfying in every respect the demands of a sound criticism."

Oh, Mr. burgomaster, they are such beautiful works! "People agreed so willingly with the tone of earnestness and energy of these two works—a tone only acquired by him who defends a good cause, and seeks the truth, and nothing but the truth; a tone which must command authority, and, supported by profound knowledge and thorough learning, was remarkably distinguished from that thoughtless noise and reckless writing too often found on the other side." Many more pages are filled with this bombast.

What could the magistracy of Haarlem answer to this drumming? As is generally the case with regard to intrusion, they were also here too polite. The civic government was authorized on the 12th August by the totally incompetent council, to inform Noordziek "that the government (of Haarlem) gratefully appreciated the untiring efforts which he and others successfully had made to maintain the honour of the Haarlem Coster, and to see it respected both at home and abroad; that they were equally thankful for the renewed proof of interest evinced by the offer of enriching the town with a statue, more adequate to the demands of the art than that erected more than a century ago, and that they would willingly accept and appreciate such a statue as an evidence of patriotic homage to the merits of the great inventor." The die was cast. In July, 1847, Noordziek published an: "Address to the

Netherland people to maintain the honour of their country," followed a year afterwards by the publication of "The Dispute, respecting the invention of printing, historically explained." This book clearly betrays Noordziek's ignorance of the question for which he laboured. Only the following decision in 1848, in the mouth of one who was said to have made a study of the subject, proved his incompetency. " The principal German candidates, who try to conquer the laurel, are Faust, Gensfleisch, Guttenberg, Jenson, Mentelin, Regiomontanus, Schöffer ; the towns which appropriate that honour, Strasburg, Basle, Cologne, Mentz, Prague, Ulm." He, who dares to write this in 1848 (when he could have read in a most superficial article of Prof. H. W. Tydeman, Mnemosyne, 1815 : " It is well *known* that only the towns of Haarlem, Mentz, and Strasburg can be admitted to the dispute"), who, in 1848, takes Gensfleisch and Gutenberg to be two different persons, who thinks that at that time there could still be any question of Mentelin, Jenson, and Regiomontanus, he knows *nothing* of the "dispute." Noordziek's opinion on the literature of the question confirms this assertion abundantly, and it is on that account that we will take a rapid view of it :—

"Junius was the first of our countrymen who took the question seriously to heart, *investigated it thoroughly*, and came openly forward as proclaimer and defender of Haarlem's right to the honour of the invention. He wrote an account of that event, with an indication of the sources from which he derived it, and the *evidence* (old wine-pots and a totally misunderstood old book) which *confirmed* it." On the contrary, Junius was the first who composed a fable from impure ingredients.

"Sixty years afterwards Scriverius thought it his duty to investigate the whole question more closely, and to come forward as the second defender. He published his *Laurecrans*, and confirmed therein the honour of Coster and the credibility of Junius with *many and powerful proofs*. In this respect the cause could not but gain in solidity and clearness " . . . .

Noordziek has never read the Laurecrans.

" Induced by Scriverius' book, the Germans *tried* to get a little beyond the question, as they could not *invalidate* the *powerful proofs* of the Cologne chronicle, of Coornhert, Van Zuren, Guicciardini, &c." Oh ! !

" In the year 1740, even a foreigner, J. C. Seiz, a German by birth, undertook the defence of Haarlem, and performed his task with energy and produced *solid proofs*, in a meritorious work, which deserves to be consulted, even now."

I quoted already the wretched chronology of this book.

" However, M. Meerman's meritorious, and—with regard to bibliographic and xylographic history—*classical* work, had a totally different effect with foreigners." How was that ? Well—

" M. Meerman deviated from the original text, the sheet-anchor of the history, by making the inventor Koster (sacristan) of the cathedral at Haarlem. Junius, on the contrary, had distinctly said that the family name Coster originated from an hereditary family-sacristanship. This interpretation of M. Meerman made the identity of *Coster* and the *Laurens Janszoon*—about whom so many particulars are found in the old archives (namely his going to a diet as councillor, his supplies to the cathedral, as a *wine-merchant*, the expenses made in his *inn* !) which explain (!), confirm (! !), and strengthen (! ! !) the account of Junius—very improbable to the foreigner, to whom it afforded an opportunity of declaring the account to be a fable."

Meerman, therefore, deviated from the original text, the sheet-anchor of this history? Now, we can understand that this deviation must annoy M. Noordziek, who in his " Eclaircissements " copied his master regarding this sheet-anchor: " Plus que jamais on est convaincu à présent que Junius, auquel on avait accordé pendant des siècles une confiance sans borne, et qu' on savait avoir été de bonne fois dans la composition de la Batavia, reste en définitive digne de conserver cette confiance, et que pas *une seule lettre* ne doit être retranchée ni modifiée dans son récit." And further : " Il n'existe donc *aucune particularité* du récit de Junius, qui ne se soit trouvée exacte par suite de recherches postérieures."

Let us now, in the face of Meerman's Koster-heresy, make up the account of the totally heretical profession of De Vries and Noordziek; for the same persons who wrote thus on Meerman and the original text, in which not a "single letter" should be altered, of which "every particular" was *confirmed* by inquiries,—those same heretic-hunters *believe* (without knowing it themselves?) *not a word of the original text*. I shall put the doctrine of the commentator by the side of the text—the doctrine of De Vries (Noordziek) by the side of that of Junius.

Junius.	De Vries and Noordziek.
1. The art of printing was invented *a*, in 1440; *b*, by Lourens Janszoon Coster (whom we meet in the archives down to 1483), *c*, member of the family Coster, who hereditarily possessed the then very profitable and honourable office of sacristan (Meerman was therefore punctiliously orthodox with his sacristanship.	1. The art of printing was invented *a*, in 1423; *b*, by Louwerijs Janszoen, who died in 1439; *c*, no sacristan, but sheriff.
2. The first book of Coster, the "Spiegel der behoudenis," was printed *a*, with wooden letters or forms (faginas formas); *b*, anopisthographic, as a firstling.	2. The "Spiegel der behoudenis" is printed *a*, with cast, metal letters; *b*, preceded by an Horarium and by Donatuses, which were opisthographic.
3. Coster printed whole figures, with a text (inde etiam pinaces totas figuratas additis characteribus expressit). Indeed, the fathers of the Church, of the "fourth jubilee," Bertius, Scriverius, Boxhorn, Seiz, De Bruyn, Meerman, Koning, Scheltema, and De Vries, have always seen a xylographer in Coster; nay, with the same facility with which Junius made the first typographer of him, they appointed him, most ridiculously, *inventor* of wood-engraving. In 1862 De Vries added a wooden block and block-books to the Costeriana, which were henceforth exhibited at Haarlem and—whereby he would be exposed himself.	3. Louwerijs Janszoen had nothing to do with those figures. "Qu'on ne lui attribue pas ce dont l'histoire (!) ne fait aucune mention, qu'on n'en fasse *ni un artiste dans l'art de dessiner ou de graver, ni l'inventeur de la xylographie, ni l'auteur de ces gravures en bois qu'il pourrait d'un text; car il n'en est fait mention dans aucun écrivain.*" But 100 pages further : "La vieille tradition connue de Harlem, *qui s'est toujours conservée la même*, nous apprend que Coster, *amateur et practicien habile de la xylographie* se promenant un jour, &c. Le récit de Junius est bien conforme à cette tradition."
4. The new merchandise (of the printed books), hitherto unknown, caused a lively demand and yielded great profits. On that account the business was to be extended, and Coster took more men in his service. (The Coster of Junius' fiction was therefore an honest printer and bookseller, who gave his goods *for what they really were:* something new and extraordinary.)	4. Louwerijs Janszoen printed for amusement, not for any profit. But yet—he begun a formal swindler's speculation, for his agents (chargés d'affaires) sold his goods for manuscripts (certainly no uncommon things at that time!). This was done by "l'habile et riche inventeur," and was imitated in this work by Thomas Pietersz, "un homme riche et considéré."
5. The inventor, however, was robbed of everything in 1441. The thief, Johan (Faust), prints *within* a year after at Mentz, in 1442.	5. The inventor was robbed after his death in 1439. The thief, Joh. Gensfleisch, prints, somewhat more than two years after, at Mentz in 1442.
6. The witness of this fact, Cornelis the bookbinder, reached at least eighty years.	6. Cornelis the bookbinder reached at least a hundred years.

In this pitiable way M. Noordziek goes on forging words. His ignorance was only surpassed by his boldness. He dared, for instance, to say of the work of Schaab, which remained hitherto unrefuted: "His work was elaborately refuted (read: chattered over) by M. Scheltema, and the author severely censured for his offensive invectives. But this censure (this prattle) however disgraceful (to Scheltema) could not prevent others (as De Vries and Noordziek) coming forward and assuming the same tone. A German (Wetter) ventured—but with greater appearance of moderation, *with more crafty argumentation* (than Schaab), and with greater *show of learning*—upon a so-called "critical history of the art of printing," no less offensive to Junius, than humiliating to the honour of our country."

M. Noordziek knows of that "crafty" book of Wetter, nothing but the title. And as for "show of learning," no more miserable example of this than his "Geschilstuk", which work, full of bombastic nonsense, contains a couple of hundred of titles of unread books, which were ready-made for him in the blue boxes of the Royal library at the Hague.

How obsequiously Noordziek trod the path of his great master is evident from two other passages in his "Geschilstuk." On page 89, we find this tirade: "There is no doubt that a worthy statue ought to be erected in honour of L. J. Coster, at the expense of the nation; it should represent the inventor in all his grandeur, and be superior in every respect to that of his antagonist Guttenberg, to whom, according to an ingenious remark, a statue is erected by a foreign artist, who, doubting, as it seemed, the claims of that pretended inventor, represented him at Mentz in a manner which clearly shows, that Guttenberg does not wish to put himself in the foreground regarding the great question of the invention of printing, and for that reason is afraid of showing to the world the loose letters he holds in his outstretched hand, but holds them as it were concealed, that nobody can see them." What, now, follows on page 91, on that very same worthless statue of Gutenberg? "More than one statue was erected in Germany in honour of Guttenberg, and even the most able judge admires the hand of the artist, who was able to sketch and finish the last erected one at Mentz."

No wonder, that the tone of M. Noordziek became intolerable, after he had obtained his purpose regarding "the hairs of Haarlem's symbolic virgin." The victory of ignorance intoxicated the victor. In his "Memorial" he dared, with incomprehensible confidence, to give an attestation of orthodoxy in doctrine and life to M. Frederik Muller, who, by a discussion with M. H. J. Koenen (in Felix Meritis, 1855, printed 1856), advanced incontrovertible objections against the tradition, which were answered by Koenen with nothing but evasions. Moreover, Frederik Muller gave evidence of his purely historical intuition, by his never-answered questions as to the identity of the sheriff Lourens Janszoon with Lourens Coster, in the "Navorscher" of 1856. Yet Noordziek incorporated the learned bookseller among the life-guards of the new statue.

Were there still heathens elsewhere on the earth who did not believe in Coster, after Noordziek had put his name on the title of a French translation of the works of De Vries? "Indeed, a voice was raised here and there," says M. Noordziek, with crushing superiority, "which objected to any honour being given to our countryman; but, by a mere perusal of the writings of such an author, we saw directly that he was not well informed regarding the question. These insignificant and ignorant antagonists have only been thought worthy of being referred to the sources, *where the whole truth was to be found*. What else could we do with respect to them but compassionately shrug the shoulders about such childish opposers, who ventured to declare for one or other party without thoroughly knowing the matter in question. I (Noordziek) mentioned those unscientific and superficial authors already, in so far they were known to me till 1848, and do not wish to point them out again." We see that this tissue of fantastic conjectures of those who do not even know over whom they throw them, is called already *science*. From the standpoint of this "science," M. Noordziek now begins to chastise the unbelieving "Bulletin du Bibliophile Belge," in which M. Helbig has been so bold as to write: "On voit sur la place de Haarlem celui (le monument) du problématique personnage Lourens Coster faisant une triste figure. Derrière cette statue se dresse en ricanant un autre monument colossal, qui la domine et l'écrase, visible pour tous, à eux seuls (les Hollandais) invisible : la statue du ridicule!" Let every one read the learned attack, with which Noordziek answers this deserved ridicule in his " Diary," which he concludes by saying: "M. Helbig has brought down this rebuke upon himself by his own fault." Has the evil since this rebuke become better? After this it is the turn of the Belgian bibliographer Ruelens. "I am compelled," says Noordziek, "to deny, provisionally, this author the right of giving his opinion in this question. *I will grant this* as soon as he has given me (!) a proof of understanding it." This is strong, a little *too* strong. Noordziek, armed with the jus promovendi with respect to bibliographers like Ruelens; it is about the same as if I allowed Kern and Hoffmann to occupy themselves with Sanscrit and Japanese. The Nestor of the bibliographers, Brunet, also, who had said with perfect truth of M. De Vries, "qui toutefois, il faut bien le connaître, a donné souvent de simples conjectures pour des faits positifs"—Brunet supplied Noordziek with "a proof that little judgment was required to get a great name as bibliographer."

In opposition to such ignoramuses, Noordziek agrees "willingly and absolutely" with the opinion of M. Vander Meersch, "that the larger towns of Italy, France, England, Spain, and Germany, owe to us the settlement of their first or principal printers, whereby the force of the argument—so often brought against us by the partisans of Guttenberg, that Mentz workmen had introduced the art of printing in most of the towns of Europe—falls entirely to the ground." He who dares to print such expressions in 1858, betrays either a disposition to renounce all feelings of shame, or such an absolute ignorance, that the author has to be treated, not as an antagonist, but as a patient. However, his voice was too strong for an invalid. Of the same nature is the following: "We have referred to the opinions given in favour of the Netherlands by Mariangelus Accursius, a Neapolitan (who knew nothing about the question, but who, at any rate, spoke only of xylographic Confessionalia!), Gucciardini of Florence (who only recorded an "on dit" in 1567!), Van Zuren, burgomaster, and Coornhert, pensionary of Haarlem, Ortels of Antwerp (all of the same value as Gucciardini!), Braun of Cologne, (who simply translates Gucciardini as far as the "fama" of Haarlem is concerned, but who says of Mentz: *To this town we owe the invention of typography!*), Von Eytzing of Austria (who also copies Gucciardini in 1583!), Quadus of Germany (who also copies Gucciardini in 1600), Atkyns of England (a reference in 1858 to the ridiculous Corsellis-fiction of Atkyns of the year 1664!), Conti of Milan (who copies, in 1572, his countryman, Gucciardini, but with addition of the year 1458, and the name of—*Gutenberg*!), Badius of Paris (who said *nothing* about Haarlem!), Mirtius, of the convent of Subiaco in Italy (who copies, in 1629, the foolish account of Conti!), &c. (&c. ??) all written *before* Junius' time, *some even a century earlier*." Does M. Noordziek really *believe* this? Does he *believe* indeed that of *all* those so-called proofs—of which not even one falls in the *first* half of the 16th century, of which the earliest was printed in 1561,—*some* were "written" a *century* before Junius, who wrote in 1568, and whose work was printed in 1588?! "And which evidences," Noordziek goes on, "are naturally linked with those given above?" He does not hesitate to answer: "Those of authors, contemporaries of Junius, who evidently drew from other sources, and finally those on whom Junius rests his account, and who never contradicted the historian, namely Gerard (?) Thomaszoon, M. Claes Lottijnszoon Gael, often sheriff of Haarlem, Quirinus Talesius, or M. Quirijn Dirkszoon." M. Noordziek!—one or two modest questions: which of those gentlemen you mention *wrote* on the Coster-legend? Who had to contradict Junius, whose book was printed after the death of all of them? Or was Gerrit Thomasz. to do it, who brought the first story into the world? To commit such literary deceptions, is *that* maintaining the honour of Holland?

From the herald who lied through ignorance or vanity, we turn for a moment to the result of his cry. We know from my correspondence with the Haarlem archivist, that the intended erection of a metal statue in honour of the sheriff Lourens Janszoon at Haarlem was the cause of a curious event, without the public having had any suspicion of it. After 1840, M. Joh. Enschedé (not aware that Koning himself had already made the discovery, but had dishonestly concealed it, and that De Vries had a copy of the documents at home) discovered the name of the chandler Lourens Janszoon Coster in the archives at Haarlem. As he was convinced that this name only answered to the vellum pedigree and the account of Junius, but nowise to the sheriff-innkeeper Lourens Janszoon, who died in 1439, he took the chandler to be the inventor of printing. Although by this, at least honest, interpretation of the tradition, he did not succeed in sweeping away the awful blundering (from Scriverius down to De Vries) with the sheriff—who never bore the family name Coster—because De Vries had entangled himself before the eyes of all Europe into a fable—yet M. Joh.

Enschedé prevented by his energy *the statue being erected to the sheriff, and the words Vir consularis and the well-known arms being placed on the pedestal.* When the archivist M. A. J. Enschedé rediscovered the Lourens Janszoon Coster, who positively lived in 1447, he also learned, a few years after the inauguration of the new sheriff, *that in 1856 a statue was erected at Haarlem* (in secret!) *to the chandler L. J. Coster.* Since the preface of Thijm to the work of Paeile (1867) the public also knows the chandler; since March, 1870, all Holland knows who *they now say* really figures in metal at Haarlem.

But after this revelation a most important question presents itself: *Did M. Noordziek know, or did he not know, anything of this secret change of persons?* According to his public acts, he did *not*. After the political events of 1848 had for a few years impeded his efforts on behalf of the new statue, he resumed the task in 1852 with fresh vigour. Among the means of filling the purse was also the publication of a work written expressly on the subject, illustrated with wood-cuts, and of which copies would be distributed among those who should contribute a certain sum to the undertaking, as an acknowledgment of their assistance. By the kindness of M. Steengracht van Duivenvoorde, the Head Committee (of the Coster-Committees) was put in possession, free of expense, of drawings by M. Bakker Korff, Jr., engraved in wood by M. Ball, and the text written by M. W. F. Otten. This original manuscript was accidentally missed for a long time; but found, after a new treatise had been compiled (by M. Noordziek) from the notes which had been preserved. This new treatise included all the interesting things which had happened since, and was published by Messrs. Enschedé and Sons at Haarlem, under the title of "Invention of the art of Printing." The consequence was that of this work more than 2,500 copies were sent in 1854 and 1855 by the permanent committee to the persons interested in it (Diary, pp. 80 and 81). Now, this work, so universally distributed, this really handsomely executed souvenir of the contributions of the Dutch to the Haarlem statue,[1] regards exclusively *the sheriff Louwerys Janszoon*, who was continually confused with the much later *L. J. Coster.* His crest, a pretty little dog, with his tongue hanging out, is represented on page 15; and on page 41 Johan Gänsfleisch, a Mentz knight, who never knew that there existed a town of Haarlem, is occupied with emptying, by candle-light, a type-case into a modern trunk. On page 54 the magisterial citizen is seated on a bench in the Hout, dressed in an ermine mantle, fumbling with a pocket-knife in his barky typography. This book of 1854 was followed by the solemn inauguration of the metal statue, July 16, 1856. A typographical exhibition was held on that occasion. The catalogue mentions, under No. 7: "Original pedigree of Lourens Jansz. Coster," the document which concerns a L. J. Coster, who in 1446 brought the first "print" into the world, and which, therefore, could be fathered on the *chandler* of that name and time. But it is followed by: "8. Receipt given and sealed by L. J. Coster, 1431." So the *innkeeper* Lourens Janszoon, who was never called Coster, was re-baptized. "9. Register of the graves (of 1439), in which the burial of L. J. Coster is noticed;" (read: in which the burial of the sheriff-innkeeper, Lourens Janszoon, is noticed). We may now compare the numbers 7 and 9 of this Barnum-museum.

At last, in 1858, the "Diary of the Coster-fêtes" was published. However curious the silence may be which prevails in this book regarding the imaginary inventor, yet the above-quoted numbers are mentioned on page 106, and therefore the *sheriff*, whose name is not *Coster*, figures also here. A passage in this last work has attracted my attention very much since I received M. A. J. Enschedé's letter. "In the beginning of 1856 the *inscriptions* were chiselled *on the pedestal*. As to how they should run, many negotiations, written as well as verbal, took place between the members of the Head Committee, and later, with regard to their form, with M. Tetar van Elven, *and lasted for more than three months.* In order to satisfy all opinions, it was

---

[1] Uitvinding der Boekdrukkunst. Haarlem, Joh. Enschedé en Zonen. 1854. 4to. [By Noordziek.]

decided, in Sept., 1855 (the chiseller of '56 therefore served only to cover the long period of the negociation about the most simple matter of the whole undertaking) that the contents should state what Holland demanded should be ascribed to Coster;— whom the statue represented;—and who had paid for the erection. These inscriptions now run:—

LOURENS JANSZOON COSTER *Homage* of the *Netherland Nation* MDCCCLVI	LOURENS JANSZOON COSTER *Hulde* van het *Nederlandsche Volk* MDCCCLVI	*Inventor* of the *Art of Printing* with *moveable Letters* cast of metal.	*Uitvinder* van de *Boekdrukkunst* met *beweegbare* uit metaal gegoten *Letters.*

So, without giving any reasons, without saying anything about those "opinions" which were to be "satisfied," M. Noordziek skips over the important question of the inscriptions. Curious! Why was the year 1423, chiselled already at Haarlem and officially fixed at the time of the fourth jubilee, omitted here? For the same reason, of course, why the title Vir consularis, and the lion rampant, with label, were omitted: because M. Joh. Enschedé *objected* to the sanction of the sheriff-humbug. But again; *did* M. Noordziek know *nothing* of all this!? Without clear evidence, charity compels me to regard him as one of the dupes, and not as one of the deceivers. If he had been initiated into the ridiculous quid-pro-quo of the legend, then the heading of this chapter should be altered. But did Noordziek *not* know the secret of this comedy—he, who had promulgated proclamations to the Dutch, who had written an entire Coster-archive for erecting a statue, who had buried himself under a mountain of scientific crimes to reach his aim—who, for the sake of the sheriff-innkeeper Louwerijs Janszoen, trampled upon logic, common-sense, and the reputation of scholars and dilettanti—did he *not* know who was put in 1856 into the place of the phantasm of his enthusiasm, his labour and toil? if not, then this cruel fact should awaken him from his dream, should convince him that he has laboured for a chimera and not for truth. Or are we allowed to speak of *history*, when people can be mistaken for three centuries long in the person who is said to have invented typography at Haarlem?! Can we imagine for a single minute that we could burn all apologies for the Haarlem pretence, from Scriverius down to the Arguments of De Vries, in order to put in 1870 *another* hero in the story of 1588?! It is a supposition that would make any one giddy. But whatever some people may be able to put up with, it is certain that the history of civilization is without example of such a NATIONAL MYSTIFICATION as took place at Haarlem in 1856. The inscription on the pedestal should have been: "Homage of the *deceived* Netherland nation." Homage to whom? Just as it falls: those who allow themselves to be deceived by the botching of Junius' account, may think that the sheriff Lourens Janszoon, who died in 1489, stands there; but those who understand the account well, can only think that it is the chandler Lourens Janszoon Coster, who still lived in 1483. M. Noordziek, at any rate, cuts the saddest figure with regard to this monumental smuggling; he wrote in his "Diary": "Junius mentions such particular circumstances respecting the inventor (!) that they leave not the least doubt about the identity of his person, and all have been confirmed in a remarkably curious way (!!) by renewed investigations in old archives (!). The number of these particulars shows that Junius pointed out the right person as the inventor, and that he added so many explanations (!) *to prevent his being confused with any other of the same name*. So much has been already published and discovered about this our ancestor, that, if we collected and explained it, *a very circumstantial and important history of the meritorious and curious man*, completer than the one existing, might be compiled." Is this not dreadfully tragic? Did not the chandler sing himself the hymn of his promotion, which was preserved in the "Diary"? It runs (p. 298):—

> "I sit in a metal garb,
> They say I look very handsome and gallant;
> All Holland shouts round my statue,
> No German is able to rob me of my glory."

M. Noordzick! assist us in removing the shame, as a penalty of your senseless zeal! Just as my criticism is a propitiation to Netherland science for the shameful dishonouring of Gutenberg and the abusing of truth, so is it your sacred duty to repair before your death the wrong you have done at the cost of our true reputation in other countries. If the stone man erected in 1722, in an uncritical time, were still standing on the Market-place, the difficulty would be very small. He could have been removed without much trouble, and we could have given him an everlasting bath in the river; but the bronze statue, inaugurated as sheriff-woodengraver-prototypographer in 1856, exposed as chandler-typographer in 1870, is a matter which ought to be seriously taken in hand, for in the face of these dates we are not allowed to refer to what our uncritical forefathers have done in their good-hearted innocence. In the stone statue we have to do with a *fable*, in the metal one with a *lie*.

XXI.

METAMORPHOSIS OF THE LEGEND.

BEFORE summing up the investigation, we ought to notice the gyrations whereby the flake became a snow-heap, which buried truth and honesty for three centuries long. I solicit urgently no superficial, but a calm and repeated reading for this apparently dry review, which may save many the perusal of a great number of books. There lies an overpowering eloquence in the chronology of the Haarlem fictions. I place the dates, the authors, and their opinions together, adding only the general observation, that all these authors have never *proved* anything, but always *said* something. No wonder that they have said *much!* Let us pay attention to the metamorphosis of every separate part of the fable, of the curious growth of every seed sown by a Haarlem innkeeper in the 16th century in his pedigree. The fictitious year 1446 retrograded to 1420, and Lourens Coster's metempsychosis moves also, not very philosophically, backwards instead of forwards; *the first print!* of which nobody knows anything—dear me! what a library has sprung from this "first print"! how liberally has it been translated on the pedestal of 1856! The innkeeper, however, does not seem to have been guilty of the robbery of the honour of foreigners; it was Junius who formed a school of thoughtless slanderers—so unpardonably thoughtless, that Koning, who acknowledges that the story of Junius is entirely based on the story of the bookbinder Cornelis, knows, even better than this bed-fellow of the thief, his christian name, and changes Jan into Frielo (a Mentz knight, by the way, who was dead at the time of the invented theft). All these metamorphoses not only destroy the "changeling" of the Haarlemers, but they contain their mutual process of destruction and falsification.

1546.[1] Gerrit Thomasz.: *Lourens Janszoon* COSTER brings the first "print" into the world, anno 1446.

---

[1] This 1546 is my conjecture, in explanation of the 1446 of the pedigree, for I am unable to find any other reason why Gerrit Thomasz. pitched upon *that* year for the first print, but that he, while devising his pedigree, thought a round century would be very appropriate to begin with. The supposition of the year 1446 having been placed there afterwards, after the document had existed for some time, just as other tamperings had taken place, is excluded—1st, by the word *Anno*, of the same hand with what goes before: what is said about Lourens Janszoon Coster is *one* whole; 2nd, if Junius had been followed, they would have stuck to the year 1440, maintained so long at Haarlem; 3rd, if an ignorant person had deducted the 128 years from the story of Junius *or* from the date of the preface, written 1570, changed into 1575, *or* from the year of the publication 1588, we would have got 1442, 1447 or 1460. The whole character of the document, however, answers to my supposition.

1560 (?). Jan Van Zuren: some person practises *for many years*, during the period *x* + *y*, the art of printing at Haarlem, until it was brought by *a foreigner* to Mentz.

1561. Dirk Volkertsz. Coornhert: The art of printing is, it is said, invented at Haarlem in a very crude manner in the year *x*, and afterwards carried off to Mentz by *an unfaithful servant*.

1567. Luigi Guicciardini: The Haarlemers assert that the art of printing was invented in their town, and brought, *after the death of the inventor* who left the art *unfinished*, to Mentz by a *servant*, who was received there with open arms. I don't know, however, whether this is true.

1568 ('88). Hadrianus Junius: A certain *Lourens Janszoon Coster* invented, on occasion of a walk in the Hout in 1440, the xylographic art of printing; he printed with it the Dutch "Spiegel der behoudenis," used afterwards also metal letters, *i.e.* practised *typography*, but was robbed on Christmas-night of the year 1441, of his invention and printing-office by *Johan*, probably *Faust*, who, together with all the *materials*, irreparably transported also the *invention* to Mentz.

1600. Petrus Bertius: L. J. *Coster* invented the art of printing by means of *fixed wood-cuts* (*i.e.* xylography), but the threefold villain (trifurcifer), *Johan Faust*, stole the art from him.

1609. Joseph Scaliger: The art of printing commenced with *wood-cuts*. My grandmother, Veronica Lodronia, possessed a small xylographic primer, much older than the earliest printed book known. This book, however, was destroyed thirty-six years after her death by a hunting-dog. (That grandmother died in 1512 or 1513, and Scaliger was born in 1540, so that he was a boy of eight or nine years of age when the bibliophagus-huntingdog, probably "bribed by Fust," tore the curious book to pieces. "This account, declared by many to be a mere effusion of Scaligerian family pride, afterwards almost generally rejected as a very improbable tradition of no historical value, *met at the time with implicit belief from most of the scholars of our country*."—De Vries.)

1628. Petrus Scriverius: Laurens Janszoon, *sheriff* of Haarlem in 1431, invented, on occasion of a walk, *xylography*, and printed the *Biblia pauperum* in 1428. He was, after the invention of *typography*, robbed in 1440 by *Johan Gutenberg*. " Junius *has . . . his faults, and cannot be held free from inadvertence*. According to what he says, the letters of the 'Spieghel onser behoudenisse,' were cut in wood, or every single letter was made of wood. Lourens, it is said, cut a sufficient quantity of these letters of the bark of beeches and put them together. But whether the Spieghel be the right Peter I doubt very much, and believe (that it was the Biblia pauperum). The types of the Spieghel were not made of wood, but of lead or tin. That these letters were cast and not cut is as evident and clear as the sun at mid-day. So that if we wished to say more about it, we should seem to light a candle by daylight. I omit even that it is totally incredible, on such a small scale, that each single letter should have been of wood, and, moreover, of the bark of trees: which are too weak and soft to bear the force of printing. No, printing was done at first in this way: a whole leaf was cut on a separate block and printed . . . As, for instance, Grammatica Donati. But to think that every letter was separately cut on wood . . . that is not so. And Junius ought to have paid more attention to this point, if he has seen the Spieghel himself; and if not, he has been misinformed."

While Scriverius thus by his own invention destroys that of Junius, he unwittingly fabricates at the same time a monster xylographer at Haarlem. For inquiries in the Haarlem archives have shown that Lourens Janszoon *Coster* was chandler and innkeeper at Haarlem from 1436, and left the place in 1483; but that the sheriff-innkeeper Lourens Janszoon died there in 1439. The fictitious Haarlem Lourens Janszoon *Coster* since Scriverius is, therefore, not only unhistorical, but also a full-grown and two-headed monster.

1630. The Haarlem printer, Adriaan Rooman, publishes a wood-cut in honour of Coster, with the inscription: M. S. *Viro Consulari* Laurentio Costero, Harlemensi,

Alteri Cadmo, & artis typographicæ, circa Annum Domini 1430, Inventori primo, bene de literis ac toto orbe merenti hanc Q. L. C. Q. statuam, quia æream non habuit pro monumento posuit civis gratiss. Adrianus Romanus Typographus. A. 1630.

1639. Marcus Zuerius Boxhorn: Laurens Coster began to print block-books in 1420.

1654. The 5th of Oct. the town of Haarlem buys at the Hague, for three hundred guilders, a small box containing the *Ars moriendi*, the *Canticum*, the *Speculum*, the *Apocalypse* (all gradually fathered on the mythic xylographer L. J. Coster, and provided with false new titles and the engraving of Rooman), three incunabula of Mentz, the Cologne chronicle, and a copy of "De proprieteyten der dingen, Haerlem, 1485." Misson invented afterwards the fable that the Dutch Spiegel, wrapped in silk, was preserved in a silver box, of which each member of the government had a key. But in 1706 the book was shown to John Bagford, Ballard, and Murray, in the summer-house of the head-master of the Latin grammar-school; it was in a wooden box, of which the servant had the key, in order to show the relique in the absence of the master. (Van Oosten de Bruyn said in 1765 that this copy was preserved in the town-library, in a glass case, of which the school directors, trustees of the library, and the head-master, had each a key.)

1722. 18 Aug. a stone statue was inaugurated in the Hortus Medicus at Haarlem, with the inscription : Æ. M. S. | Laurentio Costero | Harlemensi | Viro Consulari, | typographiæ | inventori vero, | monumentum hoc | erigi curavit | Collegium Medicum | Anno 1722. (This statue was removed in 1801 to the Market-place, but stands at present again in its old place.)[1]

1733. P. Vlaming: "Laurens Koster, inventor of printing, which fact is disputed by many, but may be confirmed by new proofs, in addition to those of Junius and Scriverius; because some years ago (1654!) a trunk was sold at the Hague, containing many things which had been concealed (!) a long time among the family of Koster, without Junius, Donza, Scriverius, or other partisans of Koster's invention, knowing anything about it (!) This box was bought for the town of Haarlem, and is at present preserved by the burgomasters of that town. This information may some day afford an opportunity for a more elaborate treatise on the subject."

1740. Seiz: The Haarlem sheriff, Laurens Jansen, invented in 1428, on a walk in the Hout, *xylography*, and printed with this art in 1431 the Temptationes Dæmonis, the *Biblia pauperum* in 1432, the *Canticum Canticorum* in 1433, the *Apocalypse* in 1434, a *Donatus* in 1435. He printed in 1436, with moveable letters cut in lead, and in 1439, a Donatus and the *Spiegel der behoudenis* with letters cast of lead. The report of the Haarlem invention attracted Gutenberg that year to Haarlem: he learns there to *cut*, but not to *cast*, letters, packs himself off in 1440 with "some of the most important tools of Koster," and carries them to Mentz. In 1442 Koster cast better letters of tin, and prints in 1443 the *Spiegel* again, in 1444 the *Speculum*, in 1450 the *Historia Alexandri Magni*. Until 1456 Koster was "busily engaged in printing books," so that the report of it came to the ears of Henry VI., King of England, in consequence of which the English also pilfered the art of printing from Haarlem. After the death of Laurens Koster, c. 1467, his printing-office ceased to exist, and his workmen began to establish printing-offices here and there in the

---

[1] Gothofredus Clarmontius: De statua laureata, quam collegium medicum Laurentio Costero, typographiæ inventori primo erexit. Amstelaed. 1723. 4to.

Laurier-krans, gevlogten om 't hoofd van Laurens Koster, eerste uitvinder der boekdrukkunst binnen Haarlem. Haarlem, 1726, 4to., with the twice falsified pedigree of Coster.

Willem Hessen: Parnasvreugde over het derde eeuwjaar van de geboorte der drukkunst door Laurens Koster. Haarlem, 1731. 4to.

Arnold Hoogvliet placed, however, the year of the invention some years afterwards again "about 1440." The statue of 1722 had, however, nothing to do with a "jubilee," as is evident from the following brochure :—

Romeyn de Hooge en de Hortus Medicus met het standbeeld van L. Jsz. Coster door Dr. C. Ekama. Haarlem, 1869. 8vo.

Netherland towns. "I wished and felt obliged to relate all this so circumstantially and accurately, *in order to correct, to stop, and to do away with the many different, cripple, confused, and contradictory accounts* of Junius, Bertius, Boxhorn, Van Meteren, Scriverius, and *those who copy them*, and whereby the world has been for more than 200 years led to think that these first Haarlem books were wood-cuts, or printed from wooden blocks, or with wooden letters, and therefore not belonging to the proper art of printing.

In 1740 a silver medal was struck in honour of " Laur. Jansz. Koster, Harl. Typ. Inv. 1428"; a second in honour of " Laur. Costerus Jan. f. Sen. Harl. Typ. Inv. 1428"; a third in honour of " Laurentivs Costervs Harlemensis, primus artis typographicae inv. circa A. 1440"; a fourth with the inscription: "M. S. Harlemvm, 1740. Typographia hic primvm inventa circa ann. 1440." We got therefore in 1740 a choice between an invention in 1428 (Scriverius' fable) and in 1440 (Junius' fable). But no one knew who was meant by the impossible Consul and Senator L. J. Coster.[1]

1743. Gerardus Meerman: L. J. *Coster* prints in 1443 the second [first] Dutch *Spiegel*.

1757. Gerardus Meerman: "*The pretentious assertion of the invention of the art of printing by Laur. Coster begins to lose credit more and more.* And all that has been told us about it by Seiz, and incorporated in Wagenaar's Hist. of Holland, are mere suppositions, and *the chronology of Coster's inventions and enterprises is a romantic fiction*. I think that the matter is sufficiently settled, and that the laurel ought to be torn from Coster's head."[2]

1761 (1765). Gerardus Meerman: *Louwerijs Janszoen, sheriff* in 1422, 1423, 1431, *treasurer* in 1426, 1430, 1434, *sexton* of the cathedral at Haarlem, born a nobleman, as bastard of one of the Brederodes, c. 1370 (because he seems to have had in 1440 a great grand-daughter, Grietje Peters, according to the supplemented pedigree of Gerrit Thomasz., who speaks of quite *another* person), who died between 1484 and 1440,—invented and practised in 1428 or 1430 the art of printing with *moveable wooden* letters. What Junius writes of Coster's invention of leaden and tin letters *is devoid of all truth*. Neither ought the firstlings of printing to be classed with xylography, *which nowise deserves the name of printing*.

Laurens was robbed on Christmas night, 1440, by *Johan Gensfleisch the elder*. The nobleman-sheriff-sexton-woodengraver-printer, Louwerijs Janszoen, printed only the first [read, last] Dutch undated edition of the Spiegel, with *moveable wooden* letters. The other (earlier!) editions, with metal letters, are of his *heirs*.

1765. Van Oosten de Bruyn: The sheriff, Lourens Janszoon, surnamed *Koster* (as he was *employed* as sacristan [Koster] of the cathedral, and *not* because his family possessed the sacristanship hereditarily, as Junius says of L. J. Coster), according to a new discovery (namely, his arms) of "distinguished birth," invented the art of printing between 1420 and 1430. "It is *impossible* to know either the exact year or the day of the invention, and we had therefore better leave it undecided, in order not to provoke the ridicule of some persons at such an unproved accuracy." I don't know precisely whether the invention consisted of *wooden* or *metal* letters, neither is it of any consequence, but the Spiegel has been printed with cast types. The block-books, which are preserved at Haarlem, have *also* been printed by Laurens Janszoon. His servant N. N. robbed him, assisted by a *second* thief, "who carried off the stolen tools."

"Laurens Janszoon, walking on a certain afternoon in the Hout, accidentally cut some letters of the bark of a beech, which he arranged reversely into lines and

---

[1] Some years before two (vroedschap) medals had been struck in reference to two Haarlem legends. "The remembrance, both of the capture of Damiate and of the invention of the art of printing, we find preserved on the two (following) medals, which it is customary to present to the members of the town-council at their meeting." They bear the words: Typographia. Harlemum. S. C.—Cf. Beschryving der nederlandsche historiepenningen ... door Mr. Gerard van Loon, 's Hage. 1723. Fol. L, 160. The invention of "Laurens Jansz. Koster" is there put at 1440.

[2] Het leeven van Jan Wagenaar. Benevens eenige brieven van en aan denzelven. Amsterdam. 1776, 8vo.

pressed upon paper; he found that the figures of those letters were impressed on the paper: be it that the hardness of the wood had only made a blank impression on the paper, or that by some sap of the wood, some colour had come upon it. For—that Laurens should have wrapped those letters in, or put them on a piece of paper, and fallen asleep afterwards; whereupon he, awakening, found that the paper, by the damp air or rain, had got wet, and the letters were impressed reversely, with some dye from the wood, on the paper, *as Scriverius' imagination was pleased to invent*, and in which he was seriously followed by Chr. Seiz—that is not to be found in Junius. Laurens, however, proceeding from this simple accident, cut in a similar way *whole lines in wood.*" . . . Perfectly understood! Laurens, therefore, discovered *printing* on a walk, after it had been known already for centuries.

1768. The Haarlem type-founder and printer, Johannes Enschedé, got made for him at Antwerp two statues, and placed them at the back of his house; the one with the inscription: "Lourentio Joannis f. *Scab. Harlem.* Artis typogr. inventori, Jo. Enschedius, typographus, et typorum fusor, hanc statuam prototypographo grati animi monumentum, posuit Harl. 1768"; the other: "Viro immortali, Hadr. Junio, ob servatam de inventione artis typogr. historiæ veritatem, Jo. Enschedius, typographus statuam hanc L. M. Q. P. 1768." About the legend he writes: "Loureus Jausen Koster was the first letter- and figure-cutter in *wooden blocks*, and also, in a defective way, the first founder of types of tin. But he used no *wooden* moveable letters, as [Junius and] later, and some still living scholars [Meerman], who know nothing of the mechanism of type-founding, assert, and who *therefore greatly swerve from the path of simple truth*. Experienced stamp-cutters and type-founders could judge better of the firstlings of printing than such scholars."

1809. Van Westreenen: "A Dutch citizen discovers, before 1436, the art of printing books with moveable wooden letters, and prints with them a school-book, called *Donatus*. It is indisputable that the efforts of the Dutch citizen extended *no further* than the *wooden moveable* letters." "The theft at Haarlem is a mere guess."[1]

1815. H. W. Tydeman: The Haarlem sheriff Laurens Janszoon, surnamed Koster, born in 1364, married Katrijn Andriesdochter, and died in 1434; he invented between 1420 and 1430 the art of printing with moveable *wooden* letters. No connexion between Haarlem and Mentz can be shown, for it appears from a document of 1441 that Johan Gensfleisch the elder made payments from property managed by him: a "strong evidence" that Meerman's supposition, that he had been the thief, "*is totally inconsistent.*" But could not one of the typographers *Jan Meydenbach* or *Jan Petersheim* have been the man?[2]—What a jurist that professor was! The monster "L. J. Koster," is, according to this account, already 119 years old at his departure from Haarlem in 1483.

1816. Jacobus Koning: Lourens Janszoon, sacristan of the cathedral, in 1417 officer of the Haarlem National Guard, member of the council in the same year and in 1418, 1423, 1429, 1432, *sheriff* in 1422, 1423, 1428, 1429 and 1431, treasurer in 1421, 1426, 1430, 1434, great-grandfather in 1440, and therefore born cc. 1370, died c. 1439, invented *xylography* and *typography*, and printed in 1430 the first [last] Dutch Spiegel with cast types. All this I am able to prove à priori by undated early printed books. The thief was *Frielo Gensfleisch.*

1817. G. van Lennep: The Essay of Koning has done *more harm than benefit to the cause of Haarlem.*

1822. Dr. Abraham De Vries: Lourens Janszoon (Koster) did *not* invent xylography, but in any case *typography* c. 1423. "The time of *Koster's* first experiment, or the birth-year of the invention, HITHERTO TOTALLY UNCERTAIN, can now be fixed

---

[1] Verhandeling over de uitvinding der boekdrukkunst: in Holland oorspronkelijk uitgedacht, te Straatsburg verbeterd en te Mentz voltooid; door W. H. J. van Westreenen. 's Hage. 1809. 8vo.

[2] Mnemosyne. Mengelingen voor wetenschappen en fraaije letteren; verzameld door Mr. H. W. Tydeman en N. G. van Kampen. I. Dord. 1815. 8vo. (pp. 123—216: Verhandeling over de uitvinding der boekdrukkunst door Laurens Jansz. Koster te Haarlem).

pretty accurately with *perfect historical certainty*. It cannot be put earlier than 1420, as *Koster was at that time already grandfather;* and not later than 1425, because already in the beginning of 1426, *no such walk* as Junius (by the year 1440!!) mentions, *could any longer take place in the Hout*. It is now A PERFECTLY PROVED CASE, that the first experiments in printing of our ingenious and meritorious countryman must have taken place before the year 1426 (when the Hout was cut down, and not even chips were left to afford an ingenious innkeeper an opportunity for inventing the art of printing), and that they date, THEREFORE, from a considerably earlier time than the first experiments of the Germans." How "historical"! "We have at last succeeded in discovering the original notice of *Koster's* death in the church registers. On the list of the dead, for whom payments were made in 1439 to the church for tolling the bells and digging graves, we find the following item: 'Item *Lou Jans soon* breet II. gul. cloe en graf.' Hereby, '*our Koster*' is meant." Anathema! who doubts it. "The work of the learned, but not very judicious, Meerman, has done more harm to the cause of Haarlem than all its antagonists."

1823. On the spot in the Hout where this Koster in 1423 cut the first letters in the bark of a beech, a memorial stone is erected. On the sides we find, among other things, the arms of "L. J. Koster, accurately copied from his seal, as it occurs on divers documents sealed by him as *sheriff*." The Dutch inscription runs : In honour of Lourens Jansz. Koster, inventor of the art of printing, (erected) by Burgomasters and Councillors of the town of Haarlem. On the IV. Jubilee 1823. Moreover, three medals were struck in silver and bronze, of which one gives the period of the invention as 1420—1425. Holland celebrates a ridiculous jubilee, and Costerianism its first orgies, to the surprise of the ghosts of Thomasz., Junius, Lourens Coster, and Louwerijs Janszoon !

1824. In the month of June a memorial stone is erected at the expense of King William I., in the cathedral at Haarlem, against the chief pillar of the south tower, consisting of a black marble slab, with an inscription in gilt letters: Honori. ct. meritis. | Laurentii. Jani. Costeri. | Harlemensis. | festo. sæculari. | quarto. | inventæ. *typographiæ*. | celebrata. Harlemi. | A. D. X. Julii. Anni CIƆIƆCCCXXIII. | Augustissimo. Belgii. Rege. | Guilielmo. Primo. |

1824. G. van Lennep : " In the 'Memorials of the fourth jubilee of the invention of the art of printing,' the first and chief duty of an historian (to be accurate and impartial; to tell simply what has happened, without concealing, distorting, or mutilating the truth with the view of pleasing the party to which he belongs, has been miserably violated." " The so-called new evidences of M. de Vries prove nothing, or at least very little." " The compiler of the Memorials says : ' We had expected that the anticipated celebration at Haarlem should rouse the jealousy of the Germans ; meanwhile they remained silent at the announcement, approach, and celebration of the jubilee.' Yet we read in the Neue Maintzer Zeitung of 26th June, 1823, a fortnight before the celebration : The *Letterbode* contains the following article : The government of Haarlem has resolved that on the 10th of the following month, the fourth jubilee of the invention of the art of printing shall be celebrated in that town, &c. But a fable, when it is celebrated by a puppet-show, can thereby be made more ridiculous, but never true. We are of the opinion of the French scholars, that it is fortunate for Mentz that M. Koning exposed, by his work, the superficiality (Seichtheit) of the basis on which Haarlem tries to claim the honour of the invention. This work, which contains arguments of which a schoolboy would feel ashamed, &c. We (Van Lennep) have pointed out the untruths of the Memorials to the Dutch nation, whom *we could not tolerate to be taken in so shamefully*."[1]

---

[1] [Mr. G. van Lennep:] Aanmerkingen op de Gedenkschriften wegens het vierde eeuwgetijde van de uitvinding der Boekdrukknnst, door Lourens Janszoon Koster. 's Gravenhage. 1824. 8vo.
Essai d'une liste chronologique des ouvrages et dissertations concernant l'histoire de l'imprimerie en Belgique et en Hollande. Par L. F. Hoffmann. Bruxelles. 1859. 8vo. Cf. Neuer Anzeiger für Bibliographie und Bibliothekwissenschaft. Herausgegeben von Dr. J. Petzholdt. 1865 (pp. 273—89, 1867 pp. 317—22.)

1833. Jac. Scheltema: The sheriff Lourens Janszoon, not at all an *innkeeper* (as the Germans had incontrovertibly *proved* from the supplement of Koning) but *sacristan* of the cathedral (what Scheltema felt bound to acknowledge himself was *not* proved) invented and exercised typography from 1420—1439. He commenced, however, with xylography. Is perhaps the brief-prenter Henne *Cruse*, whom we find at Mentz in 1440, the thief who robbed us of the invention? The Germans have to prove that it was *not* he (!).

1841. Dr. Abr. De Vries: The sheriff *L. J. Coster* has been no *sacristan* at all. His "cause" has nothing to fear but from those "who, unprepared, without any preliminary, thorough investigation, and incompetent, venture to come forward as its defenders, and in their ignorance not knowing how to distinguish the true from the false, the suitable from the useless, deny what ought to be acknowledged, grant what should be disputed. And senselessly sticking to arguments incapable of proof, deciding nothing in the question, give an appearance of doubt, intricacy, and obscurity to a subject which is in itself simple, clear, and evident, but, in the long contest between its numerous assailants and defenders, has been buried under so much dust of useless learning and misunderstanding, cavillings and untruths, that it is impossible to recognise it without removing that confused ballast. Once free, however, from that which does not belong to, but confuses it, there is needed only a clear and accurate indication of the real and well-proved facts of the history. We have to consider before all, that the question concerns no object of speculation, which can be settled by guesses and reasonings à priori (hear, hear!), but an event that happened, a *factum historicum*, which can be decided only by historical proofs (bravo!). Let us confine ourselves strictly to the real point of the question, to the proper case, which is to be proved; to the maintenance of that honour of our worthy countryman to which the verdict of history (!) evidently entitles him, laying himself no claims to any thing but the acknowledgment of the merit, which the most credible historians (? since Gerrit Thomaszoon !) positively adjudge to him: THAT HE IS THE INVENTOR OF TYPOGRAPHY, OF THE PROPER ART OF PRINTING ; THE FIRST WHO INVENTED AND PRACTISED THE ART OF PRINTING WITH MOVEABLE AND CAST LETTERS, AND SO GAVE THE EXAMPLE TO MENTZ. We ought not to ascribe to him what history (!) does not sanction. We ought not to make him an artist in drawing and engraving, *an inventor and the first practiser of xylography or printing with wooden blocks*, or an engraver of wood-cuts under which he also printed the text—for which (just as little as for the other fables which De Vries goes on to serve up) *not a single evidence can be found in any historian*. Let no one attach too much value to guesses and probabilities, founded on speculations and comparisons of early printed books of uncertain date and origin [*as Koning has done*], nor forget that those can lead to nothing but fallible and questionable inferences (hear!), and that the opinion of the most esteemed judge on this point, is, as experience teaches us, very uncertain and different. Let no one indulge too positive decisions as to which incunabula are the productions of Coster's press, but those which have been distinctly mentioned by Zell (!) and Junius ; nor must we build arguments and conclusions on vague suppositions (bravo!) as to the condition, the time of the continuance of, and the works issued from, Coster's press after his death, about which history contains not a single notice; but (observe !) let every one assert with force and energy what no thorough and impartial judgment could deny in good faith, that of all accounts concerning the history of the invention of the art of printing, there is none, decidedly none, which may in any way be compared in authority (!), simplicity (!!), completeness (!!!), and well-proved accuracy (!!!!), with that of Zell (who in 1499 purely historically says that typography was invented at Mentz 1440—50 by *Johan Gutenberg!*), and Junius (who asserts in 1568 that a certain art of *wood*-printing was invented at *Haarlem* in 1440, and not, as De Vries said, in 1428, by Lourens Janszoon *Coster!*), who declare for Holland, Haarlem, and *Coster*."

1848. Noordziek : " The whole protension of attributing to Coster the greatest part of the xylographic works which are found at Haarlem *is an error*. The supposition (of Koning) that Coster had only got through them the idea of typography is again a deviation from history; and it is stated nowhere that the descendants of *Laurens Janszoon* continued, with success, printing, which had yielded profits to its inventor." The same man, in the same book: "Coster returned every time to the ordinary manner of the printers of cards and images, to the impression with fixed letters, without ceasing, however, to occupy himself with perfecting his first discovery, which had appeared preferable to him in every respect." Of all imaginable nonsense the most nonsensical nonsense!

1845. Dr. A. De Vries: The sheriff Lourens Janszoon was *really* a xylographer, and his heirs have *really* printed.

1847. Noordziek: Oh land, land, land, listen! "Before the whole world (before the *whole* WORLD!), we should, according to *my* opinion, bring down upon ourselves a well-deserved blame of lukewarmness and indifference, if we calmly *tolerated* the Germans continuing to make a show with such a magnificent statue in honour of the imitator of the inventor, without the erection among us—a nation financially so powerful—of a proportionate mark of honour to the *real inventor*!" Oh! all ye ends of the earth, listen to the word of Balaam, the son of Beor!

M. Joh. Enschedé, meanwhile, has learned that in no case can there be any question of the sheriff-innkeeper, Lourens Janszoon (who had been bandied about for two centuries and a-quarter), but that the only Haarlem pretender-inventor of typography, who could be taken into consideration, is the later (non-sheriff) *chandler*, LOURENS JANSZOON COSTER. Seeing the danger approach of the erection of a metal statue, he opposes the repetition of the sheriff-crowing of 1823. The result of this honest, but, alas! too compassionate opposition, has been that Dr. De Vries should make no mention of the *sheriff* on the pedestal, and that M. Enschedé should not reveal the *chandler* as long as De Vries lived. In public the Coster-community, deceived by their priests, went on sacrificing to the *sheriff*.[1] M. Enschedé was weak enough to look silently on this imposture, so that it was only disclosed in 1870, in consequence of my criticism.

1848. J. J. F. Noordziek: "To this man ought undoubtedly a worthy statue to be erected, at the expense of the nation, which should represent the inventor in all his grandeur, and be superior in every respect to that of his antagonist, Gutenberg." "Coster, who was sheriff of his native town, ought to be represented in the dress of a magistrate of the 15th century."

1851. A club (Kamer der Wyngaardranken) at Haarlem place a memorial stone in front of the rebuilt Coster-house, with the inscription: "Costeri Aedes typographiæ natales." The picture which has been there until the rebuilding had as inscription: "M. S. | Viro Consulari | Laurentio Costero, | Harlemensi, | Typographiæ | Inventori . | circa annum | MCCCCXXX." The committee entrusted with the business of the memorial stone put for the first time a stop to the bandying about of the fictitious year of the fictitious invention.

1851. Dr. A. De Vries: "In the beginning the art of printing was, as we know (!), secretly practised for a long time, not only during the lifetime of the inventor, but also many years after his death (!), as a trade, it is said, in manuscripts (!), the only

---

[1] "The Netherland people," Noordziek wrote, "prepared themselves (July, 1856) to raise shouts of joy, which would resound far and wide, without mixing with them any bitterness against the *conquered foreign countries*, but acknowledging in conciliating spirit what was in accordance with truth and justice." What was that "shouting" people taken in! They danced round the new statue, which *came instead* of the old sheriff-statue, which it was "to replace" (these are the official words). I give also some proofs, derived from Noordziek's own description of "the illuminations of the town" at the occasion of the inauguration. The decorations of the railway station contained, "in a laurel of immortals, and underneath a crown, *the year of the invention of printing*, 1423," and "the arms of Lourens Janszoon Coster," *i.e.* the *lion* of the *innkeeper* Lourens Janszoon, but NOT the *dove* of the *chandler* Lourens Janszoon *Coster*. On the memorial-stone in the wood were the words: "From Haarlem's flower-garden the light arose over the earth," with the year 1423, "adopted as that in which Coster made the invaluable invention of printing with *loose, cast metal letters*." Very bad! In 1823 the year 1423 was adopted, because the trees in the wood had been cut down in 1426, and Coster could therefore not have taken his inventor's-walk later: there was not enough beech-wood. But in 1856 this whole history is muffled, and the invention of *metal* letters in 1423 put instead!

trade which was known at that time. They (the innkeeper Louwerijs Janszoen!) made all they printed as much like the handwriting of those days as possible, and sold the impressions at great profit as manuscript (!). The law-suit at Mentz, between Faust and Gutenberg, revealed (!) the secret of the (Haarlem!) art. From that time the printers in Germany and elsewhere began to advertise (!) publicly the productions of their press, and the printers disclosed their name, the place, and the time of printing. Books, provided with such inscriptions, were soon brought and spread into Holland, and the secret which had hitherto been so carefully kept concealed became very soon known (!). All reasons for further secrecy were now removed (!). *The whole history of the invention was disclosed* (!!). The busy trade in *so-called manuscripts*, which had so long (!) been carried on at Haarlem with such great profits, now appeared to have been a secret printing-office (!). People saw that the pretended MSS., sold there, were printed books (!). The man who began this *secret* trade, now (when?) discovered, had been very well known and esteemed during his lifetime. He had been an active and influential (!) member of the municipal government, had deserved well in important political matters, and was still alive in the *grateful* remembrance of his fellow-townsmen (on account of the imputed *swindler's-secret*, his *inn*, or his delegation with other members of the council?!). He was assisted and succeeded in this trade (swindling) by his son-in-law Thomas Pieterszoon, who, being from the beginning a partner of the secret, had been zealously labouring in behalf of the success of the business; he lived, and continued the paternal business (of innkeeper?), in the paternal house by inheritance." Has there ever been bungling like this since the creation?

1854. Noordziek: The SHERIFF *Lourens Janszoon*, whose seal "proves most incontrovertibly that *Coster* (!) belonged to the greatly-distinguished family of Brederode, descended from our ancient Dutch Counts, invented the art of printing in the year *x*, but he was robbed by (the dead) *Johan Gensfleisch* the elder, also in the year *x*." "The circumstantial indication of the man whom Junius meant, makes a supposition of confusion and mistake as to the person, the most *obvious absurdity*."

1856. The metal statue at Haarlem is inaugurated; it is decorated with the name *Lourens Janszoon* COSTER, but without the least indication of the time of his invention. At the typographical exhibition, however, are found the documents of the insane Costerian dualism: 1st, the falsified pedigree of *Coster*; 2nd, a receipt, sealed by the sheriff *Lourens Janszoon*; 3rd, the register of the graves, containing the notice of his burial in 1439.

All Holland is feasting in honour of the *sheriff-innkeeper* Louwerijs Janszoon, quasi-inventor at Haarlem in 1423.

1862. Dr. A. De Vries: The sheriff Lourens Janszoon invented the art of printing, and practised *xylography*.

1867. J. A. Alberdingk Thijm: The Haarlem *City-chandler*, Lourens Janszoon *Coster*, who occurs in the municipal accounts of 1441—1447, invented the art of printing. He is *identical* with the sheriff *Lourens Janszoon*, who died in 1439!—!—! —!—!—!—!—!—!—!

This insane self-ridiculing of Costerianism was a well-merited beginning of the end. The Haarlem monster was now concocted as sheriff-innkeeper-chandler-sexton-sacristan - engraver - shopkeeper - xylographer - typographer - swindler in manuscripts—grandfather in 1420—dead in 1439—alive in 1447—departed from Haarlem in 1483.

1870. M. A. J. Enschedé, archivist of Haarlem, states that the statue erected in 1856 in honour of the SHERIFF-innkeeper *Lourens Janszoon* does not concern him, but the CHANDLER (-innkeeper) Lourens Janszoon *Coster*, of later date.

The Coster-deception is exposed in the "Nederlandschen Spectator" from Dec., 1869, till May, 1870; but it is, even after this disclosure, calmly maintained by the town of Haarlem, as if *nothing* had happened!

XXII.

A MUNICIPAL SHOW-BOOTH.

LET us review, in conclusion, what is shewn in the town-hall at Haarlem to natives and foreigners. I shall observe in this enumeration the order of the official "List of documents regarding the history of the invention of printing, preserved at the town-hall at Haarlem; compiled by Dr. A. De Vries, librarian of the Town-library. 1862."

No. 1. Historia Sancti Johannis Evangelistæ ejusque visionis Apocalypticæ. A block-book of the 15th century, of *German* origin, but provided with the portrait of an unknown person of the 17th century, which is meant to represent a Haarlem sheriff of the 15th century, named *Lourens Janszoon*, but 189 years after his death baptized as *Coster*, and represented, entirely without his fault, as a xylographer.

No. 2. Historia seu providentia virginis Mariæ ex Cantico Canticorum. Nine wood-engravings of the 15th century, of Dutch origin, fathered, in the 17th century, on the aforesaid sheriff, as having been executed by him in 1480.

No. 3. Ars moriendi sive de tentationibus morientium vel tentationes dæmonis. Seven wood-engravings, ascribed in 1628 to the same "great unknown."

No. 4. Donatus-fragments, typographically printed after the year 1470, fathered on the same innkeeper, imaginary wood-cut printer, who was, in the 17th century, created a book-printer, to the detriment of another legendary book-printer, in reality a chandler, but whose name was at least Lourens Janszoon *Coster*.

No. 5. Fragment of a Doctrinale, printed in the 15th century with Dutch types, and discovered in Holland, but ascribed in 1568, by Dr. Hadrianus Junius, to a Mentz press of Johan Fust in 1442, which never existed.

No. 6. Spieghel onser behoudenisse. *Second* Dutch, undated, edition of a typographic work of about the last quarter of the 15th century, printed with worn types, fathered in 1568, by Doctor Junius, on a certain L. J. Coster at Haarlem, as a work printed in the year 1440, with wooden letters, but converted in the 18th and 19th century into *first* edition. In the same volume is bound an undated work printed c. 1470, at Utrecht by Ketelaer and De Leempt, but claimed at the end of the 16th century as a *Haarlem* product.

No. 7. Spieghel onser behoudenisse. Second copy of the same edition, the fifth and eleventh leaf of which consist of two half-leaves pasted together, and are a palpable evidence that this kind of books could not possibly have ever been sold as manuscripts, as the Costerians pretended. It is untrue that this copy "was bought at the sale of the effects of one of the descendants of Coster."

No. 8. Speculum humanæ salutis. Latin, and at the same time earliest, edition of this work, but with modern title, which fathers it on L. J. Coster, under the year 1440, contrary to the Haarlem legend (1446) and to historical truth.

No. 9. Spieghel der menscheliker behoudenisse. Manuscript on vellum of the year 1464, anterior to the printed editions, but naïvely put after them.

No. 10. Spieghel onser behoudenisse. Printed at Culemborg, by Johan Veldener, in the year 1483, with the *original* wood-cuts of the four undated editions, now cut in two: a palpable evidence that these editions originate not from the *first*, but from the *second* half of the 16th century.

Documents concerning a certain Haarlem sheriff-innkeeper *Louwerijs* Janszoen, who died in 1489; but they are here collectively fathered on a later Haarlemer, named *Lourens Janszoon Coster*. For instance :—

No. 11. Receipt on vellum, of a gift of four almshouses, passed and sealed by the

Haarlem sheriff *Louweriis Janszoen* and *Gherrit van Adrichem*, dated Whitsun-eve, 1481. Eight more sheriff-documents, of the same kind, follow; besides autographs of the same sheriff, who is called *Coster* on the list, but never had that name.

No. 12. Autographs and facsimile signatures of descendants of a certain Haarlem chandler-innkeeper, called L. J. Coster (here confused, however, with the sheriff-innkeeper Lourens Janszoon), but on whom are fathered, in 1862 only, a grandson, *Wouter* Thomaszoon, and a great-grandson, *Thomas* Thomaszoon.

No. 13. Pedigree of *Lourens Janszoon Coster*, on vellum, made in the 16th century, on which the earliest reading of the Haarlem Coster-fiction is mentioned, but was afterwards falsified. The falsification, very easily to be done on vellum, is obvious even to the naked eye. The vellum document is not continued, as the official description of Dr. De Vries tells us, till 1724, for it leaves off in the 16th century. But another pedigree is added to it, fabricated in the 18th century, and copied on *paper* by Jacobus Koning. And just as with the two fables of the Haarlem invention, so these two documents are mixed up together in one description.

No. 14. Wooden block, containing a part of a Horarium, of the beginning of the 16th century, but fathered on the Haarlem sheriff-innkeeper of the 15th century.

No. 15. Wood-cut, representing the sheriff Laurens Janszoon, executed, as is historically certain, in the 18th century, out of mere fun, by Cornelis van den Berg at Haarlem, but put here as of doubtful, therefore not as of positively certain, spuriousness.

No. 16. Painted portrait of *Erasmus*, but "which has always been thought to be a likeness of Lourens Janszoon Coster"! Underneath: Painted portrait of *Ruard Tapper*, in the former century said to be the sheriff *Lourens Janszoon*.

No. 18. Copper engraving of the portrait of L. J. Coster, engraved by Jan Ladmiraal after a picture, sketched in the beginning of the last century by Laur. van der Vinne, but which was attributed afterwards to a painter of the 15th century, Albert van Oudewater.

No. 19. Cronica van der Hilliger Stat van Coellen, printed at Cologne by Johan Koelhoff, in 1499. In this work an account is given of the invention of typography, in which it is, according to history, positively ascribed to JOHAN GUTENBERG of Mentz. But the author, however well he may have been informed about the principal matter by Ulric Zell, a disciple of the earliest Mentz press, is mistaken in some details, especially when he endeavours to explain the derivation of typography from xylography. Namely, just as the prosperity of South Netherland wood-engraving falls in the first half of the 15th century, so that of North Netherland falls in the second half, and we know that xylography continued to supply school-books by the side of the flourishing typography. A xylographic Donatus preserved at Deventer, for instance, dates from the latter part of the 15th century (according to Meerman, even 1499—1503); the letters of the wooden block at Haarlem have the greatest resemblance to those of Willem Vorsterman, who printed at Antwerp in the beginning of the 16th century. Moreover, typographic Donatuses were printed afterwards in great numbers in the North Netherlands and exported also to foreign countries. Add to this the lively trade between Holland and Cologne, which belonged to the Hanse-towns; that, chiefly from Cologne, typography spread over the Netherlands; and the geographical inaccuracy, the confusion of Holland with Flanders, of the North with the South Netherlands, is nowise surprising in an author of the middle ages. We may, therefore, read in the chronicle, accepting that this particular originated also from Zell, and not from the author of the chronicle (for that must still remain a question, and the author of the chronicle *may* be the first who had no longer a clear technical idea of the connexion between typography and xylography, and began to mix up the two modes of printing), thus:—Junker Johan Gutenberg got, about the year 1440, (a *period* expressed by a round number, not exactly a *year*), by means of Netherland block-Donatuses, the idea of our present mode of printing books. He spent some years in developing this new idea, in experiments, and was ready with his invention in 1450.

The very natural *error* of the author of the chronicle in the history of *xylography*, has been, since the 17th century, taken advantage of by the Costerians, to cover the pretence of an invention of *typography* at Haarlem, and the book in which it is found is exhibited there in all sincerity. Their argument, however, was of the same kind as that which, by dividing the first verse of Psalm 14 or 53, tries to prove atheism from the Bible.

And not only that, but it was supplied (fortunately not yet, as Mr. Humphreys wishes, in a foreign language!) with a Costerian exegesis, which converts this clear account to nonsense. For granting, for a moment, that the chronicle speaks of *typographical* Donatuses, of a *Dutch* invention, therefore, of the proper art of printing, this stronghold of Haarlem would then consist of the following labyrinth :

"Typography was *first of all* invented at Mentz, between 1440 and '50.

No, typography was *not* invented at Mentz, but it was, *before* that time (*i.e.* before the *first* invention!) invented in *Holland*.

No, typography has *really* been invented in Germany, for the *first inventor* was Gutenberg, at Mentz."

Fine reasoning! People may be amused, feel annoyed or sad, according to one's disposition or opinion, at the capers to which such logic leads. Let us again hear what De Vries says :—

"There is in this account of Zell something remarkable and naïve, which most clearly proves, that he must have been not only a grateful disciple, but even an enthusiastic admirer of Guttenberg. He is *so* delighted with him, that he tries to exalt him as much as possible, and considers it a great honour for his German countrymen, that such an ingenious man had been among them; nay, in the enthusiasm and rapture of his passionate admiration, he suffers himself to be carried away so far (?) as to ascribe to him the honour of the invention (hear!); an assertion, however, he, after further consideration (!), thinks bound, from conscientious veracity, *to retract* (eh?) and *to modify*; yet he could not make up his mind (oh!) to moderate the excessive praise (not nice!), but by expressly telling that this admired master, although not in the proper sense of the word the first inventor (*where* is that? he distinctly calls him the first inventor!), had invented this art in a much more masterly and subtile mode than the other one, and made it more and more perfect (vill meysterlicher ind subtilicher is vonden dae die selue manier was, vnd (ye lenger ye mere) kunstlicher wurden.)"

Enthusiasm, rapture, passionate admiration, carrying away, conscientious veracity —these are the same exegetic tricks, by which the rabbis have proved that the pit of Joseph was, according to the Bible-text, "empty, without water," *yet*—full of serpents. Such an explanation is condemned simply by quoting it.

What on earth was there to be invented for that "first inventor," for that enthusiastically-admired Gutenberg, whom Zell tries to exalt as much as possible, when *typography* proper *was* invented already. For there is no question of the improver of type-casting, Peter Schöffer, but of the "*first inventor*," before 1450, whose claim is even defended by a violent assault upon the error about Jenson, against those confident persons who assert that there had been printing already before. Really the author of the chronicle, whose "evidence is beyond all doubt, and cannot be untrue," places his Haarlem interpreter, by anticipation, among the "confident persons."

Here, therefore, citizens and countrymen! here you have a *museum*, with precious documents to prove that typography was invented at Haarlem, about 1423, by a certain Lourens Janszoon Coster. In order to *prove* this, we show you first an old *pedigree* of that inventor, of a chandler, and on which you may read that he brought the *first* print into the world—in 1423, you think? No, in 1446; secondly, we let you see *sheriff-documents*, about the sale of houses and other typographical particulars, signed by a certain innkeeper Lourens Janszoon, who died—the *evidence* is here in a case—in 1439; then we have even the books, printed by our two-headed Haarlem inventor; look here: it is true, you would not find anything upon them about Haarlem or the innkeeper Lourens, or the chandler Coster, neither are they earlier than 1470—80, but—out of respect for our museum, you ought to believe that they are *Haarlem* books, of between 1420—40; finally—for such a complete museum, citizens and countrymen, has never been seen before—you have here even the *portraits* of this celebrated Haarlem inventor; as a child, he strikingly resembled this old Erasmus; when his printing-office flourished he was so good-looking that no one could distinguish him from this Ruard Tapper, also a practiser of the art of printing (pressing), but of the clerical printing; but when his servant ran away in 1441, with press and invention, he assumed that sour face which you may behold in this third representation. You see, therefore, distinctly, that, in reality, he has had more heads than two, at least *three*. He is our worshipped Brahma, our highly honoured Cerberus, our thousand-headed monster; and that he allowed himself to be cheated by a miserable German, was only the consequence of his superhuman tolerance and our national forbearance.

Yes, citizens and countrymen, such a booth as here is nowhere to be found on earth: the first wood-cut print came here into the world, anno 1446; typography was stolen here in 1441; the man who invented it in 1423, died in 1439, but left this town in 1483; he himself was invented only in 1568, shuffled away in 1628, was brought to light again in 1870.

Certainly, this official fair-booth is unique on this earth. Would it not be high time to close it?

XXIII.

CONCLUSION.

The genuine documents of the *fifteenth* century, the imprints of the earliest incunabula, *all* (even the Netherland) chronicles, prove that typography was invented at Mentz before 1450 by *Johan Gensfleisch Gutenberg*. Vanity and family pride, however, brought the Faust-legend, and, assisted by narrow-minded localism, the Strasburg and Haarlem fictions, into existence, of which history is now freed for good.

The Haarlem pretence, especially, exhibited an uninterrupted series of trickery and smuggling. The sheriff-innkeeper, Gerrit Thomasz., based his (great-) grandfather Lourens Janszoon Coster, upon a dim recollection of the first typographer at Haarlem, Jacob of Zierikzee;—Junius the year 1440 upon the fictitious date of Thomaszoon's pedigree, and an undated book upon "deerste print;"—Scriverius, a second imaginary inventor, the sheriff Lourens Janszoon, upon Coster;—Meerman, an impossible sexton, upon that sheriff, and so on.

So they went on till they perpetrated the gross deception of the public in 1856, by the inauguration of a spurious statue.

Hadrianus Junius was the first who, in 1568, in order to earn the thanks of the town in which he lived, compiled a story, which would give, in a time full of superstition, an appearance of credibility to a town-gossip. Every effort to save this fiction, made public only in 1588, by evasions, is henceforth impossible, now we have disclosed the falsification of the year in the original document of Gerrit Thomaszoon's vanity. We should not forget that in bygone centuries people had a more elastic conscience with regard to literary fraud, when it could serve to increase the glory of one's country, father, or grandfather, than at present. A pia fraus is to us, who have fortunately stricter notions of morality, nonsense; but it was a legitimate means with our fathers. Since scientific criticism has begun, this chapter also of the history of morals has been enriched with so many examples, that surprise can only be the part of the ignorant. *Untrue* is the year in Junius' fable, for the document of his legend does not give 1440 but 1446; untrue is it that by "deerste print" the "Spiegel der behoudenis" could have been meant, for this work is a *typographical* figure-book, and the invention of typography was only *ready* in 1450; *untrue* are ALL Junius' descriptions of this book which he, on his own authority, fathers upon L. J. Coster; *invented* is the theft (fabricated to establish a connexion between Haarlem and Mentz, in a manner which leaves the priority to Haarlem), for in 1442 they could not print at Mentz with the tools of a prenter, whose first work appeared in 1446; *imaginary* is the person of the thief, Johan (Faust), for no press was established in Mentz before 1450; *imaginary* the evidence of the bookbinder Cornelis, for the man who dies as an octogenarian in 1522 was no servant in the year 1440, and would, moreover, have made, by his long-continued raving against the Mentz theft, the *secret* of a Haarlem invention of typography for more than a century IMPOSSIBLE.

Although Junius remained in his story correct—with respect to the name at least of the chimerical inventor L. J. *Coster*—to the great-grandfather of his friend, Gerrit Thomasz.; and with his year, 1440, within the limits at least of Coster's life (now known as having extended from 1436—83)—in the 17th century the legend cut the only two threads which connected it with its origin. Scriverius invented the year 1428, deviated entirely from the account of Junius, also, with regard to the Spiegel, and, taken in by the similarity of the christian names, he fancied he had discovered the Haarlem inventor in a certain Haarlem sheriff, *Louwerijs Janszoon*, not of the *second*, but of the *first* half of the 15th century, and who died in 1439, *one* year *before* the invention in Junius, two years before the theft, seven years *before* the "first print" of Gerrit Thomaszoon's ancestor Lourens Janszoon *Coster*. The superstition of the Costerians went on building on this mistake of Scriverius, unaware that they had no longer to do with the man to whom their original worship was devoted. Since that time everything of which untruth, deception, sophism and impudence, superstition and narrow-mindedness, is capable, has been done, to give an appearance of truth to the colossal error, that typography had been invented by the Haarlem sheriff-innkeeper *Louwerijs Janszoen*, of the *first* half of the 15th century, while the original legend claimed nothing but the first (*xylographic*) prent for *Lourens Janszoon Coster*, chandler-innkeeper of the *second* half of the 15th century. On this confusion of persons are based the works of Scriverius, Boxhorn, Meerman, Koning, Scheltema, De Vries, Noordziek, and Pacile, which, therefore, from the moment of the discovery of the mistake, disappear in smoke.

The public thought that the new statue of 1856 was also for the sheriff, who had already, in the former century, two stone statues at Haarlem. But my exegesis of the story of Junius, disclosing the mistake of the interchange of persons, even before I discovered the falsification of the pedigree, lifted up the veil: the *chandler* stands on the Market-place, the *sheriff* stands in the Hortus Medicus and in the Hout, and inscribed on several medals. And now also the true reading of the earliest document of the Coster-legend is brought to light; now the year 1446, which was falsified and partly erased, is recovered: the whole fable lies exposed. For it is at present *certain*, that Junius, who knew this year, meant, with his story of the theft, not only the removal of *the art of printing*, but of the *invention* itself, from Haarlem to Mentz, during *the lifetime of Coster, i.e.* he meant absolute nonsense.

It is no longer a guess, but a scientific result, what the most competent critics of other countries have always thought of our pretended invention at Haarlem—what Fournier, for instance, wrote, in his Observations (Paris, 1760): "Les prémices de l'Art sont dûs, suivant M. Schoepflin, à Coster, & ont été faits à Haarlem. J'ai fait voir que cet opinion est dépourvûe de fondement, de preuves, même de vraisemblance, & que Coster n'est qu'un être idéal dans l'histoire de l'Imprimerie; aucune production Typographique ne dépose en sa faveur; il n'est connu que par des préjugés nationaux, et par des recits accompagnés de contradictions et de fables ridicules."

At Haarlem, therefore, we have to do away with the following monuments: 1. The statue on the Market-place; 2. The memorial-stone in front of the Coster-house; 3. The slab in the cathedral, in remembrance of the "fourth jubilee" of 1823 (although the celebration of a first, second and third was never thought of!); 4. The memorial-stone in the Hout, with the arms of the sheriff and the year 1423; Finally, the deceptive Coster-museum ought to be abolished and the books themselves incorporated with the town library.

Let the votaries of dead conservatism, which would leave the things in being, not because they are *good* and *true*, but because they *exist*, make no illusions of their cynicism of characterless indifference. "That statue looks well there!" so the "ostriches" of the solved question console themselves. But they forget that henceforth there can be no longer any pretence of a Coster-question, but of a Coster-*scandal*, which our national honour demands should be stopped as soon as possible; they forget that henceforth not only every scientific, but also every honest man, will disavow the exposed fraud; they forget that in our time of telegraphs and railways, international intercourse and reading, there is no longer place for shuffling tactics; they forget that this criticism has found its way already beyond our borders, and that in our own country the number of radical favourers of *truth* increases, who would not feel inclined, for the sake of ease and spiritual bluntness, to help us to bear the ridicule of the Coster-bunglings; they forget that the bronze statue of 1856 is henceforth *impossible*, on account of the cause which it represents; that it is a shame to our nation, on account of the immorality of its origin; they forget that we could say with erect head to the foreigner: We were deceived, but the deception has no hold on us; for we ourselves have torn with strong hand the tissue of lies, and thrown the rags at the feet of the blockheads and deceivers.

It is now the duty of those who are convinced of the truth, to raise it by public courage to a moral power, removing what has made us ridiculous for two centuries already. Although there are persons who, immorally indifferent, *will not* take cognizance of the verdicts of science—it ought to be made plain that the honour of our country is not entrusted to them.

I have received many paternal exhortations about the "sharpness," and heard many expressions of sympathy for the victims of, my criticism. But the opinion of those who have no notion whatever of the "fecit indignatio versum," is of no importance. It would be grander, if there were less offence in a destructive criticism and more offence in the unparalleled deception of which the people of Holland have been the dupes for many years.

I have had to put up also with the thousand-and-one observations about the "good faith" with which A had done this, B that, and C something else in behalf of Costerianism, *i.e.* in the interest of a bad cause. I should wish such observers to re-consider their elastic notion of "good faith," for I am afraid that our friend Mephistopheles has hitherto been satisfied with it.

In our small country, especially, science ought to rend the chains of local eye-service. For that Holland is, properly speaking, nothing but a club of petty clubs, arises from that childish fear of plainly telling the truth. It is for that reason that the disclosure of the Coster-deceptions has not so much a literary, as a moral significance, for they are the fruit of popular delusion.

Indeed, the Coster-question is "national." And that it is so, is a sad sign.

National! One of those miserable words which corrupt the minds of the people! Anthropophagy, lepra, impurity, laziness, thievishness, all these may be "national," if we only know of what "nation," Battaks, Icelanders, Arabs, Lazzaroni, or Caffres, we speak. National by itself means *nothing:* the question is whether we mean national vices or virtues. Our "moderation" (euphemism for lukewarmness and apathy) is very national, but on that account no less detestable. And our national gin is a national plague. On the other hand—for our national perseverance (although it is too slow), spirit of independence (although it is somewhat grocer-like), cleanliness (although it is somewhat partial), language (although it is too meagre

CONCLUSION.

for song), for our national vegetables and cows — all respect! But not, for instance . . . .

Not, for instance, for our *national* Coster, for "our" Coster. He expresses our ridiculous self-adoration, and it is a *national* interest to destroy him.

METAMORPHOSIS.

ORIGIN.	AUTHORITY.	SCAPE-GOAT.	ACCUSATION.	WHEN.	THIEVES.
1546	Gerrit Thomasz.	L. J. Coster	Deerste print	1446	
1560	Van Zuren	N. N.	Poor art	x	Foreigner
1561	Coornhert	N. N.	Crude manner of printing	x	Unfaithful servant
1568	Junius	L. J. Coster	Xylographic Spieghel der Behoudenis	1440	Johan Faust
1628	Scriverius	Lourens Jansz., Sheriff	Printed the xylographic Ars moriendi & typogr. Spieghel	1428	Johan Gutenberg
1639	Boxhorn	,,	Swindler in imitated manuscripts	1420	Johan Faust
1740	Seiz	,,	Printed 10 xylogr. and typogr. books	1428-1467	Johan Gutenberg
1765	Meerman	,, Sheriff-sexton	Prints with *moveable wooden* types	1430	Johan Gensfleisch the Elder
1809	Westreenen	N. N.	,,	before 1436	Nobody
1816	Koning	Lourens Jansz., Sheriff-sacristan	Invented xylography and typography. Prints 17 books	1420-1436	Frielo Gensfleisch
1822	De Vries	,, † 1439	{ Inventor of moveable types, cast of metal, *i.e.* of Typography proper. cf. 1546 }	1423	Johan Gensfleisch
1867	Alb. Thijm	L. J., † 1439, is Sheriff-chandler 1441-47 and called L. J. Coster.		,,	Hans

THE END.

www.ingramcontent.com/pod-product-compliance
Lightning Source LLC
Chambersburg PA
CBHW020926230426
43666CB00008B/1586